# A LEVEL
# ACCOUNTING

**Ian Harrison**

Chief Examiner

Every effort has been made to trace copyright holders and to obtain their permission for the use of copyright material. The authors and publishers will gladly receive information enabling them to rectify any reference or credit in subsequent editions.
First published 1996
**Reprinted 1998, 1999**

Letts Educational
Aldine House
Aldine Place
London W12 8AW
020 8740 2266

**British Library Cataloguing in Publication Data**
A CIP record for this book is available from the British Library

ISBN 1 85758 390 6

*Note for readers:* Some of the information in this book is liable to change, particularly that which is directly influenced by Government policy. Such information is correct at time of going to press but the reader should keep in touch with current affairs to ensure an up-to-date knowledge of the subject.

Typeset by Catherine Bourne

Printed and bound in Great Britain by Ashford Colour Press, Gosport, Hants

Letts Educational is the trading name of BPP (Letts Educational) Ltd

**Acknowledgements**
Questions in Chapters 1, 2, 3, 4, 5, 6, 7, 9, 11, 12 and 13: Reproduced by kind permission of the Associated Examining Board. Any answers or hints on answers are the sole responsibility of the author and have not been provided or approved by the Associated Examining Board. Questions in Chapters 2, 3, 5, 9, 10, 11 and 13: Reproduced by kind permission of the Northern Examinations and Assessment Board. The author is responsible for the solutions given and they may not necessarily constitute the only possible solutions. Questions in Chapters 3, 6, 7 and 12: © Northern Ireland Council for the Curriculum, Examinations and Assessment. Questions in Chapters 4, 6 and 8: The University of Cambridge Local Examinations Syndicate bears no responsibility for the example answers to questions taken from its past question papers which are contained in this publication. Questions in Chapters 4 and 10: Reproduced by kind permission of the University of London Examinations and Assessment Council. The University of London Examinations and Assessment Council accepts no responsibility whatsoever for the accuracy or method of working in the answers given. Question in Chapter 14: UODLE material is reproduced by permission of the University of Cambridge Local Examinations Syndicate. The University of Cambridge Local Examinations Syndicate bears no responsibility for the example answers to questions taken from past UODLE question papers which are contained in this publication. Question in Chapter 5: Reproduced by kind permission of the Welsh Joint Education Committee.

# CONTENTS

## SECTION 1: STARTING POINTS 1

How to use this book 2
Quality of language 3
Syllabus checklists and paper analysis 3
Examination board addresses 10
Studying and revising Accounting 11
The examination 14

## SECTION 2: ACCOUNTING TOPICS 17

**Chapter 1  Double entry 18**
1.1 Provisions and reserves 19
1.2 Provision for depreciation 19
1.3 Bad debts 23
1.4 Provision for bad debts 24
1.5 Provision for discounts allowed 25
1.6 Control accounts 26
1.7 Suspense accounts and the correction of errors 29
Illustrative questions 32

**Chapter 2  Incomplete records 36**
2.1 The concept of incomplete records 37
2.2 Calculation of results for cash-based businesses 37
2.3 Preparation of final accounts for cash-based businesses 38
2.4 Calculation of results for clubs and societies 43
2.5 Preparation of final accounts for clubs and societies 43
2.6 Calculation of missing cash or missing stock 46
Illustrative questions 48

**Chapter 3  Concepts and conventions of accounting 57**
3.1 Statements of standard accounting practice (SSAPs) 58
3.2 The concepts and conventions of accounting 58
Illustrative questions 64

**Chapter 4  Partnership accounts 69**
4.1 Partnership agreements 70
4.2 Partnership profit and loss appropriation accounts 70
4.3 Capital and current accounts 71
4.4 Structural changes 72
4.5 Goodwill 75
4.6 Partnership dissolution 78
4.7 Partnership amalgamation 80
4.8 Limited company taking over a partnership 83
Illustrative questions 84

**Chapter 5  Limited company accounts 91**
5.1 What is a limited company? 92
5.2 Types of limited companies 92
5.3 Advantages and disadvantages of limited liability status 93
5.4 The profit and loss appropriation account of a limited company 93
5.5 The balance sheet of a limited company 95
5.6 Reserves 96
5.7 Debentures 99
5.8 Fixed assets 99
5.9 Published accounts of limited companies 99
5.10 The issue of shares 100
5.11 The redemption of shares 104
Illustrative questions 106

**Chapter 6  Analysis and interpretation of accounts 111**
6.1 Users and uses of financial statements 112
6.2 Functions of accounting 112
6.3 Performance evaluation 113

| | | |
|---|---|---|
| | 6.4 Profitability ratios | 116 |
| | 6.5 Financial ratios | 117 |
| | 6.6 Investment ratios | 119 |
| | 6.7 Interpretation | 122 |
| | 6.8 Limitations of ratio analysis | 123 |
| | 6.9 Accounting for inflation | 123 |
| | Illustrative questions | 125 |
| **Chapter 7** | **Cash flow statements** | **131** |
| | 7.1 Uses of cash flow statements | 132 |
| | 7.2 Construction of a cash flow statement using FRS 1 | 132 |
| | Illustrative questions | 144 |
| **Chapter 8** | **Costing for materials and labour** | **152** |
| | 8.1 Accounting for materials | 153 |
| | 8.2 Methods of stock valuation | 154 |
| | 8.3 Wage systems | 158 |
| | 8.4 Accounting for labour | 159 |
| | 8.5 Remuneration of labour | 159 |
| | 8.6 Manufacturing accounts | 161 |
| | Ilustrative questions | 165 |
| **Chapter 9** | **Costing for overheads** | **172** |
| | 9.1 Cost allocation and apportionment | 173 |
| | 9.2 Transfers of service department costs | 175 |
| | 9.3 Overhead absorption | 178 |
| | 9.4 Overhead adjustment account | 181 |
| | Illustrative questions | 182 |
| **Chapter 10** | **Budgets and budgetary control** | **188** |
| | 10.1 Budgeting | 189 |
| | 10.2 Budgetary control | 190 |
| | Illustrative questions | 195 |
| **Chapter 11** | **Standard costing and variance analysis** | **200** |
| | 11.1 Standard costing | 201 |
| | 11.2 Variances | 201 |
| | 11.3 The flexed budget | 203 |
| | 11.4 Overhead variances | 204 |
| | Illustrative questions | 208 |
| **Chapter 12** | **Capital investment appraisal** | **213** |
| | 12.1 Capital projects | 213 |
| | 12.2 Payback | 214 |
| | 12.3 The accounting rate of return | 215 |
| | 12.4 Discounted cash flows | 216 |
| | 12.5 The internal rate of return | 220 |
| | Illustrative questions | 222 |
| **Chapter 13** | **Absorption and marginal costing** | **226** |
| | 13.1 Variable and fixed costs | 227 |
| | 13.2 Marginal costing | 227 |
| | 13.3 Uses of marginal costing | 229 |
| | Illustrative questions | 239 |
| **Chapter 14** | **Social accounting** | **246** |
| | 14.1 Non-financial aspects of accounting | 246 |
| | 14.2 Social awareness | 246 |
| | 14.3 Social costs | 247 |
| | 14.4 Social costs and profitability | 247 |
| | Illustrative question | 248 |

# SECTION 3: TEST RUN

| | |
|---|---|
| **SECTION 3: TEST RUN** | **251** |
| Test your knowledge quiz | **252** |
| Test your knowledge quiz answers | **253** |
| Progress analysis | **255** |
| Mock exam | **256** |
| Mock exam suggested answers | **266** |
| Index | **274** |

# STARTING POINTS

*In this section:*

How to use this book

The structure of the book

Using your syllabus checklist

Quality of language

Syllabus checklist and paper analysis

Examination board addresses

Studying and revising Accounting

The difference between GCSE and A/AS level

Study strategies and techniques

Subject-specific skills

Revision techniques

The examination

Question styles

Examination techniques

Final preparation

# HOW TO USE THIS BOOK

## THE STRUCTURE OF THIS BOOK

The key aim of this book is to guide you in the way you tackle A-level Accounting. It should serve as a study guide, work book and revision aid throughout any A-level/AS-level course, no matter what syllabus you are following. It is not intended to be a complete guide to the subject and should be used as a companion to your textbooks, which it is designed to complement rather than duplicate.

We have divided the book into three sections. Section One, Starting Points, contains study tips and syllabus information – all the material you need to get started on your A-level study – plus advice on planning your revision and tips on how to tackle the exam itself. Use the Syllabus Checklist to find out exactly where you can find the study units which are relevant to your particular syllabus.

Section Two, the main body of the text, contains the core of A-level Accounting, It has been devised to make study as easy – and as enjoyable – as possible, and has been divided into chapters which cover the themes you will encounter on your syllabus. The chapters are split into units, each covering a topic of study.

The Chapter Objectives direct you towards the key points of the chapter you are about to read. The Chapter Roudup at the end of the chapter gives a summary of the text just covered, brings its topics into focus and links them to other themes of study. To reinforce what you have just read and learned, there are Illustrative Questions at the end of each chapter. All questions are actually taken from those recently set by the examination boards (including Scottish Higher). The tutorial notes and suggested answers provided give you practical guidance on how to answer A-level questions, and give additional information relevant to that particular topic.

In Section Three, Test Run, we turn our attention to the examination you will face at the end of your course. First, you can assess your progress using the Test Your Knowledge Quiz and analysis chart. Then, as a final test, you should attempt the Mock Exam, under timed conditions. This will give you invaluable examination practice, and, together with the specimen answers specially written by the author, will help you to judge how close you are to achieving your A-level pass.

## USING YOUR SYLLABUS CHECKLIST

Whether you are using this book to work step-by-step through the syllabus or to structure your revision campaign, you will find it useful to use our checklist to record what you have covered – and how far you still have to go. Keep the checklist at hand when you are doing your revision – it will remind you of the chapters you have revised, and those still to be done.

The checklist for each examination – A, AS or Higher Grade – is in two parts. First there is a list of topics covered by this book where are part of the syllabus. Although the checklists are detailed, it is not possible to print entire syllabuses. You are therefore strongly recommended to obtain an official copy of the syllabus for your examination and consult it when the need arises. The examination board addresses are given after the syllabus checklist.

When you have revised a topic, tick the box in the column provided and, if there are questions on it elsewhere in the book, try to answer these too.

The second part of the checklist gives y ou information about the examination, providing useful details about the time allocated for each paper and the weighting of the questions on each paper. The different types of questions which may be set are explained in detail later in this section under the heading The Examination.

## QUALITY OF LANGUAGE

Students need to be aware that, following the issue of a Code of Practice by the Schools' Curriculum and Assessment Authority, examination boards will be assessing candidates in terms of their ability to express themselves in good English. Marks will be allocated for spelling, punctuation and grammar in examinations from 1998 onwards. Some examination boards may decide to comply with this requirement before 1998. You should consult the relevant syllabus to check this detail.

Students will need to demonstrate the ability to present ideas and information in an appropriate manner and demonstrate that they can argue with clarity and in a logical structure.

All the examination boards already assess the structure and presentation of ideas in Accounting. Marks are awarded for presentation and layout of reports and accounting statements. In the future more emphasis will be placed on: correct headings to all answers; data collection; reconciliation statements; acceptable layouts.

The mark scheme for written sections of questions will incorporate marks specifically for clarity of expression, spelling, punctuation and grammar. The marks will usually be allocated using a banded mark scheme, for example, if a question instructed candidates to present their answer using a report format, marks might be allocated in the following way:

Correct heading:  2 marks (possibly 1 mark if only partially correct)

0–2 marks:  This range of marks would be awarded to an answer that lacks clarity of expression and which contained some spelling, punctuation and grammatical errors.

3–4 marks:  This range of marks would be awarded to answers that were expressed in a clear, relevant and logical manner and which had only a few errors in terms of spelling, punctuation and grammar.

## SYLLABUS CHECKLISTS AND PAPER ANALYSIS

### ASSOCIATED EXAMINING BOARD
### A level

| Syllabus topic | Covered in Unit No | ✓ |
|---|---|---|
| **Accounting information systems** | | |
| Nature and role of accounting: standards and concepts | 3.1, 3.2 | |
| Decision making | 12.1–12.5, 13.1–13.3 | |
| Limitation of accounting | 5.2, 6.8, 14.1 | |
| **Determination of business income** | | |
| Final accounts and balance sheets | 2.3, 2.5, 4.2, 4.5, 4.8, 5.4, 5.5–5.9 | |
| Provisions and reserves | 1.1, 1.2, 1.4, 1.5 | |
| Classification of assets and liabilities | 5.5–5.10 | |
| Goodwill | 4.5 | |
| Social aspects of accounting | 14.1–14.4 | |
| **Types of business entity** | | |
| Sole traders | 2.2, 2.3 | |
| Partnerships | 4.1–4.8 | |
| Limited companies | 5.1–5.11 | |
| Incomplete records | 2.1–2.6 | |

| Syllabus topic | Covered in Unit No | ✓ |
|---|---|---|
| Clubs and societies | 2.4–2.6 | |
| Published accounts | 5.9, 7.1, 7.2 | |
| Ownership and control | 5.1 | |
| Long-term capital | 5.6, 5.7, 5.10 | |
| **Accounting for forward planning and decision making** | | |
| Costs and their behaviour | 8.1–8.6, 13.1 | |
| Absorption costing | 9.1–9.4, 13.1 | |
| Marginal costing | 13.2 13.3 | |
| Overheads | 9.1–9.4, 11.4 | |
| Pricing policies | 9.1, 13.1, 13.3 | |
| Budgetary control | 10.1, 10.2 | |
| Standard costing and variance analysis | 11.1–11.4 | |
| Capital investment appraisal | 12.1–12.5 | |
| **Analysis and interpretation of accounting statements** | | |
| Ratio analysis | 6.1 – 6.8 | |

## Paper analysis

Paper 1    *3 hours*    50% of the total marks
Section A: three compulsory questions
Sections B and C: two questions in each section –
candidates must answer one question from each section

Paper 2    *3 hours*    50% of the total marks
Section A: two compulsory questions
Sections B and C: two questions in each section –
candidates must answer one question from each section

The papers will include computational questions and those requiring the use of continuous prose.

### AS level

The AS level syllabus covers the same general topic areas as the A level syllabus. The emphasis is on interpretation and analysis of financial information rather than its preparation. For example, candidates will not be required to prepare final accounts from a trial balance; they will not be required to prepare a cash flow statement or to calculate variances, but they may be required to comment on the results of such statements. The syllabus booklet states that '. . . the emphasis in the Advanced Supplementary Examination is essentially on the interpretation of accounting data rather than the construction of financial statements. Candidates will not be expected to have a detailed knowledge of the double entry book-keeping model . . .'

## Paper analysis

Paper 1    *1 hour*    40% of the total marks
           *45 mins*   All question are compulsory and based on source material

Paper 2    *2 hours*    60% of the total marks
Section A (30%): one compulsory structured question
Section B (30% ): three structured questions – candidates are
required to answer two

The papers will include computational questions and those requiring the use of continuous prose.

## UNIVERSITY OF CAMBRIDGE LOCAL EXAMINATIONS SYNDICATE
### A level

| Syllabus topic | Covered in Unit No | ✓ |
|---|---|---|
| **The accounting system** | | |
| Recording accounting data | 1.1–1.8 | |
| Classification of assets and liabilities | 5.8–5.10 | |
| Control accounts | 1.6 | |
| **Financial accounting** | | |
| Concepts | 3.1, 3.2 | |
| Sole Traders | 2.2, 2.3 | |
| Partnerships | 4.1–4.8 | |
| Limited companies | 5.1–5.11 | |
| Clubs and societies | 2.4, 2.5 | |
| Manufacturing accounts | 8.6 | |
| Goodwill | 4.5 | |
| **Financial reporting** | | |
| Published accounts | 5.9, 7.1, 7.2 | |
| Accounting standards | 3.1, 3.2 | |
| Accounting for inflation | 6.9 | |
| Limitations of accounting | 5.2, 6.8, 14.1 | |
| **Elements of managerial accounting** | | |
| Costs and their behaviour | 8.1–8.6, 9.1–9.4, 13.1 | |
| Absorption costing | 9.1–9.4 | |
| Marginal costing | 13.2, 13.3 | |
| Capital investment appraisal | 12.1–12.5 | |
| Standard costing | 11.1–11.4 | |

## Paper analysis

Paper 1    *3 hours*    50% of the total marks
Six questions: two compulsory questions with a choice of two further questions from four others

Paper 2    *3 hours*    50% of the total marks
Six questions: two compulsory questions with a choice of two further questions from four others

Questions on Managerial Accounting will be set in Paper 2 only.

## UNIVERSITY OF LONDON EXAMINATION AND ASSESSMENT COUNCIL
### A level

| Syllabus topic | Covered in Unit No | ✓ |
|---|---|---|
| **General financial accounting** | | |
| Double entry | 1.1–1.8 | |
| Limitations of accounting | 5.2, 6.8, 14.1 | |
| Concepts and conventions | 3.1, 3.2 | |
| Final accounts and balance sheets | 2.3, 2.5, 4.2, 4.5, 4.8, 5.4, 5.5–5.9 | |
| Ratio analysis and interpretation of accounts | 6.1–6.8 | |
| Incomplete records | 2.1–2.6 | |
| Goodwill | 4.5 | |
| Long-term capital | 5.6, 5.7, 5.10 | |
| FRS 1 Cash flow statements | 7.1, 7.2 | |
| Published accounts of limited companies | 5.9, 7.1, 7.2 | |

| Syllabus topic | Covered in Unit No | ✓ |
|---|---|---|
| SSAP's | 3.1, 3.2 | |
| **Management and cost accounting:** | | |
| Elements of cost | 8.1–8.5, 9.1–9.4, 11.1–11.4 | |
| Material costing | 8.1, 8.2 | |
| Labour costs | 8.3–8.5 | |
| Accounting for overheads | 9.1–9.4 | |
| Allocation, apportionment and absorption costing | 9.1-9.4 | |
| Marginal costing | 13.2, 13.3 | |
| Budgetary control | 10.1, 10.2 | |
| Capital budgeting | 12.1–12.5 | |
| Standard costing | 11.1–12.4 | |
| Social accounting | 14.1–14.4 | |

## Paper analysis

Paper 1    3 hours    50% of the total marks
Section A: 3 question, candidates required to attempt two
Section B: 3 questions, candidates required to attempt two
Section C: 2 questions, candidates required to attempt one

Paper 2    3 hours    50% of the total marks
Same format as Paper 1

Questions in Paper 1 will be set *mainly* on Part 1 of the syllabus and questions on Paper 2 will be set *mainly* on Part 2 of the syllabus.

## NORTHERN EXAMINATIONS AND ASSESSMENT BOARD
## A level

| Syllabus topic | Covered in Unit No | ✓ |
|---|---|---|
| **Introduction to financial accounting theory and practice** | | |
| Accounting concepts | 3.1, 3.2 | |
| Valuation of assets | 5.8 | |
| Valuation of stocks | 8.1, 8.2 | |
| Current cost accounting | 5.9 | |
| Current purchasing power | 5.9 | |
| Valuation of liabilities | 5.5, 5.6, 5.7 | |
| **Analytical and application skills** | | |
| Accounting procedures | 2.1–2.8 | |
| Final accounts and balance sheets | 2.3, 2.5, 4.2, 4.5, 5.4, 5.5–5.9 | |
| Analysis and interpretation | 6.1–6.8 | |
| Cash flow statements | 7.1, 7.2 | |
| Ratio analysis | 6.1–6.8 | |
| **An introduction to management and cost accounting theory and practice** | | |
| Short-run decisions | 8.1–8.5, 9.1–9.4, 13.2, 13.3 | |
| Long-run decisions | 12.1–12.5 | |
| Budgeting | 10.1, 10.2 | |
| Costing for control | 11.1–11.4 | |
| **Legal, financial and social background** | | |
| Forms of business | 2.3, 2.5, 4.2, 4.5, 4.8, 5.4, 5.5–5.9 | |
| Social accounting | 14.1, 14.4 | |

## Paper analysis

Paper 1      *3 hours*      50% of the total marks
Section A: 2 questions, candidates required to answer one
Section B: 5 questions, candidates required to answer three

Paper 2      *3 hours*      50% of the total marks
Section A: 2 questions, candidates required to answer one
Section B: 5 questions, candidates required to answer three

Questions in Paper 1 will be set *mainly* on sections 1, 2 and 4 of the syllabus and Paper 2 will be set *mainly* on sections 3 and 4.

## UNIVERSITY OF OXFORD DELEGACY OF LOCAL EXAMINATIONS
## A level

| Syllabus topic | Covered in Unit No | ✓ |
|---|---|---|
| **Financial accounting** | | |
| Double entry | 1.1–1.8 | |
| Control systems | 1.6, 1.8 | |
| Concepts and conventions | 3.1, 3.2 | |
| SSAP's | 3.1, 3.2 | |
| Provisions and reserves | 1.1, 1.2, 1.4, 1.5 | |
| Final accounts and balance sheets | 2.3, 2.5, 4.2, 4.5, 4.8, 5.4, 5.5–5.9 | |
| Sole traders | 2.2, 2.3 | |
| Partnerships | 4.1–4.8 | |
| Limited companies | 5.1–5.11 | |
| Incomplete records | 2.1–2.6 | |
| Clubs and societies | 2.4–2.6 | |
| Published accounts | 5.9, 7.1, 7.2 | |
| Goodwill | 4.5 | |
| Inflation accounting | 6.9 | |
| Analysis and interpretation of accounting statements | 6.1–6.8 | |
| **Management accounting** | | |
| Material costing | 8.1, 8.2 | |
| Costing for labour | 8.3–8.5 | |
| Allocation, apportionment and absorption costing | 9.1–9.4 | |
| Absorption costing | 9.3–9.4, 13.1 | |
| Marginal costing | 13.2, 13.3 | |
| Budgetary control | 10.1, 10.2 | |
| Standard costing and variance analysis | 11.1–11.4 | |
| Capital investment appraisal | 12.1–12.5 | |
| Social aspects of accounting | 14.1–14.4 | |

## Paper analysis

Paper 1      *3 hours*      50% of total marks
Section A (31%): 2 questions, candidates required to answer one
Section B (69%): 4 questions, candidates required to answer three

This paper will examine topics dealing with financial accounting.

Paper 2      *3 hours*      50% of total marks
Same format as Paper 1

This paper will examine topics dealing with management accounting.

### Modular course

The above details are for candidates being examined in 1997. After this, the course will become modular, comprising six 1½ hour papers. The content of this course is still addressed by this book

## AS level

There are two separate AS papers available, one on financial accounting the other on management accounting.

The financial accounting AS paper is Paper 1 of the A level examination.

The management accounting AS paper is Paper 2 of the A level examination.

## NORTHERN IRELAND COUNCIL FOR THE CURRICULUM, EXAMINATIONS AND ASSESSMENT

## A level

| Syllabus topic | Covered in Unit No | ✓ |
|---|---|---|
| Concepts and conventions | 3.1, 3.2 | |
| SSAP's | 3.1, 3.2 | |
| Final accounts and balance sheets | 2.3, 2.5, 4.2, 4.5, 4.8, 5.4, 5.5–5.9 | |
| Sole traders | 2.2, 2.3 | |
| Partnerships | 4.1–4.8 | |
| Goodwill | 4.5 | |
| Limited companies | 5.1–5.11 | |
| Published accounts | 5.9, 7.1, 7.2 | |
| FRS 1 | 7.1, 7.2 | |
| Incomplete records | 2.1–2.6 | |
| Inflation accounting | 6.9 | |
| Depreciation | 1.2 | |
| Stock valuation | 8.2 | |
| Ratio analysis | 6.1–6.8 | |
| Budgeting | 10.1, 10.2 | |
| Costing for materials | 8.1, 8.2 | |
| Labour costs | 8.3, 8.5 | |
| Overheads | 9.1–9.4, 11.4 | |
| Absorption costing | 9.1–9.4, 13.1 | |
| Marginal costing | 13.2, 13.3 | |
| Standard costing | 11.1 | |
| Variance analysis | 11.2–11.4 | |
| Capital investment appraisal | 12.1–12.5 | |

## Paper analysis

| | | |
|---|---|---|
| Paper 1 | *3 hours* | 50% of the total marks |
| | | Section A (20%): 3 questions, candidates required to answer two |
| | | Section B (30%): 6 questions, candidates required to answer four |
| Paper 2 | *3 hours* | 50% of the total marks |
| | | Paper 2 will be structured in the same way as Paper 1 |

## WELSH JOINT EDUCATION COMMITTEE
## A level

| Syllabus topic | Covered in Unit No | ✓ |
|---|---|---|
| **Objectives of accounting** | | |
| Recording financial information | 1.1–1.8 | |
| Control | 1.6, 1.8, 10.1, 10.2, 11.1–11.4 | |
| Pricing policy | 9.1, 13.1, 13.3 | |
| **Uses of accounting** | | |
| Companies Acts – disclosure requirements | 3.1, 3.2, 5.9, 7.1, 7.2 | |
| Social accounting | 14.1–14.4 | |
| Accounting concepts and conventions: SSAP 2 | 3.1, 3.2 | |
| Concepts | 3.1, 3.2 | |
| **Stewardship accounting** | | |
| Accruals accounting | 5.2 | |
| Double entry system | 1.1–1.8 | |
| Final accounts and balance sheets | 2.3, 2.5, 4.2, 4.5, 4.8, 5.4, 5.5–5.9 | |
| Sole traders | 2.2, 2.3 | |
| Clubs and societies | 2.4–2.6 | |
| Company accounts: | | |
| Published accounts | 5.9, 7.1, 7.2 | |
| Profit and loss accounts and balance sheets | 5.4–5.9 | |
| Share issue and redemption | 5.10, 5.11 | |
| FRS 1 | 7.1, 7.2 | |
| **Income measurement** | | |
| Goodwill | 4.5 | |
| Stock valuation | 8.2 | |
| Reserves and provisions | 1.1, 1.2, 1.4, 1.5 | |
| Accounting for inflation | 6.9 | |
| SSAPs | 3.1, 3.2 | |
| **Partnership accounts:** | | |
| Capital and current accounts | 4.3 | |
| Final accounts and balance sheets | 4.2–4.7 | |
| Structural changes | 4.4 | |
| Goodwill | 4.5 | |
| **Management accounting** | | |
| Costs and their behaviour | 8.1–8.6, 13.1 | |
| Absorption costing | 9.1–9.4, 11.4 | |
| Marginal costing | 13.2, 13.3 | |
| Budgetary control | 10.1, 10.2 | |
| Standard costing | 11.1–11.4 | |
| Variance analysis | | |
| **Analysis and interpretation:** | | |
| Ratio analysis | 6.1–6.8 | |
| Capital investment appraisal | 12.1–12.5 | |
| Social accounting | 14.1–14.4 | |

## Paper analysis

Paper 1     *3 hours*     50% of the total marks
Two compulsory questions (15% and 7½%)
Candidates will attempt one question from each of three pairs
The mark allocation between the three pairs will not be uniform

Paper 2     *3 hours*     50% of the marks
Paper 2 will be structured in the same way as Paper 1

## SCOTTISH EXAMINATIONS BOARD
### Higher

| Syllabus topic | Covered in Unit No | ✓ |
|---|---|---|
| **Financial accounting** | | |
| Manufacturing accounts | 8.6 | |
| Partnership accounts | 4.1–4.8 | |
| Limited company accounts | 5.1–5.11, 7.1, 7.2 | |
| Cash flow statements | 7.1, 7.2 | |
| Interpretation of accounting information | 6.1–6.8 | |
| Incomplete records | 2.1–2.6 | |
| Checks, controls and regulations | 1.1–1.8 | |
| Provisions and reserves | 1.5 | |
| **Managerial accounting** | | |
| Classification of costs | 13.1 | |
| Cost elements | 8.1–8.5, 9.1–9.4 | |
| Marginal and absorption costing | 9.1–9.4, 13.2, 13.3 | |
| Break-even analysis | 13.2 | |
| Budgets | 10.1, 10.2 | |
| Standard costing | 11.1–11.4 | |
| Decision making | 13.2, 13.3 | |

## Paper analysis

Paper 1    2¼ hours    40% of total marks
Divided into three sections:
Section A: one compulsory question
Section B: one essay-type question from a choice of three
Section C: 5 questions, candidates required to answer two

Paper 2    2¼ hours    40% of total marks
Same format as Paper 1

Paper 3    1½ hours    20% of total marks
This paper is a computer-based assignment
Candidates will be required to edit/amend and print a spreadsheet to show given accounting information

# EXAMINATION BOARD ADDRESSES

*AEB*    The Associated Examining Board
Stag Hill House,Guildford, Surrey GU2 5XJ
Tel: 01483 506506

*CAMBRIDGE*    University of Cambridge Local Examinations Syndicate
Syndicate Buildings, 1 Hills Road, Cambridge CB1 2EU
Tel: 01223 553311

*NEAB*    Northern Examinations and Assessment Board
12 Harter Street, Manchester M1 6HL
Tel: 0161 953 1180

*NICCEA*    Northern Ireland Council for the Curriculum, Examinations and Assessment
Beechill House, 42 Beechill Road, Belfast BT8 4RS
Tel: 01232 704666

| OXFORD | University of Oxford Delegacy of Local Examinations<br>Ewert House, Ewert Place, Summertown, Oxford OX2 7BZ<br>Tel: 01865 54291 |
| --- | --- |
| SEB | Scottish Examining Board (for Higher Grade)<br>Ironmills Road, Dalkeith, Midlothian EH22 1LE<br>Tel: 0131 663 6601 |
| ULEAC | University of London Examinations and Assessment Council<br>Stewart House, 32 Russell Square, London WC1B 5DN<br>Tel: 0171 331 4000 |
| WJEC | Welsh Joint Education Committee<br>245 Western Avenue, Cardiff CF5 2YX<br>Tel: 01222 265000 |

# STUDYING AND REVISING ACCOUNTING

A revision guide cannot be expected to cover every topic on every Accounting syllabus of all the various examination boards.

This book is not intended to act as a substitute for a good standard text book, it is a supplement and an aid to your study of the subject.

## THE DIFFERENCE BETWEEN GCSE AND A/AS LEVEL

Some students embark on an A level Accounting course without any prior experience, some have previously studied the subject at GCSE level, while others have gained some experience in the work place and wish to build on that experience. Many students in school or in colleges of further education enrol on a two year course. The first year will generally follow, almost perfectly, a GCSE syllabus. In the second year new topics are introduced and higher order skills are developed.

The GCSE syllabuses are an ideal foundation for the A level Accounting course . The GCSE course lays down good solid foundations on which the more difficult and taxing topics can be built. GCSE students rely heavily on being able to recall knowledge that they may have learned by rote. It is fairly easy to memorise what a sales ledger control account looks like and it is quite easy to memorise the reasons why a business might introduce the use of control accounts into its systems. It is a different matter being able to reconcile an incorrect total of debtors extracted from the sales ledger with an incorrect total resulting from the production of a control account.

A GCSE student should be able to calculate the acid test ratio for a business. An A level student would be expected to comment on the ratio and perhaps suggest remedial action for the business if the ratio was not satisfactory. As an A level student you will be assessed on your ability to:

- demonstrate a *knowledge and understanding* of accounting information systems
- *assemble and classify* accounting data
- *know and apply* accounting concepts and techniques
- *interpret and analyse* accounting information
- be able to evaluate information and alternative courses of action
- make reasoned judgements from accounting information
- communicate results in a variety of different forms to suit the users of accounting information
- understand and appreciate the role and the limitations of accounting information

You will observe that a great deal of emphasis is now placed on analysing , explaining, evaluating and interpreting data rather than just recalling information that you may have learned off by heart.

## STUDY STRATEGIES AND TECHNIQUES

Studying and revising for any examination should not be a last minute affair. In order to pass the examination you should make notes throughout the course and, in the case of a subject like Accounting, you should practice the various topics covered in the course on a regular basis.

There are certain formulae and layouts that you must learn, for example there is no other way of remembering the layout of a cash flow statement or the model to be used to calculate the gross margin that a business earns.

Revision is a continuous process. Plan your revision sessions well in advance and undertake them on a regular basis. Your teacher will have helped you in this process by setting homework and by giving you regular tests in class. Both of these types of work are a very valuable part of your revision programme. Use them to ensure that you do understand the subject of the homework or the test. Revise the topic covered in the homework or the test before you do it, then when your work is given back to you, note carefully your teacher's comments and try to rectify any basic errors pointed out.

Use each homework and test to build up a bank of knowledge and skills that you may be able to apply to subsequent pieces of work. As a subject Accounting is very much like a jigsaw puzzle, the pieces of information learned a couple of weeks ago may often be applied to complete today's work, or to help analyse a business problem.

There is no one best way of revising, all students are different and each person must find the methods that suit them best. You must learn the key concepts in each topic, this is often easier than you think; the difficult part is applying this knowledge to each question asked in the examination.

## SUBJECT-SPECIFIC SKILLS

### Numeracy

Accounting is a numeracy-based subject and a large proportion of the paper will require you to communicate information using figures. The skills needed are the ability to:

*   perform simple and complex calculations;
*   present accounting statements in a logical and coherent manner;
*   analyse accounting data resulting from your own calculations or from a given set of data;
*   demonstrate an understanding of the information;
*   evaluate alternative strategies by reasoning to arrive at a suitable conclusion.

Examiners are not only interested in the numbers that appear in your examination answer booklet, they are also interested in how you have arrived at that particular answer. If the examiner is to know the reasoning behind your answer he or she must be able to refer to your workings. You will probably rely on a calculator to do most of your workings. Show the examiner exactly how the figure was arrived at. Show your working neatly and clearly and in a logical progression. Remember the examiner is not a mind reader. The examiner must be able to follow your workings through to the answer.

EXAMPLE

A company whose financial year end is 31 December 1995 purchased equipment costing £3,600 on 31 March 1995. It is company policy to depreciate equipment at 10% per annum on cost on a monthly basis.

**Required**

Calculate the depreciation charge for the year ended 31 December 1995.           (4 marks)

**Solution**

Mary gives an answer of £27 and she is awarded 0 marks.

Megan gives an answer of £27 she is awarded 3 marks because she showed her workings: £3,600 (1) × 10% (1) × $3/4$ (1). She was awarded marks for each part.

## Communication

Accounting is a communication medium. Most information is communicated to the users of accounts by the use of figures, but as accountants we must also be able to communicate through the written word. Examination boards are beginning to award marks for this aspect of the subject and it will become increasingly more important in future examinations. Credit will be given for your ability to organise and present the information required. Many questions now require a memorandum (memo) or simple report format. Both of these require identification of the sender and the receiver, the date and a title. A report also requires some form of recommendation.

# REVISION TECHNIQUES

A revision programme should be drawn up well in advance of the examination. Draw up a weekly plan which identifies a number of times when you can devote at least two hours to your revision. Remember that, for some of you, accounting will not be the only subject that you are revising. This fact must also be taken into account when drawing up your plans. Try to determine which time of the day suits your needs best. If you are still at college or in school try to use your free time during the day. Find a quiet place in the library or in a spare classroom and build this into your revision plan. Once you have drawn up your plan try to stick to it. You will find that a regular routine will work best and pay the best dividends.

If you lose concentration during one of your revision sessions have a break. The break can either be for a drink or snack or just a change in topic or subject. This should revitalise you, ready for another spell of work. Varying your methods of revision should help you to concentrate for longer periods of time. Try the following:

- read aloud;
- explain topics to yourself;
- test yourself;
- use a friend to test you;
- use a friend to bounce ideas or answers off each other (take care that revision with a friend does not end up as a gossip session!)
- summarise answers to questions;
- practice parts of questions which will build into a whole answer;
- answer questions under examination conditions.

Ask yourself the question 'Could I explain this topic area to someone who doesn't know about accounting so that they would understand it?' If you can honestly answer yes, then you probably understand the topic; if your answer is no, then you need to spend some more time revising the topic.

Use this guide as a basis for your revision programme. Revise one topic at one of your sessions. Read the chapter. Make a mental note of the key points. Attempt one of the questions provided. Check your answer. Identify any errors or omissions you may have made and make a note so that you will not make the same mistakes again. Remember, you may have included correct information that is not included in the Guide's suggested answer, or you may have used a perfectly valid, different method of arriving at the correct answer.

When you get nearer to the examination try to extend your revision time to around three hours. This will give you practice at concentrating and sitting at a desk for the length of time that will be required in the examination room.

# THE EXAMINATION

## QUESTION STYLES

Examination questions are of three types:

- those which require only a numerical response (these are appearing less frequently nowadays);
- those that require a numerical answer followed by a written response, usually based on your findings in the numerical section;
- those requiring only a written response in the form of an essay.

### Numerical questions

Use the correct headings as shown in the question. For example, if the answer requires a budgeted balance sheet, the answer should say 'Budgeted balance sheet as at 31 December 1995'.

Make sure that you show all workings. As an examiner it is very frustrating to see figures that clearly must have been arrived at by some form of calculation, but the calculation is known only to the candidate. However, there are no marks for workings on their own. For example, if you show a perfect subscriptions account in your workings when preparing the income and expenditure account for a club, but then do not include any subscriptions in the final accounts you will not receive any marks.

On the other hand, if you include an incorrect figure as subscriptions in the income and expenditure account the examiner will look for the workings so that you can be rewarded for the correct parts of your calculation. So make your workings as clear as possible and easy to follow.

Examiners generally apply what is known as the own figure rule. This means that if you have been penalised once for making an error then the error is disregarded in future calculations. For example, if there is a mark for the net profit figure in the profit and loss account and a candidate fails to get this mark, he or she would not lose a further mark for using his or her own profit figure as an addition to the proprietor's capital account.

If you make any assumptions then state them.

### Numerical and written answers

This type of question seems to be the most popular type with examiners since they can test a range of skills. In the written sections plan what needs to be said by making a few brief notes. Arrange your thoughts into a logical progression then start your answer.

- Identify what you are going to say
- Discuss it in general terms
- Apply your thoughts to the numerical part of the question if it is appropriate

### Written response questions

Make a plan of what you intend to say. Organise the facts into a logical order. This will make sure that you do not repeat yourself (you will only be rewarded once for a particular point). Try to write as neatly as possible. If your writing is difficult to read it may be that your teacher has become familiar with it and therefore can decipher it, but the examiner will be seeing your handwriting for the first time. Do not use your own abbreviations.

## EXAMINATION TECHNIQUES

The key to success is *planning* and *timing*.

At the start of any examination make sure that you read the instructions on the front of the examination paper very carefully. They are there for your information and you are required to follow them. Note the number of questions that you are required to attempt.

Also note the instructions given when a choice of questions is available and how many questions you are to choose from different sections of the paper when applicable.

Take approximately 15 minutes reading through the paper to familiarise yourself with the topics being examined. Divide the remaining time by the number of marks available (the total number of marks available is generally shown on the front of your examination paper), you can then allocate your time according to the number of marks given to a question or to a part of a question. For example, on the AEB paper you will have 165 minutes left to achieve 200 marks. This is 0.8 minutes per mark (if 20 marks are available then you should spend 16 minutes on the question). If you do this you will have 5 minutes left at the end of the examination to read through your work. Do not relax during this 5 minutes – use it to check your work. It is easy to make the simplest of errors when you are working under examination conditions. This final look through your script may help you to find and correct one or more such errors.

During the examination, when you have used the allotted time on a question, quickly jot down anything that you have not yet included in your answer. Leave a space so that you can return to this question later, time permitting. You must move on to the next question. Many candidates fail to do justice to themselves because they spend too long on one or two questions early in the examination, leaving themselves insufficient time to either complete the full paper or to answer later questions to the same standard as the earlier ones.

When you are required to make a choice between questions, take time to read the questions carefully in order to ensure that you can do all parts of the question you finally choose. Avoid being tempted to choose a question after reading and recognising only one or two parts of it. In order to obtain high marks you need to be able to attempt all parts of a question.

In the written sections of a question identify the key word(s). The examiner puts these in the question as an indication of how you are required to respond. *State*, *list*, *describe* indicate that the examiner expects you to simply give information. If the question asks you to *evaluate* or *analyse* you will be expected to provide a developed argument which may balance the potential advantages and disadvantages of a given situation or decision.

Remember the points made previously about planning your answers. Ultimately, it will save you time and you will also present a much more logical and coherent answer for the examiner to read. It is much easier for an examiner to award marks when points are made in a clear and structured fashion. Avoid falling into the trap of recognising a word or phrase in a question which triggers that well known response 'all I know about . . .' Make sure that your answer is relevant to the question set.

Remember you can gain a good grade even if you give less than perfect answers.

## FINAL PREPARATION

### The week before the examination

Make sure that you know the exact requirements of the examination board whose papers you are sitting.

- How many questions are there on the paper?
- How many compulsory questions?
- How many sections are there in the paper?
- How many questions do you have to answer in each section?
- What overall weighting do the papers have?

Make sure that you are capable of sitting and concentrating for three hours. As the day of the examination draws closer everyone has their own keys to success. At this stage you should have a thorough knowledge of most topic areas on your syllabus but do not stop revising.

### The night before the examination

Because we are all individuals we may all have different strategies for coping with the night before. I have known candidates who have gone to the cinema the night before the examination and have gained a grade 'A'. I have also known candidates who gained a grade

'U' after going to the cinema the night before an important examination. Some people revise into the early hours of the morning with equally different results.

You must do what you feel most comfortable doing. If you do continue revising, concentrate on your weaker areas; by doing this you may just commit to short-term memory a couple of points that may improve your final grade.

Spend some time getting together the things that you will need for the examination:

- two or three pens (not red);
- two sharpened pencils (do not use these when answering the questions);
- an eraser;
- ruler;
- watch;
- calculator.

Check that you have any documentation that may be needed by the examination centre (identification, room number, seat number etc).

## The day of the examination

If you have time, you may feel the need to glance through your notes. This should help to boost your confidence and it should reinforce your short-term memory. Leave for the examination centre in plenty of time, in case your bus or car should be delayed. Remember, this is the day that you have been preparing for. It is the concluding part to all those weeks of revision preparation. It is the conclusion of one or two years of hard work at school or college.

# ACCOUNTING TOPICS

*In this section:*

Chapter 1:    Double entry

Chapter 2:    Incomplete records

Chapter 3:    Concepts and conventions of accounting

Chapter 4:    Partnership accounts

Chapter 5:    Limited company accounts

Chapter 6:    Analysis and interpretation of accounts

Chapter 7:    Cash flow statements

Chapter 8:    Material costing

Chapter 9:    Costing for overheads

Chapter 10:   Budgets and budgetary control

Chapter 11:   Standard costing and variance analysis

Chapter 12:   Capital investment appraisal

Chapter 13:   Absorption and marginal costing

Chapter 14:   Social accounting

*Each chapter features:*

■ *Units in this chapter:* a list of the main topic heads to follow.

■ *Chapter objectives:* a brief comment on how the topics relate to what has gone before, and to the syllabus. Key ideas and skills which are covered in the chapter are introduced.

■ *The main text:* this is divided into numbered topic units for ease of reference.

■ *Chapter roundup:* a brief summary of the chapter.

■ *Worked questions:* typical exam questions, with tutorial notes and our suggested answers.

■ *Question bank:* further questions, with comments on the pitfalls to avoid and points to include in framing your own answers.

# DOUBLE ENTRY

## Units in this chapter

1.1  *Provisions and reserves*
1.2  *Provision for depreciation*
1.3  *Bad debts*
1.4  *Provision for bad debts*
1.5  *Provision for discounts*
1.6  *Control accounts*
1.7  *Suspense accounts and the correction of errors*

## Chapter objectives

Advanced level examinations do not generally examine basic double entry book-keeping methods of recording financial transactions. It is assumed that all candidates for the examination are well versed in the techniques used up to the extraction of a trial balance, but certain topics do appear from time to time in advanced level papers. The popular examination questions involve techniques which are undertaken after the trial balance has been extracted from the books of account. The purpose of this chapter is to help you recall the topics that examiners often include in papers.

Key topics and concepts covered in this chapter are:

- provisions;
- reserves;
- methods of calculating depreciation;
- book-keeping for depreciation;
- asset disposal;
- bad debts;
- provision for bad debts;
- provision for discounts;
- errors and their correction;
- suspense accounts;
- journal entries.

## 1.1    PROVISIONS AND RESERVES

### PROVISIONS

**A provision** is an amount set aside out of profits for a known expense, the amount of which is uncertain.

This definition covers the amount written off profits:
- by way of depreciation of fixed assets;
- to reflect that all trade debtors may not pay their debts;
- to meet a liability, such as damages claimed by a customer.

We know that our assets depreciate – we don't know by how much.
We may know from past experience that all our debtors may not pay – we don't know how much the potential bad debts may be.
We may know that a customer is suing for damages – we do not know how much will be awarded.

### RESERVES

**A reserve** is any amount set aside out of profits which is not a provision.

Reserves are made at the discretion of the directors of a limited company.
If you have difficulty in remembering a definition in the heat of the examination room, or in expressing yourself or your knowledge, use an example and explain the effect the example will have on the profit and loss account and on the balance sheet.
Remember that:
- increases in provisions appear with expenses on the profit and loss account, thus reducing profits;
- reserves do not affect trading profits;
- transfers to reserves appear 'below the line', that is after the pre-tax profit or net loss has been calculated;
- all provisions reduce assets on the balance sheet as they are credit balances.

## 1.2    PROVISION FOR DEPRECIATION

The purchase of a fixed asset is capital expenditure. That is, the asset will yield a string of benefits (profits) to the business over a number of years.
The accruals concept states that all expenses incurred in a particular time period should be matched with the revenues that the expense has helped to generate.
A fixed asset is used over a number of years to produce goods or services, so we must spread its cost over those time periods.

**Depreciation** is the apportioning of the cost of an asset over its useful life.

### WHICH ASSETS DEPRECIATE?

SSAP 12 tells us that all fixed assets with a finite life depreciate. So all fixed assets, with the exception of land, should be depreciated.

The book-keeping entries to record depreciation are always the same, it is only the amount to be charged to the profit and loss account which changes according to the method of calculation used.

EXAMPLE 1

The depreciation on a fixed asset for the year has been calculated at £750.

**Required**
The entries in the profit and loss account and the entries in the provision for depreciation of fixed asset account.

**Solution**

**Profit & loss account**

Provision for depreciation          £750

**Provision for depreciation**

Profit & loss account     £750

*Point to note*
Always keep the fixed asset account and the provision for depreciation of fixed asset account separate. (As usual with an *always* there is an exception! You may need to put the two accounts together when preparing a set of final accounts from incomplete records.)

Although at Advanced level candidates will not be asked to describe the various methods of providing for depreciation it may be necessary to use the straight line method and the reducing balance method.

## THE STRAIGHT LINE METHOD (ALSO CALLED THE EQUAL INSTALMENT METHOD)

The cost of the fixed asset is divided equally over the assets' lifetime.

EXAMPLE 2

A van costs £17,000. Its disposal value in 5 years time is expected to be £2,000.

**Required**
Calculate the annual depreciation charge.

**Solution**
The annual depreciation charge is £3,000

$$\text{Formula} = \frac{\text{Cost} - \text{Disposal value}}{\text{Useful life in years}} \qquad \frac{£17,000 - £2,000}{5}$$

## THE REDUCING BALANCE METHOD

There are a number of variations of this method, but the most common method, used in examinations, deducts a given percentage from the net book value of the fixed asset each year.

EXAMPLE 3

A lorry costs £20,000.

**Required**
Calculate the annual depreciation to be charged to the profit and loss account if the rate of depreciation to be charged each year is 40% using the reducing balance method.

**Solution**
Deprecation to be charged in year 1 is £8,000 (20,000 × 40%)
Depreciation to be charged in year 2 is £4,800 ((20,000 − 8,000) × 40%)
Depreciation to be charged in year 3 is £2,880 ((20,000 − 8,000) − 4,800 × 40%)
and so on.

*Point to note*
Any disposal value is ignored when using this method.

Examination questions tend to ask candidates to calculate a number of years' depreciation and then to dispose of the asset.

A source of concern to many students is how to treat depreciation when an asset is sold part-way through a financial year, especially when the question stipulates that 'depreciation is to be provided for on a monthly basis'.

### EXAMPLE 4

A business whose financial year end is 30 December purchased a machine costing £20,000 on 1 July. Depreciation is charged at 10% per annum on cost calculated on a monthly basis.

**Required**

The machinery at cost account, and the provision for depreciation on machinery account, for the first two years.

**Solution**

| | **Machinery at cost** | |
|---|---|---|
| Year 1 Bank | £20,000 | |

| | **Provision for depreciation of machinery** | |
|---|---|---|
| | Year 1 P & L a/c | £1,000 |
| | (20,000 × 10%, but for only 6 months) | |
| | Year 2 P & L a/c | £2,000 |
| | (20,000 × 10% for full year) | |

What happens when an asset is sold part way through the year?

Work carefully through the following example. If you miscalculate the depreciation charge transferred to the disposal account refer to the notes after the solution.

### EXAMPLE 5

Anne Binks depreciates her office machinery using the straight line method at a rate of 10% per annum on cost, calculated on a monthly basis. Her financial year end is 31 December.

Machine JJH/32 was purchased on 1 January 1991 at a cost of £8,000.

Machine MLK/73 was purchased on 1 July 1993 at a cost of £10,000.

Machine 51/SMH was purchased on 1 October 1995 at a cost of £12,000. This amount was settled by trading in machine MLK/73 at an agreed value of £5,000, the balance being paid in cash.

**Required**

Prepare the following accounts as they would appear in the general ledger of Anne Binks for the years ended 31 December 1991, 1992, 1993, 1994, and 1995:

(a) office machinery at cost;
(b) provision for depreciation of office machinery;
(c) office machinery disposal account.

**Solution**

**Office machinery at cost**

| | | £ | | | £ |
|---|---|---|---|---|---|
| 1/1/91 | Bank | 8,000 | | | |
| 1/7/93 | Bank | 10,000 | 31/12/93 Balance c/d | | 18,000 |
| | | 18,000 | | | 18,000 |
| 1/1/94 | Balance b/d | 18,000 | 31/12/94 Balance c/d | | 18,000 |
| 1/1/95 | Balance b/d | 18,000 | 1/10/95 Disposal | | 10,000 |
| 1/10/95 | Bank | 7,000 | | | |
| 1/10/95 | Disposal | 5,000 | 31/12/95 Balance c/d | | 20,000 |
| | | 30,000 | | | 30,000 |
| 1/1/94 | Balance b/d | 20,000 | | | |

### Provision for depreciation of office machinery

|          |             | £     |          |             | £     |
|----------|-------------|-------|----------|-------------|-------|
|          |             |       | 31/12/91 | P & L a/c   | 800   |
| 31/12/92 | Balance c/d | 1,600 | 31/12/92 | P & L a/c   | 800   |
|          |             | 1,600 |          |             | 1,600 |
|          |             |       | 1/1/93   | Balance b/d | 1,600 |
| 31/12/93 | Balance c/d | 2,900 | 31/12/93 | P & L a/c   | 1,300 |
|          |             | 2,900 |          |             | 2,900 |
|          |             |       | 1/1/94   | Balance b/d | 2,900 |
| 31/12/94 | Balance c/d | 4,700 | 31/12/94 | P & L a/c   | 1,800 |
|          |             | 4,700 |          |             | 4,700 |
| 1/10/95  | Disposal    | 1,500 | 1/1/94   | Balance b/d | 4,700 |
| 31/12/95 | Balance c/d | 4,300 | 31/12/95 | P & L a/c   | 1,100 |
|          |             | 5,800 |          |             | 5,800 |
|          |             |       | 1/1/96   | Balance b/d | 4,300 |

### Office machinery disposal MLK/73

|         |             | £      |          |             | £      |
|---------|-------------|--------|----------|-------------|--------|
| 1/10/95 | Office mach | 10,000 | 1/10/95  | Depreciation | 1,500  |
|         |             |        | 1/10/95  | Machinery   | 5,000  |
|         |             |        | 31/12/95 | P&L a/c     | 3,500  |
|         |             | 10,000 |          |             | 10,000 |

*Points to note*

- Transfer the whole of the cost of the fixed asset being sold from the fixed asset account to the disposal account (not the selling price).

- Examine each profit and loss account entry in the provision for depreciation of office machinery account. Ask yourself 'how much of each entry "belongs to" the asset being sold'.

  e.g.   When MLK/73 was sold:        £
  
  | | £ | |
  |---|---|---|
  | 1991 depreciation | 0 | |
  | 1992 depreciation | 0 | |
  | 1993 depreciation | 500 | (half year) |
  | 1994 depreciation | 1,000 | (full year) |
  | 1995 depreciation | 0 | (you can only take out of the account what has already gone in) |

  The depreciation that 'belongs to' MLK/73 is £1,500 (500 + 1,000).

  The reference to charging depreciation affects the year of purchase not the year of sale.

- MLK/73 was 'sold' to the machinery supplier for £5,000.

  Two entries are needed in the office machinery account:

  | One for the trade in | DR Office machinery | CR Office machinery disposal |
  |---|---|---|
  | the other for the | | |
  | balance to be paid | DR Office machinery | CR Bank |

## WRITTEN QUESTIONS ON DEPRECIATION

These tend to concentrate on the relationship between depreciation and cash. Does depreciation provide a cache of money enabling a business to buy a new asset in the future? The straightforward answer is that there is no direct relationship between depreciation and cash.

**Depreciation** is a non-cash expense – a book entry.

A collector does not appear at your front door every Friday night to collect the depreciation on your car!

Depreciation does not provide cash for the replacement of fixed assets but, when depreciation is charged to the profit and loss account, profits are reduced.

- This *may* have a deterrent effect on the proprietor. He or she *may* withdraw less from the business as a consequence.
- Directors of a company *may* recommend a lower dividend because profits have been reduced.
- So, depreciation *may* result in funds being held in the business which might otherwise have been taken out of the business.

The same effect is also seen when a business makes a provision for bad debts.

## 1.3   BAD DEBTS

The majority of transactions in the modern business world take place using credit facilities.

Inevitably, there will always be some customers who cannot pay their debts. Immediately it is established that debtors cannot pay their debts they must be transferred out of the debtors' accounts in the sales ledger to the bad debts account in the general ledger.

**Debtors** are assets. Debtors who cannot pay are no longer assets.

If they were left in the sales ledger the current assets would be overstated (as would profits and capital). This situation would violate the concept of prudence.

At the end of each financial year all revenue expenditure accounts in the general ledger are closed by transferring the year's charge to the profit and loss account. The only items left in these accounts are any accruals or prepayments relating to the following financial year.

The bad debts account is a revenue expenditure account, and at the end of the financial year the account is closed by a transfer to the profit and loss account.

### EXAMPLE

The following balances appear in the sales ledger of Charles Draper.

|  | **Tom** |
|---|---|
| Balance b/d | £235 |

|  | **Dick** |
|---|---|
| Balance b/d | £160 |

|  | **Harry** |
|---|---|
| Balance b/d | £72 |

|  | **Mary** |
|---|---|
| Balance b/d | £84 |

During the financial year the following information is available:

Tom's business has gone into liquidation, he is only able to pay £100. Mary is unable to pay any of her outstanding debt.

These two debtors must be written off since they no longer represent assets of the business. They are written off to the bad debts account.

At the end of the financial year the bad debts account is written off to the profit and loss account.

| | £ | | £ |
|---|---|---|---|
| | | **Tom** | |
| Bal b/d | 235 | Cash | 100 |
| | | Bad debts | 135 |
| | 235 | | 235 |

| | £ | **Mary** | £ |
|---|---|---|---|
| Bal b/d | 84 | Bad debts | 84 |

**Bad debts (general ledger)**

| | | | |
|---|---|---|---|
| Tom | 135 | P & L a/c | 219 |
| Mary | 84 | | |
| | 219 | | 219 |

**Profit and loss account for the year ended 19xx**

| | | | |
|---|---|---|---|
| Bad debts❷ | £219 | Gross profit (say) | £158,000❶ |

❶ This gross profit figure includes sales on credit – including sales to Tom and Mary. We cannot eliminate these sales so,

❷ we cancel the sales out with a debit entry after the gross profit calculation.

*Points to note*

- If the bad debts were not written off, and gross profit and net profit would be overstated.

- If the debtors are not removed from the sales ledger an asset would be overstated. In both instances the concept of prudence is being applied.

## 1.4 PROVISION FOR BAD DEBTS

As well as actual bad debts there may be other outstanding debts which *could* prove to be bad. It may be necessary to make a provision for these doubtful debts.

The amount of the provision is generally calculated:

- from past experience – the managers of a business may know that in an average year 2% of the business debtors usually do not pay. They will make provision in the light of that knowledge and their knowledge of the prevailing economic conditions.

- by examining each individual debtor's balance to determine how long it has been outstanding. The provision is then made taking into account the possibility of non-payment. The longer a debt has been outstanding the more likely it is to prove to be bad. This method uses an age profile of debtors.

**Note** Some teachers and text books use the term provision for bad debts, others use the term provision for **doubtful debts**. Either heading is acceptable. In the examination your question should be headed according to what the examiner requires.

### EXAMPLE

Edna Elliot is owed £26,000 by debtors at the end of her first year of trading. It is believed that 2.5% of these outstanding debts may well prove to be bad.

**Required**

The provision for bad debts account and a profit and loss account extract as they would appear at the end of Edna Elliot's first year of trading.

**Solution**

- The profits need to be reduced by £650.

- Debtors need to be reduced by £650.

**Provision for bad debts**

| | |
|---|---|
| End year 1 P &L a/c | £650 |

**Profit and loss account for the year ended 19xx**

| | | | |
|---|---|---|---|
| | | Gross profit (say) | £158,000❶ |
| Provision for bad debts❷ | £650 | | |

❶ This figure includes sales which may not be paid. We cannot eliminate these so,

❷ we cancel the sales out with a debit entry after the gross profit calculation. The provision account is adjusted each year to reflect the total of doubtful debts in that year.

If Edna needed a provision in the following year of £800, £150 would be debited to the profit and loss account in year 2. The provision account will show:

**Provision for bad debts**

| | £ | | £ |
|---|---|---|---|
| | | Year 1 P & L a/c | 650 |
| Year 2 Balance c/d | 800 | Year 2 P& L a/c | 150 |
| | 800 | | 800 |
| | | Year 3 Balance b/d | 800 |

If in year 3 Edna Elliot needed a provision of £1,100. The provision for bad debts account would show:

**Provision for bad debts**

| | £ | | £ |
|---|---|---|---|
| | | Year 3 Balance b/d | 800 |
| Year 3 Balance c/d | 1,100 | Year 3 P & L a/c | 300 |
| | 1,100 | | 1,100 |
| | | Year 4 Balance b/d | 1,100 |

If in year 4 Edna only required a provision of £750, some of the profits previously allocated to the provision for bad debts account would need to be 'given back' to the profit and loss account. There is an over-provision.

The provision for bad debts and profit and loss account would show the following entries:

**Provision for bad debts**

| | £ | | £ |
|---|---|---|---|
| Year 4 P & L a/c | 350 | Year 4 Balance b/d | 1,100 |
| Year 4 Balance c/d | 750 | | |
| | 1,100 | | 1,100 |
| | | Year 5 Balance b/d | 750 |

**Profit and loss account for the year ended 19xx**

| | £ | | £ |
|---|---|---|---|
| | | Gross profit (say) | 158,000 |
| | | Over-provision for bad debts | 350 |

*Points to note*

- Only the increase or decrease in the provision is shown in the profit and loss account.
- The balance on the provision account is shown (like all end of year balances) on the sheet for balances, the balance sheet. It is deducted from the debtors' figure.

## 1.5 PROVISION FOR DISCOUNTS ALLOWED

The managers of some businesses create a provision for discounts allowed. They assume that some debtors, outstanding at the balance sheet date, will take advantage of available discounts, when they settle their debt.

If discounts are deducted by the debtors when they do pay, the debtors figure in the balance sheet is overstated by the amount of that discount.

The book-keeping entries are very similar to the entries required to provide for bad debts.

**Note** You may find that some teachers and some textbooks refer to **Discount on debtors**.

EXAMPLE

George Hay makes a provision for discounts allowed of 2% on debtors balances outstanding at the end of each financial year. His financial year end is 31 December.

Debtors outstanding at 31 December 1993 (his first year of trading) were      £45,900
Debtors outstanding at 31 December 1994 were                                  £51,800
Debtors outstanding at 31 December 1995 were                                  £50,500

**Required**

The provision for discounts allowed account as it would appear in the books of George Hay.

**Solution**

Provision for discounts allowed

| | £ | | £ |
|---|---|---|---|
| | | 31 December 1993 P & L a/c | 918 |
| 31 December 1994 Bal c/d | 1,036 | 31 December 1994 P & L a/c | 118 |
| | 1,036 | | 1,036 |
| 31 December 1995 P & L a/c | 26 | 1 January 1995 Balance b/d | 1,036 |
| 31 December 1995 Balance c/d | 1,010 | | |
| | 1,036 | | 1,036 |
| | | 1 January 1996 Balance b/d | 1,010 |

The extracts from the profit and loss accounts of each year would appear thus:

Profit and loss account for the year ended 31 December 1993

Provision for discount allowed            918

Profit and loss account for the year ended 31 December 1994

Provision for discount allowed            118

Profit and loss account for the year ended 31 December 1995

Over-provision for discount allowed            26

In the appropriate balance sheet the following amounts would be deducted from the debtors figure:

Balance sheet as at 31 December 1993

| | £ | £ |
|---|---|---|
| Debtors | 45,900 | |
| *Less* provision for discounts | 918 | 44,982 |

Balance sheet as at 31 December 1994

| | | |
|---|---|---|
| Debtors | 51,800 | |
| *Less* provision for discounts | 1,036 | 50,764 |

Balance sheet as at 31 December 1995

| | | |
|---|---|---|
| Debtors | 50,500 | |
| *Less* provision for discounts | 1,010 | 49,490 |

## 1.6   CONTROL ACCOUNTS

It is unusual for a question at Advanced level to require candidates to prepare straight forward control accounts; questions generally deal with events or errors that have been discovered after the control have been prepared.

Questions are designed to test candidates' knowledge of:

• how control accounts are prepared;

• the sources of information used to compile the control accounts;

• the relationship between the control accounts and the ledger balances.

The following tables show the sources of information used to draw up control accounts.

| Source | Purchase ledger control account | | Source |
|---|---|---|---|
| Previous month's control account | Balances b/d | Balances b/d | Previous month's control account |
| Cash book | Cash | Purchases | Purchase day book |
| Cash book | Discount received | | |
| Purchase returns day book | Returns outward | | |
| Journal | Transfers to sales ledger | | |
| Balances from purchase ledger | Balances c/d | Balances c/d | Balances from purchase ledger |
| | Balances b/d | Balances b/d | |

| Source | Sales ledger control account | | Source |
|---|---|---|---|
| Previous month's control account | Balances b/d | Balances b/d | Previous month's control account |
| Sales day book | Sales | Cash | Cash book |
| | | Discount allowed | Cash book |
| | | Returns inward | Sales returns day book |
| | | Transfers to purchase ledger | Journal |
| | | Bad debts written off | Journal |
| Balances from sales ledger | Balances c/d | Balances c/d | Balances from sales ledger |
| | Balances b/d | Balances b/d | |

### Points to note

- Control accounts only contain credit transactions with customers and suppliers. Ignore cash sales and cash purchases.
- Provision for bad debts (and provision for discounts) is not included in the sales ledger control account; it is a general ledger account.
- Transfers between the sales ledger and the purchase ledger are sometimes called set-offs or contra items.

It is worth spending some time making sure that you know where each figure in the control accounts has come from. Each entry is a total from a book of original entry (a day book). Some businesses keep control accounts as part of the double entry system, i.e. as general ledger accounts. They are *integrated* into the system. In this case the individual ledger accounts are only used to check against suppliers' statements and to enable the business to send out statements and reminders to credit customers. The personal ledgers contain individual accounts for memorandum purposes only.

Other businesses use their personal ledgers as part of the double entry system. The control accounts are used to check the accuracy of all the entries in the purchase and sales ledgers.

Whether the control accounts are part of the double entry system or not, they are *always prepared in the same way* (see the table above). The only time it is different for an examination candidate is where an answer requiring a double entry is necessary.

### EXAMPLE 1

A purchase of goods for resale, on credit, from Iain John for £932, had been omitted from the purchase day book of Kathy Larch.

**Required**
Journal entries to correct the error in the books of Kathy Larch.

**Solution 1**
(Where Kathy keeps control accounts as part of her double entry system.)

Journal

| | DR | CR |
|---|---|---|
| Purchases | £932 | |
| Purchase ledger control account | | £932 |

**Solution 2**
(Where Kathy's control accounts are not part of her double entry system.)

Journal

| | DR | CR |
|---|---|---|
| Purchases | £932 | |
| Iain John | | £932 |

The most popular type of question to be examined at Advanced level requires candidates to reconcile the balance shown in the control account with the total of the balances extracted from the appropriate ledger

### EXAMPLE

Maurice Naylor maintains control accounts as an integral part of his general ledger. He has prepared a sales ledger control account for January 1996 with information derived from his subsidiary books. The debit balance shown in the sales ledger control account at 31 January 1996 failed to agree with the schedule of debtors extracted from the sales ledger at that date. The total value of debtors according to the sales ledger at 31 January 1996 was £7,436.

The following errors were subsequently discovered:

❶ Mame Neal, a credit customer, had sent a cheque for £213 to Maurice on 9 January 1996. The cheque had been entered in the cash book as £312.

❷ In January a page of the sales returns day book had been overcast by £100.

❸ Discounts received of £78 had been mistakenly entered in the discounts allowed column of the cash book in January 1996.

❹ A debit balance of £412 on Oliver Pink's account in the sales ledger had been set off against his account in the purchase ledger. This entry had not been recorded in either control account.

❺ The provision for bad debts is to be increased from £617 to £891 at 31 January 1996.

❻ £29 discount allowed to Ruth Simpson had been correctly entered in the cash book but had not been entered in Ruth's account.

**Required**

(a) A calculation of total debtors for the month of January 1996 as shown in Maurice's sales ledger control account before the errors had been corrected.

(b) Calculate the total of the debtors balances at 31 January 1996 after the errors have been corrected.

**Solution**

(a)       **Maurice Naylor sales ledger control account for January 1996**

| | £ | | £ |
|---|---|---|---|
| Balance b/d | | Purchase ledger control ❹ | 412 |
| Cash ❶ | 99 | | |
| Sales returns ❷ | 100 | | |
| Discount allowed ❸ | 78 | Balances c/d | * |
| | | | |
| Balances b/d | * | | |

| | | £ |
|---|---|---|
| (b) Debtors balances as per schedule | | 7,436 |
| Increase in Mame Neal's balance ❶ | | 99 |
| Decrease in Ruth Simpson's balance ❻ | | (29) |
| | | 7,506* |

The corrected total debtors balance* from the adjusted schedule can be inserted as the correct closing debtors' balance. By working 'backwards' the opening balance can be determined as £7,641 (7,506 + 412 – 99 – 100 – 78).

The key to this type of problem is knowing whether each error involves:

| | | |
|---|---|---|
| the individual posting to the customer's account in the the ledger balances shown in the ledger ❶ and ❻ | hence affecting | the ledger balances shown in the schedule of debtors |

**or**

| | | |
|---|---|---|
| the totals in the subsidiary books, which are the source of all the figures in the control accounts ❶, ❷, ❸ and ❹ | hence affecting | the control account |

### Points to note

- Some errors affect neither the schedule of debtors nor the control account ❺.
- The provision for bad debts account will be in the general ledger.
- Only an entry in the purchase ledger or the sales ledger will have an effect on a control account.
- The numbered bullets in the accounts show where the various entries occur or are corrected.

## 1.7  SUSPENSE ACCOUNTS AND THE CORRECTION OF ERRORS

When a difference exists in a trial balance a book-keeper cannot expect a set of final accounts, produced using those figures, to balance.

The difference on the trial balance is placed into a temporary account, called a suspense account. A suspense account is where the difference on a trial balance is placed until the errors that caused the difference are located and rectified. In reality, the amount of time and effort put into eliminating the difference from the trial balance will depend on the magnitude of the difference.

If the trial balance of Tina Unsworth, the owner of a window cleaning business, did not balance by £2,000, this would probably represent a significant amount. If the trial balance of General Motors was out by the dollar equivalent of £2,000 then this would definitely be insignificant, and unless there were suspicious circumstances surrounding the difference it could justifiably be written off to the profit and loss account. However, it should still be entered in a suspense account and hopefully the error will be found.

In an examination you can be certain that, when the errors given to you in the question are corrected, the trial balance will balance. Questions involving errors and suspense accounts are often linked with journal entries. (This after all is one of the uses of the journal.)

In this type of question the examiner is testing whether:

- the candidate knows what the original entry was;
- the candidate knows what the correct entry should have been;
- the candidate can take the correct remedial action;
- the candidate knows how to use the journal.

Many candidates get confused when correcting errors because they sometimes see the same figure appearing three times – triple entry book-keeping it seems! Remember:

- The system being used is a double entry system.
- You will always need at least one double entry to correct any error.
- You may find it useful to avoid using figures for the original incorrect entry.

## EXAMPLE 1

Repairs costing £710 carried out on a lorry has been entered in the motor vehicles account.

**Required**

The journal entries correcting the error.

**Solution**

**Motor vehicles**

| | £ | | £ |
|---|---|---|---|
| Bank ❶ | xxxx | Motor vehicle expenses ❷ | 710 |

**Motor vehicle expenses**

| | £ |
|---|---|
| Motor vehicles ❸ | 710 |

❶ The incorrect £710 is included in this amount.

❷ This £710 removes the error from the motor vehicles account.

❸ The correct entry.

The journal entries are:

**Journal**

| | £ | £ |
|---|---|---|
| Motor vehicle expenses | 710 | |
| Motor vehicles | | 710 |

## EXAMPLE 2

Page 131 of the purchase day book has been undercast by £1,000 (the business does not maintain integrated control accounts in the general ledger).

**Required**

The journal entries to correct the error.

**Solution**

**Purchases**

| | £ |
|---|---|
| PDB ❶ | xxxx |
| 'other account' ❷ | 1,000 |

❶ This figure is £1,000 less than it should be.

❷ This £1,000 corrects the purchases account.

But now a double entry is needed. Where can the other entry be placed? The only other account that can be used is a suspense account.

**Suspense account**

| | | £ |
|---|---|---|
| | Purchases ❸ | 1,000 |

❸ This completes the double entry.

The journal entries are:

**Journal**

| | £ | £ |
|---|---|---|
| Purchases | 1,000 | |
| | | 1,000 |

## EXAMPLE 3

Vincent West extracted a trial balance from his ledgers at the close of business on 31 January 1996. The trial balance totals failed to agree. (Vincent does not maintain integrated control accounts in his general ledger.) In early February Vincent found the following errors:

1 The telephone account had been undercast by £100.

2 A cheque paid to Yip Deng for £134 had been posted to the credit of his account.

3 Discounts received £63 had been posted to the debit of the discounts allowed account as £36.

4 Commission paid £1,200 had been posted to the credit of the commission received account.

5 Goods returned by Alice Evans £84 to Vincent had been completely omitted from the books of account.

**Required**

(a) The journal entries to correct the errors. (Narratives are not required.)

(b) A suspense account showing clearly the original trial balance error.

**Solution**

(a)

|  | Journal | £ | £ |
|---|---|---|---|
| 1 | Telephone | 100 | |
| | Suspense | | 100 |
| 2 | Yip Deng | 268 | |
| | Suspense | | 268 |
| 3 | Suspense | 99 | |
| | Discount Allowed | | 36 |
| | Discount Received | | 63 |
| 4 | Commission received | 1,200 | |
| | Commission paid | 1,200 | |
| | Suspense | | 2 400 |
| 5 | Sales returns | 84 | |
| | Alice Evans | | 84 |

(b)

**Suspense account**

| | £ | | £ |
|---|---|---|---|
| Trial balance difference | | Telephone | 100 |
| *(Missing figure)* | 2,669 | Yip Deng | 268 |
| Discounts allowed | 36 | Commission received | 1,200 |
| Discounts received | 63 | Commission paid | 1,200 |
| | 2,768 | | 2,768 |

Workings:

**1**

**Telephone**

| | £ | | £ |
|---|---|---|---|
| Cash ❶ | xxxx | | |
| Suspense ❷ | 100 | | |

❶ This amount is £100 short.
❷ This account is now correct.

**Suspense**

| | | | £ |
|---|---|---|---|
| | | Telephone ❸ | 100 |

❸ Completes the double entry.

**2**

**Yip Deng**

| | £ | | £ |
|---|---|---|---|
| Suspense ❷ | 134 | Cash ❶ | xxxx |
| Suspense ❸ | 134 | | |

**Suspense**

| | | | £ |
|---|---|---|---|
| | | Yip Deng ❹ | 268 |

❶ This amount includes the original error.
❷ This £134 cancels out the error.
❸ The correct entry.
❹ Completes the double entry.

3
                          **Discount allowed**
                          £                                    £
    Cash book ❶          xxxx    Suspense ❷                    36
                          **Discount received**
                                  Suspense ❸                    £
                                                                63
                          **Suspense**
                          £
    Discount allowed ❹    36
    Discount received ❺   63

    ❶   This amount includes the original error.
    ❷   This £36 cancels out the error.
    ❸   The correct entry.
    ❹❺ Completes the double entry.

4
                          **Commission received**
                          £                                    £
    Suspense ❷           1,200    Cash ❶                      xxxx
                          **Commission paid**
                          £
    Suspense ❸           1,200
                          **Suspense**
                                                               £
                          Commission received ❹               1,200
                          Commission paid ❺                   1,200

    ❶   This amount includes the original error.
    ❷   This £1,200 cancels out the error.
    ❸   The correct entry.
    ❹❺ Completes the double entry.

5
                          **Sales returns**
                          £
    Alice Evans          84
                          **Alice Evans**
                                                               £
                          Sales returns                        84

Double entry is complete without the use of a suspense account.

*Point to note*
The numbered bullets show where the various errors are corrected.

---

## Chapter roundup

Chapter 1 has looked at areas that you probably studied for your GCSE examination or in the first year of your A level course.

It has refreshed your memory on the most popular A level double entry topics.

You should be able to answer questions set on the subjects covered as well as apply the principles to other problems.

---

# Illustrative questions

**1**  Toltec Ltd is a small company established on 1 April 1991. Company records reveal that machinery was purchased as follows:

|               | £      |
| ------------- | ------ |
| 1 April 1991  | 20,000 |
| 1 April 1992  | 15,500 |
| 1 July 1993   | 16,800 |

Company policy is to provide for depreciation using the straight line method at a rate of 20% per annum on cost. A full year's depreciation is charged in the year of acquisition of an asset but none in the year of disposal.

On 1 July 1994 the company purchased a machine at a cost of £7,000 and on 1 March 1995 a further machine was acquired for £1,200. A machine which had cost £4,000 on 1 April 1991 was sold for £1,000 on 30 September 1994.

*Required*

(a) Write up the following accounts for the year ended 31 March 1995:
(i) machinery at cost account;
(ii) provision for depreciation on machinery account;
(iii) disposal of machinery account. (15)
(b) State clearly the main objectives of providing for depreciation of fixed costs. (8)
(c) The annual charging of depreciation to the profit and loss account ensures the availability of cash funds for the replacement of fixed assets. Discuss this statement. (6)
(d) State why it is important to apply the concept of consistency to depreciation methods and rates. (6)
(AEB)

*Tutorial note*
Take care to transfer the machine at £4 000 to the disposal account. Spend just less than half of your time on the numerical section (13 minutes), leaving 15 minutes for the written section. Do not list the different ways of calculating depreciation in any section.

*Suggested answer*

(a) (i) **Toltec Ltd machinery at cost**

| | | | |
|---|---|---|---|
| 1 April 1994 Bal b/d | 52,300 | 30 Sept 1994 Disposal | 4,000 ❶ |
| 1 July 1994 Cash | 7,000 | 31 Mar 1995 Bal c/d | 56,500 |
| 1 Mar 1995 Cash | 1,200 | | |
| | 60,500 | | 60,500 |
| 1 April 1995 Bal b/d | 56,500 | | |

❶ The 'whole' of the asset is transferred to the disposal account *not* just the selling price.

(ii) **Provision for depreciation of machinery**

| | | | |
|---|---|---|---|
| 30 Sept 1994 Disposal | 2 400 | 1 April 1994 Bal b/d | 21,560 |
| 31 Mar 1995 Bal c/d | 30,460 | 31 Mar 1995 P & L a/c | 11,300 |
| | 32,860 | | 32,860 |
| | | 1 April 1995 Bal b/d | 30,460 |

(iii) **Disposal of machinery**

| | | | |
|---|---|---|---|
| 30 Sept 1994 Machinery | 4,000 | 30 Sept 1994 Depreciation | 2,400 |
| | | 30 Sept 1994 Cash | 1,000 |
| | | 31 Mar 1995 P & L a/c | 600 |
| | 4,000 | | 4,000 |

(b) To accord with the accruals concept – matching the use of the machine with the profits it has helped to generate. Thus ensuring that each accounting period bears part of the cost of the machine.
To spread the cost of capital expenditure over the useful life of the asset.
Since assets decline in value over their lifetime this needs to be measured.
The profits and the balance sheet value of the machine will both be reduced.

(c) Not true. Remember no-one collects the depreciation on your mountain bike every Friday night. Depreciation is a non-cash expense and so does not provide a cache of money at the end of the asset's life.
It is possible to set aside cash to ensure that replacement assets can be purchased, but this is a cash management problem.

An amount, equivalent to the rate of depreciation charged, could be invested each year which, together with the interest accruing, would equal the cost of the asset being replaced. However, increases in the price of the new asset may make the investment fall short of the replacement cost.

The charging of depreciation to the profit and loss account does reduce profits and should have a deterrent effect on the owners' perception of what could be taken out of the business in the form of drawings (in the case of a sole trader) or dividends (in the case of a limited company). Funds should therefore be retained within the business, but not necessarily in the form of cash.

(d) The same methods and rates should be used for calculating depreciation over time. This will ensure that any changes in profits are due to changes in management strategy and/or economic factors, and not due to annual changes in depreciation rates or policy.

It is important that profit figures can be compared with previous years and the users of accounts should be confident that they are comparing like with like as far as accounting policies are concerned.

Changes in the method or the rate will make it very difficult to determine the age of the assets or whether a fair value is shown on the balance sheet with regard to the age of the assets.

**2** Joan Hunter rents a business property at a monthly rental of £650. At 31 December 1994 she was five months in arrears with her rent payments. At her financial year end 31 December 1995 she was four months in arrears.

The rates of £1,800 per annum are payable half-yearly in advance on 1 April and 1 October each year.

At 31 December 1994 the rates for the half year to 31 March 1995 had not been paid but Joan cleared these arrears and the rates for 1995/6 were paid on the due date.

*Required*
(a) An explanation of the accruals concept.                                                     (10)
(b) From the information above prepare Joan Hunter's combined rent and rates account for the year ended 31 December 1995.                                 (10)
(c) Extracts from Joan Hunter's profit and loss account for the year ended 31 December 1995 and extracts from her balance sheet as at 31 December 1995 showing any entries regarding rent and rates.                                 (5)

*Tutorial note*
Plan your explanation. This will avoid repetition. If you find it difficult to express yourself, give examples trying to use information given in the question. If you find part (b) difficult, prepare separate accounts for rent and rates as workings then combine them.

*Suggested answer*

(a) The accruals concept (or matching concept) is concerned with the difference between revenues and expenses, rather than cash receipts and expenditures.

Revenue expenses are matched (in the profit and loss account) with the profits they have helped to generate.

If it was not adhered to, Joan's profits could be manipulated upwards or downwards by delaying payments or by paying some expenses in advance.

(b)                                         **Rent and rates**

| | £ | | | £ |
|---|---|---|---|---|
| During 1995 Cash (rent) | 8,450 | 1 Jan 1995 | Balance b/d (rent) | 3,250 |
| During 1995 Cash (rates) | 2,700 | | Balance b/d (rates) | 450 |
| | | 31 Dec 1995 | P & L a/c | 9,600 |
| 31 Dec 1995 Balance c/d (rent) | 2,600 | 31 Dec 1995 | Balance c/d (rates) | 450 |
| | 13,750 | | | 13,750 |
| 1 Jan 1996 Balance b/d | 450 | 1 Jan 1996 | Balance b/d | 2,600 |

(c)

**Profit and loss account (extract)
for the year ended 31 December 1995**

| Expenses: | £ |
| --- | --- |
| Rent and rates | 9,600 |

**Balance sheet (extract) as at 31 December 1995**

| Current assets | £ |
| --- | --- |
| Prepayment (rates) | 450 |
| Current Liability | |
| Accrued expense (rent) | 2,600 |

## CHAPTER 2

# INCOMPLETE RECORDS

## Units in this chapter

2.1 *The concept of incomplete records*
2.2 *Calculation of results for cash-based businesses*
2.3 *Preparation of full final accounts for cash-based businesses*
2.4 *Calculation of results for clubs and societies*
2.5 *Preparation of full final accounts for clubs and societies*
2.6 *Calculation of missing cash or missing stock*

## Chapter objectives

Much of an accountant's work is taken up in the preparation of the final accounts of cash-based organisations. These organisations do not keep a full set of ledgers. There is no need. Purchase and sales ledgers are only used to record credit transactions. By definition these organisations will not have many credit transactions.

There are two main types of organisation that fall into this category: small cash-based businesses, and clubs and societies.

This chapter deals with the calculation of profits or losses in the case of a business, and with the calculation of surpluses or deficits in the case of non-trading organisations.

The key topics and concepts covered in this chapter are:

- key stages in calculation of profit or loss;
- key stages in preparation of trading, profit and loss accounts from incomplete records;
- balance sheets;
- cash accounts;
- adjustment accounts (control accounts);
- final accounts;
- differences when preparing final accounts of clubs and societies;
- subscriptions accounts;
- income and expenditure accounts;
- cash deficiencies;
- stock losses.

## 2.1 THE CONCEPT OF INCOMPLETE RECORDS

The small cash-based business does not need a full set of ledgers to record all the businesses credit transactions – most of the business involves the exchange of goods and services by cash. Think of your local hairdresser, the local MacDonald's, etc.

The main source document used in the preparation of the final accounts of these organisations is the cash book, supplemented by bank statements, invoices and receipts. The task is to build up a more complete picture than the one that is presently shown by the cash book on its own. Examination questions are almost exclusively based on information given in a cash book, with additional material in note form.

There are two main types of questions set in examinations:

• where candidates are required to calculate the organisation's profit or loss; or

• where candidates are required to prepare a revenue statement and balance sheet.

It is important that you are able to recognise these two types of question.

## 2.2 CALCULATION OF RESULTS FOR CASH-BASED BUSINESSES

The key to recognising what a question requires is to read the question very carefully. When a question asks for a calculation (the first type mentioned in 2.1) the following procedure should be followed.

• **Stage 1** Calculate the opening capital figure (accumulated fund in the case of a non-trading organisation). Remember the accounting equation?

Fixed assets + Current assets – All external liabilities = Capital

• **Stage 2** Calculate the closing capital (accumulated fund).

• **Stage 3** Deduct opening capital (accumulated fund) from the closing capital (accumulated fund). This will indicate the profit/loss retained in the organisation. Some profits may have been taken out of the business as drawings. These need to be added to the retained profits.

• **Stage 4** Add drawings to the change in capital over the year.

Sometimes the proprietor of a business may introduce extra cash from outside the business. This extra capital will increase the closing assets of the business. It will increase the closing capital figure, which in turn will increase (decrease) the figure we have called retained profit (loss). Obviously this amount is not profit (loss) derived from the business so it must be disregarded in our calculation.

• **Stage 5** Deduct any injections of new capital into the business by the proprietor.

These stages can be summarised thus:

|  | Closing capital |
| --- | --- |
| *Deduct* | Opening capital |
| Gives retained profit | £xxxx |
| *Add* | Profit withdrawn during year (drawings) |
|  | £xxxx |
| *Less* | Capital introduced |
| Profit for the year | £xxxx |

### EXAMPLE

At 1 January 1995 Arthur had the following assets and liabilities: van £4,500, equipment £800, stock £450, bank balance £780.

He owed suppliers £320.

At 31 December 1995 Arthur had the following assets and liabilities: vans £12,300, equipment £750, stock £620, debtors £135, bank balance £945.

He owed suppliers £180 and had a Bank loan of £1,500.

During the year ended 31 December 1995 he withdrew £9,000 from the business for his household expenses, and a further £2,340 for a family holiday in Spain.

In July a distant relative of Arthur's died, leaving Arthur a legacy of £1,500. Arthur paid this sum into the business bank account in October.

### Required

A calculation of Arthur's profit for the year ended 31 December 1995.

### *Point to note*

The question uses the word **calculation**. It does *not* ask for an income statement.

### Solution

|  | £ |
|---|---:|
| Closing capital | 13,070 |
| Less opening capital | 6,210 |
| Profits retained in the business | 6,860 |
| Plus profits withdrawn during year | 11,340 |
|  | 18,200 |
| Less capital introduced during year | 1,500 |
| Profit for year ended 31 December 1995 | 16,700 |

## 2.3 PREPARATION OF FINAL ACCOUNTS FOR CASH-BASED BUSINESSES

When a question asks you to prepare a trading and profit and loss account and balance sheet (the second type mentioned in 2.1) the following stages should be followed.

- **Stage 1** Prepare an opening statement of affairs (balance sheet on the first day of the year in question).
- **Stage 2** Compile summarised cash and bank accounts. Either or both of these might be given in the question.
- **Stage 3** Construct adjustment accounts (some teachers call these **control accounts**).
- **Stage 4** Prepare the final accounts.

It is important that you learn these 4 key stages.

It is essential to follow each step methodically each time you have to prepare a set of final accounts from incomplete records. The stage that is either ignored or gives most students most problems is stage 3. It is important that you understand why these adjustment accounts are necessary. Stage 3 is necessary because the cash spent on acquiring a resource is not necessarily the same figure as the amount of that resource used to help generate the profits.

The accruals concept says that, as accountants, we must match expenses with the profits that the expenses have helped to generate in the time period under review. To illustrate this point consider the following:

- The cash going through the till during the year is not necessarily the same as the sales figure for the year. Why?
- Some of last year's customers may have paid during the year under review. Some sales take place near the financial year end and the cash due for these sales may not pass through the till until after the financial year end.

- The figures in the cash account and bank account need to be adjusted to arrive at the expense figure for entry on the profit and loss account.

This sounds rather complicated, but if we go back to first principles, back to basics, it should be simplified. Rely on double entry book-keeping principles. Use 'T' accounts.

## EXAMPLE

Belinda owns a florist shop. She does not keep proper books of account. She supplies you with the following information for the financial year end 30 November 1995.

Summarised bank account for the year ended 30 November 1995:

| | £ | | £ |
|---|---|---|---|
| Balance 1 December 1994 | 648 | Payments to creditors | 28,361 |
| Takings banked | 51,723 | Rent | 3,400 |
| | | Rates | 940 |
| | | Insurance | 822 |
| | | Advertising | 346 |
| | | Heating and lighting | 1,825 |
| | | Sundry expenses | 268 |
| | | Motor expenses | 1,348 |
| | | Drawings | 11,167 |
| | | Balance 30 November 1995 | 3,894 |
| | 52,371 | | 52,371 |

All business takings have been paid into the bank account except for the following:

| | £ |
|---|---|
| Wages | 7,140 |
| Drawings | 1,385 |

The following additional information is also available:

| Assets and liabilities at 30 November | 1994 | 1995 |
|---|---|---|
| | £ | £ |
| Stock | 340 | 410 |
| Debtors | 72 | 48 |
| Creditors | 210 | 346 |
| Rent owing | – | 600 |
| Rates prepaid | 74 | 86 |
| Fixtures at valuation | 600 | 540 |
| Van at valuation | 8,000 | 6,000 |
| Cash in hand | 117 | 211 |

**Required**

A trading and profit and loss account for the year ended 30 November 1995 and a balance sheet as at that date for Belinda's business.

**Point to note**

Because the question asked for a 'complete set' of final accounts we must go through each of the 4 stages in a very methodical way.

**Solution**

**Stage 1** Prepare an opening statement of affairs

Advanced level students should be able to do this almost as quickly as they can write the figures down. This process is not part of the answer. It is only workings. Do not be concerned with categorising items into fixed assets and current assets, etc. Write the figures down *quickly* and *neatly*.

|  | £ |  | £ |
|---|---|---|---|
| Stock | 340 | Creditors | 210 |
| Debtors | 72 |  |  |
| Rates | 74 |  |  |
| Fixtures | 600 | Capital *(Missing figure)* | 9,641 |
| Van | 8,000 |  |  |
| Bank | 648 |  |  |
| Cash | 117 |  |  |
|  | 9,851 |  | 9,851 |

Note that all the items have been written down as they appeared in the question. No attempt has been made to write them down in any particular order.

Take care to include the *bank balance*; it is commonly missed as it is often not included in the list of assets and liabilities.

**Stage 2** Compile summarised cash and bank accounts

A summarised bank account has been given as part of the question, but we do need to prepare a cash summary.

|  | £ |  | £ |
|---|---|---|---|
| Balance 1 December 1995 | 117 | Monies banked | 51,723 |
| Cash received *(Missing figure)* | 60,342 | Wages | 7,140 |
|  |  | Drawings | 1,385 |
|  |  | Balance 30 November 1995 | 211 |
|  | 60,459 |  | 60,459 |

The cash received figure is money passing through the till; some could be for previous year's sales. We only require this year's sales for this year's final accounts. Also, Belinda may not yet have received cash for some sales that took place towards the end of November. We need to include these sales in this year's final accounts.

The cash received figure needs adjusting. We do this in stage 3.

**Stage 3** Construct adjustment accounts (control accounts)

These adjustments are necessary because of the accruals concept. Some students are unsure how many adjustment accounts are necessary and which figures need to be adjusted. If you are not very confident about this stage, open an adjustment account for every item listed under additional information; the assets and liabilities listed at the start and end of the year.

To some people this may seem like going over the top, but in the examination do not leave anything to chance – every mark counts towards your final grade. The stock is adjusted on the trading account, but open an account for the other items listed.

As you gain more confidence you may find that you can miss out some of the fixed asset accounts. Usually, those that do not change at all, or those where the only change is the depreciation charge. You may do this adjustment by debiting the profit and loss account and deducting the appropriate figure from the asset in the balance sheet.

### Debtors

|  | £ |  | £ |
|---|---|---|---|
| Balance 1 December 1994 | 72 | Cash | 60,342 |
| Trading account *(Missing figure)* | 60,318 | Balance 30 November 1995 c/d | 48 |
|  | 60,390 |  | 60,390 |
| Balance b/d | 48 |  |  |

### Creditors

|  | £ |  | £ |
|---|---|---|---|
| Bank | 28,361 | Balance 1 December 1994 | 210 |
| Balance 30 November 1995 c/d | 346 | Trading account *(Missing figure)* | 28,497 |
|  | 28,707 |  | 28,707 |
|  |  | Balance b/d | 346 |

**Rent**

| | | | |
|---|---|---|---|
| Bank | 3,400 | P & L a/c *(Missing figure)* | *4,000* |
| Balance 30 November 1995 c/d | 600 | | |
| | 4,000 | | 4,000 |
| | | Balance b/d | 600 |

**Rates**

| | | | |
|---|---|---|---|
| Balance 1 December 1994 | 74 | P & L a/c *(Missing figure)* | *928* |
| Bank | 940 | Balance 30 November1995 c/d | 86 |
| | 1,014 | | 1,014 |
| Balance b/d | 86 | | |

**Fixtures**

| | | | |
|---|---|---|---|
| Balance 1 December 1994 | 600 | P & L a/c *(Depreciation missing figure)* | *60* |
| | | Balance 30 November 1995 c/d | 540 |
| | 600 | | 600 |
| Balance b/d | 540 | | |

**Van**

| | | | |
|---|---|---|---|
| Balance 1 December 1994 | 8,000 | P & L a/c *(Depreciation missing figure)* | 2,000 |
| | | Balance 30 November 1995 c/d | 6,000 |
| | 8,000 | | 8,000 |
| Balance b/d | 6,000 | | |

The only other balance in the list is the cash balance. We have already adjusted the cash figure in the summarised cash account.

It may seem superfluous to bring all the balances down, but when we come to compile the closing balance sheet all those balances will be needed.

Up to this point you have scored *no marks*. The question asked for 'a trading and profit and loss account and a balance sheet'. All we have done is to get all the information ready. All the hard work has been done. It is now simply a matter of putting this information to the correct use.

Some text books and teachers use the following method to find the figure to be used in the final accounts:

Cash paid (from cash or bank account)
*Add* Closing accrued balance (from information list)
*Less* Opening accrued balance (from information list)

**or** Cash paid (from cash or bank account)
*Add* Opening prepaid balance (from information list)
*Less* Closing prepaid balance (from information list)

The answer is the figure to be used in the final accounts.
To find the *sales* figure using this method:

| | £ |
|---|---|
| Cash paid | 60,342 |
| Add closing balance | 48 |
| | 60,390 |
| Deduct opening balance | 72 |
| Trading Account figure | 60,318  (sales for the year) |

If you feel more comfortable using this method continue to use it. The examiner wants to see the correct figure in the trading account. The workings will only be referred to if the figure in the answer is incorrect. You may score some part-marks for those workings.

This is why it is so important to *always show workings*.

**Stage 4** Prepare the final accounts.

**Belinda trading and profit and loss account
for the year ended 30 November 1995.**

|  | £ | £ | £ |
|---|---|---|---|
| Sales |  |  | 60,318 |
| Less Cost of sales |  |  |  |
| Stock 1 December 1994 |  | 340 |  |
| Purchases |  | 28,497 |  |
|  |  | 28,837 |  |
| Less Stock 30 November 1995 |  | 410 |  |
|  |  |  | 28,427 |
| Gross Profit |  |  | 31,891 |
| Less Expenses |  |  |  |
| Wages |  | 7,140 |  |
| Rent |  | 4,000 |  |
| Rates |  | 928 |  |
| Insurance |  | 822 |  |
| Advertising |  | 346 |  |
| Heating and lighting |  | 1,825 |  |
| Sundry expenses |  | 268 |  |
| Motor expenses |  | 1,348 |  |
| Depreciation – Fixtures | 60 |  |  |
| Van | 2,000 |  |  |
|  |  | 2,060 |  |
|  |  |  | 18,737 |
| Net Profit |  |  | 13,154 |

**Belinda balance sheet as at 30 November 1995**

|  | £ | £ | £ |
|---|---|---|---|
| **Fixed assets** |  |  |  |
| Fixtures at valuation |  |  | 540 |
| Van at valuation |  |  | 6,000 |
|  |  |  | 6,540 |
| **Current assets** |  |  |  |
| Stock |  | 410 |  |
| Debtors |  | 48 |  |
| Bank |  | 3,894 |  |
| Cash |  | 211 |  |
| Rates prepaid |  | 86 |  |
|  |  | 4,649 |  |
| Less Current Liabilities |  |  |  |
| Trade creditors | 346 |  |  |
| Accrued Rent | 600 |  |  |
|  |  | 946 |  |
|  |  |  | 3,703 |
|  |  |  | 10,243 |
| **Capital** 1 December 1994 |  |  | 9,641 |
| Add Profit |  |  | 13,154 |
|  |  |  | 22,795 |
| Less Drawings |  |  | 12,552 |
|  |  |  | 10,243 |

<h1>2.4 CALCULATION OF RESULTS FOR CLUBS AND SOCIETIES</h1>

The examples in 2.2 and 2.3 involved the preparation of the accounts of small cash-based businesses. The *same principles apply* when preparing the final accounts of clubs and societies. There are a number of very superficial changes made in some of the headings used in the final accounts of these organisations.

Learn these different descriptions:
* The revenue statement of a club or society is not called a profit and loss account it is an **income and expenditure account**.
* A club or society will not make a profit (loss) it will make a **surplus (deficit)**.
* The capital account of a club or society is called the **accumulated fund**.
* The summarised cash book may be called a **receipts and payments account**.

## EXAMPLE

Skirwith village badminton club had the following assets and liabilities at 31 January 1995: nets £34, stock of shuttles £12, creditor for shuttles £9.50, line paint £4.50, balance at bank £89, cash in hand £14.

On 31 January 1996 the club's assets and liabilities were: nets £16, stock of shuttles £25, creditor for shuttles £10, trophies £82, balance at bank £34, cash in hand £8.

During the year an ex-member donated £40 to purchase two trophies to be awarded to the men's and ladies' singles champions of the club.

**Required**

A calculation of the badminton club's surplus or deficit for the year ended 31 January 1996.

**Solution**

Since the question did not ask for an income and expenditure account, a computation is required. (A complete set of final accounts could not be prepared. There are insufficient details given in the question.)

|  | £ |  |
|---|---|---|
| Closing accumulated fund | 155 | (16 + 25 + 82 + 34 + 8 − 10) |
| Opening accumulated fund | 144 | (34 + 12 + 4.5 + 89 + 14 − 9.5) |
|  | 11 |  |
| Less donation received | 40 |  |
| Deficit for year | 29 |  |

*Points to note*
* This is very similar to calculating Arthur's profit in 2.2.
* The donation was added back as it was an extraordinary amount and as such should not be included in the calculation of any surplus or deficit for the year.

<h1>2.5 PREPARATION OF FINAL ACCOUNTS FOR CLUBS AND SOCIETIES</h1>

If a question asks for a set of final accounts, then we need to go carefully through the 4 stages as we did in the case of Belinda's shop in 2.3. Can you remember them?

## EXAMPLE

The following receipts and payments account for the year ended 31 December 1995 for the Mellerby Gardening Club has been prepared for you by the club's honorary treasurer:

| | £ | | £ |
|---|---|---|---|
| Bank balance 1 January 1995 | 137 | Seed purchases | 654 |
| Seed sales | 875 | Rotavator purchase | 459 |
| Subscriptions received | 1,450 | Rent | 750 |
| Show entry fees | 84 | Secretary's honorarium | 120 |
| Equipment hire | 365 | Speakers' expenses | 395 |
| Annual dinner dance ticket sales | 850 | Bank charges | 34 |
| Bank balance 31 December 1995 | 20 | Advertising | 139 |
| | | Insurance | 172 |
| | | Postages and telephone | 81 |
| | | Dinner dance expenses | 749 |
| | | Printing for dinner dance | 128 |
| | | Show prizes | 100 |
| | 3,781 | | 3,781 |

The following additional information is available:

| At 31 December | £ 1994 | £ 1995 |
|---|---|---|
| Equipment at valuation | 1,090 | 1,100 |
| Creditor for seed purchases | 70 | 45 |
| Printing bill outstanding for Dinner dance | 128 | 177 |
| Insurance prepaid | 46 | 49 |
| Subscriptions paid in advance | 60 | 35 |
| Subscriptions owed at year end | 15 | 30 |

Equipment is available for use by members at a nominal charge.
Seeds are purchased by the club and sold to members.

**Required**

An income and expenditure account for the year ended 31 December 1995 and a balance sheet as at that date for the Mellerby Gardening Club.

**Solution**

**Stage 1** Prepare an opening statement of affairs

| | £ | | £ |
|---|---|---|---|
| Equipment | 1,090 | Creditor – seeds | 70 |
| Insurance prepaid | 46 | Printing | 128 |
| Subscriptions owed | 15 | Subscriptions in advance | 60 |
| Bank balance *(do not forget this)* | 137 | Accumulated fund *(Missing figure)* | *1,030* |
| | 1,288 | | 1,288 |

**Stage 2** Compile summarised cash and bank accounts

No need – given in the question.

**Stage 3** Construct adjustment accounts (control accounts)

This is the *all important stage*. Use one account for each item of additional information.

**Equipment**

| | £ | | £ |
|---|---|---|---|
| Balance 1 January 1995 | 1,090 | Income and expenditure a/c *(Depreciation missing figure)* | *449* |
| Bank | 459 | Balance 31 December 1995 c/d | 1,100 |
| | 1,549 | | 1,549 |
| Balance b/d | 1,100 | | |

**Creditor for seeds**

| | £ | | £ |
|---|---|---|---|
| Bank | 654 | Balance 1 January 1995 | 70 |
| Balance 31 December 1995 c/d | 45 | Income and expenditure a/c *(Missing figure)* | *629* |
| | 699 | | 699 |
| | | Balance b/d | 45 |

### Printing for Dinner Dance

| | £ | | £ |
|---|---|---|---|
| Bank | 128 | Balance 1 January 1995 | 128 |
| | | Income and expenditure a/c | |
| Balance 31 December 1995 c/d | 177 | *(Missing figure)* | *177* |
| | 305 | | 305 |
| | | Balance b/d | 177 |

### Insurance

| | £ | | £ |
|---|---|---|---|
| Balance 1 January 1995 | 46 | Income and expenditure a/c | |
| | | *(Missing figure)* | *169* |
| Bank | 172 | Balance 31 December 1995 c/d | 49 |
| | 218 | | 218 |
| Balance b/d | 49 | | |

The next adjustment account is the one that seems to cause the most problems; it is the subscriptions account.

It is worth spending some time getting this one sorted out in your own mind.

### Put yourself in the position of the club treasurer

| | |
|---|---|
| People or organisations who owe you money are | **debtors** (debit balances) |
| Members who owe your club money are also | **debtors** (debit balances) |
| Subscriptions owing at the year end are | **debtors** (debit balances) |
| Subscriptions in arrears are | **debtors** (debit balances) |

At the year end some members may have paid their subscriptions for the following year. If they have taken up a university place or moved abroad to take a job, they may wish to cease membership of the club, in which case the club owes them money and until the club pays them the ex-member would be a creditor.

| | |
|---|---|
| If you owe people or organisations money they are | **creditors** (credit balances) |
| Members who are owed money are | **creditors** (credit balances) |
| Subscriptions paid in advance at the year end are | **creditors** (credit balances) |
| Subscriptions received in advance are | **creditors** (credit balances) |

Monies received during the year from members will have been debited to the cash book. We need to complete the double entry for this in the subscriptions adjustment account.

The debit can be seen in the receipts and payments account and we complete the double entry by crediting the subscriptions account.

> Subscriptions (cash) received from members is a credit entry in the subscriptions account.

You may find that you make fewer mistakes with balances on the adjustment accounts if you put closing balances *under* the account, then take them up diagonally into the body of the account. You are less likely to make careless mistakes.

### Subscriptions

| | £ | | £ |
|---|---|---|---|
| Balance 1 January 1995 | 15 | Balance 1 January 1995 | 60 |
| Income and expenditure a/c | | | |
| *(Missing figure)* | *1,490* | Bank | 1,450 |
| Balance 31 December 1995 c/d | 35 | Balance 31 December 1995 c/d | 30 |
| | 1,540 | | 1,540 |
| Balance b/d | 30 | | 35 |

Once again the hard work has been done preparing the information, but *no marks* have been scored yet because the question asked for an 'income and expenditure account and balance sheet'. It is important that you work methodically, accurately, neatly, and quickly.

**Stage 4** Prepare the income and expenditure account and balance sheet

**Mellerby Gardening Club income and expenditure account
for the year ended 31 December 1995.**

| | £ | | £ |
|---|---|---|---|
| Rent | 750 | Subscriptions | 1,490 |
| Secretary's honorarium | 120 | Profit on sales of seeds (875 – 629) | 246 |
| Speakers' expenses | 395 | | |
| Bank charges | 34 | | |
| Advertising | 139 | | |
| Insurances | 169 | Deficit for the year | 128 |
| Postages and telephone | 81 | | |
| Loss on dinner dance (850 – 749 – 177) | 76 | | |
| Loss on equipment hire (365 – 449 depn) | 84 | | |
| Loss on show (84 – 100) | 16 | | |
| | 1,864 | | 1,864 |

**Mellerby Gardening Club balance sheet as at 31 December 1995**

| | £ | | £ |
|---|---|---|---|
| Equipment at valuation | 1,100 | Accumulated fund | 1,030 |
| Insurance prepaid | 49 | Less Deficit | 128 |
| Subscriptions in arrears | 30 | | 902 |
| | | Creditors for   seeds | 45 |
| | |                 printing | 177 |
| | | Bank overdraft | 20 |
| | | Subscriptions paid in advance | 35 |
| | 1,179 | | 1,179 |

*Points to note*

- The headings have changed from those of business accounts.

- The activities have been 'netted out' to reveal to the members which activities contribute toward the finances of the club, and which activities are a drain on the club's resources. You should do this when you see that the club or society runs activities which are not central to its existence.

- The workings have been shown in brackets simply to help you. Show your workings, but show them outside the body of the answer.

- Your workings should be neat and clear so that if the examiner needs to refer to them he can find them easily and quickly. For example:

$$\text{Dinner dance } 850 - 749 - 177$$

is quite easy to follow, whereas

$$1,090 - 70 - 60 + 137 - 128 + 15 + 46$$

takes a lot more investigation on the part of the examiner to find what the calculation refers to (it is the calculation necessary to determine the Accumulated Fund at 1 January 1995).

## 2.6 CALCULATION OF MISSING CASH OR MISSING STOCK

Questions sometimes indicate that some cash or some stock has disappeared from the business during the course of the year. Part of the question will require the candidate to ascertain the missing amount.

The procedure to follow is to work out what the position should have been, had the mishap not occurred, and to compare that with the actual position.

## MISSING CASH

Imagine you had just received your wages from your part-time job. You receive £55 on the way home you buy a CD costing £13.99 and a magazine costing £1.40.

Later, as you are having a shower, your brother asks to borrow some cash from you for a couple of days. You shout from the bathroom 'help yourself'!

How would you calculate how much he had borrowed? An accountant would use the same technique.

### EXAMPLE 1

Celia owns a small stationary supply retailers business. At 1 January her cash in hand was £32, at the end of the year on 31 December it was £48. Her cash takings for the year amounted to £42,956. She banked £30,500 after taking cash drawings of £5,200 and paying the following expenses:

|  | £ |
|---|---|
| wages | 4,284 |
| rent | 2,400 |

She believes that some cash was stolen in a burglary during Christmas week.

**Required**

A calculation showing clearly the amount of cash stolen.

**Solution**

**Cash account**

| | £ | | £ |
|---|---|---|---|
| Cash in hand 1 January | 32 | Cash banked | 30,500 |
| | | Wages | 4,284 |
| Takings for year | 42,956 | Rent | 2,400 |
| | | Drawings | 5,200 |
| | | Stolen *(Missing figure)* | 556 |
| | | Cash in hand 31 December | 48 |
| | 42,988 | | 42,988 |

**Points to note**
- The question does not ask for an account, it asks for a calculation.
- There are a variety of ways to calculate the missing cash, if you use a different way and you arrive at the correct answer then that is perfectly acceptable, but show full workings.
- The solution showed a cash account as this fits in with what has been done in the previous examples. It is part of stage 2.

## MISSING STOCK

To calculate the amount of stock that has gone missing during a financial year a trading account using *actual figures* is compared to a trading account using the *figures that ought to have applied*.

### EXAMPLE 2

Dirk owns a hairdressing salon. Several boxes of expensive shampoos have been stolen, but he is unsure of the exact amount. Shampoos in stock at 1 February 1995 £450; stock at 31 January 1996 £180; purchases of shampoo during year £26 950; sales of shampoos during year £36,000. All shampoos carry a uniform mark-up of $33^{1/3}\%$ on cost.

**Required**

Calculate the amount of stock stolen from Dirk's shop

**Solution**

|  | Actual figures are | They should be |
|---|---|---|
|  | £ | £ |
| Opening stock | 450 | 450 |
| Purchases | 26,950 | 26,950 |
| Closing stock | 180 | ? ❶ |
| Sales | 36,000 | 36,000 |

A trading account can be prepared using the actual figures

|  | £ | £ |
|---|---|---|
| Sales |  | 36,000 |
| Less cost of sales: |  |  |
| Stock 1 February 1995 | 450 |  |
| Purchases | 26,950 |  |
|  | 27,400 |  |
| Stolen stock | ? ❺ |  |
| Less stock 31 January 1996 | 180 ❹ |  |
|  |  | 27,000 ❸ |
| Gross profit |  | 9,000 ❷ |

- ❶ As you can see, they are all the same, with one exception.
- ❷ Gross profit is 33.3% of cost of sales, which gives ❸ 27,000, which means that stock should be £400 not £180 as shown ❹ so stolen stock ❺ must be £220.

**Points to note**
- The other entry for the closing stock is as usual on the balance sheet.
- The other entry for the stolen stock is as an expense on the profit and loss account

---

## Chapter roundup

This chapter has dealt with an extremely popular topic with examiners. It is very difficult, if not impossible, to find an examination paper without either a set of club accounts or a set of small cash-based business accounts on it.

It is important to be able to construct the adjustment accounts. It is also vital to show all workings and to use your results from those workings in the body of your answer.

---

# Illustrative questions

**1** Bhupesh Chaughan runs a small retail shop selling costume jewellery. He does not keep a full set of accounting records, but is able to give you the following information about the financial position of the business at 1 May 1994 and 30 April 1995.

The assets and liabilities were:

|  | 1 May 1994 | 30 April 1995 |
|---|---|---|
|  | £ | £ |
| Fixtures and fittings (cost £10 000) | 9,000 | 8,100 |
| Van (E742 XBA) | 7,000 | – |
| Van (M217PFQ) | – | 6,750 |
| Stock | 6,000 | 7,000 |
| Debtors | 1,750 | 1,160 |
| Creditors | 850 | 700 |
| Insurance prepaid | 340 | 400 |
| Rent accrued due | 250 | 200 |
| Balance at bank | 1,480 | – |
| Bank overdraft | – | 9,170 |
| Cash in hand | 140 | 160 |

He has also provided the following summary of the business bank account for the year ended 30 April 1995.

| | £ | | £ |
|---|---|---|---|
| Balance 1 May 1994 | 1,480 | Purchases | 35,670 |
| Receipts from debtors for sales | 6,170 | Rent and rates | 4,170 |
| Proceeds from sale of van | | Lighting and heating | 2,140 |
| (E742XBA) | 4,500 | Advertising | 850 |
| Cash banked | 41,120 | Insurance | 1,200 |
| Balance 30 April 1995 | 9,170 | Motor expenses | 2,110 |
| | | General expenses | 3,180 |
| | | Van (M217PFQ) | 9,000 |
| | | Payments to creditors | |
| | | for purchases | 4,120 |
| | 62,440 | | 62,440 |

All the takings were from the cash sales banked after the following payments were made:

| | £ |
|---|---|
| Purchases | 1,360 |
| Wages | 15,240 |
| Drawings | 14,150 |

Bhupesh now knows that a part-time assistant who left his employment in October 1994 was systematically stealing cash from the shop; he is uncertain of the exact amount. He was not insured against this loss.

The shop normally earns a gross profit on sales of 50%.

*Required*

(a) A computation showing how much cash has been stolen from Bhupesh Chaughan's shop. (8)

(b) A trading and profit and loss account for the year ended 30 April 1995 and a balance sheet as at that date. (32)

(c) A memorandum addressed to Bhupesh indicating the measures that he could take to prevent cash being stolen in future. Include advice on how Bhupesh could improve his financial record keeping. (10)

(AEB)

*Tutorial note*
You will need to complete part (b) to gain the cash sales figure to use in part (a). In part (c) concentrate on financial measures to prevent cash being stolen. Clearly other measures are important, but you are taking an accounting examination.

*Suggested answer*
In order to determine the amount of cash stolen you need to prepare a cash account.

A trading account must be completed in order to find the level of cash sales to be included in the cash account.

(a)                                        **Cash account**

| | | | |
|---|---|---|---|
| Balance b/d | 140 | Cash banked | 41,120 |
| Cash sales | | | |
| (from trading account) | 74,420 | Purchases | 1,360 |
| | | Wages | 15,240 |
| | | Drawings | 14,150 |
| | | Stolen (missing figure) | 2,530 |
| | | Balance c/d | 160 |
| | 74,560 | | 74,560 |
| Balance b/d | 160 | | |

(b) **Bhupesh Chaughan trading and profit and loss account
for the year ended 30 April 1995**

| | £ | £ | £ |
|---|---|---|---|
| Sales | | | 80,000 |
| Less cost of sales | | | |
| Stock | | 6,000 | |
| Purchases | | 41,000 ❶ | |
| | | 47,000 | |
| Stock | | 7,000 | |
| | | | 40,000 |
| Gross profit | | | 40,000 |
| Less expenses | | | |
| Wages | | 15,240 | |
| Light and heating | | 2,140 | |
| Advertising | | 850 | |
| Motor expenses | | 2,110 | |
| General expenses | | 3,180 | |
| Rent and rates | | 4,120 ❸ | |
| Insurance | | 1,140 ❹ | |
| Stolen | | 2,530 | |
| Loss on sale of van | | 2,500 | |
| Depreciation   van | 2,250 | | |
| fixtures | 900 | 3,150 | 36,960 |
| Net profit | | | 3,040 |

*Workings*
Sales are 200% of cost of sales. Since we know that credit sales are £5,580❷ we can find the cash sales to use in part (a): £80,000 – £5,580 = £74,420.

**❶ Creditors**

| | £ | | £ |
|---|---|---|---|
| Bank | 4,120 | Balance b/d | 850 |
| Balance c/d | 700 | Purchases | 3,970 |
| | 4,820 | | 4,820 |
| | | Balance b/d | 700 |

❶ 3,970 + 1,360 + 35,670

**❷ Debtors**

| | £ | | £ |
|---|---|---|---|
| Balance b/d | 1,750 | Bank | 6,170 |
| Sales | 5,580 | Balance c/d | 1,160 |
| | 7,330 | | 7,330 |
| Balance b/d | 1,160 | | |

**❸ Rent and rates**

| | £ | | £ |
|---|---|---|---|
| Bank | 4,170 | Balance b/d | 250 |
| Balance b/d | 200 | P & L a/c | 4,120 |
| | 4,370- | | 4,370 |
| | | Balance b/d | 200 |

**❹ Insurance**

| | £ | | £ |
|---|---|---|---|
| Balance b/d | 340 | P & L a/c | 1,140 |
| Bank | 1,200 | Balance c/d | 400 |
| | 1,540 | | 1,540 |
| Balance b/d | 400 | | |

### Balance sheet as at 30 April 1995

| Fixed assets | £ | £ |
|---|---|---|
| Fixtures | 9,000 | |
| Less depreciation | 900 | 8,100 |
| Vehicle | 9,000 | |
| Less depreciation | 2,250 | 6,750 |
| | | 14,850 |
| **Current assets** | | |
| Stock | 7,000 | |
| Debtors | 1,160 | |
| Cash | 160 | |
| Prepayment | 400 | |
| | 8,720 | |

| Less current liabilities | | | |
|---|---|---|---|
| Creditors | 700 | | |
| Bank overdraft | 9,170 | | |
| Accrued expense | 200 | 10,070 | (1,350) |
| | | | 13,500 |
| **Capital** | | | 24,610 |
| Add profit | | | 3,040 |
| | | | 27,650 |
| Less drawings | | | 14,150 |
| | | | 13,500 |

(c) To

From    *(i.e. memorandum format)*

Date

### Measures to be taken to avoid stolen cash

Measures could include:

Accurate recording of cash transactions.
Collect cash from tills frequently.
Use bank facilities whenever possible – bank cash regularly.
Make as many payments as possible by cheque.
Division of duties for control purposes.
Cash payments by staff must have authorisation.

Bhupesh could improve his financial record keeping by:

Keeping a cash book in as much detail as possible.
Keeping and numbering all receipts, and invoices.
Filing and using bank statements.

**2** The treasurer of Fairoaks Golf Club has prepared the following receipts and payments account for the year ended 31 March 1995.

| Receipts | £ | Payments | £ |
|---|---|---|---|
| Balance 1 April 1994 | 520 | Bar steward's wages | 9,320 |
| Casual green fees | 1,380 | Ground staff wages | 37,780 |
| Bar takings | 10,800 | Administration costs | 3,870 |
| Subscriptions 1993/1994 | 5,400 | Operating costs | 5,460 |
| 1994/1995 | 46,600 | Rates and insurance | 2,080 |
| Balance 31 March 1995 | 2,000 | Payments to bar creditors | 7,730 |
| | | Legal costs | 460 |
| | 66,700 | | 66,700 |

Additional information.

(1)

|  | At 31 March 1994 £ | At 31 March 1995 £ |
|---|---|---|
| Bar stocks at cost | 1,850 | 460 |
| Subscriptions in arrears | 8,400 | 9,400 |
| Operating costs owing | 300 | 250 |
| Bar creditors | 950 | 1,930 |

(2) The club's fixed assets at 31 March 1994 were:
   (i) freehold land at cost £280,000;
   (ii) the club house was completed on 1 April 1979 at a cost of £110,000. Depreciation had been charged on the club house at a rate of 5% per annum on cost;
   (iii) equipment had been purchased on 1 April 1991 at a cost of £52,000. A depreciation rate of 20% per annum on cost is applied to equipment.

(3) Any outstanding subscriptions for 1993/1994 were written off on 1 March 1995 and the members involved removed from the membership roll.

(4) The legal costs were incurred in the successful defence of an unlawful dismissal claim brought by the bar steward who was dismissed following the discovery of discrepancies in the bar stocks.

*Required*

(a) A bar trading account for the year ended 31 March 1995.                    (6)

(b) (i) An income and expenditure account for the club for the year ended 31 March 1995.                                                          (13)
   (ii) A balance sheet as at 31 March 1995.                                   (12)

(c) A report from the treasurer to the members
   (i) reviewing the club's financial position (where possible illustrating your comments with figures);                                              (10)
   (ii) making suggestions as to what measures could be taken to improve the club's financial position.                                               (9)

(AEB)

*Tutorial note*
Show all adjustment accounts clearly; this will ensure that you can earn part of the marks if you make the odd error. Remember that to assess performance of a business, you must calculate financial ratios. The methods of improving the financial position should be very familiar to you – like all students you must have considered how to improve your own financial position – the club faces the same problems.

*Suggested answer*

(a)

**Fairoaks Golf Club Bar trading account for the year ended 31 March 1995**

|  | £ | £ |
|---|---|---|
| Bar takings |  | 10,800 |
| Less cost of sales |  |  |
| Stock | 1,850 |  |
| Purchases ❶ | 8,710 |  |
|  | 10,560 |  |
| Stock | 460 | 10,100 |
| Gross profit |  | 700 |
| Bar stewards wages |  | 9,320 |
| Net loss |  | 8,620 |

**❶ Purchases**

| | £ | | £ |
|---|---|---|---|
| Payments | 7,730 | Balance b/d | 950 |
| Balance c/d | 1,930 | Purchases | 8,710 |
| | 9,660 | | 9,660 |
| | | Balance b/d | 1,930 |

(b) (i) **Fairoaks Golf Club Income and expenditure account for the year ended 31 March 1995**

| | £ | £ |
|---|---|---|
| Income | | |
| Subscriptions ❶ | | 56,000 |
| Casual green fees | | 1,380 |
| | | 57,380 |
| Less expenditure | | |
| Groundsman's wages | 37,780 | |
| Administration costs | 3,870 | |
| Rates and insurance | 2,080 | |
| Legal costs | 460 | |
| Operating costs ❷ | 5,410 | |
| Loss on bar | 8,620 | |
| Subscriptions written off | 3,000 | |
| Depreciation – Club house | 5,500 | |
| – Equipment | 10,400 | 77,120 |
| Excess of expenditure over income | | 19,740 |

**❶ Subscriptions**

| | £ | | £ |
|---|---|---|---|
| Balance b/d | 8,400 | Receipts | 52,000 |
| Income and expenditure | 56,000 | Subs w/o | 3,000 |
| | | Balance c/d | 9,400 |
| | 64,400 | | 64,400 |
| Balance b/d | 9,400 | | |

**❷ Operating costs**

| | £ | | £ |
|---|---|---|---|
| Cash | 5,460 | Balance b/d | 300 |
| Balance c/d | 250 | Income and expenditure | 5,410 |
| | 5,710 | | 5,710 |
| | | Balance b/d | 250 |

(ii) **Fairoaks Golf Club balance sheet as at 31 March 1995**

| **Fixed assets** | £ | £ | £ |
|---|---|---|---|
| Freehold property | | | 280,000 |
| Club house | | 110,000 | |
| Less depreciation | | 88,000 | 22,000 |
| Equipment | | 52,000 | |
| Less depreciation | | 41,600 | 10,400 |
| | | | 312,400 |
| **Current assets** | | | |
| Bar stocks | | 460 | |
| Subscriptions in arrears | | 9,400 | |
| | | 9,860 | |
| **Less current liabilities** | | | |
| Operating costs owing | 250 | | |
| Bar creditors | 1,930 | | |
| Bank overdraft | 2,000 | 4,180 | 5,680 |
| | | | 318,080 |
| **Accumulated fund:** | | | |
| Balance 1 April 1994 | | | 337,820 |
| Less deficit | | | 19,740 |
| | | | 318,080 |

(c) To

From

Date *(i.e. report format)*

*The Club's financial position and suggestions*
*for making improvements*

(i) Bar trading is weak. Gross margin is only 6.48%. Stock turnover is slow at 42 days.

Stocks are 75% lower than they were at the start of the year. This could be due to the stock discrepancies.

The current ratio is strong (2.3:1), but £9,400 of the current assets is represented by outstanding subscriptions and given the club's previous problems in collecting overdue subscriptions, this liquid position can be viewed with scepticism. Without the outstanding subscriptions the liquidity position is poor. Liquid funds may be required in the not too distant future to replace equipment and to refurbish the club house, as both are now quite old.

(ii) Suggestions could include:

- Increased membership fees and a campaign to ensure that current members pay subscriptions in good time. Perhaps a life membership scheme could be introduced.
- Control of bar stocks and an increase in prices charged at the bar.
- Increase casual green fees.
- See if cost savings can be made.
- Use of fund raising activities e.g. discos, raffles, sub-letting parts of the premises etc.
- Sell surplus assets.
- Mortgage property.

**3** Mary Cugat has operated a small fancy goods shop for five years. An analysis of her bank records for the year ended 31 December 1993 shows:

| Payments | £ |
|---|---|
| Purchases of goods | 72,299 |
| New shop fittings | 1,837 |
| Heat and light | 935 |
| Van running expenses | 1,091 |
| New van (balance of purchase price) | 5,150 |
| Insurance | 810 |
| Bank charges | 206 |
| Rent | 2,400 |
| Personal expenses | 2,691 |
| **Receipts** | |
| Paid in from takings | 82,310 |
| Money introduced from Mary's private savings | 3,927 |

It is Mary's practice to pay all takings into the bank each week after deducting the following amounts:

| | £ |
|---|---|
| Personal drawings | 80 |
| Sales assistant's wage | 70 |
| Cleaner's wage | 20 |

Mary is proud of the fact that she did not take a holiday in 1993, working a 52 week year.

Mary makes credit sales to a small number of customers. She controls these by writing out an invoice for each credit sale and placing it in a box. When the customer pays, she stamps the invoice paid, hands it to the customer and includes the cash received in that week's takings. At 31 December 1992 the total of these outstanding invoices was £540, and Mary was confident that these would be paid. At 31 December 1993 the total of these outstanding invoices was £790, including one for £120 which Mary does not expect to be paid. During 1993 Mary tore up two outstanding invoices because, she says, she 'gave up hope of payment'. She does not remember the amount involved, but thinks that it was about £250.

Apart from debtors, Mary had the following assets and liabilities as at 1 January 1993.

| **Assets** | £ |
|---|---|
| Shop fittings net of depreciation | 4,872 |
| Van | 2,350 |
| Stock | 15,920 |
| Prepaid rent | 300 |
| Cash | 172 |
| **Liabilities** | |
| Trade creditors | 8,273 |
| Accrued heat and light | 71 |
| Bank | 195 |

During 1993 the van was traded in for £2,000 on a part exchange deal to purchase a new one. Depreciation is on the following basis.

| Shop fittings | 15% reducing balance |
|---|---|
| Van | 20% straight line |

Mary's policy is to provide a full year's depreciation in the year of acquisition and no depreciation in the year of disposal.

At 31 December 1993 stock was £16,271, prepaid rent was £300, cash was £195, trade creditors were £8,975 and accrued heat and light was £82.

*Required*

(a) Prepare a profit and loss account for the year ended 31 December 1993 and a balance sheet as at 31 December 1993 for Mary Cugat. (28)

(b) Explain three disadvantages that may arise from failing to operate a full double entry accounting system. Illustrate your answer with examples drawn from Mary Cugat's business. (12)

(NEAB)

*Tutorial note*

Use the four stages outlined in the text to answer part (a) and remember to use examples from the problems you have encountered in preparing Mary's accounts to answer part (b).

*Suggested answer*

(a) **Mary Cugat trading and profit and loss account
for the year ended 31 December 1993**

| | £ | £ |
|---|---|---|
| Sales ❶ | | 91,673 |
| Less cost of sales | | |
| Stock | 15,920 | |
| Purchases ❷ | 73,001 | |
| | 88,921 | |
| Stock | 16,271 | 72,650 |
| Gross profit | | 19,023 |
| Less expenses | | |
| Heat and light ❸ | 946 | |
| Motor expenses | 1,091 | |
| Insurance | 810 | |
| Bank charges | 206 | |
| Rent ❹ | 2,400 | |
| Wages | 3,640 | |
| Cleaning | 1,040 | |
| Bad debts | 370 | |
| Loss on sale of van | 350 | |
| Depreciation – fittings | 1,006 | |
| van | 1,430 | 13,289 |
| Net profit | | 5,734 |

## Balance sheet as at 31 December 1993

| Fixed assets | £ | £ | £ |
|---|---|---|---|
| Fittings | | 6,709 | |
| Less depreciation | | 1,006 | 5,703 |
| Van | | 7,150 | |
| Less depreciation | | 1,430 | 5,720 |
| | | | 11,423 |
| **Current assets** | | | |
| Stock | | 16,271 | |
| Debtors | | 670 | |
| Cash | | 195 | |
| Rent prepaid | | 300 | |
| | | 17,436 | |
| **Less current liabilities** | | | |
| Trade creditors | 8,975 | | |
| Bank overdraft | 1,377 | | |
| Accrued heat & light | 82 | 10,434 | 7,002 |
| | | | 18,425 |
| Capital | | | 15,615 |
| Add capital introduced | | | 3,927 |
| Profit | | | 5,734 |
| | | | 25,276 |
| Less drawings | | | 6,851 |
| | | | 18,425 |

**❶ Sales calculation**

**Debtors**

| | | | | **Total sales** | |
|---|---|---|---|---|---|
| Balance b/d | 540 | Bank | 82,310 | Credit sales | 82,560 |
| Credit sales | 82,560 | Balance c/d | 790 | Cash receipts | 8,840 |
| | 83,100 | | 83,100 | Bad debt w/o | 250 |
| Balance b/d | 790 | | | Opening cash balance | (172) |
| | | | | Closing cash balance | 195 |
| | | | | | 91,673 |

**❷ Creditors**

| | | | |
|---|---|---|---|
| Bank | 72,299 | Balance b/d | 8,273 |
| Balance c/d | 8,975 | P & L a/c | 73,001 |
| | 81,274 | | 81,274 |
| | | Balance b/d | 8,975 |

**❸ Heat and light**

| | | | |
|---|---|---|---|
| Bank | 935 | Balance b/d | 71 |
| Balance c/d | 82 | P & L a/c | 946 |
| | 1,017 | | 1,017 |
| | | Balance b/d | 82 |

**❹ Rent**

| | | | |
|---|---|---|---|
| Balance b/d | 300 | P & L a/c | 2,400 |
| Bank | 2,400 | Balance c/d | 300 |
| | 2,700 | | 2,700 |
| Balance b/d | 300 | | |

(b) Disadvantages of not operating a system of double entry book-keeping could include:

- Single entry does not provide the detail that a double entry system does.
- Inland revenue and customs and excise may require more detail than a single entry system provides.
- Certain figures are difficult to validate, e.g. cash drawings, goods for own use.
- It may be more difficult to operate a system of credit control.
- It may be more difficult to prevent fraud or losses in other areas, e.g. stock losses.

# CONCEPTS AND CONVENTIONS OF ACCOUNTING

## Units in this chapter

3.1   *Statements of Standard Accounting Practice (SSAPs)*
3.2   *The concepts and conventions of accounting*

## Chapter objectives

Life is full of rules. We drive on the left hand side of the road. If a footballer handles the ball in his own penalty area then the opposing side will be awarded a penalty. These rules have evolved over the years. We know that if we drive our car in Carlisle or in Cardiff road users will all drive on the left.

In the same way rules have evolved over time in accounting, and this is what we will be looking at in this chapter. We need to know that if a set of accounts are prepared in Scunthorpe or in Swanage that the same set of principles have been used in their preparation. We can then make judgements or comparisons, safe in the knowledge that we are comparing like with like, as far as the accounts are concerned.

The key topics and concepts covered in this chapter are:

- SSAPs 2, 4, 9, 12, 13, 17, 18, and 22;
- going concern;
- accruals;
- consistency;
- prudence;
- materiality;
- money measurement;
- business entity;
- realisation;
- dual aspect.

## 3.1 STATEMENTS OF STANDARD ACCOUNTING PRACTICE (SSAPs)

The Accounting Standards Committee (replaced by the Accounting Standards Board in 1990) was set up by the major accounting bodies to devise common standards in the production of accounting statements.

In general, examination syllabuses do not require you to have knowledge of the minutiae of all the Statements of Standard Accounting Practice (SSAPs), and *it is not essential that you can remember the numbers of the standards.*

You have already been using some of the standards in the work you have done in class over the past couple of years, although you may not have realised the fact.

### SSAP 2 DISCLOSURE OF ACCOUNTING POLICIES

The SSAP defines three terms:

* **1 Fundamental Accounting Concepts** 'broad basic assumptions which underlie the periodic financial accounts of business enterprises'. There are four of these and they have statutory backing (The Companies Act 1985).

    They are:

    * The going concern concept.
    * The accruals concept.
    * Consistency.
    * Prudence.

* **2 Accounting Bases** 'the methods which have been developed for expressing or applying fundamental accounting concepts to financial transactions and items'.

    These bases include methods of charging depreciation on fixed assets (e.g. straight line, reducing balance, etc.), methods used for the valuation of stocks and work in progress (LIFO, FIFO, AVCO.), treatment and amortisation of intangible assets, etc.

    You should recognise these too.

* **3 Accounting Policies** 'the specific accounting bases judged by business enterprises to be most appropriate to their circumstances, and adopted by them for the purpose of preparing their financial accounts'.

    These policies would determine, for example, which method was chosen to depreciate a particular fixed asset in a particular industry.

It is assumed that accounting statements will be prepared bearing in mind the three terms outlined above.

## 3.2 THE CONCEPTS AND CONVENTIONS OF ACCOUNTING

### 1 The going concern concept

The business is assumed to be going to continue in existence for the foreseeable future. The business accounts are prepared with this in mind. If the business were to close down tomorrow then perhaps the assets would be valued differently.

The major consequence of this concept is that assets are valued at cost, not what they would fetch if sold (as a going concern, the business will need its assets and is therefore not going to sell them).

The idea of valuing assets at cost may seem rather strange since the value of, say, property may have risen over the years.

Two points can be made:

*   Who does the valuation and is it accurate? Could you say with any certainty how much your house or car would fetch if sold? Valuations even by qualified surveyors must be subjective to a degree.
*   Will it make any difference to the running of the business as a going concern whether the owner believes his assets are worth £60,000 or £80,000? An increase in the value of his assets will not help him to pay his gas bill or his staff wages.

The most objective value that can be placed on any asset is the price paid for it. So, assets shown on balance sheets of sole traders and partnerships are shown at *cost*. The exception is that assets may be revalued in the accounts of limited companies. (see page 98).

## 2 The accruals concept (sometimes called the matching concept)

Accountants are interested in accounting for the resources used in the running of the business in a particular time period, not in the cash paid out to acquire those resources – the two are not necessarily the same.

For example, you ride your motor cycle to college today. The amount of petrol you have used is not necessarily the same as the amount of cash you have spent on petrol today.

Businesses pay some time later for certain resources used in the business. In other cases they have to pay before they can use the resource.

## 3 Consistency

There are a number of figures that have been used in the preparation of the final accounts of the business where the person preparing the accounts could have chosen any one of a variety of figures, e.g. the provision for depreciation of fixed assets – a straight line method could have been used or a reducing balance method; in the valuation of stock – the first in first out method or a weighted average method could have been used.

Each time a different method is used to calculate the depreciation charge or to ascertain the value of closing stock a different profit figure will result.

This would mean that:

*   within certain parameters, profits could be increased or decreased for reasons to do with the calculation of tax liability or in order to sell the business;
*   it would be extremely difficult to make comparisons between years for management and stewardship reasons;
*   it would be difficult to tell whether profits had risen or fallen because of business activity or because of a change in accounting policy.

Once the managers of a business have decided on the accounting treatment of an item, similar items should be treated using the same method.

## 4 Prudence (sometimes called conservatism)

Accountants provide for losses as soon as they are anticipated. They do not acknowledge profits until they are realised. It is much safer to understate profits than overstate them.

The concept of prudence arises since certain items are, of necessity, often estimates made when preparing periodic accounts, e.g. accrued expenses, prepaid expenses.

If managers and owners were over-optimistic then profits could be overstated, and this could result in the resources of the business being depleted by excessive drawings or excessive dividends being paid out.

There are a number of other concepts which, although not explicitly mentioned in SSAP 2, are nevertheless important to observe when preparing the final accounts of a business. These will be dealt with now.

## 5 Materiality

Capital expenditure is spending on fixed assets or their improvement. Revenue expenditure is spending on the everyday running costs of the business

Fixed assets last more than one time period. If we apply the accruals concept (see 2 above) we should spread the cost of a fixed asset over the years it is used to generate the product and hence the profits. For example, a business provides the office junior with a calculator. The cost of the calculator is £4.99. It is estimated that the calculator should last for 5 years. Technically, the calculator is a fixed asset and should therefore be depreciated annually. To do this would not be worth the time or the effort involved. The £4.99 would be treated as a revenue expense and would be debited to sundries or office expenses.

As a rule, if a user of a financial statement would be misled by the exclusion or inclusion of an item of capital expenditure in the appropriate accounts, then that item is material.

## 6 Money measurement

Only transactions that can be measured in monetary terms are recorded in the books of account.

It is very difficult to record and compare information in terms of quantifiable amounts. Which has a greater value, 7 therms of gas or one hour of a sales person's time?

All accounting information is converted into money. We can easily compare £1.74 spent on gas with £5.65 spent on a sales person's commission. It is easy to put a value on goods and services used.

Because of their subjectivity it is impossible to put a value on items such as:

- the efficiency of the management;
- the skill and efficiency of the workforce;
- good customer relations leading to a greater volume of sales in the future.

## 7 Business entity

Only financial transactions concerning the business are recorded in the business accounts.

Any private transactions involving the proprietor(s) are disregarded when arriving at the business profit or loss for the year under review. If a sole trader was to win £8,000,000 on the national lottery, the win would not be entered as part of the business income. However, if the proprietor takes some stock from the business for the use of his family this would affect the business profits; it would reduce purchases and increase drawings, and therefore should be recorded in the business accounts.

## 8 Realisation concept

Profits are normally recognised when, in legal terms, the title to the goods passes to the customer.

### 9 Dual aspect concept

There are two aspects to accounting, and they are always equal to each other. This is recognisable as the accounting equation. The assets of a business are always equal to the liabilities of the business. It is also evident in the double entry system of bookkeeping.

$$\text{Fixed assets} + \text{Current assets} = \text{Liabilities} + \text{Capital}$$

Now to continue with further consideration of SSAPs.

## SSAP 4 ACCOUNTING FOR GOVERNMENT GRANTS

If a company receives a government grant towards an item of revenue expenditure the cash or bank account is debited and the appropriate revenue account is credited. The profit and loss account therefore shows a net amount.

If a company receives a government grant towards an item of capital expenditure this 'netting' process cannot take place. The grant is apportioned to the credit of the profit and loss account over the lifetime of the asset.

## SSAP 9 STOCKS AND LONG-TERM CONTRACTS

Stocks are to be valued at the lower of cost or net realisable value.

**Cost** is defined as 'expenditure . . . incurred . . . in the normal course of business in bringing the product . . . to its present location'. This definition includes import taxes, transport costs and any handling charges.

**Net realisable value** is the selling price less any direct expenses incurred in getting the product into a saleable condition. This may be less than cost due to a drop in selling prices, damage to the product, or the product now being obsolete.

Prime cost cannot be used to value finished goods in the case of a manufacturing business; full production cost must be used.

SSAP 9 does not accept LIFO as a method of stock valuation.

A long-term contract is one which will run for more than one year. The standard allows credit to be taken for a proportion of turnover and profit on a partly finished contract if the outcome can be assessed with a reasonable degree of certainty.

## SSAP 12 ACCOUNTING FOR DEPRECIATION

The standard states that 'assets are intended for use on a continuing basis . . .'

It defines depreciation as 'the measure of wearing out, consumption or other reduction in the useful economic life of a fixed asset whether arising from use, effluxion of time or obsolescence through technological or market changes.'

This statement summarises the causes of the depreciation of assets.

It goes on to say 'Depreciation should be allocated so as to charge a fair proportion of the cost or valuation of the asset to each accounting period expected to benefit from its use.'

All assets with a finite life should be depreciated, so all assets except freehold land will be depreciated.

There are a few examples where freehold land would be depreciated. A quarry would be depreciated by using a depletion method. Can you give another example?

The method chosen for depreciating an asset should be used consistently. However, the method used to depreciate fixed assets may be changed, but only if the new method gives a fairer presentation of the profits(losses) and of the financial position.

When a company revalues assets, depreciation should be calculated on the revalued amount over the remaining lifetime of the asset. Continue to apportion the value of the asset over its useful lifetime, using the method previously used if still appropriate. (The details of the revaluation must be shown in the accounts.)

Remember, depreciation is not a savings fund where cash is set aside to enable a replacement to be bought sometime in the future, nor does depreciation help us to know what the true value of the assets are.

## SSAP 13 ACCOUNTING FOR RESEARCH AND DEVELOPMENT

The standard divides research and development under three headings and defines each.

- **Pure research** 'is experimental or theoretical work undertaken primarily to acquire new scientific or technical knowledge for its own sake rather than directed towards any specific aim or application'.

- **Applied research** is 'original . . . investigation undertaken in order to gain new scientific or technical knowledge and directed towards a specific practical aim or objective'.

- **Development costs** are defined as '. . . costs relating to the . . . use of knowledge acquired through research to produce new or substantially improved materials, devices, products, processes, systems or services . . . prior to the commencement of commercial production . . .'

Neither of the first two types of expenditure listed may be capitalised. That is, they should be treated in the same way as any other revenue expenditure and debited to the profit and loss account. If fixed assets are purchased to facilitate the research and development then they should be capitalised like any other fixed asset. Development expenditure should be written off in the year that the expenditure is incurred. However, it may be capitalised and written off over the period that the resulting product is used or sold.

The rules which must be satisfied that will allow capitalisation are:

- that there is a clearly defined project;

- that the related expenditure can be clearly identified;

- that the outcome of the project is reasonably feasible and commercially viable;

- that all costs incurred now and in the future which relate to the project will be covered by the revenues generated by the project;

- adequate resources exist to enable the project to be completed.

The standard requires that accounting policy on research and development expenditure should be stated and explained.

## SSAP 17 ACCOUNTING FOR POST-BALANCE SHEET EVENTS

A post-balance sheet event is 'an event which occurs between the balance sheet date and the date on which the financial statements are approved by the board of directors'.

SSAP 17 categorises events which occur after the balance sheet date into the following:

- **1 Adjusting events** If material (see earlier concept of materiality) then changes must be made to the financial statements before they are presented to the shareholders.

  These events provide further information on conditions which existed at the balance sheet date. Examples of adjusting events would include:

  - where an asset sale was agreed before the year end without agreement having been reached about the price;

  - where the extent of loss or damage to stock (or other asset) is determined after the balance sheet date, thus reducing it's value at the year end;

  - dividends receivable relating to the period before the balance sheet date are declared after the balance sheet date.

- **2 Non-adjusting events** arise after the balance sheet date. These should not be included in the accounts. However, if they are of material significance then they should be disclosed by way of a note to the accounts.

Examples of non-adjusting events might include:

- devaluation of the currency in a major customer's country, after the balance sheet date;
- a new issue of shares or debentures after the balance sheet date;
- the decline in the value of a fixed asset after the year end.

## SSAP 18 ACCOUNTING FOR CONTINGENCIES

Post-balance sheet events are revealed after the accounts are prepared and may require the accounts to be adjusted accordingly. A contingency does exist at the balance sheet date, but the event may or may not happen.

A prudent approach should be adopted. If in doubt, provide for a contingent loss, but leave out a contingent gain.

## SSAP 22 ACCOUNTING FOR GOODWILL

The standard defines goodwill as 'the difference between the value of a business as a whole and the aggregate of the fair view of its separable net assets'.

Goodwill may be either inherent or purchased. Inherent goodwill is non-purchased goodwill. It exists within many businesses, because of their standing, reputation, and future prospects.

Inherent goodwill should not be recorded in the books of account.
Goodwill only ever appears in the books of the purchaser.

It is the price paid by the purchaser in excess of the net book value of the assets taken over. It is the difference between the market value of the business and its book value.

Remember the purchaser cannot buy customers. The purchaser is buying access to his perception of future profits.

Purchased goodwill should not remain on the balance sheet as a permanent asset. It should be written off on acquisition against reserves. It may, under certain circumstances, be written off against profits over its useful economic life.

The main topics for examination questions in this particular area of study are:

- depreciation;
- stock;
- accruals and
- inherent goodwill.

## EXAMINATION QUESTIONS

These are generally of two types:

- A full question devoted entirely to standards or concepts, where 4 or 5 different scenarios are presented and the candidate has to advise on the correctness, or not, of the treatment. Questions 1, 2, and 3 below are examples of this type of question.
- Supplementary parts to a question which has dealt with a major topic in its own right. For example, a question may deal mainly with valuing stock using LIFO, FIFO, and AVCO. Part of the question could ask for a discussion of the concepts involved in the valuation of stock. (Prudence, consistency).

All answers to examination questions should be dealt with in three parts:

- identify the concept;
- explain the concept in general terms;
- apply the general principles to the question.

EXAMPLE

A machine which cost £45,000 has a book value of £13,500. A similar model has recently been sold by another business for £19,000. It is proposed to revalue the machine and include it in the books at the revalued price of £19,000.

**Required**

Explain how the machine should be treated in the books of account. Make reference to any accepted accounting concepts or conventions.

**Solution**

Identification – going concern concept.

General explanation of concept – unless there is evidence to the contrary it is assumed that the business will continue to trade into the foreseeable future. Value assets at cost not what they could be sold for.

Application – do not revalue. The machine should be shown on the balance sheet as follows:

| Fixed Assets | Cost | Depreciation | Net |
|---|---|---|---|
| Machine | £45,000 | £31,500 | £13,500 |

It is implicit in *all* questions that the standards and other concepts and conventions will be applied in the workings of your answer. This sounds daunting, but you have been doing this from the start of your studies.

Remember valuing assets at cost? Remember taking rates prepaid into account when you prepared a profit and loss account?

You have been using standards and concepts now for a considerable time. All that this chapter is seeking to do is to formalise them.

---

## Chapter roundup

Chapter 3 outlines the major 'rules' that govern the ways that accounts are prepared.

It has explained the ways that these principles are applied in practice. Adherence to the concepts and conventions means that business results should be the same no matter who prepares the accounts.

---

# Illustrative questions

1    Given below are five unconnected transactions made by five different businesses together with the proposed treatment of each transaction in the final accounts of the business concerned.

(1) Perry Ltd commenced trading in the early 1980s. Since then the company sales have increased by 400% and the number of customers has doubled. The company has an extremely good name in the trade. As a result the directors propose to introduce £80,000 goodwill into the balance sheet as a fixed asset.

(2) Fishwick Ltd bought new premises in 1988. The market value of these premises fell between 1988 and 1992. Consequently the premises were depreciated until 1992. Since 1992 property prices have started to rise again so the directors are proposing to discontinue the practice of providing for depreciation on premises.

(3) Patel values all his business stock at cost. He is proposing to value his closing stock of clothing at £90,000. Included in this figure is a batch of damaged sweatshirts which cost £800. After undertaking repairs costing £100 they could be sold for £850. The cost of replacing the damaged sweatshirts would be £700.

(4) Glynn Ltd commenced business in January 1990. In the first two years losses were incurred. Since 1992 the company has started to make profits. For the year ended 31 December 1993 debenture interest paid amounted to £18,000. Bank overdraft interest was £1,500. The directors would like to declare a dividend of £20,000. They propose to show an entry in the profit and loss account – interest and dividends £39,500.

(5) Nelson plc had written off a bad debt of £23,000 owed by Saunders and Co in the year ended 30 April 1991. In the current year Nelson plc has received a payment of £23,000 from the receivers of Saunders & Co. The directors are proposing to credit the £23,000 to retained earnings as the amount recovered refers to a previous year.

*Required*
Explain, giving reasons, how each proposal should have been treated and explain which generally accepted accounting conventions and principles should have been applied. (50)
(AEB)

*Tutorial note*
Remember, in this type of question, identify the concept, explain it in general terms and then apply it to the transactions being considered.

*Suggested answer*
(1) Going concern
Assumption of infinite life – so value assets at cost, not what they will fetch if sold.
A going concern is not going to sell the business.
Goodwill only appears in the books of account when it is purchased.
Inherent goodwill never appears on a balance sheet.
Perry Ltd should not include goodwill on the balance sheet.

(2) Consistency
Same method of depreciation should be applied each year.
All assets with a finite life should be depreciated.
Depreciation apportions the cost of an asset over its useful lifetime; it is not an attempt to value it.
Fishwick Ltd should continue to depreciate at the same rate as before. (They could revalue and then continue to depreciate.)

(3) Prudence
When valuing stock the lower of cost or net realisable value should be used.
Net realisable value is selling price less any expenses incurred in getting the goods into a condition to make them saleable.
Patel has the choice of cost £800, or net realisable value £750 (selling price £850 less the repair costs of £100). The batch of sweatshirts should be valued at £750. The value of Patel's closing stock is £89,950.

(4) Glynn Ltd may declare a dividend, but would this be prudent?
The company must cover previous losses.
Cash must be available to make the payment possible.
Dividends are an appropriation of profits, whereas interest is a revenue expense.
Dividends appear in the appropriation account while both sets of interest should be shown on the profit and loss account.

(5) Accruals or matching
This is not a prior year adjustment.
Credit this year's profit and loss account, but show separately from the trading profit.
It is important to record Saunders and Co's payment through the use of a bad debt recovery account.

**2** 'It is fundamental to the understanding and interpretation of financial accounts that those who use them should be aware of the main assumptions on which they are based.'

*Required*
(a) Outline briefly the four fundamental accounting concepts specifically mentioned in SSAP 2 (Disclosure of Accounting Policies). (4)
(b) Distinguish between accounting concepts, bases and policies. (4)
(c) Illustrate the link between accounting concepts, bases and policies using one SSAP (other than SSAP 2). (7)

(NICCEA)

*Tutorial note*
Keep your answers brief and to the point. Note the marks available for this question – the whole question should only take about 25 minutes.

*Suggested answer*

(a) The four fundamental accounting concepts specifically mentioned in SSAP 2 are:
Going concern
Accruals
Consistency
Prudence
*(Refer to the text for explanations of the above terms.)*

(b) SSAP 2 defines concepts as 'broad basic assumptions which underlie the periodic financial accounts of business enterprises'.
Bases are the methods which could be used when applying the concepts, e.g. there are a multitude of different methods of calculating the annual depreciation charge on fixed assets.
Policies are the bases which individual managers feel are most appropriate to be applied in their business.

(c) Research and development costs.
Concepts involved – accruals and prudence
Bases – immediate write-off
deferral policy
Policy – managers will choose according to the nature of the expenditure, e.g. the expenditure could be deferred for a clearly defined project being researched over a number of years.

**3** In relation to SSAP 9 'Stocks and long term contracts':

(a) explain:
(i) cost;
(ii) net realisable value;
(iii) attributable profit;
(iv) foreseeable losses. (16)

(b) At what amount should total stock be shown in the balance sheet, given the following circumstances? Show your calculations.

|  | Cost | Net realisable value | Replacement cost |
|---|---|---|---|
|  | £ | £ | £ |
| Line A | 1,200 | 1,500 | 1,400 |
| Line B | 2,000 | 1,000 | 1,200 |
| Line C | 800 | 900 | 850 |
| Line D | 3,000 | 3,200 | 1,800 |
| Line E | 700 | 800 | 750 |
|  | 7,700 | 7,400 | 6,000 |

(4)
(NEAB)

*Tutorial note*

Note that most of the marks are for the written sections. Plan carefully what you wish to say so that you can avoid repeating and labouring a point.

*Suggested answer*

(a) (i) Cost is defined in SSAP 9 as 'that expenditure which has been incurred in the normal course of business in bringing the product or service to its present location and condition'. This includes the purchase price plus any conversion costs to make the product ready for sale.

(ii) Net realisable value is the actual or estimated selling price less all further costs incurred in making the goods fit for sale. These costs include repairs, marketing and selling and distribution costs.

(iii) Attributable profit is 'that part of the total profit currently estimated to arise over the duration of the contract, after allowing for estimated remedial and maintenance costs and increases in costs so far as not recoverable under the terms of the contract, that fairly reflects the profit attributable to that part of the work performed at the accounting date'.

(iv) Foreseeable losses are 'losses which are currently estimated to arise over the duration of the contract, after allowing for estimated remedial and maintenance costs and increases in costs so far as not recoverable under the terms of the contract'.

(b) Replacement cost is not an acceptable method of valuing stock so these figures can be ignored.

Stocks are valued at the lower of cost or net realisable value:

|  | £ |  |
|---|---|---|
| Line A | 1,200 | (cost) |
| Line B | 1,000 | (NRV) |
| Line C | 800 | (cost) |
| Line D | 3,000 | (cost) |
| Line E | 700 | (cost) |
| Stock value | 6,700 | |

**4** Due to a heavy workload the annual stocktake of Barmic Ltd did not take place on 31 December 1993, but was completed one week later on the 7 January 1994 when the value of £26,400 was established.

The chief accountant believed the above figure to be inaccurate and a subsequent investigation revealed the following.

(i) The stocks had been valued at selling price instead of cost. Selling price is cost plus 25%.

(ii) During the week ended 7 January 1994:
goods received and invoiced were £5,000;
invoiced sales to customers were £7,750 including an overcharge of £250;
goods with a sales value of £250 were sent to a customer on approval.

(iii) The stock included items which had been valued at £300 which were damaged and should have been valued at 50% of cost.

(iv) The total of one stock sheet of £3,000 had not been included in the total stock summary.

(v) A box of samples, with a sales value of £200, had been included in the stock. These items were to be given free to potential customers.

(vi) Items which had been hired for a sales promotion had been included in stock at an amount of £1,000.

*Required*

(a) Calculate the correct value of stock at 31 December 1993 using accepted accounting rules and concepts. (16)

(b) Identify the rules and concepts which were involved in your calculations.     (4)

(NEAB)

*Tutorial note*
Beware of the calculation required to reduce the selling price of the goods to the necessary cost price.

*Suggested answer*

| (a) | | £ | (b) |
|---|---|---:|---|
| Stock as per stocktake | | 26,400 | |
| (i) | less mark up | (5,820) | Lower of cost or net realisable value |
| (ii) | goods received | (5,000) | Cost |
| | sales less £1 500 mark up | 6,000 | Lower of cost or net realisable value |
| | goods on approval | 200 | Goods only sold when title passes |
| | damaged stock | (120) | Lower of cost or net realisable value |
| (iv) | carry forward error | 2,400 | Error of omission |
| (v) | samples | (160) | Lower of cost or net realisable value |
| (vi) | sales promotion material | (800) | Revenue Expenditure |
| | | 23,640 | |

# PARTNERSHIP ACCOUNTS

## Units in this chapter

4.1 *Partnership agreements*

4.2 *Partnership profit and loss appropriation accounts*

4.3 *Capital and current accounts*

4.4 *Structural changes*

4.5 *Goodwill*

4.6 *Partnership dissolution*

4.7 *Partnership amalgamation*

4.8 *Limited company taking over a partnership*

## Chapter objectives

This chapter examines the nature of partnership; the preparation of partnership accounts; the main changes that take place in partnerships, and the book-keeping procedures required to record these changes.

Key topics covered in this chapter are the treatment of:

* profits when a partnership agreement exists;

* profits in the absence of an agreement;

* changes in profit sharing ratios;

* the introduction of a new partner;

* the retirement of a partner;

* the dissolution of the partnership;

* the takeover of a partnership by a limited company.

## 4.1    PARTNERSHIP AGREEMENTS

A partnership is one type of business which has more than one owner. It is defined by the Partnership Act 1890 as

'the relationship which subsists (exists) between persons carrying on a business in common with a view of profit'.

It is usual for a partnership to have a written agreement (although the agreement could be an oral one). The agreement normally covers:

* the duties of the partners
* the way profits are to be shared, and
* the financial arrangements if there is any change in the composition of the partnership.

If there is no partnership agreement, then the Partnership Act 1890 lays down the following rules which must apply:

* Partners should contribute equal amounts of capital.
* No partner is to be entitled to interest on his/her capital.
* No partner is to be entitled to a salary.
* No partner is to be charged interest on drawings.
* Residual profits and losses are to be shared equally.
* Any loan made to the business by a partner will carry interest at the rate of 5% per annum.

In an examination question if no details of profit share are given, then the candidate must assume that no agreement exists and so the Partnership Act comes into play.

## 4.2    PARTNERSHIP PROFIT AND LOSS APPROPRIATION ACCOUNTS

The 'final accounts' for all businesses are the same in most respects.

| Manufacturing account | Factory account |

| Trading account | Warehouse account |

| P & L account | Administration (office) account |

It is only at this point that changes take place. When the accounts are prepared for a sole trader the profit (or loss) is carried down to the capital account.

The profit in a partnership is shared among the partners, so a further account is needed.

| Appropriation account | Profit (loss) sharing account |

This account takes the profits (or losses) earned by the business and shows how these are divided amongst the partners.

# 4.3   CAPITAL AND CURRENT ACCOUNTS

The balance sheet of a partnership differs from that of a sole trader in that, since there is more than one owner, there must be more than one capital account, showing the financial involvement of all the partners in the business.

Indeed, the capital employed in the business is usually divided into partners' capital accounts and partners' current accounts.

Included in the partners' capital accounts are:
* deliberate injections of capital at any time during the partnership life;
* any goodwill adjustments; and
* any profits or losses arising on revaluation of fixed assets (generally when a structural change takes place).

Included in the current accounts are:
* all entries relating to the current years profits;
* any errors that may have been made relating to previous years' profits.

Both of these two accounts taken together are the equivalent of the sole traders' capital account.

Partners may have agreed to share the profits in a number of ways in order to take into account such things as work load or the amount of capital that a partner may have invested.

Although partners, like all owners of businesses, receive a share of profits, for convenience sake, the profit is shown on the appropriation account under the headings salaries, interest on capital and share of residual profits or losses.

* Partnership salaries are usually allocated to partners to reflect their work load.
* Interest on capital reflects the injection of capital that each partner has made.
* The residual profit is the reward that each partner receives for the risk taking element of the business.

**Note** Despite the names, all these elements are **profits**. The entrepreneur (the partner) receives profits.

Occasionally there is provision in the partnership agreement to charge the partners interest on any drawings they make. This is a notional charge (that is, the partners do not pay cash into the business as they would pay interest to a bank for a loan). It is charged to act as a cost to those partners who draw cash out of the business in the early part of the accounting period.

## EXAMPLE

Arthur and Brenda are in partnership. Their capital and current accounts as at 1 January 1994 show:

| | Capital Balances | Current Balances | | Drawings |
|---|---|---|---|---|
| | £ | £ | | £ |
| Arthur | 20,000 | 2,500 (credit) | Arthur | 8,500 (on 30 June) |
| Brenda | 30,000 | 1,500 (credit) | Arthur | 8,500 (on 30 December) |
| | | | Brenda | 6,000 (on 30 April) |
| | | | Brenda | 6,000 (on 31 August) |
| | | | Brenda | 6,000 (on 31 December) |

The partnership agreement provides for the following:
* profits and losses are shared between Arthur and Brenda in the ratio 2:1
* Arthur is to be credited with a salary of £3,000 per annum
* interest on capital at 8% per annum is allowed
* interest on drawings is charged at 10% per annum.

The profit for the year is £47,975.

**Required**

(a) The partnership profit and loss appropriation account for the year ended 31 December 1994.

(b) The partnership capital and current accounts as at 31 December 1994.

**Solution**

(a) 
## Arthur and Brenda profit and loss appropriation account
### for the year ended 31 December 1994

| | | £ | £ | | | £ | £ |
|---|---|---|---|---|---|---|---|
| Salary A | | | 3,000 | NP | | | 47,975 |
| Interest on capital | A | 1,600 | | Interest on drawings | A | 425 | |
| | B | 2,400 | 4,000 | | B | 600 | 1,025 |
| Profit share | A | 28,000 | | | | | |
| | B | 14,000 | 42,000 | | | | |
| | | | 49,000 | | | | 49,000 |

(b)
## Capital accounts

| | A | B |
|---|---|---|
| Balance b/d | £20,000 | £30,000 |

## Current accounts

| | A | B | | A | B |
|---|---|---|---|---|---|
| | | | Balance b/d | 2,500 | 1,500 |
| Drawings | 17,000 | 18,000 | Salary | 3,000 | |
| Interest on drawings | 425 | 600 | Interest on capital | 1,600 | 2,400 |
| Balance c/d | 17,675 | | Profit | 28,000 | 14,000 |
| | | | Balance c/d | | 700 |
| | 35,100 | 18,600 | | 35,100 | 18,600 |
| Balance c/d | | 700 | Balance c/d | 17,675 | |

*Points to note*

- Brenda has withdrawn more profits than she was credited with during the year. Hence the debit balance (she is a debtor, she owes the business £700 on her current account).

- The traditional horizontal format has been used in the profit and loss appropriation account. This shows clearly the debits for salaries etc in the appropriation account followed by the credits in the current account. If students have been taught the vertical layout and feel comfortable using it they should continue to do so. Generally candidates will be given credit for using any acceptable form of layout.

- The columnar layout of the capital and current accounts saves time but once again if students prefer to show separate accounts this is acceptable.

    However, if a question asks for a particular layout students must form their answer according to the question.

- Interest on drawings calculation:

Arthur: $8500 \times \dfrac{10}{100} \times \dfrac{6}{12} = 425$     Brenda: $6000 \times \dfrac{10}{100} \times \dfrac{8}{12} = 400$

$6000 \times \dfrac{10}{100} \times \dfrac{4}{12} = 200$

# 4.4    STRUCTURAL CHANGES

If there are any changes in the structure of a partnership then one partnership ceases to exist and another takes its place.

These structural changes can be caused through:

- the admission of a new partner
- the retirement or death of an existing partner
- a change in the profit sharing values between existing partners.

## EXAMPLE 1

Carol and Denis decide to admit Ethel as a partner on 1 July. The financial year end is 31 December.

We have two distinct businesses: Carol and Denis were in business from 1 January to 30 June and Carol, Denis and Ethel were in business from 1 July to 31 December.

It follows that we should prepare a set of final accounts for both businesses. One set of accounts to be prepared up to 30 June and another set will be prepared to show the 'new business activities' from 1 July to 31 December.

## EXAMPLE 2

Fred and Greta are in partnership sharing profits and losses 2:1 respectively. Their year end is 31 December. They decide to admit Hannah as a partner with effect from 1 July. Fred, Greta and Hannah will share profits and losses 2:2:1 respectively. The profit for the year ended 31 December is £30,000. The profit has accrued evenly throughout the year.

**Required**

The profit and loss appropriation accounts for the year ended 31 December.

**Solution**

**Fred and Greta profit and loss account for the six months ended 30 June**

| | | £ | | £ |
|---|---|---|---|---|
| Share of profits | Fred | 10,000 | NP | 15,000 |
| | Greta | 5,000 | | |
| | | 15,000 | | 15,000 |

**Fred, Greta and Hannah profit and loss appropriation account for the six months ended 31 December**

| | £ | | £ |
|---|---|---|---|
| Fred | 6,000 | NP | 15,000 |
| Greta | 6,000 | | |
| Hannah | 3,000 | | |
| | 15,000 | | 15,000 |

Although this illustrates the fundamentals of the treatment of the appropriation account, common sense would suggest that if partners were to invite others to join the partnership they would look at their business before the new partner joined to see if the business assets reflected the true worth of the business at that time.

Remember that assets are valued at cost on the balance sheet, not what they may fetch if sold (the going concern concept).

## EXAMPLE 3

Iain and Jane have been in partnership for over 30 years sharing profits and losses in the ratio of 2:1 respectively. Their year end is 31 December. They decide to admit Keith into the partnership with effect from 1 May. The partnership balance sheet prior to Keith's admission as a partner is:

**Iain and Jane balance sheet as at 30 April**

| | £ | | | £ |
|---|---|---|---|---|
| Premises at cost | 4,000 | Capital | Iain | 15,000 |
| Vehicles at cost | 14,000 | | Jane | 10,000 |
| Stock | 5,000 | | | |
| Debtors | 3,000 | | | |
| Bank | 1,500 | Creditors | | 2,500 |
| | 27,500 | | | 27,500 |

Over the past 20 years the price of premises has risen. A recent valuation values the partnership premises at £40,000.

**Required**

Show the necessary accounts in the books of the partnership to show the increase in the value of the premises.

**Solution**

This rise in value has taken place while Iain and Jane have been the proprietors, so the profit (due to inflation) belongs to them. The increase did not arise after Keith's admission so he should not benefit.

The book keeping entries would be:

### Premises

| | £ |
|---|---|
| 30 April balance | 4,000 |
| 30 April revaluation | 36,000 |

### Capital – Iain

| | | £ |
|---|---|---|
| | 1 January balance | 15,000 |
| | Revaluation | 24,000 |

### Capital – Jane

| | | £ |
|---|---|---|
| | 1 January balance | 10,000 |
| | Revaluation | 12,000 |

### Revaluation account

| | £ | | £ |
|---|---|---|---|
| 30 April – Iain | 24,000 | 30 April Premises | 36,000 |
| 30 April – Jane | 12,000 | | |
| | 36,000 | | 36,000 |

Once this adjustment is made the entries to record Keith's admission can be made.

It may seem strange to use a revaluation account when we could debit premises with £36,000 and credit Iain and Jane with £24,000 and £12,000 respectively. We use a revaluation account because there may be a number of assets which have been revalued.

> The revaluation account is used to collect all the necessary adjustments.

## EXAMPLE 4

Lisa and Mark are in partnership sharing profits and losses equally, they decide to admit Noel into the partnership at 1 January 1995.

### Lisa and Mark balance sheet as at 31 December 1994

| | £ | | | £ |
|---|---|---|---|---|
| Premises at cost | 12,000 | Capital accounts | Lisa | 24,000 |
| Machinery at cost | 8,000 | | Mark | 20,000 |
| Vehicles at cost | 17,000 | | | |
| Stock | 4,000 | | | |
| Debtors | 5,000 | Creditors | | 4,000 |
| Bank | 2,000 | | | |
| | 48,000 | | | 48,000 |

The following asset valuations have been agreed between Lisa, Mark and Noel

| | |
|---|---|
| Premises | £46,000 |
| Machinery | £6,000 |
| Vehicles | £13,000 |
| Stock | £3,700 |

All other asset and liability values are agreed at book value.

Noel is to introduce £10,000 cash capital.

**Required**

(a) Revaluation account recording the change in the partnership assets.

(b) The partners' capital accounts after admitting Noel to the partnership.

(c) The partnership balance sheet as at 1 January after the admission of Noel as a partner.

(a)
Revaluation account

| | £ | | £ |
|---|---|---|---|
| Machinery | 2,000 | Premises | 34,000 |
| Vehicles | 4,000 | | |
| Stock | 300 | | |
| Profit on revaluation | 27,700 | | |
| | 34,000 | | 34,000 |

(b)
Capital accounts

| | Lisa £ | Mark £ | Noel | | Lisa £ | Mark £ | Noel £ |
|---|---|---|---|---|---|---|---|
| | | | | Balance b/d | 24,000 | 20,000 | |
| | | | | Revaluation | 13,850 | 13,850 | |
| Bank balance | 37,850 | 33,850 | 10,000 | Bank | | | 10,000 |
| c/d | 37,850 | 33,850 | 10,000 | | 37,850 | 33,850 | 10,000 |
| | | | | Balance b/d | 37,850 | 33,850 | 10,000 |

(c) **Lisa, Mark and Noel balance sheet as at 1 January after the admission of Noel**

| | £ | | £ |
|---|---|---|---|
| Premises | 46,000 | Capital accounts | |
| Machinery | 6,000 | Lisa | 37,850 |
| Vehicles | 13,000 | Mark | 33,850 |
| Stock | 3,700 | Noel | 10,000 |
| Debtors | 5,000 | Creditors | 4,000 |
| Bank | 12,000 | | |
| | 85,700 | | 85,700 |

## 4.5  GOODWILL

As well as revaluing the tangible assets of the business when a new partner is admitted (or when an old partner retires), intangible assets, such as the reputation or good name of the business; the future prospects; the strength of the workforce; the location of the business, and others should be considered.

When a successful business is sold the vendor(s) will generally price the business at a sum greater than the value of the net assets.

### EXAMPLE 1

The balance sheet of a fish and chip shop may be as follows:

| **Fixed assets** | £ | | £ |
|---|---|---|---|
| Equipment | 12,000 | **Capital – Oliver** | 19,250 |
| Fixtures and fittings | 6,000 | | |
| **Current assets** | | **Current liabilities** | 750 |
| Stock | 350 | | |
| Bank | 1,650 | | |
| | 20,000 | | 20,000 |

Oliver decides to sell his business, he may advertise it at £50,000. If the business is sold to Peter at this price

(a) Oliver sells at a profit of £30,750;

(b) Peter has purchased goodwill of £30,750.

Peter's opening balance sheet would be as follows:

| Fixed assets | £ | | £ |
|---|---|---|---|
| Goodwill | 30,750 | Capital – Peter | 50,000 |
| Equipment | 12,000 | | |
| Fixtures and Fittings | 6,000 | | |
| **Current Assets** | | **Current liabilities** | 750 |
| Stock | 350 | | |
| Bank | 1,650 | | |
| | 50,750 | | 50,750 |

Why would Peter pay £30,750 more than the business assets are worth? He is buying access to future profits. He must believe that he can make himself a great deal of profit in the future.

Goodwill can appear in the books of any business organisation when it is purchased. It is normal practice to write off this intangible asset in the year of purchase since goodwill can be destroyed very easily and the exact value can only be ascertained when the purchaser agrees a price.

- When a partnership structure changes (page 72) 'one partnership ceases to exist and another takes its place.' It is as if the 'old' partnership was selling all its assets to the 'new' partnership.
- Generally the 'old' business would sell to the 'new' business at what the business might fetch if sold on the open market, that is after revaluing the assets and valuing goodwill.

## EXAMPLE 2

Quentin and Ruth are in partnership sharing profits and losses 3:2 respectively. Their balance sheet as at 31 March 1994 is as follows:

| Fixed assets | £ | | £ |
|---|---|---|---|
| Premises at cost | 27,000 | Capital – Quentin | 26,000 |
| Machinery at cost | 13,000 | – Ruth | 22,000 |
| **Current assets** | | **Current liabilities** | 2,000 |
| Stock | 6,000 | | |
| Debtors | 3,000 | | |
| Bank | 1,000 | | |
| | 50,000 | | 50,000 |

Quentin and Ruth admit Shirley as a partner with effect from 1 April 1994. Shirley will pay £20,000 as her share of capital. The new profit sharing ratio will be 2:2:1.

The partners agree the following valuations:

| | |
|---|---|
| Premises | £50,000 |
| Machinery | £10,000 |
| Stock | £5,000 |
| Goodwill | £30,000 |

All other assets and liabilities at their book value.

**Required**

The accounts in the partnership books to record the admission of Shirley as a partner.

**Solution**

### Revaluation account

| | £ | | £ |
|---|---|---|---|
| Machinery | 3,000 | Premises | 23,000 |
| Stock | 1,000 | Goodwill | 30,000 |
| Capital – Quentin | 29,400 | | |
| Capital – Ruth | 19,600 | | |
| | 53,000 | | 53,000 |

**Capital accounts**

| | Quentin £ | Ruth £ | Shirley | | Quentin £ | Ruth £ | Shirley £ |
|---|---|---|---|---|---|---|---|
| | | | | Balance b/d | 26,000 | 22,000 | |
| | | | | Revaluation | 29,400 | 19,600 | |
| Balance c/d | 55,400 | 41,600 | 20,000 | Cash | | | 20,000 |
| c/d | 55,400 | 41,600 | 20,000 | | 55,400 | 41,600 | 20,000 |
| | | | | Balance b/d | 55,400 | 41,600 | 20,000 |

As can be seen in the balance sheet of Quentin, Ruth and Shirley, goodwill is shown. In the general ledger it will appear thus:

**Goodwill**

| | |
|---|---|
| Balance b/d | £30,000 |

If the account is written out, then the partners must stand the 'loss' in their profit sharing ratios of 2:2:1.

The balance sheet as at 1 April after the admission of Shirley was:

| | £ | | | £ |
|---|---|---|---|---|
| Goodwill | 30,000 | Capital | Quentin | 55,400 |
| Premises | 50,000 | | Ruth | 41,600 |
| Machinery | 10,000 | | Shirley | 20,000 |
| Stock | 5,000 | Current liabilities | | 2,000 |
| Debtors | 3,000 | | | |
| Bank | 21,000 | | | |
| | 119,000 | | | 119,000 |

As stated on page 62 it is not usual to show goodwill in the books; if it is then the goodwill account should be written out of the general ledger. In the balance sheet of Quentin, Ruth and Shirley, goodwill is shown. The account will appear in the General Ledger. If the account is to be written out of the ledger the partners must stand the 'loss' in their profit sharing ratios of 2:2:1.

**Goodwill**

| | £ | | | £ |
|---|---|---|---|---|
| Balance | 30,000 | Capital | Quentin | 12,000 |
| | | | Ruth | 12,000 |
| | | | Shirley | 6,000 |
| | 30,000 | | | 30,000 |

**Capital**

| | Quentin £ | Ruth £ | Shirley £ | | Quentin £ | Ruth £ | Shirley £ |
|---|---|---|---|---|---|---|---|
| Goodwill | 12,000 | 12,000 | 6,000 | Balance b/d | 55,400 | 41,600 | 20,000 |
| Balance c/d | 43,400 | 29,600 | 14,000 | | | | |
| | 55,400 | 41,600 | 20,000 | | 55,400 | 41,600 | 20,000 |
| | | | | Balance b/d | 43,400 | 29,600 | 14,000 |

In questions involving goodwill, remember that the original partners probably spent many years building up the reputation of the business and the quality of product etc, so the value of the goodwill should be reflected in their capital accounts.

If we write off any asset, e.g. a vehicle, a computer or goodwill, the partners capitals will reflect this writing off. Since goodwill will be written out of the 'new' partnership books the 'new' partner's capital accounts must bear this.

Should a partner retire or leave the business, this would have to be recorded in the books of account.

EXAMPLE 3

Trevor, Una and Victor are in partnership sharing profits and losses in the ratio of 3:2:1. On 31 January Trevor retires from the business. The partnership balance sheet as at that date is as follows:

| | £ | | | £ |
|---|---|---|---|---|
| Premises | 30,000 | Capital | Trevor | 20,000 |
| Plant and Machinery | 18,000 | | Una | 20,000 |
| Vehicles | 12,000 | | Victor | 25,000 |
| Stock | 7,000 | Current liabilities | | 5,000 |
| Debtors | 2,000 | | | |
| Bank | 1,000 | | | |
| | 70,000 | | | 70,000 |

The following valuations had been agreed between Trevor, Una and Victor:

| | |
|---|---|
| Premises | £50,000 |
| Plant and machinery | £16,000 |
| Vehicles | £8,000 |
| Goodwill | £40,000 |

All other assets and liabilities are valued at book value.

**Required**

The balance sheet as at 1 February immediately after Trevor's retirement. The partnership have negotiated a bank loan to pay Trevor's settlement.

**Solution**

### Revaluation account

| | £ | | £ |
|---|---|---|---|
| Plant and machinery | 2,000 | Premises | 20,000 |
| Vehicles | 4,000 | Goodwill | 40,000 |
| Capital | 54,000 | | |
| | 60,000 | | 60,000 |

### Capital account

| | Trevor £ | Una £ | Victor £ | | Trevor £ | Una £ | Victor £ |
|---|---|---|---|---|---|---|---|
| Cash | 47,000 | | | Balance b/d | 20,000 | 20,000 | 25,000 |
| Balance c/d | | 38,000 | 34,000 | Revaluation | 27,000 | 18,000 | 9,000 |
| | 47,000 | 38,000 | 34,000 | | 47,000 | 38,000 | 34,000 |
| | | | | Balance b/d | | 38,000 | 34,000 |

### Balance sheet as at 31 January 1994 (after Trevor's retirement)

| | £ | | | £ |
|---|---|---|---|---|
| **Fixed assets** | | | | |
| Goodwill | 40,000 | Capital | Una | 38,000 |
| Premises | 50,000 | | Victor | 34,000 |
| | | | | 72,000 |
| Plant and machinery | 16,000 | **Loan – bank** | | 47,000 |
| Vehicles | 8,000 | **Current liabilities** | | 5,000 |
| **Current assets** | | | | |
| Stock | 7,000 | | | |
| Debtors | 2,000 | | | |
| Bank | 1,000 | | | |
| | 124,000 | | | 124,000 |

If goodwill had to be written off, it would be written off to Una and Victor's capital accounts in their new profit sharing ratios.

## 4.6 PARTNERSHIP DISSOLUTION

A partnership may be dissolved by:

- the death or retirement of a partner;
- the bankruptcy of a partner;
- agreement of the partners.

On a dissolution the assets of the business should be disposed of and the liabilities settled. The settlement should be in the following order

- creditors;
- partners loans;
- partners capitals.

The mechanism used is a realisation account which is rather like a trading and profit and loss account. Unless the question indicates anything to the contrary, assume that the partnership will collect the money from debtors and pay the business creditors. All assets to be disposed of are entered on the debit side of the realisation account. The proceeds of any sales and take overs are entered on the credit side. The resulting profit or loss is then entered in the partners' capital accounts.

## EXAMPLE

William, Yvonne and Anne are in partnership they share profits and losses 3:3:2. They agree to dissolve their partnership on 31 December 1994 when their balance sheet appeared as follows:

| Fixed assets | | £ | Capital accounts | | £ |
|---|---|---|---|---|---|
| Premises | | 52,000 | William | | 30,000 |
| Plant and Machinery | | 8,000 | Yvonne | | 20,000 |
| Vehicles (3 cars) | | 6,000 | Anne | | 20,000 |
| | | 66,000 | | | 70,000 |
| | | | | | |
| **Current assets** | | | **Current accounts** | | |
| Stock | 9,000 | | William | 2,000 | |
| Debtors | 7,000 | | Yvonne | 1,200 | |
| Bank | 4,000 | 20,000 | Anne | 800 | 4,000 |
| | | | **Loan – Yvonne** | | 10,000 |
| | | | **Current liabilities** | | 2,000 |
| | | 86,000 | | | 86,000 |

The following assets are sold for cash:

| Premises | £60,000 |
|---|---|
| Plant and machinery | £5,000 |
| Stock | £7,500 |

The vehicles are taken over by the partners at the following agreed valuation:

| Car 1 by William valued at | £2,500 |
|---|---|
| Car 2 by Yvonne valued at | £3,000 |
| Car 3 by Anne valued at | £1,500 |

The debtors pay £6,700 in settlement.
The creditors are paid £1,800 in settlement.
Dissolution expenses amount to £2,000.

## Required
The realisation account, cash account and capital accounts to close the partnership books.

## Solution

**Realisation account**

| | | | | | |
|---|---|---|---|---|---|
| Disc allowed | | 300 ❶ | Disc received | | 200 ❷ |
| Premises | | 52,000 ❹ | Cash | | 60,000 ❺ |
| Plant and machinery | | 8,000 ❹ | Cash | | 5,000 ❻ |
| Vehicles | | 6,000 ❹ | Cash | | 7,500 ❼ |
| Stock | | 9,000 ❹ | Capitals (cars) | William | 2,500 ❽ |
| Costs | | 2,000 ❾ | | Yvonne | 3,000 ❽ |
| Profit on realisation | | | | Anne | 1,500 ❽ |
| William | 900 | | | | |
| Yvonne | 900 | | | | |
| Anne | 600 | 2,400 ❿ | | | |
| | | 79,700 | | | 79,700 |

**Cash account**

| | | | | |
|---|---|---|---|---|
| Balance b/d | 4,000 | Creditors | | 1,800 ❷ |
| Debtors | 6,700 ❶ | Costs | | 2,000 ❾ |
| Realisation (Premises) | 60,000 ❺ | Loan Y | | 10,000 ❸ |
| Realisation (P & M) | 5,000 ❻ | Capital | William | 30,400 ⓫ |
| Realisation (Stock) | 7,500 ❼ | | Yvonne | 19,100 ⓫ |
| | | | Anne | 19,900 ⓫ |
| | 83,200 | | | 83,200 |

**Capital account**

| | William £ | Yvonne £ | Anne £ | | William £ | Yvonne £ | Anne £ |
|---|---|---|---|---|---|---|---|
| Realisation (cars) | 2,500 | 3,000 | 1,500 ❶ | Balances b/d | 30,000 | 20,000 | 20,000 |
| | | | | Current a/c | 2,000 | 1,200 | 800 |
| Cash | 30,400 | 19,100 | 19,900 ⓫ | Profit on realisation | 900 | 900 | 600 ❿ |
| | 32,900 | 22,100 | 21,400 | | 32,900 | 22,100 | 21,400 |

❶ and ❷ the debtors and creditors accounts were closed using the cash book.

❸ Yvonne was paid the money the business owes her for the outstanding loan.

❹ all assets except debtors and bank were transferred to the realisation account at their book value thus closing all other asset accounts in the general ledger.

❺, ❻, ❼ and ❽ each asset was disposed of by debiting cash or capitals in the case of the cars.

❾ the costs were included in our realisation account.

❿ the profit (or loss) was then calculated and entered on the partners capital account. You could then see clearly that William had a credit balance of £30,400 on his capital account. Yvonne had a credit balance of £19,100 on her capital account and Anne had a credit balance of £19,900.

They were all creditors – so the cash was taken from the cash account to settle their debts ⓫ – the business owed them money.

Do not attempt to share out the cash. The cash payments to the partners should close the cash account.

It may well be that one or more partners may have a debit balance on their capital accounts when all the dissolution entries have been made. The partner owes the business money. That partner will pay into the bank (debit cash) the appropriate amount from his private resources. The Garner v. Murray (1904) rule states that: if that partner cannot settle his debt the remaining partners must bear this loss in the last agreed capital account ratios (i.e. the balances on the capital accounts at the last balance sheet date).

## 4.7 PARTNERSHIP AMALGAMATION

If two or more partnerships amalgamate the entries in the partnerships' books are similar to those outlined in Unit 4.4. Realisation accounts will be used to close down the 'old' partnerships' books. The 'new' partnership will be debited with the agreed valuation of assets taken over.

### EXAMPLE

Brad and Cedric and Denise and Elaine are two partnerships. The profit sharing ratios were 2:1 for Brad and Cedric and equally for Denise and Elaine. They have decided to amalgamate their businesses under the name of Denric & Co from 1 January 1996.

The balance sheets of the two partnerships as at 31 December 1995 were as follows:

**Brad and Cedric**

| | £ | | | £ |
|---|---|---|---|---|
| Premises | 40,000 | Capitals | Brad | 48,000 |
| Machinery | 10,000 | | Cedric | 20,000 |
| Vehicles | 17,000 | Current accounts | Brad | 2,200 |
| Stock | 2,000 | | Cedric | 1,800 |
| Debtors | 1,500 | | | |
| Bank | 2,000 | Creditors | | 500 |
| | 72,500 | | | 72,500 |

**Denise and Elaine**

| | £ | | | £ |
|---|---|---|---|---|
| Machinery | 18,000 | Capitals | Denise | 15,000 |
| Vehicles | 8,000 | | Elaine | 15,000 |
| Stock | 4,000 | Current accounts | Denise | 2,000 |
| Debtors | 2,000 | | Elaine | (200) |
| Bank | 800 | Creditors | | 1,000 |
| | 32,800 | | | 32,800 |

All four partners agreed that:

- The assets of the two partnerships be valued as follows:

| | Brad and Cedric | Denise and Elaine |
|---|---|---|
| | £ | £ |
| Premises | 60,000 | – |
| Machinery | 8,000 | 16,000 |
| Vehicles | 14,000 | 8,000 |
| Stock | 2,000 | 4,000 |
| Debtors | 1,300 | 1,500 |

- The partners provide £35,000 capital each for the new partnership.
- Profits and losses in the new partnership be shared equally.
- All adjustments to capital and current accounts be made in cash.

**Required**

(a) Statements showing:
  (i)  the profit or loss attributed to each partner on dissolution of Brad and Cedric's partnership;
  (ii) the profit or loss attributed to each partner on dissolution of Denise and Elaine's partnership.
(b) The capital accounts of:
  (i)  Brad and Cedric;
  (ii) Denise and Elaine;
  on the dissolution of their partnerships.
(c) The balance sheet as at 1 January 1996 of Denric & Co.

**Solution**

*Points to note*

- Close down the books of the old partnerships one at a time. Do not attempt to do all entries at the same time.
- When both old partnerships have been dissolved construct the new business's balance sheet.
- Remember, keep the two partnerships separate for as long as possible.

(a) (i) **Brad and Cedric realisation account**

| | £ | | | £ |
|---|---|---|---|---|
| Premises | 40,000 | Denric & Co | Premises | 60,000 |
| Machinery | 10,000 | | Machinery | 8,000 |
| Vehicles | 17,000 | | Vehicles | 14,000 |
| Stock | 2,000 | | Stock | 2,000 |
| Debtors | 1,500 | | Debtors | 1,300 |
| Profit on realisation | | | | |
| Brad | 9,867 | | | |
| Cedric | 4,933 | 14,800 | | |
| | | 85,300 | | 85,300 |

(b) (i) **Capital accounts**

| | B | C | | B | C |
|---|---|---|---|---|---|
| | £ | £ | | £ | £ |
| | | | Balances b/d | 48,000 | 20,000 |
| | | | Current accounts | 2,200 | 1,800 |
| Cash | 60,067 | 26,733 | Profit on realisation | 9,867 | 4,933 |
| | 60,067 | 26,733 | | 60,067 | 26,733 |

(a) (ii) **Denise and Elaine realisation account**

| | £ | | | ££ |
|---|---|---|---|---|
| Machinery | 18,000 | Denric & Co Machinery | | 16,000 |
| Vehicles | 8,000 | Vehicles | | 8,000 |
| Stock | 4,000 | Stock | | 4,000 |
| Debtors | 2,000 | Debtors | | 1,500 |
| | | Loss on realisation | | |
| | | Denise | 1,250 | |
| | | Elaine | 1,250 | 2,500 |
| | 32,000 | | | 32,000 |

(b) (ii) **Capital accounts**

| | D | E | | D | E |
|---|---|---|---|---|---|
| | £ | £ | | £ | £ |
| Current a/c | | 200 | Balances b/d | 15,000 | 15,000 |
| Loss on realisation | 1,250 | 1,250 | Current account | 2,000 | |
| Cash | 15,750 | 13,550 | Profit on realisation | – | |
| | 17,000 | 15,000 | | 17,000 | 15,000 |

Although not asked for the bank/cash account is shown as workings:

| | | £ | | | £ |
|---|---|---|---|---|---|
| Balances from | B & C | 2,000 | Cash to | Brad | 60,067 |
| | D & E | 800 | | Cedric | 26,733 |
| Cash from | Brad | 35,000 | | Denise | 15,750 |
| | Cedric | 35,000 | | Elaine | 13,550 |
| | Denise | 35,000 | | | |
| | Elaine | 35,000 | Balance c/d | | 26,700 |
| | | 142,800 | | | 142,800 |

In reality Brad would not pay cash into Denric's bank account and then withdraw cash; all the amounts would be netted out, so:

| | |
|---|---|
| Brad would receive | £25,067 |
| Cedric would pay | £8,267 |
| Denise would pay | £19,250 |
| Elaine would pay | £21,450 |

(c)

### Denric & Co balance sheet as at 1 January 1996

| | £ | | | £ |
|---|---|---|---|---|
| Premises | 60,000 | Capitals | Brad | 35,000 |
| Machinery | 24,000 | | Cedric | 35,000 |
| Vehicles | 22,000 | | Denise | 35,000 |
| Stock | 6,000 | | Elaine | 35,000 |
| Debtors | 2,800 | | | |
| Bank | 26,700 | Creditors | | 1,500 |
| | 141,500 | | | 141,500 |

**Note** Some syllabuses state that realisation accounts will not be examined. This does not mean you cannot use one as part of your workings. All it means is that an examiner may not ask directly 'prepare the realisation account of . . .' Most teachers will teach realisation accounts, so do use them if you feel comfortable with them.

## 4.8 LIMITED COMPANY TAKING OVER A PARTNERSHIP

The partners in a partnership may decide that they wish to form a limited company, and there may be times when a partnership is bought out by a limited company. In both cases the book keeping treatment is the same.

### EXAMPLE
Frank and Geraldine are in partnership sharing profits and losses in the ratio 3:2 respectively.

They agree to sell their business to Hugo Ltd. The purchase consideration of £100,000 being made up of 60,000 £1 ordinary shares. The partners agree that the shares in Hugo Ltd will be distributed in the capital ratios of the partnership.

**Point to note**
The purchase consideration is £100,000. Remember that £1 shares may be worth more than £1 or less than £1. The shares in Hugo Ltd are obviously worth more than £1.

Frank and Geraldine's balance sheet before the take-over is:

| | £ | | | £ |
|---|---|---|---|---|
| Net assets | 80,000 | Capital | Frank | 50,000 |
| | | | Geraldine | 30,000 |
| | 80,000 | | | 80,000 |

**Required**
The entries to close the books of Frank and Geraldine.

**Solution**

### Realisation account

| | £ | £ | | £ |
|---|---|---|---|---|
| Sundry net assets | | 80,000 | Hugo Ltd | 100,000 |
| Profit on realisation | | | | |
| Frank | 12,000 | | | |
| Geraldine | 8,000 | 20,000 | | |
| | | 100,000 | | 100,000 |

### Capital accounts

| | F £ | G £ | | | F £ | G £ |
|---|---|---|---|---|---|---|
| Shares in Hugo Ltd | 62,500 | 37,500 | Balances | | 50,000 | 30,000 |
| Cash to Frank | | 500 | Profit on realisation | | 12,000 | 8,000 |
| | | | Cash from Geraldine | | 500 | |
| | 62,500 | 38,000 | | | 62,500 | 38,000 |

### Hugo Ltd

| | | £ | | | | £ |
|---|---|---|---|---|---|---|
| Realisation | | 100,000 | Capitals | Frank | | 62,500 |
| | | | | Geraldine | | 37,500 |
| | | 100,000 | | | | 100,000 |

---

## Chapter roundup

Chapter 4 has looked at the composition of partnerships, and the effects of either having or not having a partnership agreement.

It has explained why partnerships change in structure and how to deal with those changes in the partnership books.

You should now be able to show the adjustments necessary to record changes when assets are revalued and goodwill is introduced then written off.

---

# Illustrative questions

**1** Brass and Smith have been partners for many years. They operate a foundry which produces a variety of metal goods which are sold from a shop attached to the foundry. The accounting year end is 31 December and profits and losses are shared between Brass and Smith in the ratio 2:1 respectively.

On 1 April 1993 they decided to admit Fender as an additional partner and from that date profits and losses would be shared between Brass, Smith and Fender in the ratio 4:2:1 respectively. On the same date goodwill was valued at £21,000. Goodwill has not appeared in the partnership accounts in the past and it was agreed that this policy should be continued. Fender paid £19,000 into the partnership to cover both his capital contribution and his share of goodwill. All adjustments relating to goodwill were to be processed through the partners' capital accounts.

It was further agreed that from 1 April 1993 interest of 5% per annum would be allowed on the capital account balances at that date (after making the adjustments for goodwill), and that interest would be charged on drawings as follows – Brass £360, Smith £240 and Fender £150. It was also agreed that from 1 April 1993 Smith and Fender would be allowed salaries of £8,000 per annum and £12,000 per annum respectively.

The following is a list of balances as at 31 December 1993 after the preparation of the profit and loss account:

| | £ |
|---|---|
| Vehicles at cost | 32,000 |
| Foundry equipment at cost | 69,000 |
| Freehold land at cost | 65,000 |
| Provision for depreciation on vehicles | 24,000 |
| Provision for depreciation on foundry equipment | 51,750 |
| Capital accounts (before making the adjustment for goodwill) | |
| Brass | 38,000 |
| Smith | 19,000 |
| Fender | 19,000 |

|  | £ |
|---|---|
| Bank overdraft | 4,800 |
| Cash in hand | 1,250 |
| Accrued expenses | 1,050 |
| Creditors | 21,120 |
| Debtors | 25,950 |
| Expenses pre-paid | 600 |
| Stock at cost | 7,920 |
| Drawings: Brass | 12,000 |
| Smith | 8,000 |
| Fender | 5,000 |
| Net profit for the year | 48,000 |

**Note** Profits are deemed to have accrued evenly throughout the year.

*Required*
(a) Prepare the profit and loss appropriation accounts of the partnership covering the year ended 31 December 1993. (15)

(b) Compile, for year ended 31 December 1993:
(i) the partners' capital accounts; (6)
(ii) the partners' current accounts. (6)

(c) Prepare the partnership balance sheet as at 31 December 1993. (6)

(d) Discuss **three** possible problems that are distinctive to the functioning of a partnership. (9)
(AEB)

*Tutorial note*
Remember that when a change takes place in the structure of a partnership that one business ceases to exist and immediately after this a new partnership takes its place. Prepare two appropriation accounts – one for the 3 months to 31 March 1993 and one for the next nine months. Complete the double entry by crediting the current accounts. Concentrate on the problems associated with working with others in part (d).

*Suggested answer*
(a) **Brass and Smith profit and loss appropriation account**
**for the three months ended 31 March 1993**

|  |  | £ | £ |
|---|---|---|---|
| Net profit |  | 12,000 |  |
| Share of profit | Brass | 8,000 |  |
|  | Smith | 4,000 | 12,000 |

**Brass, Smith and Fender profit and loss appropriation account**
**for the nine months ended 31 December1993**

|  |  | £ | £ |
|---|---|---|---|
| Net profit |  |  | 36,000 |
| Add interest on drawings | Brass | 360 |  |
|  | Smith | 240 |  |
|  | Fender | 150 | 750 |
|  |  |  | 36,750 |
| Less salaries | Smith | 6,000 |  |
|  | Fender | 9,000 | 15,000 |
|  |  |  | 21,750 |
| Less interest on capital | Brass | 1,500 |  |
|  | Smith | 750 |  |
|  | Fender | 600 | 2,850 |
|  |  |  | 18,900 |
| Share of profits | Brass | 10,800 |  |
|  | Smith | 5,400 |  |
|  | Fender | 2,700 | 18,900 |

85

(b)

**Capital accounts**

| | Brass £ | Smith £ | Fender £ | | Brass £ | Smith £ | Fender £ |
|---|---|---|---|---|---|---|---|
| Goodwill | 12,000 | 6,000 | 3,000 | Balance b/d | 38,000 | 19,000 | |
| | | | | Goodwill | 14,000 | 7,000 | |
| Balance c/d | 40,000 | 20,000 | 16,000 | Cash | | | 19,000 |
| | 52,000 | 26,000 | 19,000 | | 52,000 | 26,000 | 19,000 |
| | | | | Balance b/d | 40,000 | 20,000 | 16,000 |

**Current accounts**

| | £ | £ | £ | | £ | £ | £ |
|---|---|---|---|---|---|---|---|
| Drawings | 12,000 | 8,000 | 5,000 | Salaries | | 6,000 | 9,000 |
| Interest on | | | | Interest on | | | |
| drawings | 360 | 240 | 150 | capital | 1,500 | 750 | 600 |
| Balance c/d | 7,940 | 7,910 | 7,150 | Share of profits | 18,800 | 9,400 | 2,700 |
| | 20,300 | 16,150 | 12,300 | | 20,300 | 16,150 | 12,300 |
| | | | | Balance b/d | 7,940 | 7,910 | 7,150 |

(c) **Brass, Smith and Fender balance sheet as at 31 December 1993**

| | Cost £ | Depreciation £ | Net £ |
|---|---|---|---|
| Fixed assets | | | |
| Freehold property | 65,000 | | 65,000 |
| Foundry equipment | 69,000 | 51,750 | 17,250 |
| Vehicles | 32,000 | 24,000 | 8,000 |
| | 166,000 | 75,750 | 90,250 |
| Current assets | | | |
| Stock | | 7,920 | |
| Debtors | | 25,950 | |
| Cash | | 1,250 | |
| Prepayments | | 600 | |
| | | 35,720 | |
| Less current liabilities | | | |
| Creditors | 21,120 | | |
| Bank overdraft | 4,800 | | |
| Accruals | 1,050 | 26,970 | 8,750 |
| | | | 99,000 |
| Capital accounts | | | |
| Brass | | 40,000 | |
| Smith | | 20,000 | |
| Fender | | 16,000 | 76,000 |
| Current accounts | | | |
| Brass | | 7,940 | |
| Smith | | 7,910 | |
| Fender | | 7,150 | 23,000 |
| | | | 99,000 |

(d) Unlimited liability of the partners.

Responsibilities of the partners in the day-to-day running of the business.

Need for agreement on profit shares.

Need for agreement when the structure of the partnership changes i.e. when a partner leaves or when a new partner is admitted.

**2** The following information relates to the partnership of Bowler and Derby (until 30 September 1994) and Bowler, Derby and Topper (from 1 October 1994).

(1) The net profit for 1994 was £24,000. The profit sharing ratios changed on 1 April 1994 from Bowler 40%, Derby 60%, to equal shares. No adjustments were required to the partnership goodwill at that date. The profit sharing ratio changed again on 1 October 1994 when Topper was admitted as a partner. The share of profit became Bowler 40%, Derby 40%, Topper 20%.

(2) Topper was unable to introduce cash into the partnership, but brought in fixtures and fittings with an agreed value of £20,000.

(3) On Topper's admission to the partnership, goodwill was valued at 1¹/₂ times the average net profit for 1991, 1992 and 1993. The net profit figure for 1991 was £12,000 and for 1993 was £16,000. Unfortunately a fire had destroyed the records for 1992, but it was known that tax on profits had been paid totalling £2,500, and the relevant tax rate in that year was 20% on the first £5,000 profits and 25% thereafter.

(4) No goodwill account was opened in the partnership's books.

(5) Topper had drawings of £1 500 in the 3 months to 31 December 1994.

*Required*

(a) Calculate the profit share for each of the three partners for 1994 (5)

(b) Show a journal entry recording the transfer of goodwill between partners at 1 October 1994. (5)

(c) Show Topper's capital account for the 3 months ended 31 December 1994 in as much detail as possible. (5)

(ULEAC)

*Tutorial note*

When a goodwill account is opened, the original partners should be credited; after all they created it. Write if off to the debit of the new partners capital accounts.

*Suggested answer*

(a) **Bowler and Derby profit and loss appropriation account**
**for the three months ended 31 March 1994**

|  |  | £ | £ |
|---|---|---|---|
| Net profit |  |  | 6,000 |
| Share of profits | Bowler | 2,400 |  |
|  | Derby | 3,600 | 6,000 |

**Bowler and Derby profit and loss appropriation account**
**for the six months ended 30 September 1994**

|  |  | £ | £ |
|---|---|---|---|
| Net profit |  |  | 12,000 |
| Share of profits | Bowler | 6,000 |  |
|  | Derby | 6,000 | 12,000 |

**Bowler Derby and Topper profit and loss appropriation account**
**for the three months ended 31 December 1994**

|  |  | £ | £ |
|---|---|---|---|
| Net profit |  |  | 6,000 |
| Share of profits | Bowler | 2,400 |  |
|  | Derby | 2,400 |  |
|  | Topper | 1,200 | 6,000 |

Profit share for each partner:
Bowler  (2 400 + 6,000 + 2 400 ) = £10 800
Derby  (3 600 + 6,000 + 2 400 ) = £12,000
Topper                             = £ 1 200

(b) **Journal**

|  |  |  | £ | £ |
|---|---|---|---|---|
| Goodwill |  |  | 19,500 |  |
| Capital | Bowler |  |  | 9,750 |
|  | Derby |  |  | 9,750 |
| Capital | Bowler |  | 7,800 |  |
|  | Derby |  | 7,800 |  |
|  | Topper |  | 3,900 |  |
| Goodwill |  |  |  | 19,500 |

*Points to note*

- Goodwill is valued at 1¹/2 times the average net profits

| | |
|---|---|
| 1991 | £12,000 |
| 1992 | £11,000 |

  (tax paid £2,500; £1,000 on first £5,000 profits £1,500 tax has been paid at 25% on the next £6,000 so total profits must be £5,000 + £6,000)

| | |
|---|---|
| 1993 | 16,000 |
| Total profits for the three years | £39,000 |

- Average profits for the three years is £39,000/3 = £13,000
- Goodwill is valued at 1.5 × £13,000 = £19 500.

(c)

**Capital account: Topper**

| | £ | | £ |
|---|---|---|---|
| Goodwill | 3,900 | Fixtures | 20,000 |
| Drawings | 1,500 | Appropriation account | 1,200 |
| Balance c/d | 15,800 | | |
| | 21,200 | | 21,200 |

**3** On 1 May 1994, H. Pandit and T. Rowe entered into partnership; the partnership agreement included the following provisions:

(i) T. Rowe to be credited with a partner's salary of £15,000 p.a.

(ii) A current account and a capital account is to be maintained for each partner.

(iii) Interest at the rate of 5% p.a. to be credited for partners' capital account balances.

(iv) Interest at the rate of 10% p.a. to be charged for partners' cash drawings.

(v) The balance of net profits or net losses to be transferred to H. Pandit and T. Rowe in the ratio 3:1 respectively.

(vi) The following net assets of the existing businesses to be transferred to the partnership on 1 May 1994.

| | | £ |
|---|---|---|
| From H. Pandit | Fixtures and fittings | 16,000 |
| | Motor vehicle | 10,000 |
| From T. Rowe | Motor vehicle | 13,000 |
| | Stock | 16,300 |
| | Debtors | 7,400 |
| | Creditors | 3,100 |

(vii) The agreed values of the businesses transferred to the partnership were as follows:

| | £ |
|---|---|
| From H. Pandit | 42,000 |
| From T. Rowe | 34,000 |

(viii) No goodwill account is to be raised in the partnership's books of account.

Additional information for the year ended 30 April 1995:

(1) The partnership's trial balance as at 30 April 1995 includes the following items:

| | £ | £ |
|---|---|---|
| Net profit for the year ended 30 April 1995 | | 43,500 |
| Drawings – H. Pandit | 16,500 | |
| T. Rowe | 14,700 | |

(2) Interest on partners' cash drawings has been determined as follows:

| | £ |
|---|---|
| H. Pandit | 800 |
| T. Rowe | 650 |

(3) Provision has not yet been made in the partnership's books for the following goods, at cost, withdrawn for the use of partners:

| | £ |
|---|---|
| H. Pandit | 300 *r* |
| T. Rowe | 110 |

*Required*

(a) The partnership's profit and loss appropriation account for the year ended 30 April 1995. (8)

(b) The partners' capital accounts and current accounts for the year ended 30 April 1995. (11)

(c) H. Pandit is concerned that the partnership agreement does not permit a goodwill account to be maintained. He now questions the exclusion of goodwill from the partnership's accounts. As the partnership's accountant, prepare a reply to H. Pandit. (6)

(UCLES)

*Tutorial note*

Remember that only entries which derive from partnerships' trading profits should be entered in partners' current accounts. Entries for acquisition of assets and/or entries to adjust or create goodwill should be entered in partners' capital accounts.

Part (c) will require only 3 well-developed points to gain the marks. Remember – always state the obvious as well as the more obscure points.

*Suggested answer*

(a) **Pandit and Rowe profit and loss appropriation account for the year ended 30 April 1995**

| | | £ | £ |
|---|---|---|---|
| Adjusted net profit for the year❶ | | | 43,910 |
| Add interest on drawings | Pandit | 800 | |
| | Rowe | 650 | 1,450 |
| | | | 45,360 |
| Less salary Rowe | | | 15,000 |
| | | | 30,360 |
| Less interest on capital | Pandit | 1,485 | |
| | Rowe | 1,495 | 2,980 |
| | | | 27,380 |
| Share of profits | Pandit | 20,535 | |
| | Rowe | 6,845 | 27,380 |

❶ Profit for year as per trial balance 43,500 + goods for own use 300 + 110.

(b) **Capital accounts**

| | Pandit £ | Rowe £ | | Pandit £ | Rowe £ |
|---|---|---|---|---|---|
| Goodwill❷ | | 3,700 | Sundry net assets | 26,000 | 33,600 |
| Balances c/d | 29,700 | 29,900 | Goodwill | 3,700 | |
| | 29,700 | 33,600 | | 29,700 | 33,600 |
| | | | Balances b/d | 29,700 | 29,900 |

**Current accounts**

| | £ | £ | | £ | £ |
|---|---|---|---|---|---|
| Drawings | 16,500 | 14,700 | P&L appropriation a/c | | |
| Goods own use | 300 | 110 | salary | | 15,000 |
| Interest on drawings | 800 | 650 | interest on capital | 1,485 | 1,495 |
| Balance c/d | 4,420 | 7,880 | balance of profits | 20,535 | 6,845 |
| | 22,020 | 23,340 | | 22,020 | 23,340 |
| | | | Balance b/d | 4,420 | 7,880 |

❷ The goodwill adjustment is made as follows:

| | £ | £ |
|---|---|---|
| Pandit Goodwill | 16,000 | |
| Capital Pandit | | 16,000 |
| Rowe Goodwill | 400 | |
| Capital Rowe | | 400 |

This 'creates' the goodwill given by both partners to the partnership. Now it needs eliminating.

| | £ | £ |
|---|---|---|
| Capital Pandit | 12,000 | |
| Rowe | 4,000 | |
| Goodwill | | 16,000 |

This eliminates Pandit's goodwill.

| | £ | £ |
|---|---|---|
| Capital Pandit | 300 | |
| Rowe | 100 | |
| Goodwill | | 400 |

These entries have eliminated Rowe's goodwill.

(c) Inherent goodwill should not be recorded. Goodwill is only recorded when a business is purchased, in effect when Pandit and Rowe entered into partnership they were 'purchasing' a 'new' business. Note (viii) stated that goodwill should not be kept in the books of account. In any case goodwill should be written off immediately. It is almost impossible to identify reasons that contribute to the existence of goodwill and its valuation.

# LIMITED COMPANY ACCOUNTS

## Units in this chapter

5.1   *What is a limited company?*
5.2   *Types of limited company*
5.3   *Advantages and disadvantages of limited liability status*
5.4   *The profit and loss appropriation account of a limited company*
5.5   *The balance sheet of a limited company*
5.6   *Reserves*
5.7   *Debentures*
5.8   *Fixed assets*
5.9   *Published accounts of limited companies*
5.10  *The issue of shares*
5.11  *The redemption of shares*

## Chapter objectives

We have considered the accounts of sole traders and partnerships in earlier chapters. In this chapter we look at the third type of business organisation, the limited company. A limited company is treated as a separate legal entity. This means that in the eyes of the law a company is a 'person' who can sue and be sued just like you and me. The major advantage that the owners of a limited company have is that their liability is limited to the amount of share capital that they have subscribed.

The key topics and concepts covered in this chapter are:

- limited liability;
- ownership and control;
- private and public limited companies;
- appropriation of profits;
- share capital;
- preference shares and ordinary shares;
- revenue and capital reserves;
- share premium;
- revaluation reserves;
- capital redemption reserve;
- debentures;
- tangible and intangible fixed assets;
- investments;
- rights issues;
- forfeiture of shares;
- bonus issues.

## 5.1 WHAT IS A LIMITED COMPANY?

A limited company is an organisation that has a separate legal identity to that of its owners. The owners' (shareholders) liability is limited to the shares they buy in the company.

A company can be a very small business, or a giant multi-national business with branches and subsidiary companies trading all over the world. The majority of businesses are sole traders and partnerships. However, both of these types of business have a major drawback: their owners have unlimited liability. Unlimited liability means that the owners have responsibility for all debts incurred by their businesses.

In the majority of cases this is of no significance. However, if the business is making losses on a regular basis then the continuing existence of the business is in doubt. If the business does fail, and the business assets are insufficient to meet the claims of creditors, the sole trader or the partners of that business may have to meet the claims of creditors from private assets. (**Note** A business may make a net loss in one or two years, yet may be capable of continuing because it has built up resources (reserves) in past profitable years.)

The other major drawback for unlimited businesses is that there are fewer opportunities of finding extra capital if the proprietors wish to expand the business. The owners of limited companies do not face these problems.

An investor who owns shares in a limited company has limited liability. That means that a shareholder cannot be asked to contribute more capital to pay off creditors if the company goes into liquidation, provided that the shares are fully paid.

The only restriction to the amount of capital a limited company can raise, or the number of shareholders it has, is the authorised share capital.

Shareholders cannot all be involved in the day-to-day running of the company, so they delegate this responsibility to the board of directors. The directors manage the business, making the operational decisions. In small private limited companies the shareholders may also be the directors. If shareholders owning a majority of the ordinary shares in a company are dissatisfied with the way the board of directors direct the company, they can vote the directors off the board and replace them with their chosen replacements.

In a limited company there is a divorce of ownership and control. That is, the owners of the business (shareholders) do not exert direct control over the day-to-day running of the business; they leave this to their elected representatives (directors).

## 5.2 TYPES OF LIMITED COMPANIES

The companies which are the subject of questions at Advanced level are either:
- private limited companies (A. Blinkerson Ltd) or
- public limited companies (C. Djartah plc)

Private limited companies do not sell their shares to the general public at large, public limited companies do.

If a private limited company needs more capital, the directors must find other people wishing to invest in that company. As a result private limited companies are often family businesses, with members of the family or close friends owning all the shares. Directors of public limited companies who wish to raise new capital will advertise this fact and the general public may subscribe to the offer.

There is no difference in the way that the accounts and other financial statements are prepared for private limited companies and public limited companies.

## 5.3 ADVANTAGES AND DISADVANTAGES OF LIMITED LIABILITY STATUS

The **advantages** of limited liability status have been given as:
* limited liability for shareholders;
* the directors ability to raise larger amounts of capital for use within the company.

These advantages are **counterbalanced** by certain legal requirements:
* the annual accounts must be audited by a professionally qualified accountant (this is not the case with sole traders or partnerships);
* companies must complete an annual return and file their accounts with the Registrar of Companies. These filed accounts may be inspected by the public;
* companies are subjected to much more 'red tape' (laid down in the Companies Acts 1985 and 1989) than sole traders and partnerships;
* a copy of the company's annual audited accounts must be sent to each shareholder and debenture holder.

All this involves extra expenditure.

## 5.4 THE PROFIT AND LOSS APPROPRIATION ACCOUNT OF A LIMITED COMPANY

As pointed out in the chapter on partnership accounts, the final accounts of all businesses are fairly similar.

A company may prepare a manufacturing account, a trading account and a profit and loss account but, like a partnership, a limited company has more than one owner. So, companies need a profit and loss appropriation account.

This shows how the profits are used by the company. (**Note** 'Profit and loss appropriation account' may read 'Appropriation account' in some texts.)

The purpose of a company's profit and loss appropriation account is very similar to that of a partnership's: it simply shows what has happened to the business's profits.

In the case of a partnership all the profits are distributed to the partners in some way. In the case of the company some of the profits will be retained in the business to provide finance for expansion or the replacement of assets. The company's appropriation account generally has a credit balance remaining as a revenue reserve at the end of the year. The balance remaining in the appropriation account at the year end will open the appropriation account in the following year.

We will examine the appropriation account as it would appear in the general ledger using debits and credits. Later a vertical layout will be used as this layout is generally used when accounts are published.

EXAMPLE

Edward Fleabane plc has made a net profit on ordinary activities after interest charges for the year ended 31 January 1996 of £347,500 ❾.

During the year the following interim dividends were paid:

|  | £ |  |
|---|---|---|
| Ordinary share dividend | 42,000 | ❸ |
| Preference share dividend | 8,000 | ❹ |

The directors recommend:

|  | £ |  |
|---|---|---|
| a provision for corporation tax | 80,000 | ❶ |
| a transfer to general reserve | 25,000 | ❷ |
| a final dividend: ordinary shares | 68,000 | ❺ |
| preference shares | 8,000 | ❻ |
| The retained profits at 31 January 1995 | 639,400 | ❽ |

**Required**

(a) The profit and loss appropriation account for the year ended 31 January 1996 for Edward Fleabane plc.

(b) The appropriate extracts from the balance sheet as at 31 January 1996.

**Solution**

(a)            **Edward Fleabane plc profit and loss appropriation account
for the year ended 31 January 1996**

|  |  | £ |  |  | £ |  |
|---|---|---|---|---|---|---|
| Corporation tax |  | 80,000 ❶ | Balance brought forward | | 639,400 | ❽ |
| Transfer to general reserve |  | 25,000 ❷ | Net profit | | 347,500 | ❾ |
| Dividends paid |  |  |  | | | |
|   Ordinary shares | 42,000 ❸ |  |  | | | |
|   Preference shares | 8,000 ❹ | 50,000 |  | | | |
| Dividends proposed |  |  |  | | | |
|   Ordinary shares | 68,000 ❺ |  |  | | | |
|   Preference shares | 8,000 ❻ | 76,000 |  | | | |
| Balance carried forward |  | 755,900 ❼ |  | | | |
|  |  | 986,900 |  | | 986,900 | |
|  |  |  | Balance brought forward | | 755,900 | ❼ |

*Points to note*

The credit entries for the above debit entries are:

|  |  |  |
|---|---|---|
| Corporation tax a/c | 80,000 | ❶ |
| General reserve | 25,000 | ❷ |
| Bank | 42,000 | ❸ |
| Ordinary dividend | 68,000 | ❺ |
| Bank | 8,000 | ❹ |
| Preference dividend | 8,000 | ❻ |

The debit entries for the above credit entries are:

❽ Last year's profit and loss appropriation account. Also see ❼.

❾ Profit and loss account.

The numbered bullets show where the same amounts appear in the different accounts. Notice the main difference between this appropriation account and that of a partnership. Previous years' profits are brought into play ❽ and this year's profits that have not been appropriated ❼ are carried forward to be included in next year's appropriation account.

(b)         **Edward Fleabane plc balance sheet (extracts) as at 31 January 1996**

|  | £ |
|---|---|
| Share capital and reserves |  |
| General reserve | 25,000 |
| Current liabilities |  |
|   Taxation | 80,000 |
|   Proposed ordinary dividend | 68,000 |
|   Proposed preference dividend | 8,000 |

## 5.5 THE BALANCE SHEET OF A LIMITED COMPANY

The balance sheet of a limited company is essentially the same as any other balance sheet. There are some differences, and these are itemised below.

### Share capital

The *authorised share capital* is stated in the memorandum of association. It sets the limit to the number of shares that the company can sell.
The *issued share capital* is the shares that have been issued to the shareholders.

Both the authorised and issued share capital can be made up of preference shares and ordinary shares.

*Preference shares* are entitled to a fixed dividend before the ordinary shareholders receive their dividend. In the case of a company being wound up the preference shares rank before the ordinary shareholders to receive the return of their capital. This makes preference shares a safer form of investment.

(**Note** Dividends are not guaranteed on preference or ordinary shares. Dividends require profits *and* cash resources to be available.)

Preference shareholders are not guaranteed to receive the return of their capital in a winding up. They *rank before the ordinary shares* so they do stand a much better chance of getting their investment back if there are limited funds available for distribution.

- Most preference shares are *cumulative*. If dividends fail to be paid, dividend arrears must be paid in future years as soon as profits allow.

- Preference shares *do not usually have voting rights*. (In some cases if the preference shares do not receive a dividend they may be entitled to a vote at company meetings).

- Preference shares *may be redeemable*. This means that at some time in the future the company will repurchase the shares from the holder.

- They *may be convertible* meaning that they may be exchanged for ordinary shares at some future date stated in the accounts.

Once an investor has purchased shares in a limited company the money is 'locked in to the company' and the investor cannot demand the money back from the company. Also, under normal circumstances a company cannot buy back its own shares. A shareholder wishing to dispose of shares must sell them to someone else by using the stock market.

*Ordinary shares (equity)* must wait until the preference shareholders have been paid out if the company is wound up. This means that the ordinary shareholders will only be paid the remainder, which could be much less than they paid for the shares – it might even be nothing. Ordinary shares are therefore a more risky investment as far as a prospective shareholder is concerned. The ordinary shareholders must also wait until the preference share dividend has been allocated before they can receive a share of the profits.

- If the company is successful the ordinary shareholders share of profits will be large. This will generally mean good dividends and good retained profits and, in the event of a winding up, the ordinary shareholders may receive a payment in excess of the nominal value of the shares.

- Each ordinary share carries one vote at the company annual general meeting and at extraordinary meetings. This means that if any one person or organisation holds more than 50% of the ordinary shares they are effectively in control of that company.

- Each share has a nominal or par value, e.g. 10p, 50p, £1 etc.

- When a company issues new shares it may be able to sell those shares at a price in excess of the nominal value. These shares will be issued at a premium. If a company issues some extra £1 shares at a price of £1.86, the shareholder is buying a £1 ordinary share and is paying 86p as a premium. The 86p is credited to a share premium account (see later).

(**Note** If a shareholder purchased 100 second-hand £1 shares from a stockbroker and paid £186 this would not be recorded in the companies books. The extra £86 is *not* a share premium.)

The book-keeping entries for a share issue are dealt with later.

## 5.6 RESERVES

The profit of a partnership or a sole trader belongs to the owners of that business and it is credited to their capital or current accounts. Some of the profits will be removed from the business by way of drawings, the remainder of the profit is 'ploughed back' and may be used for the purchase of fixed assets and the like.

### EXAMPLE 1

Three businesses make a net profit of £25,000. (For the sake of comparisons the profit is shown net of cash taken out of the businesses by way of drawings and dividends).

**Business 1** Mary is a sole trader. Her drawings amount to £18,000. At the end of the year her balance sheet would look like this.

**Balance sheet of Mary, sole trader**

|  | £ |  | £ |
|---|---|---|---|
| Assets | 10,000 | Capital | 10,000 |
| Additional assets | 7,000 | Retained profit | 7,000 |
|  | 17,000 |  | 17,000 |

**Business 2** Joan and Keith are in partnership sharing profits and losses equally. Each has withdrawn £9,000 during the year.

**Balance sheet of partnership**

|  | £ |  |  |  | £ |
|---|---|---|---|---|---|
| Assets | 10,000 | Capital: | Joan | 6,000 |  |
| Additional assets | 7,000 |  | Retained profit | 3,500 | 9,500 |
|  |  |  | Keith | 4,000 |  |
|  |  |  | Retained profit | 3,500 | 7,500 |
|  | 17,000 |  |  |  | 17,000 |

**Business 3** Bodkins Ltd is a limited company with an ordinary issued share capital of 10,000 £1 ordinary shares. The directors pay a dividend to the shareholders of 1.80p per share.

**Balance sheet of Bodkins Ltd**

|  | £ |  | £ |
|---|---|---|---|
| Assets | 10,000 | Issued share capital | 10,000 |
| Additional assets | 7,000 | Retained profits | 7,000 |
|  | 17,000 |  | 17,000 |

*Points to note*

- The retained profits cannot be credited to each individual shareholder. In a large company there will be thousands of them. The retained profits are shown as one figure under the heading of retained profits, retained earnings, or more generally profit and loss account

- All profits belong to the ordinary shareholders, so in the event of an immediate winding up each shareholder in Bodkins Ltd would receive £1.70.

*These retained profits are a reserve.*

You should now refer back to the appropriation account of Edward Fleabane plc on page 94. The balance carried forward £755 900 is retained profit; it is made up of previous years' retained profits and also this year's retained profit. You can see this more clearly if we redraft the appropriation account into the more usual vertical format.

**Edward Fleabane plc profit and loss appropriation account for the year ended 31 January 1996**

| | £ | £ | |
|---|---|---|---|
| Net profit for the year | | 347,500 | ❾ |
| Less Corporation tax | | 80,000 | ❶ |
| Net profit after tax | | 267,500 | |
| Transfer to general reserve | | 25,000 | ❷ |
| | | 242,500 | |
| Dividends: on ordinary shares | 110,000 | | ❸❺ |
| on preference shares | 16,000 | 126,000 | ❹❻ |
| Retained profit for the year | | 116,500 | |
| Retained profit brought forward | | 639,400 | ❽ |
| Retained profit carried forward | | 755,900 | ❼ |

Do remember that these profits are not cash. Some of the profit will have been used during the year to purchase stock, replace or renew fixed assets etc.

The **retained earnings** and **general reserve** are both **revenue reserves**, that is they have arisen as a result of retaining trading profits within the company.

As we saw in the simple example on page 96, Bodkins' retained profits have been used to finance the expansion of the company by the purchase of further fixed assets.

> Retained profits are a major source of finance available to all successful businesses.

Do not fall into the trap in the examination of saying that reserves are money put aside for future use. Think of your own situation: you do not want cash for its own sake, you want cash to be able to go out or to buy a new CD player or a car. Similarly, a company will not keep its retained profits in the form of cash since cash has no earning power. Any profits that are cash will be quickly turned into assets which do have earning power.

**Revenues reserves** are the most flexible form of reserve and are used to fund dividends payments to shareholders.

Companies also have **capital reserves**. These arise from capital transactions and adjustments to the capital structure of the company. They are not available for the payment of cash dividends.

The three main capital reserves are: the **share premium account**, the **revaluation reserve** and the **capital redemption reserve**.

## SHARE PREMIUM ACCOUNT

> A share premium account arises when a company sells shares at a price greater than the nominal value of the shares.

Remember, if you sell some shares through a stockbroker at a higher price than you paid for them this will not give rise to a share premium. This is a private transaction and does not figure in the company's records.

If you answer a question in an examination be specific. Do not say 'a share premium account arises when shares are sold for more than their nominal value' this is not so. You must say that when a company issues shares at a price in excess of the nominal value a share premium account is opened.

The book-keeping entries are fairly straightforward.

EXAMPLE 2

Klumpers Ltd offer 100,000 ordinary shares of 20p each for sale at £1.75. All monies were paid on application.

**Required**

The journal entries to record the share issue (narratives are not required).

**Solution**

|  | Dr £ | Cr £ |
|---|---|---|
| Cash | 175,000 | |
| Ordinary share capital | | 20,000 |
| Share premium account | | 155,000 |

# REVALUATION RESERVE

Many companies revalue some of their fixed assets to reflect an increase in the value of the assets, and to ensure that the balance sheet shows the permanent change in value of the assets.

Why do companies revalue their assets while sole traders and partnerships do not? It is because if the assets do not reflect a current market price the company could be subject to a hostile take-over bid by a predatory rival company. The increase in the value of the fixed assets is matched with an increase in reserves which in turn will affect the share price in the market place. The revaluation reserve, being a capital reserve, is not available for dividend purposes. It is a 'profit' due to inflationary pressures which will not be realised as cash until the asset is sold.

### EXAMPLE 3

The summarised balance sheet of Clox plc shows:

|  | £ |
|---|---|
| Fixed assets at cost | 250,000 |
| Net current assets | 60,000 |
|  | 310,000 |
| Share capital | 200,000 |
| Retained earnings | 110,000 |
|  | 310,000 |

The directors of the company revalue the fixed assets at £300,000.

**Required**
Show the balance sheet as it would appear after the assets have been revalued.

**Solution**

**Clox plc balance sheet after revaluation of fixed assets**

|  | £ |
|---|---|
| Fixed assets at valuation | 300,000 |
| Net current assets | 60,000 |
|  | 360,000 |
| Share capital | 200,000 |
| Revaluation reserve | 50,000 |
| Retained earnings | 110,000 |
|  | 360,000 |

*Point to note*
Any capital reserves appear before revenue reserves on the balance sheet.

# CAPITAL REDEMPTION RESERVE

When shares are redeemed without the company issuing some new shares to cover the redemption, a sum equal to the nominal value of the shares must be transferred from the retained earnings (revenue reserve) to a capital redemption reserve (capital reserve).

This has the effect of 'locking away' profits that otherwise would have been available for distribution to shareholders. It is a reserve which is designed to protect the interests of the company's creditors.

## 5.7 DEBENTURES

Many companies raise additional capital by issuing debentures. A debenture is a loan to the company and is generally secured against the company's assets. The security may be fixed, that is it relates to a specific asset or group of assets or it may be a floating charge where no specific assets are identified. If the company were to be wound up, the debenture holders are in a safer position than either the preference shareholders or the ordinary shareholders because of this security.

Like all forms of borrowing, the debt has to be serviced and the interest will normally be paid half yearly. The interest that the company pays to the debenture holders, like all interest payable, is a charge against profits and appears on the profit and loss account. The interest is not an appropriation of profits. It must be paid whether the company is profitable or not.

Debentures are not part of the share capital. Debenture holders are not shareholders. When you draft a balance sheet make the examiner aware that you know this by showing the debentures as a deduction from the net assets of the company.

## 5.8 FIXED ASSETS

Fixed assets should be shown under the following headings:

- **Tangible fixed assets**

  These comprise assets which can be seen and touched. They would include Land, buildings, machinery, vehicles etc.

  In a published set of company accounts only the net total will be shown. The details would be shown as an appendix. In your examination you can show the detail in the body of your answer if necessary. These are:

  - the cost of the assets both at the start and end of the year;

  - any acquisitions (purchases) and disposals during the year;

  - details of the year's depreciation and the aggregate depreciation at the date of the balance sheet.

  If assets have been revalued during the year, the names of the valuers or their qualifications must be noted, together with the basis of revaluation.

- **Intangible assets**

  Non-physical assets such as goodwill, the ownership of a patent or copyright would come under this heading.

  Remember that inherent goodwill should not be included in any set of final accounts.

- **Investments**

  Like other assets these should be valued cost or market value whichever is the lower.

## 5.9 PUBLISHED ACCOUNTS OF LIMITED COMPANIES

The accounts that limited companies produce have to be used by the managers of that limited company for decision making purposes. If the accounts used by the managers were published in this useful form, rivals might gain access to much information which could undermine the company.

> Although legally a limited company must send its shareholders and lenders a set of accounts, the law protects the company by allowing it to publish an 'abridged' version.

Check with your teacher or a copy of the board's syllabus to see if you need to be able to produce a set of accounts for publication. The largest board (AEB) does not require this knowledge. If it is necessary, consult one of the standard texts for the details.

## 5.10  THE ISSUE OF SHARES

Check with your syllabus how much detailed knowledge you require with reference to double entry. The AEB syllabus does not require a detailed knowledge.

The issued share capital of a limited company can be increased in three ways:

- By selling shares to the general public for cash.
- By a rights issue. Shares are sold to existing shareholders, usually at a slight discount.
- By a bonus issue. Shares are given to existing shareholders, without any cash being paid to the company.

### Selling shares to the general public

Money is sent by the prospective shareholders, usually in instalments. Money will be sent to the company with an **application form**. In contract law terms this represents an offer to purchase the shares. The company will indicate its acceptance of the offer by sending the investor a letter of **allotment**; this will ask for the second instalment. The investor will then be required to pay some further instalments known as **calls**.

### A rights issue

A rights issue is similar in process to an issue to the general public. The shares are offered to existing shareholders in a ratio based on the shareholder's present holding of shares. For example, one new share for every five already held. If the existing shareholder does not wish to take up the issue, he may sell the rights to another person. The book-keeping entries are the same for both of these types of issue.

EXAMPLE 1

The Gander plc offers 100,000 ordinary shares of £1 each for sale to the public at £1.60 on the following terms:

On application: 25 pence per share
On allotment: 85 pence per share (including 60p premium)
First and final call: 50 pence per share

Applications were received for 157,000 shares. The directors rejected applications for 7,000 shares and their money was returned. The remaining shares were allotted to the remaining applicants on a pro rata basis. The excess application money was held by the company to reduce the amount due on allotment.

**Required**
The ledger accounts to record the above transactions.

**Solution**

### Cash

| | £ | | £ |
|---|---|---|---|
| Application and allotment | 39,250 ❶ | Application and allotment | 1,750 ❷ |
| Application and allotment | 72,500 ❸ | | |
| Call | 50,000 ❼ | | |

### Application and allotment account

| | £ | | | £ | |
|---|---|---|---|---|---|
| Cash | 1,750 | ❷ | Cash | 39,250 | ❶ |
| Ordinary share capital | 25,000 | ❹ | Cash | 72,500 | ❸ |
| Ordinary share capital | 25,000 | ❺ | | | |
| Share premium | 60,000 | ❻ | | | |
| | 111,750 | | | 111,750 | |

### Call

| | £ | | | £ | |
|---|---|---|---|---|---|
| Ordinary share capital | 50,000 | | Cash | 50,000 | ❼ |

### Ordinary share capital

| | | | £ | |
|---|---|---|---|---|
| | | Application and allotment | 25,000 | ❹ |
| | | Application and allotment | 25,000 | ❺ |
| | | Call | 50,000 | ❽ |

### Share premium account

| | | | £ | |
|---|---|---|---|---|
| | | Application and allotment | 60,000 | ❻ |

❶ Money sent by applicants.

❷ Money returned to unsuccessful applicants.

❸ The applicants owe £85,000 on allotment, but the company has received £12,500 overpayment by the successful applicants; only the difference needs to be paid.

❹ ❺ and ❻ the 'temporary' application and allotment account is closed down by transferring the appropriate amounts to the ordinary share capital account and the share premium account.

❼ The call money is received.

❽ The call account (another 'temporary' account) is closed with a transfer to the ordinary share capital account.

The above entries would have been exactly the same if this had been a rights issue.

## Forfeiture of shares

Once again check your syllabus to see if this topic is examinable.

Occasionally a shareholder fails to pay the calls when they fall due. The articles of the company may provide that the shareholder should forfeit the shares. The shareholder will lose the instalments already paid to the company.

### EXAMPLE 2

During the year ended 29 February 1996 Konkers plc made an offer of shares to the public. The details were as follows:

200,000 ordinary shares of £1 were issued and payable as follows:

| | Pence per share |
|---|---|
| On application 31 March 1995 | 30 |
| On allotment (including 40 pence premium per share) on 1 June 1995 | 70 |
| On first and final call on 1 December 1995 | 40 |

Applications were received for 223,000 shares. The directors made the following decisions:

• to return cheques for 3,000 shares.

• to allot the remaining shares on the basis of 10 shares for every 11 shares applied for.

• The balance of the money received on application was to be applied to the amounts due on allotment.

• On the call, one applicant who had been allotted 500 shares failed to pay the amount due. His shares were declared forfeit. They were reissued on 1 February 1996 at a price of 90 pence per share fully paid.

## Required
The ledger accounts to show the above transactions.

## Solution

### Cash

| | £ | | | £ | |
|---|---|---|---|---|---|
| Application and allotment | 66,900 | ❶ | Application and allotment | 900 | ❷ |
| Application and allotment | 134,000 | ❸ | | | |
| Call | 79,800 | ❻ | | | |
| Forfeit shares | 450 | ⓫ | | | |

### Application and allotment

| | £ | | | £ | |
|---|---|---|---|---|---|
| Cash | 900 | ❷ | Cash | 66,900 | ❶ |
| Ordinary share capital | 120,000 | ❹ | Cash | 134,000 | ❸ |
| Share premium | 80,000 | ❺ | | | |
| | 200,900 | | | 200,900 | |

### Call

| | £ | | | £ | |
|---|---|---|---|---|---|
| Ordinary share capital | 80,000 | ❾ | Cash | 79,800 | ❻ |
| | | | Forfeit shares | 200 | ❼ |
| | 80,000 | | | 80,000 | |

### Ordinary share capital

| | £ | | | £ | |
|---|---|---|---|---|---|
| Forfeit shares | 500 | ❽ | Application and allotment | 120,000 | ❹ |
| | | | Call | 80,000 | ❾ |
| | | | T Blank | 500 | ❿ |

### Forfeit shares

| | £ | | | £ | |
|---|---|---|---|---|---|
| Call | 200 | | Ordinary share capital | 500 | ❽ |
| T Blank | 50 | | | | |
| Share premium | 250 | ⓭ | | | |
| | 500 | | | 500 | |

### Share premium account

| | | | £ | |
|---|---|---|---|---|
| | | Application and allotment | 80,000 | ❺ |
| | | Forfeit shares | 250 | ⓭ |

### T Blank

| | £ | | | £ | |
|---|---|---|---|---|---|
| Ordinary share capital | 500 | ❿ | Cash | 450 | ⓫ |
| | | | Forfeit shares | 50 | ⓬ |

❶  Money sent by applicants.

❷  Money returned to unsuccessful applicants

❸  The applicants owe £140,000 on allotment, but the company received £6,000 overpayment by the successful applicants; only the difference needs to be paid.

❹  and ❺ The application and allotment account is closed by transferring the appropriate amounts to the ordinary share capital account and the share premium account.

❻  The call money is received; it is £200 short (500 x 40 pence)

❼  The shortfall is transferred to the forfeit shares account.

❽  The share capital is adjusted to take into account the fact that only 199,500 shares have been issued now.

❾  The call account is closed off to the ordinary share capital account.

❿  The ordinary share capital account is restored to 200,000 ordinary shares issued by selling the shares to T Blank.

⓫  Blank pays for the shares.

⓬  The discount on the shares is transferred to the forfeit shares account.

⓭  The balance of the forfeit shares account is posted to the share premium account.

## Bonus shares

When bonus shares are issued by a limited company it is called a scrip issue. The shares are given to existing shareholders by using reserves. For this reason it is also referred to as a capitalisation issue.

> Bonus shares are issued to existing shareholders without payment.
>
> The company's reserves provide permanent finance for the company. The transfer from reserves to share capital by a book entry has no effect on the capital structure of the company. The shareholders are no better or worse off than they were before the bonus issue.

The book-keeping entries are:
- Debit the reserves that are to be used. Credit a bonus account.
- Debit the bonus account and credit the share capital account.

### EXAMPLE 3

The following is an extract from the balance sheet of Sashi plc.

|  | £ |
|---|---|
| **Share capital and reserves** | |
| Share capital: ordinary shares | 400,000 |
| Share premium | 280,000 |
| Revaluation reserve | 100,000 |
| Profit and loss account | 238,000 |

The directors propose a scrip issue on the basis of one bonus share for every share already held. It is company policy to maintain reserves in the most flexible form.

### Required

The journal entries to record the scrip issue.

### Solution

**Journal**

|  | Dr | Cr |
|---|---|---|
|  | £ | £ |
| Share premium | 280,000 | |
| Revaluation reserve | 100,000 | |
| Profit and loss account | 20,000 | |
| Bonus account | | 400,000 |

The two capital reserves are used first and the remainder of the required sum is transferred from the profit and loss account. The profit and loss account is used last because it is the most flexible of a companies reserves.

The bonus account is used to 'collect' the transfers from the various reserves.

| | | |
|---|---|---|
| Bonus account | 400,000 | |
| Ordinary share capital account | | 400,000 |

The bonus account is a 'temporary' account. It is closed by transfer to the ordinary share capital account.

*Points to note*
- The issue of bonus shares gives the balance sheet a more realistic look. After the bonus issue the share capital is likely to be more in line with the permanent assets of the company. The summarised balance sheet of Sashi plc is as follows:

|  | £ |
|---|---|
| Fixed assets at cost | 1,300,000 |
| Net current assets | 218,000 |
|  | 1,518,000 |
| Less 7% debenture stock | 500,000 |
|  | 1,018,000 |

**Share capital and reserves**

| | |
|---|---:|
| Share capital: ordinary shares | 400,000 |
| Share premium | 280,000 |
| Revaluation reserve | 100,000 |
| Profit and loss account | 238,000 |
| | 1,018,000 |

After the bonus issue as outlined above the balance sheet would look thus:

| | |
|---|---:|
| Fixed assets at cost | 1,300,000 |
| Net current assets | 218,000 |
| | 1,518,000 |
| Less 7% debenture stock | 500,000 |
| | 1,018,000 |

**Share capital and reserves**

| | |
|---|---:|
| Share capital: ordinary shares | 800,000 |
| Profit and loss account | 218,000 |
| | 1,018,000 |

Hopefully you can see that before the bonus issue 'permanent' fixed assets amount to £1,300,000 'permanent' capital to only £400,000. After the bonus issue 'permanent' fixed assets amount to £1,300,000 and 'permanent' capital is now £800,000. The fixed assets and the capital are now more closely aligned.

- The bonus issue does not use the cash resources of the company, except in the administration costs that are incurred. This may allow cash resources to be used elsewhere in the company, perhaps to greater benefit.

- It may be impractical for the company to pay a dividend due to a shortage of cash. Bonus shares may be issued in lieu of the dividend.

- The bonus issue will not affect voting rights, as each shareholder has the same proportion of the overall share capital.

- The bonus issue makes it easier for an individual shareholder to sell part of his holding. He has more shares valued at a lower price, they are therefore more marketable.

- If the company can sustain its dividend per share each shareholder will receive a larger total dividend than was enjoyed before the bonus issue.

## 5.11  THE REDEMPTION OF SHARES

We have already said that once an investor buys shares in a limited company, the cash paid is 'locked in' to that company. The shareholder cannot demand his money back from the company. The exception to this rule is when a company issues **redeemable shares**.

These are generally preference shares (although it is possible for a company to issue redeemable ordinary shares, this is extremely rare). Examination questions on redemption usually feature redeemable preference shares.

The Companies Act requires that if shares are redeemed either:
- a new issue of shares should be issued to provide sufficient funds to match the nominal value of the shares redeemed; OR
- an amount that matches the nominal value of the shares redeemed must be transferred from revenue reserves (profit and loss account) to a capital redemption reserve.

This act maintains the permanent capital of the company and is a measure to protect the creditors of the company.

EXAMPLE

The summarised balance sheet of Derwat plc is shown:

|  | £ |
|---|---|
| Net assets | 240,000 |
| Cash | 25,000 |
|  | 265,000 |
| Ordinary share capital | 150,000 |
| Redeemable preference shares | 20,000 |
| Profit and loss account | 95,000 |
|  | 265,000 |

(1) The redeemable preference shares are redeemed at par. £20,000 new ordinary shares are issued at par to provide funds for the redemption.

(2) The redeemable preference shares are redeemed at par. There is no new issue of shares.

(3) The redeemable preference shares are redeemed at par. £13,000 new ordinary shares are issued at par to provide some funds for the redemption.

**Required**

For each of the above cases prepare a balance sheet to show the position of Derwat plc. after the redemption.

**Solutions**

(1) Derwat plc balance sheet after redemption:

|  | £ |
|---|---|
| Net assets | 240,000 |
| Cash (25 + 20 – 20) | 25,000 |
|  | 265,000 |
| Ordinary share capital (150 + 20) | 170,000 |
| Redeemable preference shares (20 -20) | – ❶ |
| Profit and loss account | 95,000 |
|  | 265,000 |

(2) Derwat plc balance sheet after redemption:

|  | £ |
|---|---|
| Net assets | 240,000 |
| Cash (25 – 20 ) | 5,000 |
|  | 245,000 |
| Ordinary share capital | 150,000 |
| Redeemable preference shares (20 – 20) | – ❷ |
| Profit and loss account (95 – 20) | 75,000 |
| Capital redemption reserve | 20,000 ❸ |
|  | 245,000 |

(3) Derwat plc balance sheet after redemption:

|  | £ |
|---|---|
| Net assets | 240,000 |
| Cash ( 25 – 20 + 13) | 18,000 |
|  | 258,000 |
| Ordinary share capital (150 + 13) | 163,000 |
| Redeemable preference shares (20 – 20) | – ❹ |
| Profit and loss account (95 – 7) | 88,000 |
| Capital redemption reserve | 7,000 ❺ |
|  | 258,000 |

❶ ❷ and ❹ would not be shown.

❸ from the profit and loss account.

❺ from the profit and loss account – £20,000 redeemed but only £13,000 issued.

---

## Chapter roundup

Chapter 5 shows how the accounts of limited companies differ from those of other business organisations.

You should be able to distinguish between funds provided by investors who have bought shares in a company and those provided by lenders. Shareholders and debenture holders have different rights.

You should be able to comment on the entries in the books of account that make limited companies different from other organisations.

---

# Illustrative questions

---

**1**  The chief accountant of Corchester Ltd had prepared the following balance sheet as at 1 July 1994.

|  | £000 | £000 |
|---|---|---|
| Fixed assets | | |
| Freehold property | | 100 |
| Other fixed assets | | 480 |
| | | 580 |
| Current assets (including bank) | 440 | |
| Less current liabilities | 200 | 240 |
| | | 820 |
| Financed by | | |
| Issued and paid up share capital | | |
| 400,000 ordinary shares of £1 each | 400 | |
| 150,000 8% redeemable preference | | |
| shares of £1 each | 150 | |
| | | 550 |
| Reserves | | |
| Capital redemption reserve | 100 | |
| Share premium account | 50 | |
| General reserve | 45 | |
| Profit and loss account | 75 | 270 |
| | | 820 |

The directors had decided to carry out the following transactions during July and August 1994.

(1)  **8 July 1994.** A rights issue of one ordinary share for every four held was made at £1.20 per share. All shareholders took up their rights.

(2)  **1 August 1994.** A bonus issue was made of one ordinary share for every ten held, based on the revised ordinary share capital. This was carried our by utilising equal amounts from the revenue reserves.

(3)  **5 August 1994.** 40,000 preference shares were redeemed at a premium of 5p per share. This was achieved out of profits with the exception of the premium which was covered by the share premium account.

(4)  **15 August 1994.** The freehold property was revalued at £130,000.

(5)  **19 August 1994.** Fixed assets costing £10,000 were purchased on credit.

*Required*

(a)  A balance sheet as at 19 August 1994 after the completion of all transactions indicated above.  (20)

(b)  Describe the features of:
(i)   a rights issue of shares;  (5)
(ii)  a bonus issue of shares.  (5)

(c) Explain the difference between capital and revenue reserves. (5)

(AEB)

*Tutorial note*

In part (a), take each transaction in turn and ensure that all its implications are carefully recorded before you consider the next one. Parts (b) and (c) are designed to test the precision of your knowledge.

*Suggested answer*

**Corchester Ltd balance sheet as at 19 August 1994**

|  | | £000 | £000 |
|---|---|---:|---:|
| **Fixed assets** | Freehold property | | 130 |
| | Other | | 490 |
| | | | 620 |
| **Current assets** | | 518 | |
| Less current liabilities | | 210 | 308 |
| | | | 928 |
| **Capital and reserves** | | | |
| Ordinary shares of £1 each fully paid | | | 550 |
| 8% Preference shares of £1 each fully paid | | | 110 |
| Revaluation reserve | | | 30 |
| Capital redemption reserve | | | 140 |
| Share premium account | | | 68 |
| General reserve | | | 20 |
| Profit and loss account | | | 10 |
| | | | 928 |

**Note** The capital redemption reserve has been increased by £40,000 since no new issue of shares has been made to cover the redemption

(b) (i) Rights issue

Points might include: shares sold to existing shareholders on a pro rata basis; shareholders can either take up or sell their rights to someone else; company raises finance.

(ii) Bonus issue

Points might include: also called a scrip issue; shares issued free to existing shareholders; reserves are capitalised, any type of reserve may be used; increases share capital and reduces reserves.

(c) Capital reserves are generally statutory reserves, that is the law decrees that they be created. Capital reserves are not available for the distribution of dividends. They can only be used for capital purposes, e.g. to issue bonus shares, to provide premiums on the redemption of shares etc.

Revenue reserves are transfers from the profit and loss appropriation account. They can be used in future years to help increase the profits shown in the profit and loss appropriation account. This in effect means that they are available for dividend purposes as well as the issue of bonus shares.

**2** Bash plc has prepared its draft accounts for the year ending 31 March 1995 which include the following balance sheet:

| | Cost | Depreciation | Net |
|---|---:|---:|---:|
| **Fixed assets** | £ | £ | £ |
| Property | 100,000 | – | 100,000 |
| Vehicles | 76,000 | 15,000 | 61,000 |
| Equipment | 52,000 | 32,000 | 20,000 |
| | 228,000 | 47,000 | 181,000 |
| **Current assets** | | | |
| Stock | | 75,000 | |
| Debtors | | 42,000 | |
| Bank | | 81,000 | |
| | | 198,000 | |

| | Cost £ | Depreciation £ | Net £ |
|---|---|---|---|
| **Creditors due for payment in less than one year** | | | |
| Trade creditors | | 21,000 | |
| Net current assets | | | 177,000 |
| | | | 358,000 |
| | | | |
| 200,000 £1 ordinary shares, fully paid | | | 200,000 |
| 50,000 10% redeemable preference shares, fully paid | | | 50,000 |
| Share premium account | | | 30,000 |
| Retained earnings | | | 78,000 |
| | | | 358,000 |

The preference dividend for the year has been paid in full.

On checking the accounts it is discovered that no entries have been made for the following:

(i)  To celebrate its Silver Jubilee the company issued bonus shares to the ordinary shareholders, on 1 April 1994, on a 1 for 10 basis, utilising the Share Premium Account.

(ii) During March 1995 a vehicle owned by the company, which cost £16,000, and had a written down value of £4,000, was involved in an accident. On 30 March the company's insurers agreed to pay £2,000 in compensation. The cheque was received on 15 April 1995.

(iii) The directors have decided to accept an independent valuation of £175,000 as a basis for revaluing its property as at 31 March 1995.

(iv) A final stock check revealed that stock which had been included in the stocktake at £5,000 cost could only be sold for scrap at £2,000.

(v)  On 31 March 1995 the preference shares were redeemed at par.

(vi) The directors have decided to propose a 10% ordinary dividend.

*Required*
Redraft the balance sheet as at 31 March 1995 having taken all the above points into consideration. (Clearly show all your workings.)  (20)
(NEAB)

*Tutorial note*
This question is similar in construction to Q1 (Corchester) so you must follow the same guidelines.

*Suggested answer*

### Bash Ltd balance sheet as at 31 March 1995

| | Cost £ | Valuation £ | Depreciation £ | Net £ |
|---|---|---|---|---|
| Fixed assets | | | | |
| Property | | 175,000 | | 175,000 |
| Vehicles | 60,000 | | 3,000 | 57,000 |
| Equipment | 52,000 | | 32,000 | 20,000 |
| | 112,000 | 175,000 | 35,000 | 252,000 |
| Current assets | | | | |
| Stock | | | 72,000 | |
| Debtors | | | 42,000 | |
| Bank | | | 31,000 | |
| Insurance claim | | | 2,000 | |
| | | | 147,000 | |

|  | Cost £ | Valuation £ | Depreciation £ | Net £ |
|---|---|---|---|---|
| Creditors due for payment in less than one year |  |  |  |  |
| Trade creditors |  | 21,000 |  |  |
| Proposed ordinary dividend |  | 22,000 | 43,000 | 104,000 |
|  |  |  |  | 356,000 |
| Capital and reserves |  |  |  |  |
| 220,000 £1 ordinary shares, fully paid |  |  |  | 220,000 |
| Share premium account |  |  |  | 10,000 |
| Revaluation reserve |  |  |  | 75,000 |
| Capital redemption reserve |  |  |  | 50,000 |
| Retained earnings |  |  |  | 1,000 |
|  |  |  |  | 356,000 |

The workings are fairly straightforward. Only the retained earnings are shown:

|  | £ |
|---|---|
| Balance | 78,000 |
| Loss on vehicle ❶ | (2,000) |
| Stock loss ❷ | (3,000) |
| Transfer to capital redemption reserve ❸ | (50,000) |
| Proposed dividend | (22,000) |
|  | 1,000 |

❶ Cost £16,000 – depreciation £12,000
   WDV £4,000 – Insurance claim £2,000

❷ Stock should be valued at the lower of cost (£5,000) or net realisable value (£2,000).

❸ No new issue of shares to finance the redemption.

**3** (a) *Briefly* explain the distinction between *authorised share capital* and *issued share capital*. (5)
   (b) Explain the nature of *share premium* and its treatment in company accounts. (5)
   (c) Explain the conditions under which a *revenue reserve* may become a *capital reserve*. (5)
   (d) Indicate how a company's return to shareholders' funds may be affected by its level of gearing. (5)
   (WJEC)

*Tutorial note*
Spend a quarter of the time allocated to this question on each section. The examiner is testing precise knowledge. Clarity of expression will help in this type of question.

*Suggested answer*
(a) The authorised share capital is stated in the company's memorandum of association and sets the upper limits of the number of shares that the company may issue. The issued share capital is made up of the shares that have actually been issued to the shareholders.

(b) When shares are issued by a company at a price in excess of the nominal value, the difference between the nominal value and the issue price is a share premium and the amount must be credited to the share premium account. The account is a statutory reserve and it may be applied:
   (i) for the issue of bonus shares;
   (ii) to write off the expenses incurred in forming a company (preliminary expenses);
   (iii) to write off any expenses incurred in the issue of shares or debentures;
   (iv) to write off commission paid or discount allowed on an issue of shares or debentures;

(v)  to provide any premium payable on the redemption of shares or debentures.

(c)  If a company redeems shares or buys back any of its own shares, and does not provide the finance required by the issue of a new issue of shares, a transfer must be made from revenues reserves to a capital redemption reserve.

(d)  A highly geared company has a high proportion of its capital in the form of fixed interest borrowing. This capital requires servicing whatever level of profit is made by the company. This does not pose a problem when profits are high, but when profits are low it will affect the level of dividends payable and also the level of retained profits. Interest on the borrowed funds is a charge to the profit and loss account, so the higher the level of gearing the higher the interest charges, and the lower the profits available for shareholders.

# ANALYSIS AND INTERPRETATION OF ACCOUNTS

## Units in this chapter

6.1  *Users and uses of financial statements*
6.2  *Functions of accounting*
6.3  *Performance evaluation*
6.4  *Profitability ratios*
6.5  *Financial ratios*
6.6  *Investment ratios*
6.7  *Interpretation*
6.8  *Limitations of ratio analysis*
6.9  *Accounting for inflation*

## Chapter objectives

Financial statements are prepared to convey information. Accounting is a communication medium. Much data can be extracted from accounting statements. Figures in isolation are fairly meaningless, because relationships are important and figures that are taken in isolation can sometimes be misleading. Financial statements use only absolute numbers. A statement that a man earns $35,000 per year is rather meaningless unless we know whether we are talking about American dollars, Singapore dollars, Zimbabwe dollars. Even then we need more information about the cost of living, average earnings etc.

The same is true about accounting information. A business makes a net profit of £100,000 during the year ended 31 December 1995. Has this been a good year? If the business under review was Marks and Spencer plc what would your answer be? If the business was Knitwits Wool Shop in the High Street, I dare say your answer would be different.

This chapter deals with the calculation of the most commonly examined ratios and the interpretation of ratios.

The key topics and concepts covered in this chapter are:

- needs of the users;
- functions of accounting;
- comparability;
- profitability ratios;
- liquidity ratios;
- gearing;
- investment ratios;
- interpretation of results;

- limitations of the analysis;
- historic cost accounting;
- current purchasing power accounting;
- current cost accounting.

## 6.1 USERS AND USES OF FINANCIAL STATEMENTS

Many people are 'users' of accounts and require financial information from businesses. Who are these 'users' of accounts? Who requires financial information?

What are they interested in? With one or two exceptions, all are probably most interested in the survival of the business. The exceptions could be competitors or a pressure group.

This survival depends on the business's ability to generate:
- profits – profitability
- cash – liquidity

Profits are necessary for the long-term survival of the organisation and cash is needed for the day-to-day running of the organisation, i.e. short-term survival. Which of the users are mainly interested in profitability? Which of the users are mainly interested in liquidity?

In order to be able to answer questions relating to profitability and liquidity we need to assess the performance of the organisation. The starting point in performance evaluation is the final accounts that are produced by organisations.

## 6.2 FUNCTIONS OF ACCOUNTING

Accounts are produced for two reasons:
- stewardship purposes
- management purposes

Many organisations use finance provided by other parties. Most of the finance provided for a limited company is provided by the shareholders. Finance may be provided by a bank. The finance used by the local squash club is provided by the members.

All these providers wish to know that their cash is safe and that they gain benefits from their provision of finance. Financial statements report to the members on how their organisation has performed.

In order to run a business, managers require information; this is obtained from the detailed final accounts of the business in question – from the manufacturing, trading and profit and loss account and from the balance sheet. However, most users of accounts will only have access to a set of published accounts. These published accounts lack the detail of the accounts that the managers will use.

**Stewardship function** An organisation often uses other people's cash to help run the business . It has an obligation to show those providers of finance how their investment has been used. They can then make a judgement as to whether they should continue to provide the finance or to withdraw it.

This function is evident at the Annual General Meeting of a public limited company when the directors present the financial statement in the company report to the shareholders. It is also seen when the Treasurer presents the squash club's income and expenditure account. Members can then see what has happened to their subscriptions, their weekly match fees and the profit on the Christmas raffle.

**Management function** The managers' of a business use the detailed figures provided in the accounts to decide which products should continue to be sold. Which branches/departments should remain open and where, perhaps, cost savings can be made.

# 6.3 PERFORMANCE EVALUATION

How do the users the accounts decide whether the profitability and/or the liquidity is acceptable? In the same way that you may decide whether your week-end job in the supermarket is well paid or not.

- you will possibly *compare* your earnings with what you earned last year;
- you will possibly *compare* your earnings with what your friends earn;
- you will possibly *compare* your earnings with the average earnings in the business sector in which you work;
- you may even *compare* your earnings with what you plan to spend in the future.

Performance evaluation is about making comparisons. Ratio analysis and interpretation of information are about making comparisons.

The users of accounts will follow a similar procedure to the one you use when looking at your wage slip at the end of the week. They will ask:

- 'Is the business performing better or worse than in previous years?'
- 'Is the business performing better or worse than a similar business?'
- 'Is the business performing better or worse than the sector as a whole?'
- 'Is the business performing better or worse than budgeted?'

The following comparisons are generally made:

| Performance of the organisation this year | *with* | • Own results in previous years. |
| | | • Results of similar businesses. |
| | | • Average results of the sector within which it exists. |
| | | • A previously set standard, i.e. a budget. |

Examination questions tend to concentrate on the first two areas mentioned above. The question will give either summarised accounting statements for one business for, say, two or three years or summarised accounting statements for two organisations in the same line of business.

The question may be structured, that is, it could ask you to calculate a set number of profitability ratios and a set number of liquidity ratios. Some questions may simply ask you to comment on the liquidity and/or profitability of a business based on some final accounts that you have prepared in a previous section of the question.

When textbooks or examiners refer to ratios they are using the generic term. Your answer could be either a true ratio, e.g. 3.7 : 1; or a percentage, e.g. 14.9%; or a time period, e.g. 42 days. Questions generally also ask for interpretation based on your calculations. Most students find this quite a daunting task.

Remember examiners cannot expect you to have the same depth of knowledge that they would expect from a top city analyst or a professional accountant. These professionals can usually make a better attempt at the analysis than you can because:

- they have been analysing and interpreting accounts as a living for a good number of years – you have been studying accounting for only two years or so.

- they have very much more information to base their interpretation on; they will probably have a large data base on the business in question. They may also have many researchers and helpers working with them – you will be on your own when you sit the examination.

- they have a greater length of time available to study the accounts and to think about them before coming to any conclusions – you will have only 45 minutes at the most when you attempt a question in the examination hall.

Even taking all these factors into account the 'experts' can still make errors – remember Polly Peck? Remember Maxwell?

The examiner cannot and will not expect a perfect answer from you. So all you can do is say what you see.

Many textbooks sub-divide the commonly used ratios into:

- profitability;
- financial;
- utilisation of resources;
- investment.

Also, in some cases, into:

- primary;
- secondary;
- tertiary.

Questions will not usually be set asking you to categorise your answers in this way. At Advanced level most questions generally test the candidates knowledge in calculating profitability and liquidity financial ratios. You should concentrate your efforts into *learning* these ratios. Occasionally questions are asked about gearing and dividend yield. (In a text book you may find these listed under the heading of investment ratios.)

Whichever ratio you use *always state the model or formula* that you are using.

Each of the more common ratios is calculated in the following example, using the 1995 figures only.

### Ardale, Bank and Co Ltd trading and profit and loss account
### for the year ended 31 December 1995

| 1994 £000 | | £000 | £000 |
|---|---|---|---|
| 10,500 | Sales | | 12,600 |
| | Less cost of sales: | | |
| 610 | Stock 1 January 1995 | 760 | |
| 4,350 | Purchases | 4,450 | |
| 4,960 | | 5,210 | |
| (760) | Less Stock 31 December 1995 | 800 | |
| 4,200 | | | 4,410 |
| 6,300 | Gross profit | | 8,190 |
| | Less expenses: | | |
| 1,280 | Distribution costs | 2,158 | |
| 2,925 | Administration costs | 3,876 | |
| 4,205 | | | 6,034 |
| 2,095 | Net profit on ordinary activities before interest | | 2,156 |
| 95 | Interest payable | | 105 |
| 2,000 | Net profit on ordinary activities before taxation | | 2,051 |
| 430 | Tax on profit on ordinary activities | | 480 |
| 1,570 | Profit for the year on ordinary activities after tax | | 1,571 |
| (35) | Preference dividend paid | 35 | |
| (400) | Proposed ordinary dividend | 440 | 475 |
| 1,135 | Retained profits for financial year | | 1,096 |

### Balance sheet as at 31 December 1995

| 1994 £000 | | £000 | £000 |
|---|---|---|---|
| | **Fixed assets** | | |
| 2,400 | Freehold land and buildings | | 2,700 |
| 1,000 | Plant and machinery | | 1,250 |
| 850 | Vehicles | | 900 |
| 80 | Office equipment | | 100 |
| 4,330 | | | 4,950 |
| | **Current assets** | | |
| 760 | Stock | 800 | |
| 540 | Debtors | 1,160 | |
| 34 | Bank | 20 | |
| 1,334 | | 1,980 | |
| | **Creditors**: amount falling due within one year | | |
| 240 | Trade creditors | 320 | |
| 430 | Taxation | 480 | |
| 400 | Dividends | 440 | |
| 1,070 | | 1,240 | |
| 264 | **Net current assets** | | 740 |
| 4,594 | | | 5,690 |
| 700 | **Creditors**: amount falling due after one year | | 700 |
| 3,894 | **Net assets** | | 4,990 |
| | **Capital and reserves** | | |
| | Called up share capital: | | |
| 1,250 | Ordinary shares of 50p each | | 1,250 |
| 500 | 7% Preference shares of £1 each | | 500 |
| 450 | Share premium account | | 450 |
| 1,694 | Profit and loss account | | 2,790 |
| 3,894 | **Shareholders' funds** | | 4,990 |

**Note** The market price of the company's ordinary shares at close of business today is £3.90 each. The market price a year ago was £4.10.

## 6.4 PROFITABILITY RATIOS

### RETURN ON CAPITAL EMPLOYED (ROCE)

This is an important ratio and is often known as the primary ratio.

It is a measure of the overall profitability of the business. Many of the other ratios are elements of the ROCE. Changes in mark-up, expenses, assets, etc. all have an influence on ROCE.

It shows the percentage return on the capital invested in the business. It shows how much profit has been earned for every £100 invested in long-term capital. It indicates how efficiently management is using the business resources to earn profits.

There is a variety of methods used to calculate ROCE. It is important, in order that the results can be used for comparative purposes, that the same method of calculation is used over time or when comparing the results of different businesses.

$$\frac{\text{Net profit before interest and taxation}}{\text{Capital employed}^* \text{ at the start of the year}} \times 100\%$$

$^*$(Closing capital employed less current year's retained profit)

$$\frac{2,156}{4,594} \times 100 = 46.93\%$$

Some students may have been taught to use the closing capital employed figure or an average figure for the year.

Using the closing capital employed figure the answer would be

$$\frac{2,156}{5,690} \times 100 = 37.89\%.$$

Using the average figure the answer would be

$$\frac{2,156}{5,142} \times 100 = 41.93\%.$$

Students are strongly advised to learn one method and use it consistently. Choose the method you feel most comfortable using — it will probably be the one your teacher has explained to you. Whichever model you do use *always state the formula*.

### RETURN ON OWNER'S EQUITY (ROOE)

This is a refinement of the ROCE calculation. It measures the return on the funds invested by the shareholders.

$$\frac{\text{Net profit before interest and tax but excluding any preference dividends}}{\text{Owners equity (ordinary issued share capital + all reserves) at the start of the year}}$$

$$\frac{2,121}{3,394} \times 100 = 62.49\%.$$

Again, some students may prefer to use the closing figure or an average figure for the owners equity, in which case the results would be 47.24% and 53.81% respectively.

Both of these ratios should be as large as possible. It is, however, impossible to give guidance as to what a 'good' figure would be, without having information about previous years' performance or about the particular industry as a whole. Without other information the return could be compared with the return that capital could currently obtain if invested in a bank or building society.

A major weakness when using either of these ratios is that due to the use of historic cost as a basis for accounting systems the value of some assets may be inaccurate, in which case the capital employed figure must also be inaccurate.

Consider the accounting equation:

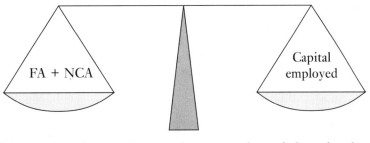

If the assets are incorrectly valued     then     the capital employed must also be incorrectly valued

## THE MARGIN RATIO AND THE MARK-UP RATIO

The margin ratio is $\dfrac{\text{Gross profit}}{\text{Sales}} \times 100\%$

$\dfrac{8,190}{12,600} \times 100 = 65\%$

The mark-up ratio is $\dfrac{\text{Gross profit}}{\text{Cost of sales}} \times 100\%$

$\dfrac{8,190}{4,410} \times 100 = 185.71\%$

Both the margin and the mark-up will be affected by the cost price and the selling price of the final product. An alteration in the selling price might be due to a management decision to increase market share. The percentage will vary according to the type of business. Students are advised not to use both of these ratios in answering a question, as they are too similar. Use one or the other.

## NET MARGIN RATIO

$\dfrac{\text{Net profit before tax}}{\text{Sales}} \times 100\%$

$\dfrac{2,051}{12,600} \times 100 = 16.28\%$

This ratio calculates the profitability of the sales. It varies widely from business to business so there is no ideal percentage for all businesses

## 6.5    FINANCIAL RATIOS

These ratios mainly assess the ability of the business to pay creditors who require payment within one year (in reality they will usually require payment very much more quickly than this). Consequently, these ratios are often required by examiners under the heading of liquidity ratios.

## THE CURRENT RATIO (ALSO KNOWN AS THE WORKING CAPITAL RATIO)

*There is no ideal ratio.* The ratio shows how many times the current assets are covering the current liabilities. Generally the ratio should be in excess of unity (greater than 1 : 1), although some businesses prosper with a ratio of less than this.

Students should look for trends when looking at the current ratio. A low current ratio may indicate that the business may have difficulty in meeting its immediate obligations in the future. A large increase in the ratio could indicate that the business is tying its resources up in non-productive assets.

$$\frac{\text{Current assets}}{\text{Current liabilities}}$$

$$\frac{1,980}{1,240} = 1.6 : 1$$

Note that ratios should be expressed as 'something' : 1.

## THE ACID TEST RATIO (ALSO KNOWN AS THE QUICK ASSET RATIO)

Again, any trend should be observed when using this ratio.

The ratio is calculated without stock since often stock is the least liquid of the current assets. If the debtors of the business pay in less time than the creditors are paid then provided the acid test ratio is greater than one the business will always have sufficient cash to pay its immediate creditors.

$$\frac{\text{Current assets excluding stock}}{\text{Current liabilities}}$$

$$\frac{1,180}{1,240} = 0.95 : 1$$

With both of the above ratios an apparently less than satisfactory ratio may be due to the existence of a bank overdraft. This fact in itself may not be cause for concern. If the bank is prepared to continue, or even increase the overdraft facility, then the business will have access to liquid resources, and is in no immediate danger of liquidation.

## DEBTORS' COLLECTION PERIOD

$$\frac{\text{Debtors} \times 365 \text{ days}}{\text{Credit sales}}$$

$$\frac{1,160}{12,600} \times 365 = 33.6 \text{ days}$$

A question may not distinguish between cash and credit sales. In such cases it is acceptable to use the total sales figure. Do remember to use the same figures when making comparisons.

This ratio measures how long, on average, it takes the business to collect its debts. Generally the longer that debts are outstanding the more likely they are to be irrecoverable. It is also advisable to have a shorter debtors collection period than the creditors payment period. This is not the case with Ardale, Bank and Co Ltd (see page 121). On average they are paying their suppliers before customers pay their debts. There may be a very good reason for this (keeping suppliers happy, taking advantage of extremely generous discounts, etc), but it could warrant investigation.

## CREDITORS' PAYMENT PERIOD

$$\frac{\text{Creditors} \times 365 \text{ days}}{\text{Credit purchases}}$$

$$\frac{320}{4,450} \times 365 = 26.2 \text{ days}$$

This measures the average time taken to pay creditors. This is very short and unless there is a good reason for this rapid payment (see comment above) it should be extended. Too long a payment period may be an indication that the business has cash flow problems.

## RATE OF STOCK TURNOVER (ALSO KNOWN AS THE RATE OF STOCKTURN, OR JUST STOCKTURN)

$$\frac{\text{Cost of sales}}{\text{Average stock held during year}}$$

$$\frac{4,410}{780} = 5.65 \text{ times a year, or stock is held for 64 days } \left(\frac{365}{5.65}\right)$$

In every 'bundle' of stock a large amount of cash and profit may be tied up. A rapid turnover of stock will release both cash and profit. The more often stock can be sold the more benefit the business will get. It may seem, then, that the best rate of stock turnover would be 365 times per year, but if the stock levels are too low it would result in losing customers if goods are not available to be sold when demanded. In some industries the need to hold large quantities of stock for long periods has almost been totally eradicated with the use of JIT (just in time) stock ordering.

## 6.6    INVESTMENT RATIOS

### GEARING

Again, there are a number of ways to calculate this figure. Choose one that you find easy to understand and to calculate and stick with it. The concept of gearing is really fairly simple.

> How much long-term capital have the owners provided and how much has been provided by others?

The 'other' providers of long-term capital are usually preference shareholders, debenture holders and institutions (banks etc.)

In the case of Ardale, Bank and Co Ltd the owners (shareholders) have provided £4,490,000 (ordinary shares + all reserves) while others have provided £1,200,000 (preference shares + long term creditors)

Two main measures are used:

- expressing fixed return funding (preference shares and other long term borrowing) as a percentage of total capital employed:

$$\frac{\text{Fixed return funding}}{\text{Capital employed}} \times 100\%$$

- expressing fixed return funding as a percentage of equity:

$$\frac{\text{Fixed return funding}}{\text{Equity (ordinary shares} + \textit{all} \text{ reserves)}} \times 100\%$$

Using the first measure, 21% of all capital employed in the business has been provided by people other than the ordinary shareholders. £1,200,000 out of the total of £5,690,000. The gearing ratio using this measure is 21%. A figure in excess of 50% using this measure would indicate a highly geared company. Less than 33% would be low geared. Using the second measure, the people other than the ordinary shareholders have provided £1,200,000, compared to £4,490,000 provided by the ordinary shareholders (26.7%). A figure in excess of 100% using this measure would be high gearing while less would be low gearing.

As a general rule you could remember this:

$$\left\{ \begin{array}{l} \text{High geared} \\ \text{High debt} \\ \text{High risk} \end{array} \right\} \qquad \left\{ \begin{array}{l} \text{Low geared} \\ \text{Low debt} \\ \text{Low risk} \end{array} \right\}$$

In times of good profits a highly geared company will have few problems servicing the large proportion of fixed return funding, but when profits are low (or negative) the fixed return funding still has to be serviced and this may put the future of the company at risk.

## EARNINGS PER SHARE (EPS)

This ratio is often used as a measure of a company's success. It shows the profit earned, before extraordinary items (thus allowing valid comparisons), in pence per share. SSAP 3 requires that all listed companies show this ratio in their published accounts. It indicates to shareholders how profitable their investment is. It is difficult to use for inter-company comparisons, but is a useful indicator for year on year comparisons in one business.

$$\frac{\text{Net profit} - \text{preference dividend}}{\text{Number of issued ordinary shares}}$$

$$\frac{1,536,000}{2,500,000} = 61.44 \text{ pence}$$

## PRICE/EARNINGS RATIO (P/E)

This is used as an indicator of how confident investors are in a company, in the future. Since the ratio compares current market price with EPS an increase in market price will increase this ratio. Demand for shares is dependent on investors' perceptions of a company's future performance. A high P/E indicates expected future growth or an overvalued share. A low P/E indicates expected poor performance in the future or an undervalued share.

$$\frac{\text{Market price of ordinary share}}{\text{Earnings per share}}$$

$$\frac{£3.90}{61.44\text{p}} = 6.34$$

## DIVIDEND YIELD

Shareholders invest in a company in order to gain a return on that investment, (they also hope that the market price of the share will rise and allow them to sell their holding at a profit – a capital gain).The yield shows the actual income return an investor can expect, based on the current market price of the shares.

$$\frac{\text{Ordinary dividend}}{\text{Market price of ordinary share}}$$

$$\frac{440,000}{9,750,000} \times 100 = 4.5\%$$

## DIVIDEND COVER

This shows the likelihood that the company can continue paying the current rate of ordinary share dividend. A high figure is good since all profits, whether distributed or ploughed back, belong ultimately to the ordinary shareholders. The benefits will be seen by the shareholders as high dividends or increasing reserves, which will be reflected in the market price of the shares.

$$\frac{\text{Profits available for dividends}}{\text{Dividends}}$$

$$\frac{1,536,000}{440,000} = 3.49 \text{ times}$$

## INTEREST COVER

This shows how many times the profits cover the current interest payments.

$$\frac{\text{Profits available to pay interest}}{\text{Interest}}$$

$$\frac{1,571,000}{105,000} = 14.96 \text{ times}$$

You should now practice the calculations using the 1994 figures from the accounts of Ardale, Bank & Co Ltd. Put your results into the grid below. As you calculate your results write down the model you have used.

| Ratio | Model | 1994 | 1995 |
|---|---|---|---|
| **Profitability ratios** | | | |
| ROCE | | | 46.93% |
| ROOE | | | 62.49% |
| Margin | | | 65% |
| Mark-up | | | 185.71% |
| Net profit margin | | | 16.28% |
| **Liquidity ratios** | | | |
| Current ratio | | | 1.6:1 |
| Acid test ratio | | | 0.95:1 |
| Debtors collection period | | | 33.6 days |
| Creditors payment period | | | 26.2 days |
| Stock turnover | | | 64 days |
| **Investment ratios** | | | |
| Gearing | | | 21% |
| Earnings per share | | | 61.44p |
| Price/earnings ratio | | | 6.34 |
| Dividend yield | | | 4.5% |
| Dividend cover | | | 3.49 times |
| Interest cover | | | 14.96 times |

## 6.7  INTERPRETATION

You will also be expected to be able to make comments on the ratios that you have calculated. Remember what was said on page 114. The examiner is not looking for a perfect answer – there may not be one!

**Remember:**

- Say what you see.

- Keep it simple – you will not have every piece of information needed to make a very sophisticated comment.

- Be explicit – do not simply say that a ratio has improved. If profits go from £20.00 to £20.01 this is an improvement, but £20.00 to £1,000,020.00 is also an improvement! Quantify your answers, use figures, e.g. profits have risen from £20.00 to £1,000,020, This puts the results into some kind of context. Better still, give the percentage change.

Compare your results with the ones given. Here are some of the comments you should have come up with.

- The **ROCE** has fallen from 60.56% in 1994 to 46.93% in 1995. Although net profit has increased, the capital employed has increased by a larger proportion. Also the net margin has fallen along with asset utilisation (sales/assets).

- The **margin** has increased from 60% in 1994 to 65% in 1995. This is due to an increased selling price. Cost of sales has increased by only 5% while sales have increased by 20%. (Remember, selling more of the product only affects the total sales figure it does not affect the margin or the mark-up.)

- The **net margin** has fallen from 19.95% in 1994 to 16.28% in 1995. This is due to an increase in expenses. They have risen from 41% of sales (60%–19%) in 1994 to 49% a year later. This should warrant investigation.

- All these comments are fairly straightforward and are based on the figures that are available in the company's final accounts. Do not try to be too clever and make up possible scenarios. Stick to the facts: 'say what you see'.

- The **current ratio** has improved from 1.25:1 in 1994 to 1.6:1 in 1995.

- The **acid test ratio** has also shown a much improved position rising from 0.54:1 in 1994 to 0.95:1 in 1995. Both still seem to be on the low side, since the more liquid current assets still do not cover the company's short term creditors. However, without further information about the sector in which the business operates, no definite conclusion can be drawn from the figures.

- There may be a need to investigate why the **debtors' payment period** has increased from 18.8 days in 1994 to 33.6 days in 1995, and why, although the company has lengthened the time it takes to pay its creditors from 20.1 days in 1994 to 26.2 days in 1995, it is still a shorter period than that taken to receive payments from its debtors.

- The **rate of stock turnover** has gone from 59 days in 1994 to 64 days in 1995. This could be due to increased selling prices (see margin above) or a general slowing down in the economy (this could account for debtors taking longer to pay their debts too). Once again, detailed comments about how long goods should stay in stock would depend on the goods being sold.

- The company has remained **low geared** in 1995. The ratio has fallen from 26% in 1994 to its present level of 21%. Without any further issues of preference shares or further long-term borrowing, the ratio will decrease over time. As profits are retained total capital will increase. One of the effects of the low gearing ratio can be seen in that interest cover is some 15 times.

- The **EPS** has remained static at around 61.4 pence.

- The **price earnings ratio** is low, (1994, 6.68; 1995, 6.34) but without further information, comment cannot be made. This may be an acceptable figure. The low figure may be due to poor performance within the sector or the shares may be under-valued.

- The **dividend yield** has risen slightly from 3.9% in 1994 to 4.5% in 1995. This is due to an increased ordinary dividend being proposed and the market price of the ordinary shares falling slightly.

- The **dividend cover** has fallen slightly from 3.84 times in 1994 to 3.49 times in 1995 due to the increased proposed dividend in 1995, while the available profits have stayed almost the same over the two years.

- Profits are still more than three times greater than the proposed dividend payment. The lack of liquid resources (see acid test ratio) may mean that a bank overdraft facility may need to be negotiated in order to pay the dividends if approved at the annual general meeting of the Company.

- Ardale, Bank & Co Ltd's profits would have to fall by a factor of around 15 before it would find difficulty in paying its present **interest charges**. This is a slight drop since last year when the comparative figure was 16.53 times.

## 6.8    LIMITATIONS OF RATIO ANALYSIS

Ratio analysis is widely used as a performance indicator, but it does have it's limitations and you must be aware of these, otherwise you might draw the wrong conclusions from your calculations.

- The merit of using historic cost is that it is objective. Its use, however, does tend to invalidate some results over a long time period. There was a time when people earned an annual income of £20 – a 5% pay rise for them would be a very different figure to a pay rise of 5% for me or you. The value of assets shown on the balance sheet is unlikely to be the same as the market value of the assets.

- Emphasis is on past results. Is the past a totally reliable indicator of future results? If a particular football team wins the premier league one year, does it mean that they will win it the next year and for five years after that?

- Published accounts give an overall view – perhaps this disguises inefficient sections of the business. One department may yield a return on its capital employed of 45%, another may have a return of 4%, yet overall, the business may have a return of 20%.

- Accounts show only the monetary aspects of the business. They do not show management or staff strengths or weaknesses. Inherent goodwill is not recorded.

- The external environment which influences the business is constantly changing. These changes may only be evident after some considerable time lag. A devaluation of the currency will cause any imported materials to the product to rise in price, but the increased costs may not be felt for some time if the business carries large stocks.

- Different organisations have different structures, methods of financing their operations, and expense and revenue patterns. They use different accounting techniques, methods of measurement and different conventions. No matter how alike two businesses appear from outside, all businesses are different.

- The final accounts of a business are prepared on a particular date. The balance sheet as at that date may well be unrepresentative of the normal position of the business.

## 6.9    ACCOUNTING FOR INFLATION

Before you continue to read on check with your teacher or your syllabus to see whether accounting for inflation is on your examination syllabus.

The first two points in 6.8 stressed the historic cost basis of our accounting system. The main *advantages* of the historic cost method of preparing financial accounts are:

- It is objective.
- It is relatively easy to understand, even by those who have not studied accounting
- It is easy to apply to the double entry system of book-keeping.
- Auditors can verify figures quite easily from source documents.
- It is the only system accepted by the inland revenue.

The major *disadvantage* is that results can be distorted by the changing value of money. In times of inflation:

- stocks cost more to replace than the original cost;
- debtors gain since they settle their debts with a devalued currency;
- creditors lose since they receive a devalued currency.

While most people would agree that historic cost accounting (HCA) is an imperfect system, no acceptable alternative has yet been devised. Over the past twenty years or so two attempts have been made to overcome the drawbacks of HCA – current purchasing power accounting, and current cost accounting.

## CURRENT PURCHASING POWER ACCOUNTING

This system uses the retail price index to convert the figures arrived at by HCA. The conversion does not apply to debtors, creditors, or cash and bank balances.

The system has HCA figures as its starting point, so its retains some of the advantages of HCA, but it also has some of the drawbacks. The system was abandoned in the mid 1970's.

## CURRENT COST ACCOUNTING

This system was adopted in 1980 after the Sandilands report. It required companies to present, as part of their final published accounts, a current cost profit and loss account and a current cost balance sheet.

The current cost profit and loss account required *four* adjustments:

- **1 The depreciation adjustment** showing the additional depreciation necessary to provide for the replacement cost of the fixed assets rather than depreciation based on their original historic cost.

- **2 The cost of sales adjustment** represents the difference between the cost of sales charged in the HCA trading account and the current cost of sales at the date of sale. Since purchases and sales can be assumed to have been purchased constantly throughout the year the value of purchases and sales will reflect average prices for the year. It is, therefore, only the stocks which need to be adjusted to reflect the changes in price levels over the year.

- **3 The monetary working capital adjustment** is based on the application of the same principles of current value to debtors and creditors as was applied to depreciation and stock. It represents the extra finance required to maintain the value of the working capital during inflationary periods.

- **4 The gearing adjustment** reduces the total of the other three adjustments to reflect the proportion of the gain or loss due to inflation borne by the external lenders of finance.

The current cost balance sheet shows fixed assets and stocks at their replacement cost. This replacement cost is calculated by using the same indices as those used above.

The adjustment to these assets is credited (or debited if there is a deficit on adjustment) to a capital maintenance reserve. The reserve also receives the entries made to adjust depreciation, cost of sales, monetary working capital and gearing.

> ## Chapter roundup
>
> Chapter 6 has shown the different ways of measuring the performance of a business.
>
> It has explained that these ratios must be used for making comparisons and that used in isolation they have very little value. It is also important that comparisons are made 'like with like'.
>
> You should be able to comment on each of the ratios, but do remember to use figures and state the obvious as well as the less obvious.

# Illustrative questions

**1** Three companies have the same long-term finance as follows:

|  | **Alex Ltd** | **Bob Ltd** | **Charles Ltd** |
|---|---|---|---|
|  | £ | £ | £ |
| 6% Debentures | 400,000 | 300,000 | – |
| 8% Preference Shares | 400,000 | 300,000 | 400,000 |
| £1 Ordinary Shares | 200,000 | 400,000 | 600,000 |
| Market value per share | 4 | 3 | 2.50 |

Net profit **before** calculation of debenture interest is £100,000 in each case.
**Note** Ignore taxation in your answers.

*Required*

(a) Calculate the net profit for each company **after** debenture interest has been applied. (3)

(b) Assume that all of Bob Ltd's profits are to be distributed:
   (i) How much ordinary dividend is payable by Bob Ltd altogether? (1)
   (ii) What percentage dividend is payable on ordinary shares? (1)
   (iii) Calculate:
   Bob Ltd's ordinary dividend yield as a percentage; (1)
   Bob Ltd's price/earnings ratio. (1)
   (iv) Explain the term 'earnings per ordinary share' and give a formula for calculating it. (2)

(c) (i) Which of the three companies is most highly geared? Explain your answer. (2)
   (ii) In years of high profits, is it better to be an ordinary shareholder or a debenture holder? Justify your answer. (3)
   (iii) Apart from shareholders and investors, suggest organisations or groups of people who might be interested in a company's investment ratios. (2)

(d) Comment briefly on the following changes which have occurred to the ratios for Charles Ltd between 1994 and 1995.

|  | 1994 | 1995 |
|---|---|---|
| Gross Profit Ratio | 20% | 33% |
| Stock Turnover Rate | 5 times | 7 times |
| Net Profit Ratio | 12% | 13% |
| Current Ratio | 2.5:1 | 1.4:1 |
| Quick(Acid Test) Ratio | 1.1:1 | 0.8:1 |
| Average Age of Debtors | 20 days | 30 days |
| Average Age of Creditors | 40 days | 30 days |
| Fixed Assets: sales | 40% | 30% |
| Return on Total Assets | 15% | 16% |

(9)

(UCLES)

*Tutorial note*

In this type of question always state the model (formula) that you are using. Take careful note of what the question requires and respond accordingly, e.g. explain or comment. Comments should be very brief since there is only 1 mark available for each ratio.

*Suggested answer*

(a)

|  | Alex Ltd | Bob Ltd | Charles Ltd |
|---|---|---|---|
|  | £ | £ | £ |
| Net profit before interest | 100,000 | 100,000 | 100,000 |
| Debenture interest | 24,000 | 18,000 | – |
| Net profit after interest | 76,000 | 82,000 | 100,000 |

(b) (i)

|  | £ |
|---|---|
| Net profit after interest | 82,000 |
| less preference dividend | 24,000 |
| Profits available for ordinary shareholders | 58,000 |

(ii) Percentage dividend payable $= \dfrac{£58,000}{£400,000} \times 100 = 14.5\%$

(iii) Ordinary dividend yield $= \dfrac{\text{rate of dividend declared}}{} \times \dfrac{\text{nominal value of share}}{\text{market price of share}}$

$$= 14.5 \times \dfrac{£1}{£3}$$

$$= 4.83\%$$

Price/earnings ratio $= \dfrac{\text{market price of share}}{\text{earnings per share}}$

$$= \dfrac{£3}{14.5}$$

$$= 20.69$$

Earnings per share $= \dfrac{\text{earnings in pence}}{\text{number of ordinary shares}} = \dfrac{5,800,000}{400.000} = 14.5\text{p}$

(iv) It is the profits earned by the company after the payment of tax and preference dividends. It shows the profits attributable to the ordinary shareholders. The profits will then be distributed or retained as part of the shareholders' funds

(c) (i) Alex Ltd. is more highly geared than the other two companies. The company has a greater proportion of its long-term fixed interest capital provided by investors who are not ordinary shareholders.

Gearing $= \dfrac{\text{fixed cost capital}}{\text{total capital}}$

|  | Alex Ltd | Bob Ltd | Charles Ltd |
|---|---|---|---|
| $=$ | $\dfrac{£800,000}{£1,000,000}$ | $\dfrac{£600,000}{£1,000,000}$ | $\dfrac{£400,000}{£1,000,000}$ |
| $=$ | 80% | 60% | 40% |

(ii) It would be better to be an ordinary shareholder. The only limits to the dividends they could receive are: the dividend policy of the directors; the available profits; the cash available to pay the dividends. The debenture holders, on the other hand, can only ever receive £6 (less income tax) for every £100 they have invested.

(iii) Other interested parties will include: employees; bank managers; prospective investors; researchers; the press etc.

(d) Gross profit has increased from 20% to 33% – 13% more than 20% (13/20 × 100) – making a 65% increase over the year. This may be due to better buying policy or an increase in selling price.

Stock turnover has increased from 73 days to 52 days. This means that both cash and profits are being released at a faster rate than previously.

Net profit ratio has increased from 12% to 13%. Profit and loss account expenses have risen from 8% in 1994 to 20% in 1995. This should warrant investigation.

Both the current ratio and the acid test ratio have deteriorated significantly. It is very difficult to arrive at any major conclusions because of lack of detail, and lack of information regarding the type of business. However, both ratios are very low and action should be taken to inject some working capital into Charles Ltd in the near future.

Debtors are taking longer to settle their debts. This is a worrying development. Credit control measures should be reviewed in order to determine what has caused the lengthening of the credit period.

Creditors are being paid more quickly. If this is due to creditor pressure there may not be much that the managers of Charles Ltd can do. However, if earlier payment is part of management policy then attention should be drawn to the debtors collection time. A return to the situation shown in 1994 (re debtors and creditors) would help restore a healthier liquid position.

The fixed asset to sales ratio shows an improvement. Either the same fixed assets employed in 1994 are generating more sales, or the same sales volume is being generated by fewer fixed assets. Whichever is the reason, fixed assets are being employed to produce a greater sales revenue.

This is one of the many ROCE measurements. The net profit after tax expressed as a percentage of total assets has increased from 15% to 16%.

**2** The directors of Keats & Co Ltd are faced with strong competition from similar companies and are seeking more information that may help them retain their trading position. It has been suggested that various ratios will give an indication of the performance of the company and help the directors to make vital decisions. The following are the summarised financial statements of the company:

### Trading and profit and loss accounts for the year ended 31 December

| | 1990 £000 | 1990 £000 | 1991 £000 | 1991 £000 |
|---|---|---|---|---|
| Turnover | | 9,000 | | 12,000 |
| less: Cost of sales | | 6,300 | | 9,120 |
| Gross profit | | 2,700 | | 2,880 |
| less Expenses | | 1,700 | | 1,820 |
| Net profit | | 1,000 | | 1,060 |
| less Corporation tax | 540 | | 580 | |
| Dividends | 420 | 960 | 460 | 1,040 |
| | | 40 | | 20 |
| Retained earnings b/f | | 240 | | 280 |
| Retained earnings c/f | | 280 | | 300 |

### Balance sheet as at 31 December

| | 1990 £000 | 1990 £000 | 1991 £000 | 1991 £000 |
|---|---|---|---|---|
| Fixed assets (at cost less depreciation) | | 9,300 | | 10,200 |
| Current assets | | | | |
| Stock | 1,560 | | 3,020 | |
| Debtors | 1,520 | | 2,940 | |
| Balance at bank | 640 | | – | |
| | 3,720 | | 5,960 | |
| Less current liabilities | | | | |
| Creditors | 1,540 | | 2,780 | |
| Tax and dividends | 960 | | 1,040 | |
| Bank overdraft | – | | 1,800 | |
| | 2,500 | | 5,620 | |
| Working capital | | 1,220 | | 340 |
| | | 10,520 | | 10,540 |
| Financed by: | | | | |
| Share capital (fully issued and paid up) | | 6,000 | | 6,000 |
| General reserve | 1,440 | | 1,440 | |
| Profit and loss a/c | 280 | 1,720 | 300 | 1,740 |
| 10% debentures | | 2,800 | | 2,800 |
| | | 10,520 | | 10,540 |

**Note** All sales are on a credit basis only.

*Required*

(a) Calculate **three** liquidity and **three** profitability ratios for 1990 and 1991. (9)

(b) Comment on the company's position as revealed by these ratios. (10)

(c) A brief report critically evaluating the use of ratios in a business. (6)

(AEB)

*Tutorial note*

Again include your model as part of your answer. In part (b) be objective with your comments. Stick to the facts. In part (c) remember to respond in report format.

*Suggested answer*

(a) Three liquidity ratios could include:

$$\text{Current ratio} = \frac{\text{Current assets}}{\text{Current liabilities}} = \quad \frac{3{,}720}{2{,}500} = 1.48 : 1 \qquad 1990$$

$$\frac{5{,}960}{5{,}620} = 1.06 : 1 \qquad 1991$$

$$\text{Acid test ratio} = \frac{\text{Current assets less stock}}{\text{Current liabilities}} = \frac{2{,}160}{2{,}500} = 0.86 : 1 \qquad 1990$$

$$\frac{2{,}940}{5{,}620} = 0.52 : 1 \qquad 1991$$

$$\text{Debtor collection} = \frac{\text{Debtors} \times 365}{\text{Credit sales}} = \frac{1{,}520 \times 365}{9{,}000} = 61.6 \text{ days} \quad 1990$$

$$\frac{2{,}940 \times 365}{12{,}000} = 89.4 \text{ days} \quad 1991$$

Three profitability ratios could include:

|  |  | 1990 |  | 1991 |  |
|---|---|---|---|---|---|
| $\text{ROCE} = $ | $\dfrac{\text{Profit before tax}}{\text{Capital employed}} = $ | $\dfrac{1{,}000 \times 100}{10{,}520}$ | $= 9.5\%$ | $\dfrac{1{,}060 \times 100}{10{,}540}$ | $= 10.1\%$ |
| $\text{Gross margin} = $ | $\dfrac{\text{Gross profit}}{\text{Sales}} = $ | $\dfrac{2{,}700 \times 100}{9{,}000}$ | $= 30\%$ | $\dfrac{2{,}880 \times 100}{12{,}000}$ | $= 24\%$ |
| $\text{Net margin} = $ | $\dfrac{\text{Net profit}}{\text{Sales}} = $ | $\dfrac{1{,}000 \times 100}{9{,}000}$ | $= 11.1\%$ | $\dfrac{1{,}060 \times 100}{12{,}000}$ | $= 8.8\%$ |

(b) A poor liquidity position has worsened. The company now only has 52 pence available to meet each £1 of current debt. Overdraft has increased significantly and has been used to purchase new fixed assets. Debtors are now taking much longer to settle their debts. This indicates poor credit control and could lead to a higher incidence of bad debts.

Higher sales have been achieved by a reduction in selling price, the result is a lowering of the margins. The lower margin will restrict growth of resources through retained profits.

(c) To

From  *(i.e. report format)*

Date

### A critical evaluation of accounting ratios

The advantages could include:

they reveal trends;

which aids management in their decision making through analysis of the results;

they help comparisons;

most aspects of a business can be covered.

Disadvantages could include:

the causes of changes are not revealed by the ratios;

it is extremely difficult to ensure that 'like with like' is being compared, changes in economic climate, changes in staff, changes in attitudes etc make valid comparisons almost impossible;
results are dependent on the accuracy of the data being used;
data is prepared using historic cost figures.

**3**   The following information relates to two separate companies for the year ended 31 December 1994.

**Draft income statements**

|  | Moira Ltd | Down Ltd |
|---|---|---|
|  | £000 | £000 |
| Trading profit | 400 | 500 |
| Debenture interest | (100) | – |
| Profit before tax | 300 | 500 |
| Taxation | (120) | (200) |
| Profit after tax | 180 | 300 |
| Dividends:   Ordinary | (100) | (80) |
|                  Preference | (18) | (45) |
| Retained profit for the year | 62 | 175 |
| Market price per ordinary share at 31 December 1994 | £4 | £5 |

**Balance sheets (extracts)**

|  | £000 | £000 |
|---|---|---|
| Capital and reserves |  |  |
| Ordinary shares (£1 each) | 250 | 250 |
| 9% Preference shares (£1 each) | 20 | 500 |
| Share premium | 80 | – |
| Revaluation reserve | 50 | – |
| Profit and loss account | 120 | 850 |
|  | 520 | 1,600 |
| Long-term liabilities |  |  |
| 10% Debentures | 1,000 | – |
|  | 1,520 | 1,600 |

*Required*
(a) Calculate the following investment ratios for the two companies for the year to 31 December 1994:
   (i)   interest cover;
   (ii)  earnings per share;
   (iii) ordinary dividend cover;
   (iv) dividend yield;
   (v)  price/earnings ratio.                                                              (5)

(b) What information can be derived from each of the ratios calculated above. (10)

(c) Which one of the two companies would you advise a potential investor offers the 'better' investment opportunity.                                                                (5)
                                                                                              (NICCEA)

*Tutorial note*
Restrict yourself to simple observations that can be deducted from the question. In part (c) remember to offer clear and unambiguous advice derived from (a) and (b).

*Suggested answer*

(a) (i)   Interest cover   $= \dfrac{\text{profit available to pay interest}}{\text{interest payable}}$

$= \dfrac{£400}{£100} = 4$ times (Moira Ltd only)

(ii) Earnings per share = $\dfrac{\text{profit available for dividends (after tax and preference dividend) in pence}}{\text{number of ordinary shares}}$

For Moira Ltd = $\dfrac{£162,000}{£250,000}$ = 64.8 pence

For Down Ltd = $\dfrac{£225,000}{£250,000}$ = £1.02

(iii) Ordinary dividend cover = $\dfrac{\text{profit after tax and preference dividend}}{\text{ordinary dividend paid}}$

For Moira Ltd = $\dfrac{£162,000}{£100,000}$ = 1.62 times

For Down Ltd = $\dfrac{£255,000}{£80,000}$ = 3.19 times

(iv) Dividend yield = Ordinary dividend declared $\times \dfrac{\text{Nominal value of ordinary shares}}{\text{Market value of ordinary shares}}$

For Moira Ltd = 40% $\times \dfrac{£1}{£4}$ = 10%        For Down Ltd = 32% $\times \dfrac{£1}{£5}$ = 6.4%

(v) Price earnings ratio = $\dfrac{\text{Market price of share}}{\text{Earnings per share}}$

For Moira Ltd = $\dfrac{£4}{64.8p}$ = 6.17%%        For Down Ltd = $\dfrac{£5}{1.02p}$ = 4.9%

(b) *Interest cover* shows the ability of a company to service its long-term borrowing out of current profits. Low interest cover would signal to the ordinary shareholders that payment of dividends might be jeopardised if profit levels cannot be maintained in the future.

*Earnings per share* is often used by potential investors when deciding whether the return on their investment is worth the risk taken. It is a measure of how successful a company is.

*Dividend cover* shows the relationship between how much profit was available for ordinary dividends and the dividends declared. It also shows the ability of a company to maintain its dividend in the future. High dividend cover could indicate a cautious dividend policy or a policy to invest profits in the business in order to ensure security in the future.

The *dividend yield* indicates the return an investor can expect when purchasing ordinary shares in a company.

The *price earnings ratio* is the number of times the current market price exceeds the current earnings per share. It shows how many current year's dividends would be needed to purchase the shares at today's price.

(c) In the short run Moira Ltd would appear to be a better investment since the yield on the shares is greater at 10%. In the longer term Down Ltd has the advantage of larger earnings per share. The smaller yield and the higher dividend cover shows that more of the company's profits are being ploughed back. Moira Ltd. is more highly geared with a gearing ratio of 67% (£1,020/£1,520). If profits were to fall significantly the debenture interest of £100,000 must still be paid. Down Ltd has a gearing ratio of 31% (£500/£1,600). Advice would be based on the time horizon for the investment.

# CASH FLOW STATEMENTS

## Units in this chapter

7.1   *Uses of cash flow statements*
7.2   *Construction of a cash flow statement using FRS 1*

## Chapter objectives

FRS 1 Cash Flow Statements replaced SSAP 10 in 1991. As a new topic it is very popular with examiners. Check with your teacher or consult your examination syllabus to see if answers must be in the FRS 1 format. The largest examination board does not require a detailed knowledge of the FRS 1 statement. Having said that, good presentational skills should always be your aim.

The Accounting Standards Board (ASB) took the view, in 1991 'that a cash flow statement forms an essential element of the information required for accounts to give a true and fair view of the state of affairs of large companies at the end of the financial year, and of the profit or loss for the year'.

The chapter will show how to calculate the necessary components for the production of a cash flow statement in good form.

The key topics and concepts covered in the chapter are:

- FRS 1 layout;
- movements in assets;
- depreciation;
- working capital;
- share capital;
- calculation of profit;
- reconciliation of operating profit to cash flow;
- analysis of changes in cash and cash equivalents;
- revaluation of freehold land;
- bonus shares.

## 7.1 USES OF CASH FLOW STATEMENTS

- The trading and profit and loss accounts concentrate on the determination of profits or losses, since profits should ensure the long-term survival of the business.
- The balance sheet concentrates on the state of affairs of the business.
- Cash flow statements concentrate on cash.

These three statements taken together show summaries of most of the financial information required by the users of accounting information. The cash flow statement takes information from a variety of sources to show an overall picture of the monies flowing into and out of the business during the financial year.

> The statement concentrates on liquidity and may help to explain why, for example, a business needed a bank overdraft in a year when profits were buoyant.

The statement is intended to show information that is not available from examining the profit and loss account and balance sheet. It is intended to fill in gaps in the available published information. The opening balance sheet of a company shows the state of affairs of that company on the first day of the year. The closing balance sheet shows the position on the last day of the year. What has gone on *during* the year?

The profit and loss account bridges the gap from one important perspective: *profits*. The cash flow statement bridges the gap from the equally important perspective of *cash*.

This concentration on liquidity is very important, since the inability to generate cash resources is the biggest single reason for many businesses going into liquidation. The importance of cash to a business is recognised by the ASB. All but the smallest companies are required to produce the statement. Even though small companies, sole traders, and partnerships do not have to produce a cash flow statement, they may find that it is a useful addition to their year end accounting information.

## 7.2 CONSTRUCTION OF A CASH FLOW STATEMENT USING FRS 1

There are three possible layouts for a cash flow statement:
- Exposure draft (ED) 54 direct method,
- ED 54 indirect method, and
- FRS 1.

You should concentrate on using FRS 1.

Questions will generally present two consecutive balance sheets of a company. By comparing the opening balance sheet with the closing one, you can determine the changes that have taken place during the year. Some of the changes are due directly to cash coming into the company or cash going out. Some of the changes will need to be adjusted to arrive at the actual cash movement.

Break your answer into two parts:
1 A clear, neat *layout*.
2 Accurate *calculations*.

## EXAMPLE 1

The following balance sheets were prepared for Waterbury plc as at the dates shown:

| | 28 February 1995 | | 29 February 1996 | |
|---|---|---|---|---|
| | £000 | £000 | £000 | £000 |
| **Fixed assets** | | | | |
| Premises at cost | 3,850 | | 6,200 | |
| Less Depreciation | 1,696 | | 2,162 | |
| | | 2,154 | | 4,038 |
| Machinery at cost | 2,065 | | 2,405 | |
| Less Depreciation | 736 | | 946 | |
| | | 1,329 | | 1,459 |
| Vehicles at cost | 903 | | 903 | |
| Less Depreciation | 416 | | 641 | |
| | | 487 | | 262 |
| | | 3,970 | | 5,759 |
| **Current assets** | | | | |
| Stock | 400 | | 500 | |
| Debtors | 180 | | 176 | |
| Bank | 44 | | 51 | |
| Cash | 17 | | 28 | |
| | 641 | | 755 | |
| **Less Creditors less than a year** | | | | |
| Trade creditors | 170 | | 184 | |
| Taxation | 182 | | 195 | |
| Dividends proposed | 150 | | 160 | |
| | 502 | | 539 | |
| | | 139 | | 216 |
| | | 4,109 | | 5,975 |
| **Less Creditors more than a year** | | | | |
| 8% Debenture stock | | 600 | | 600 |
| Net Assets | | 3,509 | | 5,375 |
| **Capital and reserves:** | | | | |
| Issued share capital | | 1,400 | | 2,100 |
| Share premium | | 560 | | 910 |
| Profit and loss | | 1,549 | | 2,365 |
| | | 3,509 | | 5,375 |

*Points to note*
- No interim dividends were paid.
- No disposals of fixed assets have taken place.

**Required**

A cash flow statement for the year ended 29 February 1996, for Waterbury plc.

**Solution**

**(1) Layout**

*Learn* the following standard headings; they are important. If your answer is in the FRS 1 format the headings are a requirement.

Operating activities.
Returns on investments and servicing of finance.
Taxation.
Investing activities.
Financing.

Some students learn lists like this by remembering capital letters, e.g. **ORTIF**, or by using a mnemonic such as **Oprah Returns Tax In Finland**.

In addition, two notes to the statement are usually required in examination questions:

- **Reconciliation of operating profit to net cash flow from operating activities.** This note takes the profit for the year and adjusts the figure to reveal the cash flow generated for the year.

- **Analysis of changes in cash and cash equivalents during the year.** This note takes the balances of cash and cash equivalents at the start of the year, makes the adjustment calculated in the cash flow statement, and the result should be the balances of cash and cash equivalents at the end of the year.

Use the correct main heading, **Waterbury plc cash flow statement for the year ended 29 February 1996,** and put the correct section headings in place.

Leave six lines between each heading. You will not have six entries under each heading, but you may make an error or two that needs to be crossed out (neatly). This will give you enough space to put in the figures from your calculations.

## (2) The calculations

Compare the figures given in the balance sheet prepared for the first day of the year (last day of last year), with the figures given in the balance sheet prepared for the last day of this year.

Any difference is due to cash coming in to the company or cash going out of the company during the year. Initially, list these changes under the headings of *cash coming in* and *cash going out*. This categorisation will be used as preparation for the production of a well-presented statement for your answer. Start at the top of the balance sheets and systematically work down to the last item, noting the changes under the two headings above.

Premises on the first day of the year had cost £3,850,000; on the last day of the year premises had cost £6,200,000. Waterbury plc must have bought some additional premises during the year at a cost of £2,350,000 – cash must have been spent to acquire these extra premises.

| Cash coming in | Cash going out | |
| --- | --- | --- |
| | Purchase of premises | £2,350,000 |

The next item on the balance sheets is depreciation. Let us consider depreciation before we deal with it. The double entry treatment for depreciation is:

| Debit profit & loss account | Credit provision for depreciation account |
| --- | --- |
| (or manufacturing account) | |

To help you understand why depreciation should be included in the cash flow statement, imagine Barry is a trader who pays all expenses immediately with cash and does not allow any customer credit facilities. A week's transactions are summarised below in Barry's trading and profit and loss account. Any profit shown in the revenue account must be equal to the increase in Barry's cash balances.

| | £ | | £ |
| --- | --- | --- | --- |
| Purchases | 200 | Sales | 500 |
| Expenses | 160 | | |
| **Net profit** | **140** | | |
| | 500 | | 500 |

Barry's cash book for the week would show:

| | £ | | £ |
| --- | --- | --- | --- |
| Sales revenue | 500 | Purchases | 200 |
| | | Expenses | 160 |
| | | **Cash balance carried forward** | **140** |
| | 500 | | 500 |

Barry's cash is equal to his profit. As a good accounting student, you tell Barry that he will have to include some depreciation in the revenue statement to reflect the use of the van he uses to pick up his purchases (accruals concept). You adjust his revenue statement accordingly:

| | £ | | £ |
| --- | --- | --- | --- |
| Purchase | 200 | Sales | 500 |
| Expenses | 160 | | |
| Depreciation of van | 40 | | |
| Net profit | 100 | | |
| | 500 | | 500 |

The profits have fallen but the cash remains the same at £140.

Depreciation reduces profits but does not reduce cash.

Cash flows are needed for a cash flow statement. Profits need to be adjusted to take into account non-cash items that have reduced profits but have had no effect on the cash flows of the company. We need to compensate for these items. If we know the profit figure we should be able to arrive at the cash figure quite simply.

Barry's profit, after we adjusted his revenue statement to take into account the use of his van, was £100. To find the cash flow into the business we need to add the depreciation to his reported profit. Then we have his cash in-flow.

|  | £ |
| --- | --- |
| Profit | 100 |
| Add depreciation | 40 |
| Cash in-flow | 140 |

Now back to Waterbury plc. The depreciation on premises for Waterbury plc for the year ended 29 February 1996 is £466,000. This amount will have been debited to the profit and loss account, thus reducing the profits, but it will not have reduced the cash balances of the company. We need to add the depreciation figure to the profit for the year. Since the profit will have resulted in cash coming into the company depreciation also needs to go in the 'cash coming in' column.

| Cash coming in | £ | Cash going out | £ |
| --- | --- | --- | --- |
| Depreciation on premises | 466,000 | Purchases of premises | 2,350,000 |

Do the same calculations for the other assets. Your table should say:

| Cash coming in | £ | Cash going out | £ |
| --- | --- | --- | --- |
| Depreciation of premises | 466,000 | Purchase of premises | 2,350,000 |
| Depreciation of machinery | 210,000 | Purchase of machinery | 340,000 |
| Depreciation of vehicles | 225,000 | | |

Disposals of assets will be dealt with later.

Adjustments need to be made in order to cancel out the effects that the accruals concept has had on the profit figure. Remember, *expense figures in the profit and loss accounts show the value of resources used, not the money spent to acquire the resources.*

The next item on the way down the balance sheets is stock. The stock figure has gone from £400,000 at the start of the year to £500,000 at the year end. The company has bought more stock. These purchases use cash. So:

| Cash coming in | | Cash going out | |
| --- | --- | --- | --- |
| | | Increase in stocks | £100,000 |

Next are debtors. At the start of the year they amounted to £180,000; at the end of the year they were only £176,000, a reduction of £4,000 implying a cash inflow.

The next two items on the balance sheet (bank and cash) are ignored, because this is the whole point of the statement: *to identify any changes in cash and cash equivalents and to analyse what has caused the changes.*

Creditors on the first day of the year were owed £170,000; by the end of the year they were owed £184,000, an increase of £14,000. This implies a cash inflow. The lists of inflows and outflows now looks like this:

| Cash coming in | £ | Cash going out | £ |
| --- | --- | --- | --- |
| Depreciation of premises | 466,000 | Purchase of premises | 2,350,000 |
| Depreciation of machinery | 210,000 | Purchase of machinery | 340,000 |
| Depreciation of vehicles | 225,000 | Increase in stock | 100,000 |
| Decrease in debtors | 4,000 | | |
| Increase in creditors | 14,000 | | |

Under the heading 'creditors less than a year' we see that the company owed the Inland Revenue £195,000. This figure has been entered on the profit and loss appropriation account of the company, and so will have reduced the profits, but it will not be paid to the authorities for some time yet. Although it has reduced Waterbury's profits it has not reduced the cash in the year we are considering.

To find the cash flow *this year* we need to add it back to our profits like Barry's depreciation. Similarly, proposed dividends appear as a short-term creditor, the cash outflow will occur in the next financial year also, so these too need to be added to our profit to arrive at the cash generated by the business through its trading activities.

| Cash coming in | £ | Cash going out |
|---|---|---|
| Taxation | 195,000 | |
| Proposed dividends | 160,000 | |

In last year's cash flow statement the same adjustment were made. But, last year's tax and last year's proposed dividends were 'creditors less than a year' on the balance sheet at the start of the year. These dividends will have been paid by the company in the year under consideration.

| Cash coming in | Cash going out | £ |
|---|---|---|
| | Last year's tax liability | 182,000 |
| | Last year's proposed dividend | 150,000 |

The issued share capital has increased by £700,000. The company obviously sold some more shares; this would bring cash into the company. The share premium account has increased by £350,000. The company clearly sold the new shares at a premium of 50p per share, so raising the extra money – more cash coming in.

The retained profits have increased by £816,000 over the year – a cash inflow. Finally, an entry needs to be made for the debenture interest. It has to be included in both columns:

| Cash coming in | £ | Cash going out | £ |
|---|---|---|---|
| Debenture interest | 48,000 | Debenture interest | 48,000 |

The final table now looks like this:

| Cash coming in | £ | Cash going out | £ |
|---|---|---|---|
| Depreciation of premises | 466,000 | Purchase of premises | 2,350,000 |
| Depreciation of machinery | 210,000 | Purchase of machinery | 340,000 |
| Depreciation of vehicles | 225,000 | Increase in stock | 100,000 |
| Decrease in debtors | 4,000 | Taxation (last year's liability) | 182,000 |
| Increase in creditors | 14,000 | Dividends (last year's proposed) | 150,000 |
| Taxation (this year's liability) | 195,000 | Debenture interest | 48,000 |
| Dividends (this year's proposed) | 160,000 | | |
| Share issue | 700,000 | | |
| Share Premium Account | 350,000 | | |
| Increase in P & L account | 816,000 | | |
| Debenture interest | 48,000 | | |

These cash flows now need to be put under the correct headings. Can you remember the layout of the headings? (Oprah Returns Tax In Finland.)

**Waterbury plc cash flow statement for the year ended 29 February 1996**

| | £000 | £000 |
|---|---|---|
| Operating activities: Net cash inflow | | 2,038 |
| Returns on investments and servicing of finance | | |
|    Debenture interest paid | (48) | |
|    Dividends paid | (150) | |
| Net cash outflow from returns on investments and servicing of finance | | (198) |
| Taxation | (182) | |
|    Corporation tax paid | | (182) |
| Investing activities | | |
|    Payments to acquire tangible fixed assets (2,350 + 340) | (2,690) | |
|    Net cash outflow from investing activities | | (2,690) |
| Net cash outflow before financing | | (1,032) |
| Financing | | |
|    Issue of ordinary shares (including premium) | 1,050 | |
| | | 1,050 |
| Increase in cash and cash equivalents | | 18 |

*Points to note*

- Reconciliation of operating profit to net cash inflow from operating activities:

| | £000 |
|---|---|
| Operating profit · | 1,219 |
| Depreciation (466 + 210 + 225) | 901 |
| Decrease in debtors | 4 |
| Increase in creditors | 14 |
| Increase in stock | (100) |
| Net cash inflow from operating activities | 2,038 |

- Calculation of operating profit:

| | £000 |
|---|---|
| Retained profits | 816 |
| Corporation tax | 195 |
| Proposed dividends | 160 |
| Debenture interest | 48 |
| Operating profit | 1,219 |

- Analysis of changes in cash and cash equivalents in the year:

| | £000 |
|---|---|
| Balance at 1 March 1995 | 61 |
| Net cash inflow | 18 |
| Balance at 29 February 1996 | 79 |

- More detail of this analysis may be given as follows. Analysis of the balances of cash and cash equivalents as shown in the balance sheet:

| | 1995 | 1996 | Change in year |
|---|---|---|---|
| | £000 | £000 | £000 |
| Cash at bank | 44 | 51 | 7 |
| Cash in hand | 17 | 28 | 11 |
| | 61 | 79 | 18 |

Let us examine other areas that seem to give some students problems:

- Calculation of the profit figure to use in the reconciliation statement.
- The cash flows resulting from the disposals of fixed assets.
- Treatment of the revaluation of freehold land.
- Treatment of the issue of bonus shares.

## Calculation of the profit figure for use in the reconciliation statement

Some examination questions give an appropriation account while others do not.

### EXAMPLE 2

**Neal, Herringbone & Co Ltd balance sheet extracts as at 31 December 1995**

| 1994 | | £000 |
|---|---|---|
| | Creditors: amounts falling due within one year | |
| 180 | Taxation | 192 |
| 150 | Proposed dividend | 145 |
| | Share capital and reserves: | |
| 936 | Profit and loss account | 1,242 |
| 90 | General reserve | 140 |

**Neal, Herringbone & Co Ltd profit and loss account extract
for the year ended 31 December 1995**

|  | £000 | £000 |
|---|---|---|
| Profit before tax |  | 748 |
| Taxation |  | 192 |
| Profit after tax |  | 556 |
| Transfer to general reserve | 50 |  |
| Ordinary interim dividend paid | 55 |  |
| Proposed dividend | 145 | 250 |
| Retained profit for the year |  | 306 |
| Retained profit b/fwd |  | 936 |
| Retained profit c/fwd |  | 1,242 |

*Points to note*
- Interest charges for the year are £84,000.
- Interest received for the year is £20,000.

## Required

A calculation of profit before tax and interest for the year ended 31 December 1995 for Neal, Herringbone & Co Ltd.

## Solution

If only the balance sheet was given in the question then the calculation of profit would be:

|  | £000 |  |
|---|---|---|
| Increase in profit and loss account | 306 |  |
| Taxation (this year's figure ) | 192 |  |
| Transfer to reserve | 50 | ❶ |
| Proposed dividend (this year's figure) | 145 |  |
| Dividends paid | 55 |  |
| Interest paid | 84 | ❷ |
| Interest received | (20) |  |
|  | 812 |  |

❶ Added back – reduced profit but not cash.

❷ Adjusted but also included in body of statement.

If the profit and loss appropriation account was given in the question then the calculation is so much simpler:

|  | £000 |
|---|---|
| Profit before tax | 748 |
| Interest paid | 84 |
| Interest received | (20) |
|  | 812 |

As you can see, both arrive at the same figure.

Use the following example to identify the cash flows involved when a profit is made on the sale of an asset.

## EXAMPLE 3

A piece of machinery costing £67,000, that had been depreciated by £41,000, was sold for £30,000.

## Required

Show the appropriate cash flows for the above transaction.

## Solution

Cash inflows:   Sale of machinery £30,000
                Profit on the sale  (£4,000)   (treat as a negative inflow rather than an outflow).

## EXAMPLE 4

A computer costing £28,000, that had depreciated by £21,000, was sold for £5,000.

**Required**
Show the appropriate cash flows for the above transaction.

**Solution**

Cash inflows:  Sale of computer           £5,000
               Loss on sale of computer   £2,000

Workings:

**Computer at cost**

|  |  |  |
|---|---|---|
|  | Disposal | £28,000 |

**Provision for depreciation of computer**

| Disposal | £21,000 |
|---|---|

**Disposal of computer**

|  | £ |  | £ |
|---|---|---|---|
| Computer | 28,000 | Depreciation | 21,000 |
|  |  | Cash | 5,000 |
|  |  | P & L account | 2,000 |
|  | 28,000 |  | 28,000 |

It is well worth spending some time going through these examples very thoroughly to make sure you understand where the cash flows are and how the figures have been arrived at.

## Treatment of the revaluation of freehold land and treatment of the issue of bonus shares

These are changes which take place during the financial year which will have an impact on the company's balance sheet, but are not the result of any movements in cash or cash equivalents.

EXAMPLE 5

**Fellside plc balance sheet extracts as at 31 January**

|  | 1995 | 1996 |
|---|---|---|
|  | £000 | £000 |
| Freehold land and buildings | 1,650 | 2,880 |
| Ordinary share capital | 7,500 | 10,000 |
| Share premium | 900 |  |
| Profit and loss account | 2,743 | 3,971 |

During the year ended 31 January 1996 Fellside plc revalued their freehold land and buildings. There were no additions or disposals. Fellside does not charge depreciation on freehold land or buildings.

During the year the company made a bonus issue of 1 ordinary share for every 3 held at 31 January 1995. The Company's capital reserves were fully used; the profit and loss account was used to fund the remainder of the capitalisation.

**Required**
Show the cash flows which have resulted from the transactions indicated.

**Solution**
There have been no cash flows as a result of the revaluation or as a result of the bonus issue. The ledger accounts show the following:

**Freehold land and buildings**

|  | £000 |  | £000 |
|---|---|---|---|
| Balance 1 February 1995 b/d | 1,650 | 31 January 1996 c/d | 2,880 |
| ❶Revaluation reserve | 1,230 |  |  |
|  | 2,880 |  | 2,880 |
| Balance 1 February 1996 | 2,880 |  |  |

**Revaluation reserve**

|  |  |  |  |
|---|---|---|---|
| ❷Bonus account | 1,230 | ❶Freehold Land & Buildings | 1,230 |

**Share premium account**

| | | | |
|---|---|---|---|
| ❸Bonus account | 900 | Balance 1 February 1995 b/d | 900 |

**Profit and loss account**

| | | | |
|---|---|---|---|
| ❹Bonus account | 370 | Balance 1 February 1995 | 2,743 |
| Balance 31 January 1996 c/d | 3,971 | Profits for year ended 31 January 96. | 1,598 |
| | 4,341 | | 4,341 |
| | | Balance 1 February 1996 | 3,971 |

**Bonus account**

| | | | |
|---|---|---|---|
| ❺Ordinary Share capital | 2,500 | ❷Revaluation reserve | 1,230 |
| | | ❸Share premium | 900 |
| | | ❹Profit & Loss | 370 |
| | 2,500 | | 2,500 |

**Ordinary share capital**

| | | | |
|---|---|---|---|
| | | Balance 1 February 1995 | 7,500 |
| | | ❺Bonus account | 2,500 |

*Point to note*

The numbered bullets in the accounts show where the same figure appears in the different accounts.

## The cash flows resulting from the disposals of fixed assets

EXAMPLE 6

The summarised balance sheets of Drossney Ltd as at 30 November are as follows:

| | £000 | 1994 £000 | £000 | £000 | 1995 £000 | £000 |
|---|---|---|---|---|---|---|
| Fixed assets at cost | | 1,842 | | | 2,032 | |
| Less depreciation | | 807 | 1,035 | | 978 | 1,054 |
| Current assets | | | | | | |
| Stock | | 1,878 | | | 2,252 | |
| Debtors | 1,148 | | | 1,200 | | |
| Less provision for bad debts | 55 | 1,093 | | 56 | 1,144 | |
| Bank | | 317 | | | | |
| Cash | | 42 | | | 26 | |
| | | 3,330 | | | 3,422 | |
| Less creditors: less than one year: | | | | | | |
| Trade creditors | 600 | | | 801 | | |
| Taxation | 170 | | | 138 | | |
| Dividends | 328 | | | 105 | | |
| Bank overdraft | | 1,098 | 2,232 | 65 | 1,109 | 2,313 |
| | | | 3,267 | | | 3,367 |
| Less creditors: more than one year | | | | | | |
| 7% Debentures | | | 1,000 | | | 750 |
| | | | 2,267 | | | 2,617 |
| Capital and reserves: | | | | | | |
| Issued share capital | | | 1,800 | | | 2,000 |
| Share premium | | | 120 | | | 210 |
| Profit and loss | | | 347 | | | 407 |
| | | | 2,267 | | | 2,617 |

*Points to note*

- During the year fixed assets costing £570,000, which had been depreciated by £342,000, had been sold for £217,000.
- Corporation tax paid during the year was £165,000.
- An interim dividend amounting to £15,000 was paid during the year.
- Debenture interest paid during the year was £70,000.

**Required**
A cash flow statement for Drossney Ltd for the year ended 30 November 1995.

**Solution**
*Workings*
We need to draw up some 'T' accounts to determine the cash flows.

**Fixed assets**

| | £000 | | £000 |
|---|---|---|---|
| Balance 1 December 1994 | 1,842 | Disposal ❶ | 570 |
| Bank *(Missing figure)** | 760 | Balance 30 November 1995 c/d | 2,032 |
| | 2,602 | | 2,602 |
| Balance b/d | 2,032 | | |

**Depreciation of fixed assets**

| | £000 | | £000 |
|---|---|---|---|
| Disposal ❷ | 342 | Balance 1 December 1994 | 807 |
| Balance 30 November 1995 c/d | 978 | P & L a/c *(Missing figure)** | 513 |
| | 1,320 | | 1,320 |
| | | Balance b/d | 978 |

**Disposal of fixed assets**

| | £000 | | £000 |
|---|---|---|---|
| Fixed assets ❶ | 570 | Depreciation of fixed assets ❷ | 342 |
| | | Bank* | 217 |
| | | P & L a/c *(Missing figure)** | 11 |
| | 570 | | 570 |

The opening and closing balances on the accounts are derived from the two balance sheets. The assets that were sold are transferred to the disposal account ❶ along with the depreciation that 'belongs' to the assets sold ❷.

You can see that these workings are a rich source of marks in this type of question. Each figure marked * is a cash flow, or is the figure to be used in the cash flow statement, and will gain you marks for its identification.

The missing figure on the debit side of the asset account can only be

* the purchase of an asset or
* a revaluation.

Since the question does not mention a revaluation of fixed assets we must assume that Drossney Ltd has purchased more assets.

The missing figure on the credit side of the depreciation account must be this year's depreciation. On the profit and loss account it has reduced profits but has had no effect on the company's cash, therefore it has to be added to the profit figure to arrive at the cash generated. Since the profit represents a cash inflow we treat the depreciation as an inflow too.

The loss on disposal will have been debited as an expense on the profit and loss account. The entry has reduced the profit but, like depreciation it is merely a book entry, no cash has moved. It has to be added to the profit just like the depreciation figure for the year. The cash flow is the £217,000 the buyer paid. The cash received for the sale is debited to the bank and credited to the disposal account.

**Drossney Ltd cash flow statement for the year ended 30 November 1995**

| | £000 | £000 |
|---|---|---|
| Operating activities: Net cash inflow | | 683 |
| Returns on investments and servicing of finance | | |
| Debenture interest paid | (70) | |
| Dividends paid | (343) | |
| Net cash outflow from returns on investments and servicing of finance | | (413) |
| Taxation | (165) | |
| Corporation tax paid | | (165) |

|  | £000 | £000 |
|---|---|---|
| Investing activities |  |  |
| Payments to acquire tangible fixed assets | (760) |  |
| Receipts from sales of tangible fixed assets | 217 |  |
| Net cash outflow from investing activities |  | (543) |
| Net cash outflow before financing |  | (438) |
| Financing |  |  |
| Issue of ordinary shares (including premium) | 290 |  |
| Redemption of debentures | (250) |  |
| Net cash inflow from financing |  | 40 |
| Decrease in cash and cash equivalents |  | (398) |

Reconciliation of operating profit to net cash inflow from operating activities:

|  | £000 |
|---|---|
| Operating profit | 383 |
| Depreciation | 513 |
| Increase in debtors | (52) |
| Increase in creditors | 201 |
| Increase in stock | (374) |
| Loss on disposal of fixed asset | 11 |
| Increase in provision for bad debts | 1 |
|  | 683 |

Calculation of operating profit:

|  | £000 |
|---|---|
| Retained profit | 60 |
| Corporation tax provision | 133 |
| Proposed dividends | 105 |
| Interim dividend | 15 |
| Debenture interest | 70 |
|  | 383 |

Analysis of changes in cash and cash equivalents:

|  | £000 |
|---|---|
| Balance 1 December 1994 | 359 |
| Net cash outflow | (398) |
| Balance 30 November 1995 | (39) |

Analysis of the balances of cash and cash equivalents as shown in the balance sheet:

|  | £000 | £000 | £000 |
|---|---|---|---|
| Cash at bank | 317 | (65) | (382) |
| Cash in hand | 42 | 26 | (16) |
| Balance 30 November 1995 | 359 | (39) | (398) |

You may understand the concept more clearly by imagining a personal example. If you believe your personal stereo is worth £25.00 and you sell it to a friend for £20.00, the cash flow is £20.00, the loss is merely in your mind.

If you feel confident you may have drawn out the actual cash flow statement. You can start to put the figures into it. If not, list the cash flows as before.

| **Cash in** |  | **Cash out** |  |
|---|---|---|---|
|  | £ |  | £ |
| Sale of fixed assets | 217,000 | Purchase of fixed assets | 760,000 |
| Depreciation of fixed assets | 513,000 |  |  |
| Loss on disposal of fixed assets | 11,000 |  |  |

Continuing down the balance sheet in a systematic way:

|  |  |
|---|---|
| Increase in stock | 374,000 |
| Increase in debtors | 52,000 |

The increase in the provision for bad debts is rather like extra depreciation of the debtors, so it can be treated in the same way that the extra depreciation was treated.

Increased provision for bad debts     £1,000

The changes in cash and bank balances will be calculated in our analysis later.

Increase in creditors £201,000

If the question indicates the amount of tax paid, and it is different from last year's liability an account should be prepared.

**Taxation**

| | £ | | £ |
|---|---|---|---|
| Bank* | 165,000 | Balance 1 December 1994 c/d | 170,000 |
| Balance 30 November 1995 c/d | 138,000 | P & L a/c *(Missing figure)** | 133,000 |
| | 303,000 | | 303,000 |
| | | Balance b/d | 138,000 |

The opening and closing balances in the account came from the information on the two balance sheets. The bank figure (tax actually paid) was given in the question. The only missing piece of information was the entry on the profit and loss account. This figure is only a book entry – it is an informed estimate of what the directors believe the company may have to pay in corporation tax. It has reduced the profit, but not the cash (the payment of £165,000 reduced the cash). It needs to be added back to the profit as a cash inflow.

Since the question did not show an appropriation account an adjustment to the profit figure needs to be made for this year's tax and dividends paid and provided for.

| | | £000 | |
|---|---|---|---|
| Net profit before appropriations | | 313,000 ❸ | |
| Less taxation | 133,000 ❷ | | |
| dividends paid | 15,000 ❷ | | |
| proposed | 105,000 ❷ | 253,000 | |
| Retained profits for the year | | 60,000 ❶ | |

❶ Use this figure, calculated from the balance sheet.

❷ Add taxation and dividends to arrive at the figure that is needed ❸.

Taxation (this year's) £133,000     Taxation paid (last year's liability) £165,000

Last year's proposed dividend was paid during this year, so is a cash outflow. This year's proposed dividend needs to be added to the profit since it is not yet a cash outflow (it will be paid in the next financial year, if ratified at the company's annual general meeting by the shareholders).

Proposed dividend (this year's) £105,000     Dividends paid (last years proposed)£328,000

In the simplified example above it says that dividends need to be added to the calculation of the profit to arrive at the operating profit. The interim dividend also needs to be added back. It is a cash outflow since it has been paid during the year.

Dividends paid £15,000     Dividends paid £15,000

Debenture interest paid is treated in the same way as the interim dividends.

Debenture interest paid £70,000     Debenture interest paid £70,000

Continuing down the balance sheet: on the first day of the year the company had a long term debt of £100,000. By the end of the year only £750,000 was owed to the debenture holders. Part of the loan has been repaid.

Redemption of debentures £250,000

The share capital has increased by £200,000 and the share premium has increased by £90,000.

Issue of shares £290,000

And finally, the retained profits for the year.

Retained profit £60,000

There are changes which take place during the financial year which will have an impact on the company's balance sheet but is not the result of any movements in cash or cash equivalents.

## Chapter roundup

Chapter 7 shows how to construct a cash flow statement. This a fairly new topic and therefore popular with examiners.

Cash is a vital element in the survival of a business in the short term. Without cash a business would not survive for very long.

You should be able to calculate business transactions which cause money to be received by a business and to identify the actions that cause outflows of cash.

Once these cash flows have been identified you should be able to formalise them into a cash flow statement.

# Illustrative questions

1  Armstrong Stearstree plc is a manufacturing company which produces components for the motor industry. The balance sheet of the company as at 31 May 1994 was as follows:

| 1993 £000 | | 1994 £000 | £000 |
|---|---|---|---|
| | Fixed assets (Note 1): | | |
| 8,645 | Land and buildings | | 10,900 |
| 1,600 | Machinery | | 945 |
| 500 | Vehicles | | 450 |
| 10,745 | | | 12,295 |
| | Investments at cost (market value at | | |
| 2,400 | 31 May 1994 £2,200,000) | | 2,400 |
| | Current assets | | |
| 820 | Stock | 950 | |
| 260 | Debtors | 450 | |
| 132 | Cash at bank and in hand | 87 | |
| 1,212 | | 1,487 | |
| | Creditors: amounts falling due within one year | | |
| 318 | Creditors | 510 | |
| 180 | Proposed dividend | 190 | |
| 180 | Corporation tax | 200 | |
| 678 | | 900 | |
| 534 | Net current assets (liabilities) | | 587 |
| 13,679 | Total assets less current liabilities | | 15,282 |
| | Creditors: amounts falling due after more than one year | | |
| 500 | 12% debenture stock | | 500 |
| 13,179 | | | 14,782 |
| | Capital and reserves | | |
| 5,750 | Called up share capital | | 6,000 |
| 2,200 | Share premium account | | 2,350 |
| – | Revaluation reserve | | 1,500 |
| 5,229 | Profit and loss account (Note 2) | | 4,932 |
| 13,179 | | | 14,782 |

*Notes to the balance sheet*

(1) Fixed assets

|  | 31 May 1993<br>£000 | 31 May 1994<br>£000 |
|---|---|---|
| Land and buildings: | | |
| Cost | 10,500 | 11,650 |
| Revaluation | | 1,500 |
| Depreciation to date | (1,855) | (2,250) |
| Net book value | 8,645 | 10,900 |
| Machinery | | |
| Cost | 4,000 | ? |
| Depreciation to date | (2,400) | ? |
| Net book value | 1,600 | ? |
| Vehicles | | |
| Cost | 900 | 1,000 |
| Depreciation to date | (400) | (550) |
| Net book value | 500 | 400 |

During the year ended 31 May 1994 machinery which had originally cost £400,000 was sold for £275,000. The depreciation charged on this machinery up to 31 May 1993 was £150,000. No additions to machinery were made during the year. There were no disposals of land, buildings or motor vehicles during the year.

(2) The summarised profit and loss appropriation account for the year ended 31 May 1994 is as follows:

|  | £000 | £000 |
|---|---|---|
| Net profit for the year before taxation | | 203 |
| Provision for corporation tax | | 200 |
| Net profit for the year after taxation | | 3 |
| Balance brought forward | | 5,229 |
| | | 5,232 |
| Interim dividend | | |
| (paid on 2 February 1994) | 110 | |
| Proposed final dividend | 190 | 300 |
| Balance carried forward | | 4,932 |

*Required*

(a) Prepare a cash flow statement for Armstrong Stearstree plc for the year ended 31 May 1994                                                                                      (36)

(b) Explain how the preparation of a cash flow statement can be of use to a company's shareholders.                                                                          (14)

*Tutorial note*

Prepare your cash flow statement by putting the headings in place (remember Oprah!). Gain the easy marks quickly (changes in stocks, debtors etc), then show detailed workings for your calculations to determine cash flows involved in the movement assets. In part (b) go through the statement and explain what has happened to produce the figures in each section.

*Suggested answer*

(a)

**Armstrong Stearstree plc cash flow statement
for the year ended 31 May 1995**

| | £000 | £000 |
|---|---:|---:|
| Net cash flow from operating activities | | 1,060 |
| Returns on investment and servicing of finance | | |
| Interest payable | (60) | |
| Dividends paid | (290) | |
| Net cash outflow from returns on investment and servicing of finance | | (350) |
| Taxation | (180) | |
| Corporation tax paid | | (180) |
| Investing activities | | |
| Purchase of tangible fixed assets | (1,250) | |
| Sale of tangible fixed assets | 275 | |
| Net cash outflow from investing activities | | (975) |
| Net cash outflow before financing | | (445) |
| Financing | | |
| Issue of shares | 400 | |
| Net cash inflow from financing | | 400 |
| Decrease in cash and cash equivalents | | (45) |

**Reconciliation of operating profit to net cash inflow
from operating activities**

| | £000 |
|---|---:|
| Operating profit | 263 |
| Depreciation 395 + 405❶ + 150 | 950 |
| Increase in creditors | 192 |
| Increase in stocks | (130) |
| Increase in debtors | (190) |
| Profit on disposal of machinery❷ | (25) |
| Net cash inflow from operating activities | 1,060 |

❶ **Depreciation of machinery**

| | | | | |
|---|---:|---|---:|
| Disposal | 150 | Balance b/d | 2,400 |
| Balance c/d | 2,655 | Profit and loss account | 405 |
| | 2,805 | | 2,805 |
| | | Balance b/d | 2,655 |

❷ **Disposal of machinery**

| | | | |
|---|---:|---|---:|
| Machinery | 400 | Depreciation | 150 |
| Profit and loss account | 25 | Cash | 275 |
| | 425 | | 425 |

**Analysis of changes in cash and cash equivalents**

| | £000 |
|---|---:|
| Balance 1 June 1993 | 132 |
| Net cash outflow | (45) |
| Balance 31 May 1994 | 87 |

(b) Cash flow statement concentrates on liquidity. This is important as liquidity problems often cause business failure.

Shows liquidity picture between balance sheet dates.

Explains why profits and losses are different from changes in cash and cash equivalents.

Clearly shows changes in assets and liabilities: movements in assets; issues of shares and debentures.

Shows sources of internal financing and extent of external financing during the year.

**2** Patel Johnstone plc is a company which manufactures kitchen equipment. The company balance sheet as at 31 May 1995 was as follows:

| 1994 £ | | 1995 £ | £ |
|---|---|---|---|
| | Fixed assets (Note 1) | | |
| 220,000 | Premises | | 264,000 |
| 100,000 | Machinery | | 72,400 |
| 40,000 | Vehicles | | 22,500 |
| 360,000 | | | 358,900 |
| 30,000 | Investments | | 30,000 |
| | Current assets | | |
| 19,000 | Stock | 23,000 | |
| 8,000 | Debtors | 7,000 | |
| 4,000 | Bank balance | – | |
| 1,000 | Cash balance | 2,000 | |
| 32,000 | | 32,000 | |
| | Creditors: amounts falling due within one year | | |
| 6,000 | Creditors | 9,000 | |
| – | Bank overdraft | 15,400 | |
| 12,000 | Proposed ordinary dividend | – | |
| 5,600 | Proposed preference dividend | 5,600 | |
| 23,600 | | 30,000 | |
| 8,400 | Net current assets (liabilities) | | 2,000 |
| 398,400 | | | 390,900 |
| | Creditors: amounts falling due after more than one year | | |
| 100,000 | 12% debentures 1994 (Note 2) | | – |
| – | 7% debentures 2025 (Note 2) | | 40,000 |
| 298,400 | | | 350,900 |
| | Capital and reserves | | |
| 150,000 | Ordinary share capital | | 230,000 |
| 70,000 | 8% Preference share capital | | 70,000 |
| 30,000 | Share premium account | | – |
| 34,400 | Retained earnings | | 36,900 |
| 14,000 | General reserve | | 14,000 |
| 298,400 | | | 350,900 |

### Notes to the balance sheet

(1) Fixed assets

| | 31 May 1994 £ | 31 May 1995 £ |
|---|---|---|
| Premises | | |
| Cost | 250,000 | |
| Valuation | | 300,000 |
| Depreciation | 30,000 | 36,000 |
| Net book value | 220,000 | 264,000 |
| Machinery | | |
| Cost | 180,000 | ? |
| Depreciation | 80,000 | ? |
| Net book value | 100,000 | 72,400 |
| Vehicles | | |
| Cost | 175,000 | 210,000 |
| Depreciation | 135,000 | 187,500 |
| Net book value | 40,000 | 22,500 |

(i) During the year ended 31 May 1995 the premises were re-valued at £300,000.

(ii) During the year ended 31 May 1995 a machine which had cost £24,000 six years ago was sold for £10,000.

(iii) The accumulated depreciation charged on this machine to the year ended 31 May 1994 amounted to £14,500.

(iv) No machinery was acquired during the year.

(v) There were no disposals of premises or vehicles during the year.

(2) The 12% debentures were redeemed at par on 30 November 1994 (no transfer to a capital redemption reserve was made).

On the same date a new issue of 7% debentures was made at par, and all were sold.

(3) A bonus issue of shares had been made during the year to 31 May 1995. The revaluation reserve and the share premium account had been utilised for this purpose.

*Required*

(a) Prepare a cash flow statement for Patel Johnstone plc for the year ended 31 May 1995. (32)

(b) Explain the reasons for producing a cash flow statement. (12)

(c) Outline **two** measures which may be taken to improve a poor working capital situation. (6)

(AEB)

*Tutorial note*

Refer to the comments for Q1 Armstrong Stearstree for notes for parts (a) and (b).

*Suggested answer*

(a)
### Patel Johnstone plc cash flow statement for the year ended 31 May 1995

|  | £ | £ |
|---|---|---|
| Net cash inflow from operating activities |  | 91,600 |
| Returns on investments and servicing of finance |  |  |
| Ordinary dividends paid | (12,000) |  |
| Preference dividend paid | (5,600) |  |
| Debenture interest paid | (7,400) |  |
| Net cash outflow from returns on investments and servicing of finance |  | (25,000) |
| Investing activities |  |  |
| Payments to acquire new vehicles | (35,000) |  |
| Receipt from sale of machinery | 10,000 |  |
| Net cash outflow from investing activities |  | (25,000) |
| Net cash inflow before financing |  | 41,600 |
| Financing |  |  |
| Redemption of debentures | (100,000) |  |
| Issue of debentures | 40,000 |  |
| Net cash outflow from financing |  | (60,000) |
| Decrease in cash and cash equivalents |  | (18,400) |

### Reconciliation of operating profit to net cash inflow from operating activities

|  | £ |
|---|---|
| Retained profits | 2,500 |
| Depreciation    premises | 6,000 |
| machinery❶ | 18,100 |
| vehicles | 52,500 |
| Profit on sale of machinery❷ | (500) |
| Increase in stocks | (4,000) |
| Decrease in debtors | 1,000 |
| Increase in creditors | 3,000 |
| Interest on debentures❸ | 7,400 |
| Preference share dividends | 5,600 |
| Net cash inflow from operating activities | 91,600 |

**❶**                   **Depreciation of machinery**

| | | | | |
|---|---|---|---|---|
| Disposal | 14,500 | Balance b/d | | 80,000 |
| Balance c/d | 83,600 | P & L a/c | | 18,100 |
| | 98,100 | | | 98,100 |
| | | Balance b/d | | 83,600 |

**❷**                   **Disposal of machinery**

| | | | | |
|---|---|---|---|---|
| Machinery | 24,000 | Depreciation | | 14,500 |
| P & L a/c | 500 | Cash | | 10,000 |
| | 24,500 | | | 24,500 |

**❸**   Debenture interest has been calculated as 12% on £100,000 for 6 months and 7% on £40,000 for 6 months.

**Analysis of changes in cash and cash equivalents during the year**

| | £ | £ |
|---|---|---|
| Cash at bank as at 31 May 1994 | 4,000 | |
| Cash in hand as at 31 May 1994 | 1,000 | 5,000 |
| Net cash outflow | | (18,400) |
| Bank overdraft as at 31 May 1995 | (15,400) | |
| Cash in hand as at 31 May 1995 | 2,000 | (13,400) |

(b)  The organisation may be required to produce a cash flow statement.
The statement helps to 'bridge the gap' between balance sheet dates.
It gives a fuller picture of the financial activities of the business.
It highlights the significant components of cash flows within the business.
Cash flows may be more understandable than profit statements to the non-accountant.
Plus other comments as shown in previous question.

(c)  Sell surplus assets. Sell external investments. Issue shares and or debentures. Borrow long-term from banks etc.

**3**   Set out below are the financial statements and appropriate notes of Bangor plc for the year ended 31 December 1994.

**Balance sheet at 31 December**

| | 1993 | | 1994 | |
|---|---|---|---|---|
| | £000 | £000 | £000 | £000 |
| Fixed assets | | | | |
| Tangible assets (Note 1) | | 740 | | 940 |
| Current assets | | | | |
|     Stock | 152 | | 80 | |
|     Debtors | 240 | | 336 | |
|     Bank | 260 | | 308 | |
| | 652 | | 724 | |
| Creditors: amount falling due within one year | | | | |
|     Trade creditors | 152 | | 104 | |
|     Taxation | 240 | | 200 | |
|     Dividends | 40 | | 80 | |
| | 432 | | 384 | |
| Net current assets | | 220 | | 340 |
| Total assets less current liabilities | | 960 | | 1,280 |
| Creditors: amounts falling due after more than one year | | | | |
|     Bank loans (1996-98) | | (100) | | (200) |
| | | 860 | | 1,080 |
| Capital and reserves | | | | |
|     Called-up share capital (ordinary shares) | | 500 | | 600 |
|     Retained profit | | 360 | | 480 |
| | | 860 | | 1,080 |

### Profit and loss account for the year ended 31 December 1994

|  | £000 |
|---|---|
| Operating profit (Note 2) | 420 |
| Interest payable | (20) |
| Profit on ordinary activities before tax | 400 |
| Taxation | (200) |
| Profit on ordinary activities after tax | 200 |
| Dividends | (80) |
| Retained profit for the year | 120 |
| Retained profit brought forward | 360 |
| Retained profit carried forward | 480 |

## Notes to the balance sheet

| (1) Tangible assets | £000 |
|---|---|
| Cost At 1 January 1994 | 1,400 |
| Additions during the year | 340 |
| At 31 December 1994 | 1,740 |
| Accumulated depreciation | |
| At 1 January 1994 | 660 |
| Charge for the year | 140 |
| At 31 December 1994 | 800 |
| Net book value at 31 December 1994 | 940 |

(2) The operating profit is stated after charging:

|  | £ |
|---|---|
| Depreciation | 140 |
| Auditors remuneration | 8 |
| Directors remuneration | 12 |

*Required*

(a) Prepare a cash flow statement to include relevant notes for the year ended 31 December 1994. (12)

(b) Outline the major purpose of FRS 1 and indicate which users of financial reports will be interested in the information contained in a cash flow statement. (8)

(NICCEA)

*Tutorial note*
Refer to the notes for Q1 and Q2.

*Suggested answer*

### Bangor plc cash flow statement for the year ended 31 December 1994

|  | £000 | £000 |
|---|---|---|
| Net cash inflow from operating activities | | 488 |
| Returns on investments and servicing of finance | | |
| Interest paid | (20) | |
| Dividends paid | (40) | |
| Net cash outflow from returns on investments and servicing of finance | | (60) |
| Taxation | | |
| Corporation tax paid | | (240) |
| Investing activities | | |
| Payments to acquire tangible fixed assets | (340) | |
| Net cash outflow from investing activities | | (340) |
| Net cash inflow before financing | | (152) |
| Financing | | |
| Issue of ordinary share capital | 100 | |
| Increase in bank loans | 100 | |
| Net cash inflow from financing | | 200 |
| Increase in cash and cash equivalents | | 48 |

### Reconciliation of operating profit to net cash inflow from operating activities

| | £ |
|---|---|
| Operating profit | 420 |
| Depreciation | 140 |
| Decrease in stock | 72 |
| Increase in debtors | (96) |
| Decrease in creditors | (48) |
| Net cash inflow from operating activities | 488 |

### Analysis of changes in cash and cash equivalents in the year

| | £ |
|---|---|
| Balance at bank 1 January 1994 | 260 |
| Net cash inflow | 48 |
| Balance at bank 31 December 1994 | 308 |

(b) FRS 1 was introduced in 1991. Its major purpose is to report, in a standard format, on how a company has generated cash and how it has used its cash resources during the year.

The standard format highlights the key components of cash flows, and it also aids comparison between companies.

Cash flow statements highlight liquidity. So, creditors, shareholders, and lenders of finance are among those users of accounts who would pay particular attention to the statement.

# COSTING FOR MATERIALS AND LABOUR

## Units in this chapter

8.1   *Accounting for materials*
8.2   *Methods of stock valuation*
8.3   *Wage systems*
8.4   *Accounting for labour*
8.5   *Remuneration of labour*
8.6   *Manufacturing accounts*

## Chapter objectives

A major function of the cost accountant in any business is to determine unit costs as an aid to the planning and control of that business.

The costs of a product are calculated as follows:

|  | £000 |
|---|---|
| Direct materials | 123 |
| Direct labour | 456 |
| Other direct expenses | 78 |
| Prime cost | 657 |
| Production overheads | 910 |
| Total production cost | 1,567 |
| Administrative overheads | 111 |
| Selling and distribution overheads | 134 |
| Total cost | 1,812 |

In this chapter we shall look at the accounting procedures for materials and labour. We will consider costing for overheads in Chapter 9.

The requirements of the different Advanced level syllabuses vary. Most candidates do not need to know the detailed procedures involved in ordering and receiving goods or on the details of paying labour. You need to consult an appropriate text book if your syllabus requires this detailed knowledge.

The key topics and concepts covered in this chapter are:

- stores ledger;
- FIFO method of issuing against requisition;
- LIFO method of issuing against requisition;
- AVCO (weighted average) method of requisition;
- inventory valuation;
- periodic valuation;

- perpetual valuation;
- SSAP 9;
- work in progress;
- direct and indirect labour;
- calculating gross pay;
- time based remuneration;
- piece work remuneration;
- incentive schemes;
- manufacturing accounts;
- provision for unrealised profit.

## 8.1 ACCOUNTING FOR MATERIALS

In a manufacturing business materials are an important element in the production of goods. The importance of materials is often overlooked by those outside the business. A glance at a manufacturing company's balance sheet could reveal that the business has a greater proportion of its resources tied up in stocks of raw materials than it has tied up in cash.

The manufacturing business is dependent on a constant supply of materials in order to satisfy its customers with delivery of the finished product. If the business has insufficient stocks of materials it could cause a hold-up in the production process, and this could mean the loss of a customer. If a business is carrying too much stock it is tying up resources that could be used more profitably elsewhere. The management of materials requires close co-operation between a number of departments and a number of personnel. The quality of the end product depends on this co-operation. Generally, a large organisation will have a purchasing office. Its function is to purchase goods of the correct quality and specification. It reacts to a purchase requisition which is instigated by the department requiring the materials. This division of the functions means that specialisation in the purchasing function can take place. The purchasing office can thoroughly investigate quality, delivery dates, and price.

The purchasing department will place the order with a supplier. It will give copies of the order to the relevant departments:

- the department that sent the requisition;
- the goods inward department;
- the finance department.

When the materials are delivered they will be checked against the delivery note that the carrier presents to the goods inward department. If the goods inward department is satisfied that the materials are in the right condition and that the order is complete it will transfer them to the appropriate department or central stores.

The basic accounting record for materials is the **stores ledger**. This account is computerised now in most businesses. There will be a separate account for each type of material used in the processes undertaken in the business and a separate account for all components, etc purchased.

You should note that the stores ledger account, in reality, may be incorporated into the double entry system in operation within the business. Questions based on this type of system are outside the scope of Advanced level syllabuses.

The accounts used are not unlike those that you have come across when looking at bank statements.

The headings, which should be self explanatory, are: Date, Receipts, Issues and Balance. When the store's department (where the items of stock are kept ready to be issued to the

purchasing or production department) receives and acts on a requisition (request) for materials, the department or cost centre receiving the materials will be charged with their value by the stores.

Entries in the receipts column should present no problems; the goods are entered at the price paid for them. Issues of stock do pose a problem. Prices of items purchased are constantly changing. What price will be charged for the materials by stores when they are used in the production process?

If the materials can be easily identified, they can be transferred to production at their purchase price. The problem arises if the materials cannot easily be identified.

Identification may be difficult when:

- materials are homogeneous. For example, a mechanic uses an air filter when servicing a Ford Escort. Some of the filters may have been in stock for some months. Should the air filter be charged to the service at the price paid in October 1995 or should it be charged out at the price paid only a fortnight ago?

- materials have been changed in some way. For example, the local timber merchant buys felled trees. The trees are sawed and planed and sold as fence posts and planks of wood. How does the timber merchant arrive at a price to charge customers for each post or plank?

The following methods of valuing issues of stock are those most frequently used:

**FIFO (First in first out)** As the name suggests, this method assumes that the first goods received by the purchasing department will be the first ones to be delivered to the requisitioning department.

However, this is only an assumption. For example, a Ford Mondeo needs a replacement carburettor. The mechanic requisitions a new carburettor from stores. The store keeper will not waste time seeking out the first carburettor he purchased. He will simply issue the first one that comes to hand.

**LIFO (Last in first out)** This method assumes that the goods received most recently are the first ones to be issued for use.

**AVCO (weighted average cost)** This method recalculates the average cost of goods held in stock each time a new delivery is received. Issues are then made at the weighted average cost.

Each of these different approaches to the issue of stock has implications for the stocks remaining in the books at the financial year end.

## 8.2 METHODS OF STOCK VALUATION

Some businesses will keep very detailed records of stock receipts and issues, making entries in the stores ledger every time goods are received or sent to a requisitioning department. This method of recalculating the stock value after every transaction is known as the **perpetual method**.

This method would be used by an organisation which needs to cost the work it does very carefully. Physical verification takes place every time goods are received or issued.

Other businesses will simply value their stock once a year. This is known as a **periodic method**. It will be used by your local mini-market or take-away.

Let us examine the results given by using the perpetual method.

EXAMPLE

During the month of July the following were the receipts and issues of the component LCJS/21:

| | Receipts | | Issues | |
|---|---|---|---|---|
| 4 July | 10 @ | £8 | 9 July | 6 |
| 15 July | 9 @ | £10 | 23 July | 7 |
| 26 July | 12 @ | £13 | 30 July | 11 |

**Required**

The stores ledger account for LCJS/21 for the month of July, using FIFO, LIFO, and AVCO methods of issuing stock from central stores.

**Solution**

**FIFO**

| Date | Receipts £ | Issues | Balance |
|------|-----------|--------|---------|
| 4 July | 10 @ £8 | | 80.00 |
| 9 July | | 6 @ £8 | 32.00 *(4 @ £8)* |
| 15 July | 9 @ £10 | | 122.00 *(4 @ £8 + 9 @ £10)* |
| 23 July | | 4 @ £8<br>3 @ £10 | 60.00 *(6 @ £10)* |
| 26 July | 12 @ £13 | | 216.00 *(6 @ £10 + 12 @ £13)* |
| 30 July | | 6 @ £10<br>5 @ £13 | 91.00 *(7 @ £13)* |

**LIFO**

| Date | Receipts | Issues | Balance £ |
|------|----------|--------|-----------|
| 4 July | 10 @ £8 | | 80.00 |
| 9 July | | 6 @ £8 | 32.00 *(4 @ £8)* |
| 5 July | 9 @ £10 | | 122.00 *(4 @ £8 + 9 @ £10)* |
| 23 July | | 7 @ £10 | 52.00 *(4@£8 + 2 @ £10)* |
| 26 July | 12 @ £13 | | 208.00 *(4 @ £8 + 2 @ £10 + 12 @ £13)* |
| 30 July | | 11@£13 | 65.00 *(4 @ £8 + 2 @ £10 + 1 @ £13)* |

**AVCO**

| Date | Receipts | Issues | Balance £ |
|------|----------|--------|-----------|
| 4 July | 10 @ £8 | | 80.00 |
| 9 July | | 6 @ £8 | 32.00 *(4 @ £8)* |
| 15 July | 9 @ £10 | | 122.00 *(Average cost 122/13 = £9.38)* |
| 23 July | | 7 @ £9.38 | 56.28 *(£9.38 × 6)* |
| 26July | 12 @ £13 | | 212.28 *(Average cost 212/18 = £11.79)* |
| 30 July | | 11 @ £11.79 | 82.53 *(£11.79 × 7)* |

Check each of the above tables very carefully.

This is a popular topic with examiners.

Since each of these methods gives a different closing stock figure it should be obvious that the gross profits produced in the respective trading accounts will be different.

Test yourself. If the selling price of an LCJS/21 was £20.00 what would the respective gross profits be?

Gross profit  using FIFO would be £245.00
          using LIFO it would be £219.00
          and using AVCO it would be £236.53.

Now we will calculate the closing stock figure by using the **periodic method**. You will see that it is much less complicated.

We consider the month of July as a complete period. During the month, purchases of LCJS/21 components were 31 and issues were 24 so there must be 7 remaining in stock. Using FIFO we assume that the first components purchased were the first ones issued, so the 7 that are left must be from the last batch. Closing stock should therefore be valued at £91.00 (7 × £13). We have arrived at the same figure as when we used the perpetual method. This is not just a coincidence. FIFO will give the same result whether you use the perpetual or the periodic method.

Using LIFO the last components purchased are deemed to be the ones issued first, so the 7 left in stock are assumed to be from the very first batch of 10 bought. Stock is valued at £56.00 (7 × £8). Which should you use?

Use the perpetual method for LIFO and AVCO unless instructed to do otherwise, but use the periodic method for FIFO because it is quicker and easier.

In the modern world, businesses with computer facilities will generally use the perpetual method, since the computer can take all the complications out of recording and recalculating stock records every time stock is received or issued. In many cases, as goods pass through the check-out the stock records are updated immediately. In some instances a business may have a direct computer link with a supplier to ensure rapid replacement when stocks get to re-order levels.

It must be emphasised, once again, that all the methods of calculating the value of stock issues mentioned above are not necessarily the actual way that stock is issued.

For example, the owner of a fruit and vegetable shop could choose LIFO as his method, but it is unlikely that this would be the way that he would choose to sell his fruit. If he did, he could have 1-month-old peaches rotting in his shop!

SSAP 9 states that stocks (and work in progress) should be *valued at the total of the lower of cost and net realisable* of the separate items of stock or work in progress. (It allows grouping of similar items).

It also states that while FIFO, AVCO and standard cost are acceptable bases for valuing stock, LIFO and replacement cost are unacceptable.

## ADVANTAGES AND DISADVANTAGES OF EACH METHOD

### FIFO

*Advantages:*

- It is the method that most people feel intuitively is right, since it assumes that stock issues are made in the order in which they are received.
- Issue prices are based on the prices actually paid for the stock.
- Closing stock values are based on the most recent prices paid.
- It is an acceptable method for the purposes of the Companies Act 1985, SSAP 9 and for taxation purposes.

*Disadvantages:*

- Issues from stock are not at the most recent prices paid and this could influence the costing of work done.
- In times of rising prices FIFO values stock at the highest prices, which lowers the cost of sales figure and thus increases the profit figure. This goes against the prudence concept.

### LIFO

*Advantages:*

- The value of closing stock is based on prices actually paid for the stock.
- Issues are valued at the most recent prices.

*Disadvantages:*

- It is less realistic than FIFO since it assumes that the most recent purchases will be issued before the older stock.
- The most recent purchase prices are not used for stock valuation.
- LIFO is unacceptable for the purposes of SSAP 9 and for taxation.

### AVCO

*Advantages:*

- Since prices are averaged it recognises that issues from stock have equal value to the business and that variations in those prices are minimised.

- It allows comparison of profit figures to be made on a more realistic basis, since marked changes in the price of stock issues is ironed out.

- The value of closing stocks will be fairly close to the latest prices paid for purchases (the method is weighted towards the most recent purchases).

- AVCO is acceptable for the purposes of SSAP 9 and the Companies Act 1985.

*Disadvantages:*

- It requires a new calculation every time new stock is purchased.

- The price charged for issues of stock will not agree with the price paid to purchase the stock.

# WORK IN PROGRESS

In a manufacturing business there will be three types of stock: the business will have stocks of raw materials waiting to go through the manufacturing process; stocks of finished goods waiting to be delivered to customers; and stocks of partly finished goods (goods which have not been completed before the financial year end). These unfinished goods are known as **work in progress (WIP)**.

The same rule applies to work in progress as applies to stocks of finished goods or stocks of raw materials and components, that is, *the lower of cost or net realisable value is used*. The major problem associated with work in progress is one of identifying the proportion of the various factors of production that have gone into the manufacture of the partly finished goods. On many occasions, if the item is large, the actual requisitions of labour and materials will form the basis of the WIP calculation.

However, in some cases it is difficult to identify precisely the costs that have gone into the manufacture of, say, a mass-produced personal stereo or a ball pen. In such cases the accountant will make a judgement as to how complete the product is, in order to calculate the proportion of the labour, raw materials and overheads that should be included in the WIP valuation.

## EXAMPLE 1

A company produces ball pens. There are 450,000 pens that are only partly finished. The costs incurred in a complete pen are:

|  | pence |
|---|---|
| Direct materials | 8 |
| Direct labour | 2 |
| Overhead | 4 |
| Total cost | 14 |

The company accountant takes the view that for the purposes of valuing WIP the following applies:

| Direct materials | 80% complete |
|---|---|
| Direct labour | 75% complete |
| Overhead | 25% complete |

**Required**

A calculation of WIP relating to the ball pens.

**Solution**

The work in progress for one pen:

| Direct materials | $8p \times 80\% = 6.40p$ |
|---|---|
| Direct labour | $2p \times 75\% = 1.50p$ |
| Overhead | $4p \times 25\% = 1.00p$ |
| WIP value for one pen | 8.90p |

So for 450,000 pens the WIP figure will be $450,000 \times 8.90p - £40,050$.

**Product costs** are the costs incurred in the factory in the process of manufacturing the product. They include all direct expenses and the production overhead. All the other costs of a non-manufacturing nature incurred by the business, such as the administration costs, the selling and distribution costs and the financial charges are termed **period costs**, and are treated as expenses of the period in which they occur.

Another problem arises when the product on process remains incomplete at the financial year end. Some of the period costs will relate to the partly finished goods. In this case, the partly finished goods are expressed as fully finished goods. For example if 600 units are only $1/3$ finished, this is the equivalent of 200 units of finished goods. It is assumed that the 600 units will have 'consumed' the same costs as 200 completed goods.

### EXAMPLE 2

At the financial year end a company has produced 10,000 toys, a further 800 toys are 25% complete. The total costs involved in the production process for the year for the toys were £28,050.

**Required**

(1) The cost per toy.

(2) The value of the WIP.

**Solution**

(1) Total production is equivalent to 10,200 (10,000 + (25% × 800))

(2) Since the 800 toys are 1/4 complete it is assumed that they will have incurred $1/4$ of the total costs.

The value of the work in progress $= \dfrac{£2.75}{4} = 68.75\text{p per toy.}$

The total value of the work in progress is £550 (68.75p × 800).

## 8.3  WAGE SYSTEMS

The second important element in the production of goods is the input from labour.

Staff who work on the production process are classified as labour. If staff work directly on the product, the cost of employing them is known as **direct labour cost**.

Staff who work in the factory providing the support services for direct labour, the cleaning staff, the maintenance engineers, the supervisory staff and many others, are known as **indirect labour**. Indirect labour costs appear in the manufacturing account under the heading of overheads.

The main aim of a business organisation is survival. In order to survive a business must be profitable. To be profitable the business has to rely to a great extent on the staff employed by the business. A wage system is of fundamental importance to the employees and to the business. Wages represent the income of the workers, but also form a significant part of the cost of running the business.

So a wage system:

• has to motivate the staff;

• may be responsible, in part, for the relationship which exists between management and staff;

• may have an influence on staff turnover ,

• may help to increase productivity by encouraging efficiency; increasing output and, hopefully, reducing overheads.

A poor wage system can have the opposite effect, leading to low morale, poor workmanship, high staff turnover, etc, with dire consequences for the quantity and quality of output. All of these will have an effect on the profitability of the business.

The cost of labour looked at in isolation is rather meaningless. The cost must be set in the context of the output achieved. This concept is known as **productivity**.

## 8.4   ACCOUNTING FOR LABOUR

In some factories workers have a **personal clock card**. On arrival at work the employee 'clocks on' by inserting the clock card into a time recording machine. The machine stamps the card with the starting time. At the end of the work period the employee repeats the process and 'clocks off' when leaving the business premises.

The clock card records the time the employee has spent on the business premises, but it does not record the actual time spent working. The employee records each job or task done on a **job card** or a **time sheet**. Theoretically, the totals of the time sheets should agree with the total of the hours shown on the clock card each week. In reality they may not agree, because of time lost due to machinery failure or raw material shortages, or the time taken to change from one job to another. Any non productive time is classed as **idle time**. It cannot be attributed to a particular job, so it is accounted for separately as an overhead. Idle time needs to be carefully controlled since it is non-productive time and it represents an additional overhead.

Details from the clock cards and time sheets are entered on a **summary sheet**, and individual workers' gross pay is calculated from the totals. The gross wage is entered on **payroll sheets**. Statutory deductions (national insurance contributions and pay as you earn tax) and voluntary deductions (savings, pension contributions, etc) are calculated, leaving the employees net wage. The payroll department will then arrange for the net wage to be paid to the employee.

## 8.5   REMUNERATION OF LABOUR

There are three main methods of calculating an employee's gross wage:

- Time-based remuneration
- Piece-work remuneration
- Bonus schemes

### TIME RATES

Time rates calculate gross rates of pay by multiplying the number of hours worked by the agreed wage rate per hour. So if an employee works 38 hours and the rate is £6.00 per hour the gross wage will be £228.00 (38 × £6).

Hours worked over the agreed contractual requirements are usually paid at overtime rates. This is an extra payment above the agreed hourly rate. It could be 'time and a half', that is one and a half times the usual hourly rate, or 'double time', that is twice the usual hourly rate. Overtime is an overhead cost unless it is at the request of a customer in order to speed up the completion of a job in which case it is simply part of direct wages. Many businesses run this system for all staff. In some businesses only the indirect labour is employed on this form of remuneration. The calculations are straightforward and employees know exactly how much they will earn from week to week.

It can be argued, however, that this form of remuneration can lead to staff only doing a minimum level of work during their normal contractual hours so that they have to do extra work at overtime rates.

**High day rates** may be introduced to overcome some of the disadvantages of time work. This system offers higher than normal rates for continuous higher than normal performance. This system is designed to attract high-quality staff who will benefit from greater rewards; the business will benefit by increased productivity.

EXAMPLE 1

Time-rate employees are paid £6.00 per hour for a 38 hour week. They produce 18 units per hour.

High day rate employees are paid £8.00 per hour for a 38 hour week. They produce 25 units per hour.

**Required**

The unit costs per product for each type of employee.

**Solution**

The respective unit costs per product are:

| | |
|---|---|
| Time-rate workers | 33.3p ❶ |
| High day-rate workers | 32.0p ❷ |

❶ Production = 38 × 18 = 684; wage costs 38 × £6 = 228.

❷ Production = 38 × 25 = 950; wage costs 38 × £8 = 304.

## PIECE WORK

Workers are paid an agreed amount for each complete unit or batch of units produced. A worker may be paid £2.50 for every batch of three units produced. If the worker produces 126 batches in one week, the gross pay would be £315.00.

It is argued that this method encourages speed and efficiency. The counter argument is that there is a greater need for quality controls with the inherent costs involved; that workers may be penalised for problems outside their control like machinery break-down, shortages of materials, etc; that workers may be tempted to rush their work which may result in poor workmanship; that this system is not suitable for all types of work or all types of workers.

## Time/piece rates

To overcome some of the problems associated with straight piece work, many firms provide a guaranteed minimum weekly wage. This removes some of the uncertainty about the size of the worker's wage.

## PREMIUM BONUS SCHEMES

The principle behind these schemes is to encourage workers to save time in the production process.

If a job should normally take 8 hours to complete and a worker finishes the job in 6 hours. There has been a saving of 2 hours. The premium bonus scheme would pay the worker the normal time-based rate (hours worked × rate per hour) plus the premium bonus. The three most commonly used premium bonus schemes are the Halsey scheme, the Halsey-Weir scheme and the Rowan scheme.

With the **Halsey scheme**, the reward is based on half the time saved.

EXAMPLE 2

10 hours are allowed to complete a job; the worker takes 8 hours to complete the job; the basic rate of pay is £8.00 per hour.

| | | |
|---|---|---|
| Gross pay is calculated: 8 hours × £8.00 = | £64.00 | |
| 1 hour × £8.00 = | £8.00* | |

*bonus based on 1 hour which is 50% of time saved

The **Halsey-Weir scheme** is a variation of the Halsey scheme. This scheme pays 30% of the time saved.

The **Rowan scheme** rewards the worker with a bonus based on the relationship between the time actually taken and the time allowed for the job.

EXAMPLE 3

10 hours are allowed to complete a job; the worker takes 8 hours to complete the job; the basic rate of pay is £8.00 per hour.

Gross pay is calculated: 8 hours × £8.00 = £64.00
1.6 hours × £8.00 = 12.80*
*bonus based on 8 tenths of hours saved = 1.6 hours

These incentive bonuses are charged to direct labour costs, since this is the wage that has been earned in producing the product.

## 8.6 MANUFACTURING ACCOUNTS

You have produced countless trading and profit and loss accounts in your study of accounting. These final accounts are prepared for business organisations that trade, that is they buy in goods and then sell them on. Obviously, many businesses actually make the products that they sell. Such organisations need to prepare a manufacturing account as part of their final accounts.

> The **manufacturing account** simply shows the costs of running and maintaining the factory in which the product is made.

The manufacturing account is shown preceding the trading account. It can be seen as the link between cost accounting and financial accounting. It has its place in both areas. The manufacturing account has **two** main sections:

### The prime cost section

This section contains all the factors of production that can be directly attributed to the product: direct materials; direct labour; other direct expenses, e.g. royalties.

For example, in every pair of Levi's that you buy, you can see the materials, you also know that someone has stitched them together. Those materials and that person's wage are direct costs.

### The overheads section

This section contains all the other expenses that have been necessary to run the factory. These expenses cannot be directly attributed to the product being manufactured, and include: indirect materials; indirect labour; other indirect expenses.

For example, it would be difficult to say how much lubricating oil used on the sewing machines has gone into the manufacture of the jeans, how much of the supervisors' wages, how much factory rent, how much of the depreciation of the sewing machines and any other factory machinery used in the production process etc. is attributable directly to the jeans. These are all necessary expenses in running the factory and so should be shown in the overheads section.

All other overheads of the business are debited to the profit and loss account. For example, the selling and distribution costs of getting the jeans to the retailer, the wages of administration staff, the depreciation of the computers in the accounts department, etc, all appear, as usual, in the profit and loss account.

Learn the layout of the manufacturing account shown on the following page.

**Manufacturing, trading and profit and loss account
for the year ended December 19xx**

|  | £ | £ |
|---|---|---|
| Raw materials |  | *** |
|    Opening stock ❶ |  | *** |
|    Purchases |  |  |
|    Carriage inwards ❷ |  | *** |
|    Closing stock ❶ |  | *** |
| Cost of raw materials consumed |  | *** |
| Manufacturing wages |  | *** |
| Royalties ❸ |  | *** |
| **Prime cost** |  |  |
| Factory overheads | *** |  |
| Indirect labour | *** |  |
| Power Factory rent and rates | *** |  |
| Factory light and heat | *** |  |
| Factory insurance | *** |  |
| Depreciation of plant and machinery ❹ | *** | *** |
| Add opening work in progress adjustment ❺ |  | *** |
| Less closing work in progress |  | *** |
| Factory cost of goods produced ❻ |  | *** |
| Sales ❼ |  | *** |
| Less cost of sales |  |  |
| Opening stock: finished goods | *** |  |
| Factory cost of goods produced ❽ | *** |  |
| Less closing stock finished goods | *** |  |
| Gross profit ❾ |  | *** |
| Add other income |  | *** |
|  |  | *** |
| Less: |  |  |
|    Selling and distribution costs | *** |  |
|    Administration costs | *** |  |
|    Finance costs | *** | *** |
| Net profit |  | *** |

❶ This is the usual stock adjustment that is necessary to determine how many materials have been used in the manufacturing process.

❷ Note that carriage inward has been added to the purchases of raw materials – it increases the cost of whatever is purchased.

❸ Royalties are paid to the owners of the patent or process for every unit sold.

❹ This is a factory expense since plant and machinery are found in the factory.

❺ This is another necessary stock adjustment.

❻ The total cost of running the factory.

❼ This is the start of the trading account.

❽ This figure takes the place of the purchases figure which was used when the business was simply a trading organisation.

❾ This is the start of the profit and loss account – it is the same as all the other profit and loss accounts that you have ever done.

## PROVISION FOR UNREALISED PROFIT

Some manufacturing businesses transfer the goods produced in their own factory to the warehouse (the trading account) at a price in excess of the total cost of production.

The difference between this transfer price and the total cost of production is a manufacturing profit. This profit loading is designed to give some credit to the factory personnel for contributing to the overall gross profit of the business. Goods bought in from an outside supplier may have cost more than it costs the business to produce them.

Manufacturing profit is an attempt to recognise the part that the factory has played in the overall profitability of the business.

## EXAMPLE 1

J. Ipon plc manufacture goggles for the engineering industry. Finished goods are transferred from the factory to the trading account at a profit of 25% on total factory cost.

The following information applies to the year ended 29 February 1996.

|  |  | £000 |
|---|---|---|
| Stocks: | Raw materials 1 March 1995 | 23 |
|  | Raw materials 29 February 1996 | 25 |
|  | Work in progress 1 March 1995 | 30 |
|  | Work in progress 29 February 1996 | 29 |
|  | Finished goods 1 March 1995 | 39 |
|  | Finished goods 29 February 1996 | 41 |
| Prime cost |  | 752 |
| Factory overheads |  | 239 |
| Selling and distribution expenses |  | 61 |
| Administration expenses |  | 87 |
| Sales |  | 1,691 |

### Required

A manufacturing, trading and profit and loss account for the year ended 29 February 1996 for J. Ipon plc.

### Solution

|  |  | £000 |
|---|---|---|
| Prime cost❶ |  | 752 |
| Factory overheads |  | 239 |
|  |  | 991 |
| Add WIP 1 March 1995 |  | 30 |
|  |  | 1,021 |
| Less WIP 29 February 1996 |  | 29 |
| Factory cost of goods produced❷ |  | 992 |
| Add factory profit |  | 248 |
| Transfer to trading account |  | 1,240 |
| Sales❸ |  | 1,691 |
| Less cost of sales: |  |  |
| Opening stock | 39 |  |
| Transfer from manufacturing a/c | 1,240 ❹ |  |
|  | 1,279 |  |
| Less closing stock | 41 | 1,238 |
| Gross profit on trading❺ |  | 453 |
| Less: |  |  |
| Selling and distribution expenses | 61 |  |
| Administration expenses | 87 | 148 |
| Net profit on trading |  | 305 |
| Add manufacturing profit |  | 248 |
|  |  | 553 ❻ |

❶ The stocks of raw material adjustment has already been done in arriving at this figure.

❷ This figure has to be increased by 25% giving the factory profit.

❸ The trading account.

❹ This is the value of the goods traded.

❺ The profit and loss account.

❻ The total profit for the year.

Stocks of finished goods may be valued using the total factory cost which could include the profit loading. If this is the case, the method of valuing the closing stock of finished goods will contravene two important accounting concepts:

- The *concept of prudence* states that stocks should be valued at the lower of cost and net realisable value.

- According to the *realisation concept* profit cannot be recognised until the goods pass to the customer.

If the valuation of closing stock of finished goods does include an element of factory profit it must be eliminated in the profit and loss account. The net profit will be overstated by the amount of the unrealised profit. The profit included in the closing stock of finished goods in the balance sheet must be eliminated since the current assets are also overstated by this amount.

The provision for unrealised manufacturing profit is very similar in appearance to the other provision account that you have used in your studies.

### EXAMPLE 2

Alim plc manufactures components for the motor industry. The following information relates to the first two years in business:

| Year ended | 31 January 1995 | 31 January 1996 |
|---|---|---|
| | £000 | £000 |
| Sales | 651 | 1,487 |
| Factory cost of goods produced transferred | 420 | 972 |
| Opening stock of finished goods | – | 120 |
| Closing stock of finished goods | 120 | 360 |
| Selling and distribution and administration costs | 212 | 409 |

The company transfers goods to the trading account at cost plus 20%.

*Point to note*

The stock values of £120,000 and the £360,000 include the profit loading of 20%, so each figure is cost + 20%, or 120% of cost price.

**Required**

(a) The provision for unrealised profit account for the years ended 31 January 1995 and 1996.

(b) The profit and loss accounts for both years.

(c) Extracts from the company balance sheets as at 31 January 1995 and as at 31 January 1996.

**Solution**

(a)

**Provision for unrealised profit**

| | | | | |
|---|---|---|---|---|
| | | 31 Jan 95 P & L a/c | 20 ❶ | |
| 31 Jan 96 Balance c/d | 60 | 31 Jan 96 P & L a/c | 40 ❷ | |
| | 60 | | 60 | |
| | | 1 Feb 96 Balance b/d | 60 | |

*Points to note*

❶  $120 \times \dfrac{20}{120} \ (\dfrac{1}{6}) = 20$

❷  $360 \times \dfrac{20}{120} = 60$, *but* 20 already provided for at 31 January 1995.

(b)

**Alim trading and profit and loss accounts
for the year ended 31 January**

| | 1995 | | 1996 | |
|---|---|---|---|---|
| | £000 | £000 | £000 | £000 |
| Sales | | 651 | | 1,487 |
| Less cost of sales: | | | | |
| Opening stock | – | | 120 | |
| Transfer from manufacturing account | 420 | | 972 | |
| | 420 | | 1,092 | |
| Closing stock | 120 | | 360 | |
| | | 300 | | 732 |
| | | 351 | | 755 |
| Less selling, distribution, administration expenses | | 212 | | 409 |
| Net profit on trading | | 139 | | 346 |
| Add manufacturing profit | 70 | | 162 | |
| Less increase in provision for unrealised profit | 20 | 50 | 40 | 122 |
| Net profit | | 189 | | 468 |

*Point to note*

The manufacturing profit must be 20/120 of the factory cost of goods manufactured figure, so 20/120 of £420 = £70 and 20/120 of £972 = £162.

(c)    **Alim plc balance sheets (extracts) as at 31 January 1995 and 1996**

| | 1995 | | 1996 | |
|---|---|---|---|---|
| | £000 | | | £000 |
| Current assets | | | | |
| Stocks of finished goods | 120 | | 360 | |
| Less provision for unrealised profit | 20 | 100 | 60 | 300 |

**Point to note**

The stocks are now shown on the balance sheet at cost.

---

## Chapter roundup

Chapter 8 had dealt with accounting for materials and labour. Check your syllabus on how much detail you require to know. The two main topic areas examined from this chapter are methods of stock valuation and manufacturing accounts. Remember LIFO, FIFO and AVCO are only methods of valuing issues of stock, they do not determine the order in which stock is issued. Remember to identify raw materials consumed, prime cost and total production cost when preparing a manufacturing account. If there is an element of factory profit included in the stocks of finished goods, a provision for unrealised profit must be used.

---

# Illustrative questions

**1**   Owing to staff shortages, Harold Green's annual stocktaking did not take place on 31 March 1994.

However, stock in trade, at cost, at 30 September 1993 was £43,400 and the following information for the six months ended 31 March 1994 has now been obtained from the business record:

(i)   Goods costing £2,100 have been withdrawn for Harold Green's own use.

(ii) Goods costing £10,000 were stolen from the business in January 1994; the insurance company has now paid Harold Green £4,000 in full settlement.

(iii) Goods costing £2,000 in stock at 30 September 1993 still remain unsold and are now regarded as valueless.

(iv) Goods costing £3,100 were sent on a sale or return basis to Mary Gibson in March 1994. The goods were unsold on 31 March 1994.

(v) Purchases during the six months ended 31 March 1994 amounted to £320,000 at list prices; a trade discount of 12.5% off list prices was obtained on all purchases. Credit notes for £4,200 were received for goods returned to suppliers as unsuitable or damaged.

(vi) Sales during the six months ended 31 March 1994 amounted to £406,000 whilst sales returns were £3,000. A gross profit of 40% is obtained on the cost of all goods sold.

(vii) An office desk costing £500 was transferred from stock to furniture and fittings at cost on 1 January 1994. This desk is being used in the manager's office.

*Required*
(a) A computation of the value of Harold Green's stock at 31 March 1994.    (10)
(b) Harold Green's trading account for the six months ended 31 March 1994.    (9)
(c) In what circumstances is it necessary to open a provision for unrealised profit account?    (6)
(UCLES)

*Tutorial note*
Remember that the selling price of the goods is 140% of cost price and that sales and sales returns must be reduced to cost for the purposes of valuing stock.

The key to part (c) is that all stocks must be valued at cost or net realisable value (NRV), whichever is the lower, so when stock contains an element of profit it must be eliminated.

*Suggested answer*

(a) **Harold Green, computation of the value of stock at 31 March 1994**

| | £ |
|---|---|
| Stock at 30 September 1993 | 43,400 |
| (i) Goods for own use | (2,100) |
| (ii) Goods stolen | (10,000) |
| (iii) Valueless goods | (2,000) |
| (iv) Goods on sale or return | No adjustment necessary |
| (v) Purchases | 280,000 |
| Purchase returns | (4,200) |
| (vi) Sales (reduced to cost price) | (290,000) |
| Sales returns (at cost price) | 2,143 |
| (vii) Office desk transferred to furniture and fittings | (500) |
| Stock at 31 March 1994 | 16,743 |

(b) **Harold Green trading account for the six months ended 31 March 1994**

| | £ | £ | £ |
|---|---|---|---|
| Sales | | | 406,000 |
| Less returns | | | 3,000 |
| | | | 403,000 |
| Less cost of sales | | | |
| Stock 1 October 1993 | | 43,400 | |
| Purchases | 280,000 | | |
| Less goods for own use | 2,100 | | |
| returns | 4,200 | 273,700 | |
| | | 317,100 | |
| Less stolen goods | 10,000 | | |
| valueless goods | 2,000 | | |
| goods to furniture and fittings | 500 | | |
| Stock 31 March 1994 | 16,743 | 29,243 | 287,857 |
| Gross profit | | | 115,143 |

(c) When profit is introduced into a set of final accounts, for internal use, before it is earned it is necessary to open a provision for unrealised gross profit. The two most common examples are when:
(i) a profit on manufacturing is required, and
(ii) when goods are sent to a branch from a central purchasing department at amounts above cost.
The provision is equal to the amount of profit brought into the accounts on unsold stock. The provision ensures that credit is not taken for the profit before it is earned.

**2** The following list of balances as at 31 March 1995 has been extracted from the books of Kitchen Tables Limited, a small manufacturing company:

| | £ |
|---|---|
| Stock at 31 March 1994: | |
| Raw materials | 3,500 |
| Finished goods (as transferred from the manufacturing account) | 14,520 |
| Work in progress at 31 March 1994 | 13,940 |
| Raw materials purchases | 50,550 |
| Direct factory wages | 39,500 |
| Indirect factory wages | 14,700 |
| Indirect factory materials | 3,900 |
| Factory maintenance and repairs | 9,740 |
| Factory heat, light and power | 14,130 |
| Sales | 225,920 |
| Head office administrative expenditure | 23,290 |
| Sales and distribution expenditure | 17,891 |
| Freehold buildings: | |
| at cost | 45,000 |
| provision for depreciation | 6,750 |
| Plant and machinery: | |
| at cost | 164,000 |
| provision for depreciation | 90,200 |
| Debtors | 20,009 |
| Creditors | 9,600 |
| Balance at bank | 4,420 |
| Ordinary shares of £0.50 each, fully paid | 60,000 |
| Share premium account | 30,000 |
| Retained earnings | 15,300 |
| Provision for unrealised profit at 31 March 1994 | 1,320 |

Additional information:
(i) Raw material stocks at cost at 31 March 1995 are £2,910.
(ii) Finished goods stocks at 31 March 1995, as transferred from the manufacturing account, amounted to £18,502.
(iii) Work in progress, at cost, at 31 March 1995 has been valued at £16,500.
(iv) All goods manufactured are transferred from the manufacturing account to the trading account at cost plus 10%.
(v) It is company policy to provide for depreciation at the following annual percentages on the cost of fixed assets:

| | % |
|---|---|
| Freehold property | 2.5 |
| Plant and machinery | 10.0 |

Freehold property depreciation is apportioned 2/5 to the factory and 3/5 to the administrative and related overheads.
(vi) The board of Kitchen Tables Limited is recommending a dividend is paid for the year ended 31 March 1995 of £0.20 per share.

Owing to a temporary lack of orders, the company's factory is facing a period of half-time working during the last four months of 1995.

However, the directors of Kitchen Tables Limited are considering whether to accept an export order at a price which would only cover manufacturing costs. The order, if accepted, would provide two months' work for the factory.

*Required*

(a) A manufacturing, trading and profit and loss account for the year ended 31 March 1995. (12)

(b) A balance sheet as at 31 March 1995. (7)

(c) A report to the board of Kitchen Tables Limited outlining the relevant factors when making a decision whether to accept the export order or not. (6)

*Tutorial note*

Remember to always identify raw materials consumed, prime cost and total manufacturing cost when preparing a manufacturing account. The total provision for unrealised profit should be deducted from the stock of finished goods in the balance sheet. Part (c) considers the marginal costs and revenues of a special contract.

*Suggested answer*

(a) **Kitchen Tables Ltd manufacturing trading and profit and loss account for the year ended 31 March 1995**

|  | £ | £ |
|---|---|---|
| Stocks of raw materials 1 April 1994 | 3,500 | |
| Purchases of raw materials | 50,550 | |
|  | 54,050 | |
| Less stocks of raw materials 31 March 1995 | 2,910 | 51,140 |
| Direct wages | | 39,500 |
| **Prime cost** | | 90,640 |
| Manufacturing overheads | | |
|     Indirect wages | 14,700 | |
|     Indirect Materials | 3,900 | |
|     Maintenance and repairs | 9,740 | |
|     Heating, light and power | 14,130 | |
|     Depreciation – Freehold buildings | 450 | |
|                  Plant and machinery | 16,400 | 59,320 |
| Total manufacturing costs | | 149,960 |
| Work in progress 1 April 1994 | | 13,940 |
|  | | 163,900 |
| Work in progress 31 March 1995 | | 16,500 |
| Cost of finished goods manufactured | | 147,400 |
| Factory profit | | 14,740 |
| Transfer price to trading account | | 162,140 |
| Sales | | 225,920 |
| Less cost of sales | | |
| Stock of finished goods 1 April 1994 | 14,520 | |
| Cost of finished goods from manufacturing account | | |
|     at transfer price | 162,140 | |
|  | 176,660 | |
| Less Stock of finished goods 31 March 1995 | 18,502 | 158,158 |
| Gross profit | | 67,762 |
| Less expenses | | |
|     Administrative expenditure | 23,290 | |
|     Selling and distribution expenditure | 17,891 | |
|     Depreciation – freehold buildings | 675 | 41,856 |
|  | | 25,906 |
| Add factory profit | 14,740 | |
| Less increase in provision for | | |
|     unrealised gross profit | 362 | 14,378 |
| Net profit on ordinary activities | | 40,284 |
| Proposed ordinary dividend | | 24,000 |
| Retained profit for the year | | 16,284 |
| Retained profit brought forward | | 15,300 |
| Retained profit carried forward | | 31,584 |

(b)         **Balance sheet as at 31 March 1995**

| Fixed assets | Cost £ | Depreciation £ | Net £ |
|---|---|---|---|
| Freehold buildings | 45,000 | 7,875 | 37,125 |
| Plant and machinery | 164,000 | 106,600 | 57,400 |
| | 209,000 | 114,475 | 94,525 |

| Current assets | | | |
|---|---|---|---|
| Stocks – Raw materials | | 2,910 | |
| Work in progress | | 16,500 | |
| Finished goods (18,502 – 1,682) | | 16,820 | |
| Debtors | | 20,009 | |
| Balance at bank | | 4,420 | |
| | | 60,659 | |
| Less creditors: amounts falling due within one year | | | |
| Creditors | 9,600 | | |
| Proposed dividends | 24,000 | 33,600 | 27,059 |
| | | | 121,584 |

| Capital and reserves | |
|---|---|
| Ordinary shares of 50p each fully paid | 60,000 |
| Share premium account | 30,000 |
| Profit and loss account | 31,584 |
| | 121,584 |

(c) To

From

Date *(i.e. in report format)*

*Factors to be considered when making a decision
whether or not to accept an export order*

Factors could include:

How many of the manufacturing and other overheads are fixed and how many are variable. This will determine the contribution that the order makes.

Will the order displace other work being undertaken in the factory?

Are there more lucrative options available?

By accepting the order will economies of scale be achieved?

Will the order result in further orders being placed in the future?

**3**  John Roberts commenced trading on 1 January 1989 with an initial capital of £50,000 used to open a business bank account. John Roberts is a dealer in the Ajax Mark 1 De Luxe Motor Caravan and his caravan transactions during 1989 were as follows:

| 1989 | Purchases | Sales |
|---|---|---|
| January | 2 at £20,000 each | |
| February | | 1 at £30,000 |
| March | 3 at £21,000 each | |
| May | | 2 at £35,000 each |
| July | 2 at £23,000 each | |
| September | | 3 at £36,000 each |
| October | 2 at £24,000 each | |
| November | | 1 at £37,000 |

John Roberts' expenses during 1989 totalled £60,000, a very high figure due to entering a very competitive market at a time when the demand for caravans has been very subdued.

John Roberts has decided that his drawings must always be equal to his profit in each financial year.

All transactions are on a cash, non-credit basis, and all receipts and payments are passed through the bank account.

The following are appropriate general price indices:

| | |
|---|---|
| 1 January 1989 | 100 |
| October 1989 | 105 |
| 31 December 1989 | 110 |

The Ajax Mark 1 De Luxe Motor Caravan cost price at 31 December 1989 was 15% greater than during October 1989.

*Required*

(a) Balance sheets as at 31 December 1989 showing the maximum amount that John Roberts can withdraw from his business at the end of 1989 and yet leave his capital intact using each of the following models:

   (i) Historical cost either using the *first in first out* or *last in first out* methods of stock valuation;

   (ii) Current cost accounting using *first in first out* method of stock valuation;

   (iii) Current purchasing power using *first in first out* method of stock valuation.

(19)

(b) A concise note comparing the objectives of the current cost accounting model and the current purchasing power accounting model.

(6)

(UCLES)

*Tutorial note*

Current cost accounting adjusts the stock using the specific index which applies to the stock. Current purchasing power uses the general price index.

*Suggested answer*

(a) (i)

**John Roberts (historical cost) balance sheet as at 31 December 1989**

| | £ |
|---|---|
| Stock (using first in first out basis) | 48,000 |
| Balance at bank | 38,000 |
| | 86,000 |
| Capital | 50,000 |
| Net profit | 36,000 |
| | 86,000 |

**John Roberts (historical cost) balance sheet as at 31 December 1989**

| | £ |
|---|---|
| Stock (using last in first out basis) | 44,000 |
| Balance at bank | 38,000 |
| | 82,000 |
| Capital | 50,000 |
| Net profit | 32,000 |
| | 82,000 |

(ii)

**John Roberts (current cost accounting) balance sheet as at 31 December 1989**

| | £ | |
|---|---|---|
| Stock | 55,200 | £48,000 × 115/100 |
| Balance at bank | 38,000 | |
| | 93,200 | |
| Capital | 50,000 | |
| Current cost reserve | 7,200 | |
| Current cost operating profit | 36,000 | |
| | 93,200 | |

(ii) **John Roberts (current purchasing power) balance sheet
as at 31 December 1989**

|  | £ |  |
|---|---|---|
| Stock | 50,286 | £48,000 × $^{110}/_{105}$ |
| Balance at bank | 38,000 |  |
|  | 88,286 |  |
| Capital | 55,000 | £50,000 × $^{110}/_{100}$ |
| Retained profits | 33,286 |  |
|  | 88,286 |  |

(b) Current cost accounting model uses specific price indices.
It seeks to maintain physical capital.
It discourages distributions in excess of current cost operating profit
Current purchasing power accounting model uses general price indices.
The emphasis is on maintaining capital intact in terms of its purchasing power.
All parts of the final accounts and balance sheet are shown in terms of monetary
units at a given date.

# COSTING FOR OVERHEADS

## Units in this chapter

9.1 *Cost allocation and apportionment*
9.2 *Transfers of service department costs*
9.3 *Overhead absorption*
9.4 *Overhead adjustment account*

## Chapter objectives

We saw in the last chapter how, by preparing a manufacturing account, the total cost of running a factory was arrived at. We looked at the elements which make up the prime costs of a manufacturing business.

In this chapter we consider the other main element in determining the cost of a product; the factory overheads.

The key topics and concepts covered in this chapter are:

- cost centres;
- cost allocation;
- cost apportionment;
- apportionment of service departments' costs;
- transfers by elimination;
- transfers by continuous allotment;
- transfers by simultaneous equation;
- labour hour rate;
- labour cost rate;
- machine hour rate;
- unit produced rate.

## 9.1 COST ALLOCATION AND APPORTIONMENT

It is important that a manufacturing business can tell what each product or group of products costs to produce in order that a selling price can be fixed. The selling price will recover the costs incurred in operating the factory and provide profits for the business.

It is a relatively simple matter to allocate direct costs to a cost centre, or cost unit. A cost centre or cost unit may be a product, a department, a machine, a job or a project to which costs can be associated. The cost centres are usually determined by the type of business. If the business is run on a departmental basis the primary cost centre will be the department. If it is organised around jobs, the jobs would be the cost centre.

It is more difficult to share overheads among different cost centres, or cost units. One reason is that the actual overheads will not be quantified until the financial year end.

When it is possible to identify costs and charge them to cost centres or cost units, the process is called **cost allocation**. When it is difficult (or even impossible) to allocate costs, it is necessary to divide the costs between cost centres or cost units in some pre-determined proportions. This process is called **cost apportionment**.

A manufacturing business intends to sell its products at a profit. The profit is the excess of the selling price over all costs.

Selling price – total cost = profit.

In order to arrive at the selling price the business must be able to determine the costs of the factors of production that have gone into the product. If a business is to be profitable it must cover all costs, including rent of premises, lighting and heating, insurance, advertising etc.

### EXAMPLE 1

Anne knits sweaters at home for sale. The wool she uses costs £14 and the time take to complete a sweater is 16 hours. Anne charges her time out at £3 per hour. To cover her costs she charges £62 for one of her sweaters. By charging £62 for a sweater Anne has absorbed all her costs.

Anne's sweaters are in great demand, so she asks Bernard to help her; she pays Bernard £3 per hour. If Anne continues to charge £62 for her sweaters she will not make a profit on the sweaters that Bernard knits for her. She increases her selling price to £75 per sweater. Anne is now covering all her costs and making a small profit, £13 per sweater, on Bernard's work.

Demand is still increasing for Anne's product, so she rents a small business unit on an industrial estate. She employs Claire and Don and purchases some knitting machines.

Anne is able to sell 520 sweaters per year. Her products must absorb all the costs of running the business. She must estimate what her total expenses are likely to be for the year and allocate the costs to each sweater knitted. She can then determine a selling price which will recover the costs and give her the profit margin she would like.

Anne estimates her costs for the year will be:

|  | £ |
|---|---|
| Wool | 2,000 |
| Wages | 17,000 |
| Rent of unit | 2,080 |
| Rates | 900 |
| Electricity | 800 |
| Advertising | 360 |
| Motor expenses | 1,320 |
| Depreciation of machines | 500 |
|  | 24,960 |

For the sake of simplicity it has been assumed that all production will be sold. In order for Anne to absorb all her costs she must recover £48 per sweater (£24,960/520).

You can see that this is a fairly straightforward process. Everyone going into business will have had to go through this process at some time to make sure that they can cover all their expenses. The major problem arises when Anne decides to extend her range of products. She believes that there is a profitable market in producing and selling woollen hats, cardigans, and waistcoats. How does she arrive at the cost for each product?

The **allocation** of direct costs is fairly straightforward. The cost of the wool (direct materials) used in each product can easily be calculated. The time taken by each knitter on the product (direct labour) can be calculated, but what of the overheads?

It is very much more difficult to determine how much of the estimated charge for rent will go into the manufacture of a sweater or a hat or a cardigan. How much of the estimated advertising costs should be charged to each? The solution is to **apportion** the estimated overheads to each of the products.

The apportionment should be done in a rational, sensible way. Arbitrary methods should be avoided. Costs which can be identified with a cost centre should be allocated to that cost centre. When a cost cannot be identified with a particular cost centre the costs must be apportioned in a fair way.

Some costs cannot be allocated to a specific cost centre, but may arise from the activities of a number of cost centres. Rent may be paid for the premises as a whole. The owner of the building will expect one payment, despite the fact that the business may have a structure which has numerous cost centres.

The aim of the business is to arrive at a total cost for each finished product.

Total cost = Prime cost + Factory overheads + Other overheads

The direct costs (prime costs) are relatively easy to allocate, but the overheads are less easy. Any costs which cannot be allocated must be apportioned in some fair way. Some costs which would prove difficult to allocate would include: rent, rates, insurances, power costs, heating and lighting costs (unless departmental meters were installed).

## EXAMPLE 2

Ardale Engineering Ltd has the following estimated costs which cannot be allocated directly to its three departments:

|  | £ |
|---|---|
| Rent | 250,000 |
| Rates | 90,000 |
| Power | 200,000 |
| Supervisory wages | 64,000 |
| Depreciation of machinery (10% p.a.) | 100,000 |
|  | 704,000 |

Additional information:

Total factory area is 300,000 m² of which   department A occupies 150,000 m²
department B occupies 100,000 m²
department C occupies 50,000 m²

Power used in each department:   A 25,000 Kwh
B 40,000 Kwh
C 35,000 Kwh

Cost of machinery in each department:   A £250,000
B £150,000
C £600,000

Staff employed in each department   A 30 workers
B 40 workers
C 10 workers

## Required

An overhead analysis sheet for Ardale Engineering Ltd.

**Solution**

| Overhead | Total cost | Basis of apportionment | Dept A | Dept B | Dept C |
|---|---|---|---|---|---|
| | | | £ | £ | £ |
| Rent | 250,000 | Area | 125,000 | 83,333 | 41,667 |
| Rates | 90,000 | Area | 45,000 | 30,000 | 15,000 |
| Power | 200,000 | Kwh | 50,000 | 80,000 | 70,000 |
| Supervisory wages | 64,000 | Number of workers | 24,000 | 32,000 | 8,000 |
| Depreciation of machinery | 100,000 | Cost | 25,000 | 15,000 | 60,000 |
| | 704,000 | | 269,000 | 240,333 | 194,667 |

When the overheads have been allocated and apportioned to the departments, the estimated total costs for each department can be determined.

# 9.2 TRANSFERS OF SERVICE DEPARTMENT COSTS

In every organisation there will exist some non-production departments. These departments are necessary to provide the back up services for the production departments. Can you think of some departments which might be necessary to promote the efficient running of the factory, yet do not produce finished goods for sale?

Examples would include: maintenance; stores; canteen; factory administration.

These departments do not sell a product to the final customer; they cannot recover their costs by incorporating them into the selling price of their product. They exist to provide services to the production department. Yet their costs must also be recovered by the business.

The estimated costs of the departments that provide services for the production departments must be apportioned to each production department. In this way each production department will recover its own overheads *and* some of the overheads of the non-producing departments.

Sometimes servicing departments will keep detailed records of the work that has been done in other departments. These costs can be allocated to the appropriate department. If this type of record is not kept, some basis for apportionment must be applied. If a business had only one servicing department its costs could be apportioned in a straightforward way.

## EXAMPLE 1

The estimated overhead costs for Fellside Construction Ltd have been allocated and apportioned as follows:

| | £ |
|---|---|
| Department E | 120,000 |
| Department F | 100,000 |
| Department G | 40,000 |
| Canteen | 21,000 |

**Required**
An overhead analysis sheet for Fellside Construction Ltd.

**Solution**
The canteen costs need to be apportioned between the three production departments. They can recover their own costs *and* the canteen costs.

| Overhead | Total | Basis of apportionment | Dept E | Dept F | Dept G | Canteen |
|---|---|---|---|---|---|---|
| | £ | | £ | £ | £ | £ |
| Total | 281,000 | | 120,000 | 100,000 | 40,000 | 21,000 |
| Canteen | | ? | 10,000 | 8,000 | 3,000 | (21,000) |
| | | | 130,000 | 108,000 | 43,000 | 0 |

Do you know how the canteen costs have been apportioned? What information would you have needed to apportion the canteen costs? The piece of information that was missing was the number of employees working in each department. 10 people work in department E, 8 in department F, and 3 in department G. This was deliberately omitted. Would you have used this information?

How would you apportion maintenance costs? Perhaps by the numbers of machines in each department, the hours the machinery is in use in each department, the age of the machinery in each department or the repair jobs done in each department? Different businesses will use different methods of apportionment. You will be given information in the examination which will indicate the basis of apportionment that you should use, unless the basis should be known to you, e.g. rent according to floor space.

When one non-production department services another non-production department the apportionment becomes more complicated. Maintenance engineers may service the kitchen equipment, while the canteen may provide refreshments and meals for the maintenance staff.

There are three main methods of dealing with inter-departmental transfers of overheads:

- elimination method, sometimes called the simplified method,
- continuous allotment method, and
- algebraic or simultaneous equation method.

## EXAMPLE 2

Townhead Manufacturers plc has three production departments (A, B, and C) and two departments (P, and R) to service them. Estimated overhead costs for February have been allocated and apportioned as follows:

| | Production departments | | | Service departments | |
|---|---|---|---|---|---|
| | A | B | C | P | R |
| | £ | £ | £ | £ | £ |
| Overheads | 18,000 | 15,000 | 12,000 | 5,000 | 8,000 |

The service departments' overheads are to be apportioned as follows:

| | | | | | |
|---|---|---|---|---|---|
| Department P | 40% | 30% | 20% | | 10% |
| Department R | 25% | 45% | 10% | 20% | |

**Required**

Show how the service overhead departments P and R could be apportioned by using:

(a) the simplified (elimination) method,

(b) the repeated distribution method,

(c) the algebraic method.

**Solution**

(a) The simplified method:

**Townhead Manufacturers plc**

| | Production departments | | | Service departments | |
|---|---|---|---|---|---|
| | A | B | C | P | R |
| | £ | £ | £ | £ | £ |
| Overheads | 18,000 | 15,000 | 12,000 | 5,000 | 8,000 |
| Apportionment of dept R's costs | 2,000 | 3,600 | 800 | 1,600 | (8,000) |
| | 20,000 | 18,600 | 12,800 | 6,600 | – |

*Point to note*

Always start with the service department with the largest total costs, in this example, this is department R.

Department R's costs have been apportioned to the other departments that it services. Department P's costs must now be apportioned.

| | £ | £ | £ | £ | £ |
|---|---|---|---|---|---|
| (Totals from above) | 20,000 | 18,600 | 12,800 | 6,600 | – |
| Apportionment of | | | | | |
| dept P's costs | 2,640 | 1,980 | 1,320 | (6,600) | 660 |
| | 22,640 | 20,580 | 14,120 | – | 660 |

R's costs are now ignored.

Strictly speaking, this simplified method is slightly inaccurate. Although department P services department R (10% of department P's work is undertaken in department R) the method ignores the 'final' £660 costs apportioned to department R. The 'inaccuracy' is just over 1% (£660 out of total costs of £58,000), but we must remember that the figures for overheads are *estimates*; the actual figures will only be known with accuracy after the financial year end. The estimates themselves may be inaccurate.

(b) The repeated distribution method.

**Townhead Manufacturers plc**

| | Production departments | | | Service departments | |
|---|---|---|---|---|---|
| | A | B | C | P | R |
| | £ | £ | £ | £ | £ |
| Overheads | 18,000 | 15,000 | 12,000 | 5,000 | 8,000 |
| Apportionment of R's costs (£8,000 split 25:45:10:20) | 2,000 | 3,600 | 800 | 1,600 | (8,000) |
| | 20,000 | 18,600 | 12,800 | 6,600 | – |
| Apportionment of P's costs (£6 600 split 40:30:20:10) | 2,640 | 1,980 | 1,320 | (6,600) | 660 |
| | 22,640 | 20,580 | 14,120 | – | 660 |
| Apportionment of R's costs (£660 split 25:45:10:20) | 165 | 297 | 66 | 132 | (660) |
| | 22,805 | 20,877 | 14,186 | 132 | – |
| Apportionment of P's costs (£132 split 40:30:20:10) | 53 | 40 | 26 | (132) | 13 |
| | 22,858 | 20,917 | 14,212 | – | 13 |
| Apportionment of R's costs (£13 split 25:45:10:20) | 3 | 6 | 1 | 3 | (13) |
| | 22,861 | 20,923 | 14,213 | 3 | – |
| Apportionment of P's costs (£3 split 40:30:20:10) | 1 | 1 | 1 | – | – |
| | 22,862 | 20,924 | 14,214 | – | – |

The overheads of both service departments have been apportioned to the production departments repeatedly until all the service costs have been transferred in full to the production departments:

$$£22,862 + £20,924 + 14,214 = £58,000$$

You can see that this could be quite a lengthy and laborious task when done manually. Clearly, a computer spreadsheet would speed matters up and would ensure accuracy in the calculations.

(c) The algebraic method.

For those who have a mathematical bent the algebraic method will produce the same end result that the repeated distribution method gave, but it is much quicker.

Let P = department P
Let R = department R

The amounts to be absorbed into production departments A, B, and C is based on the following two equations:

P = £5,000 + 20%R❶    (P's costs are £5,000 + 20% of R's costs)
R = £8,000 + 10%P❷    (R's costs are £8,000 + 10% of P's costs)

If we multiply equation ❶ by 5 we have an equation with R (not just 20% of R), so equation ❶ becomes

$$5P = £25,000 + R \quad ❸$$

We know that R = £8,000 + 10%P from equation ❷ so if we substitute equation ❶ into equation ❸ we get:

$$5P = £25,000 + £8,000 + 10\%P$$

so

$$5P = £33,000 + 10\%P$$

If we deduct 10%P from both sides of the equation

$$5P - 10\%P = £33,000 + 10\%P - 10\%P$$
$$4.9\,P = £33,000$$

and then divide both sides of the equation by 4.9 we get:

$$4.9P/4.9 = £33,000/4.9$$
$$P = £6,734.69$$

Since we now know the value of P, we can substitute £6,735 for P in equation ❷:

$$R = £8,000 + 10\% \text{ of } P$$

so

$$R = £8,000 + 10\% \text{ of } £6,735$$
$$R = £8,000 + £674$$
$$R = £8,674$$

These are the costs which need to be apportioned to the production departments in the ratios of the work done by the servicing departments.

40% of department P's costs to department A is 40% of £6,735 = £2,694
30% of department P's costs to department B is 30% of £6,735 = £2,021
20% of department P's costs to department C is 20% of £6,735 = £1,347

25% of department R's costs to department A is 25% of £8,674 = £2,169
45% of department R's costs to department B is 45% of £8,674 = £3,903
10% of department R's costs to department C is 10% of £8,674 = £867

The total cost allocated and apportioned to department A is £22,863 (£18,000 + £2,694 +2,169)

The total cost allocated and apportioned to department B is £20,924 (£15,000 + £2,021 + £3,903).

The total cost allocated and apportioned to department C is £14,214 (12,000 + £1,347 + £867).

The total of all the overheads has been allocated and apportioned to the production departments (cost centres). These costs must now be absorbed into the production cost of the product, and these costs must be recovered by the business. A proportion of the overheads must be added to each cost unit that passes through the cost centre.

## 9.3 OVERHEAD ABSORPTION

How is the proportion of the overheads to be absorbed by the product arrived at? The main methods used are: direct labour hour rate, direct labour cost rate, machine hour rate and produced rate.

### DIRECT LABOUR HOUR RATE

The estimated total of all the overheads allocated and apportioned to the producing department for an accounting period is divided by the estimated number of hours worked in that department during the same accounting period.

## EXAMPLE 1

The total overheads for department QB1 are estimated to be £80,850.

The total hours worked in the department during the same time period is estimated to be 21,000.

### Required

Calculate the overhead recovery rate for department QB1 using the direct labour hour rate method.

### Solution

Department QB1 overhead recovery rate $= \dfrac{£80,850}{21,000} = £3.85$ per labour hour.

# DIRECT LABOUR COST RATE

The estimated total of all the overheads allocated and apportioned to the producing department for an accounting period is divided by the estimated cost of direct labour for the same accounting period.

## EXAMPLE 2

The total overheads for Department JP6 is estimated at £141,996.

The total direct labour costs for Department JP6 in the same time period is estimated at £302,120.

### Required

Calculate the overhead recovery rate for Department JP6 using the direct labour cost rate method.

### Solution

Department JP6 overhead recovery rate $= \dfrac{£141,996}{£302,120} = 47$ pence per £ of direct labour cost.

# MACHINE HOUR RATE

The estimated total of all the overheads allocated and apportioned to the producing department for an accounting period is divided by the estimated number of machine hours worked in the same accounting period.

## EXAMPLE 3

The total overheads for department CA10 are estimated to be £484,906. The total machine hours worked in the department are estimated to be 71,520

### Required

Calculate the overhead recovery rate for department CA10 using the machine hour method.

### Solution

Department CA10 overhead recovery rate $= \dfrac{£484,906}{71,520} = £6.78$ per machine hour.

# UNIT PRODUCED RATE

The estimated total of all the overheads allocated and apportioned to the producing department for an accounting period is divided by the estimated number of units to be produced in the same accounting period.

## EXAMPLE 4

The total overheads for Department BB7 is estimated at £182,850. The total number of units to be produced in Department BB7 in the same time period is estimated to be 345,000.

### Required

Calculate the overhead recovery rate for Department BB7 using the unit produced rate.

### Solution

Department BB7 overhead recovery rate $= \dfrac{£182,850}{£345,000} = 53$ pence per unit produced.

# WHICH METHOD OF OVERHEAD ABSORPTION SHOULD BE USED?

In an examination you will be asked to use a particular basis for calculating the overhead recovery rate.

### EXAMPLE 5

The estimated overheads for Townhead manufacturers plc using the simplified method of apportionment were:

Department A: £22,640    Department B: £20,580    Department C: £14,120

In Department A management use a machine hour rate as the method of recovering overheads.

In Departments B and C a direct labour hour rate is used as the basis for recovery of overheads.

Machine hours worked in Department A are estimated to be 5,660.
Labour hours worked in Department B are estimated to be 1,029
Labour hours worked in Department C are estimated to be 2,824

**Required**

(a) Calculate the overhead recovery rates for each department.

(b) Use your results from part (a) to calculate the cost of job SMH/65 which incurs the following costs:

|  |  | £ |
|---|---|---|
| Department A: | Direct materials | 230 |
|  | Direct labour | 105 |
|  | Machine hours | 4 |
| Department B: | Direct materials | 18 |
|  | Direct labour hours @ £5.40 per hour | 6 |
| Department C: | Direct materials | 3 |
|  | Direct labour hours @ £6.30 per hour | 2 |

**Solution**

(a) Department A $\dfrac{£22,640}{5,660 \text{ hours}}$ = 4 per machine hour

Department B $\dfrac{£20,580}{1,029 \text{ hours}}$ = £20 per labour hour

Department C $\dfrac{£14,120}{2,824 \text{ hours}}$ = £5 per labour hour

(b)                                    **Job SMH/65**

|  |  |  | £ | £ |
|---|---|---|---|---|
| Department A | Direct materials |  |  | 230.00 |
|  | Direct labour |  |  | 105.00 |
| Department B | Direct materials |  |  | 18.00 |
|  | Direct labour |  |  | 32.40 |
| Department C | Direct materials |  |  | 3.00 |
|  | Direct labour |  |  | 12.60 |
| Prime cost |  |  |  | 401.00 |
| Overheads absorbed: | Department A 4hrs @ £4 | 16.00 |  |  |
|  | Department B 6hrs @ £20 | 120.00 |  |  |
|  | Department C 2hrs @ £5 | 10.00 |  | 146.00 |
| Total production cost |  |  |  | 547.00 |

# WHAT ARE THE RELATIVE MERITS OF EACH METHOD OF RECOVERING OVERHEADS?

The choice of which method to use will be decided by the management of the business.

It seems sensible to use the direct labour hour method when the overhead is related to time, and the cost centre is labour intensive.

The direct labour cost rate may be considered if the business is labour intensive. The main criticisms of this method is that higher rates of pay will attract a higher proportion of the overhead, so the use of skilled workers will attract a greater proportion of overhead than the use of unskilled labour. Also, overheads are time related, e.g. rent, rates etc, they are not a function of direct wages.

The machine hour rate would seem more appropriate in a capital intensive business, since many overheads are related to the use of machinery, e.g. power, depreciation etc.

The unit produced method is best suited to a business that produces one product or a range of products that are almost identical and take approximately the same time to produce.

## 9.4 OVERHEAD ADJUSTMENT ACCOUNT

### OVER ABSORPTION AND UNDER ABSORPTION OF OVERHEADS

The overheads are based on predictions of future levels of activity. It would be highly unlikely that the actual figure incurred on overheads would agree with the figures forecast a year or so beforehand. Differences between the amount of estimated overheads absorbed into the product costing and the actual overheads incurred will result in an over or under recovery of overheads.

The over or under absorption of overheads are posted to an overhead adjustment account. At the end of the accounting period any balance on this account is written off to the profit and loss account.

Over absorption will have occurred if:

* The actual level of output is greater than the forecast (budgeted) output;
* The actual overhead is less than the forecast amount.

Under absorption will have occurred if:

* The actual level of output is less than the forecast (budgeted) output;
* The actual overhead is greater than the forecast amount.

### EXAMPLE

Townhead Manufacturers plc's budget for overhead expenditure of £210,000 is based on a production level of 70,000 units. Their overhead absorption rate is £3 per unit (210,000/70,000).

**Required**

Calculate the over absorption or under absorption of overheads if

(a) Actual output was 71,000 units and expenditure on overheads was as forecast.

(b) Actual output was 68,000 units and expenditure on overheads was as forecast.

(c) Actual output was 70,000 (as forecast) and expenditure on overheads was £215,000

(d) Actual output was 70,000 (as forecast) and expenditure on overheads was £190,000

**Solution**

(a) Over recovery was $1,000 \times £3 = £3,000$

(b) Under recovery was $2,000 \times £3 = £6,000$

(c) Under recovery was $£215,000 - £210,000 = £5,000$

(d) Over recovery was $£210,000 - £190,000 = £20,000$

### OTHER OVERHEADS

The other costs of running a business must also be recovered. Selling costs, distribution costs, and administration costs must all be recovered if the business is to prosper. These costs will be recovered through the mark up that the business adds to the cost of goods sold.

Selling, distribution and administration costs are treated as period costs and as such are debited to the profit and loss account.

> ## Chapter roundup
>
> Chapter 9 has dealt with allocation and apportionment of overheads and their ultimate absorption into the product by way of labour or machine hours. It has introduced the concept of variances.
>
> You should be able to allocate overheads to departments using a rational method, then absorb the total overheads into a job or contract.

# Illustrative questions

**1** Horden Products Ltd manufactures goods which could involve any or all of three production departments. These departments are simply entitled A, B and C. A direct wages cost percentage absorption rate for the recovery of production overheads is applied to individual job costs.

Details from the company's budgets for the year ended 31 March 1995 are as follows:

|  | Dept. A | Dept. B | Dept. C |
| --- | --- | --- | --- |
| Indirect materials | £23,000 | £35,000 | £57,000 |
| Indirect wages | £21,000 | £34,000 | £55,000 |
| Direct wages | £140,000 | £200,000 | £125,000 |
| Direct labour hours | 25,000 | 50,000 | 60,000 |
| Machine hours | 100,000 | 40,000 | 10,000 |

The following information is also available for the production departments.

|  | Dept. A | Dept. B | Dept. C |
| --- | --- | --- | --- |
| Area (square metres) | 30,000 | 20,000 | 10,000 |
| Cost of machinery | £220,000 | £160,000 | £20,000 |
| Horse power of machinery | 55 | 30 | 15 |

Other budgeted figures are:

|  | £ |
| --- | --- |
| Power | 120,000 |
| Rent, rates, light, heat | 90,000 |
| Insurance (machinery) | 20,000 |
| Depreciation | 80,000 |

Machinery is depreciated on the basis of 20% on cost.

Job No. 347 passed through all three departments and incurred the following actual direct costs and times.

|  | Direct Material £ | Direct Wages £ | Direct Labour Hours | Machine Hours |
| --- | --- | --- | --- | --- |
| Dept. A | 152 | 88 | 35 | 60 |
| Dept. B | 85 | 192 | 90 | 30 |
| Dept. C | 52 | 105 | 45 | 10 |

A sum amounting to 30% of the production cost is added to every job to enable a selling price to be quoted.

*Required*

(a) A statement to show the total production overheads per department and calculate the absorption rate which the company has adopted. (28)

(b) Calculate the selling price to be quoted for Job No. 347. (8)

(c) Using the available data, calculate absorption rates when based on:
    (i)   direct labour hour rate; (3)
    (ii)  machine hour rate. (3)

(d) Explain clearly the meaning of the following terms relating to overheads:
    (i)   allotment; (3)
    (ii)  allocation; (3)
    (iii) apportionment. (2)
    (AEB)

*Tutorial note*
On the overhead analysis statement indicate clearly you basis or apportionment. Show all workings in part (b). Carefully differentiate your explanation in part (d). Once again if you cannot express yourself clearly, use examples.

*Suggested answer*

(a) **Horden Products Ltd production overhead analysis statement**

| Cost | Basis | Dept A £ | Dept B £ | Dept C £ |
|---|---|---|---|---|
| Indirect materials | Allocation | 23,000 | 35,000 | 57,000 |
| Indirect wages | Allocation | 21,000 | 34,000 | 55,000 |
| Power | Machine horse power | 66,000 | 36,000 | 18,000 |
| Rent rates etc | Area | 45,000 | 30,000 | 15,000 |
| Insurance | Cost of machinery | 11,000 | 8,000 | 1,000 |
| Depreciation | 20% on cost | 44,000 | 32,000 | 4,000 |
| | | 210,000 | 175,000 | 150,000 |

**Absorption rate**

Department A $\dfrac{210}{140} \times 100 = 150\%$

For every £1 spent on direct wages £1.50 overheads will be absorbed.

Department B $\dfrac{175}{200} \times 100 = 87.5$

For every £1 spent on direct wages 87.5p overheads will be absorbed.

Department C $\dfrac{150}{125} \times 100 = 120\%$

For every £1 spent on direct wages £1.20 overheads will be absorbed.

(b) **Selling price for Job No 347**

| | £ | £ | |
|---|---|---|---|
| Direct materials | | 289 | (152 + 85 + 52) |
| Direct wages | | 385 | (88 + 192 + 105) |
| Direct costs | | 674 | |
| Overheads  Dept A | 132 | | (150% of £88) |
|            Dept B | 168 | | (87.5% of 192) |
|            Dept C | 126 | | (120% of 105) |
| | | 426 | |
| Total production cost | | 1,100 | |
| Profit 30% of production cost | | 330 | |
| Selling price | | 1,430 | |

(c) (i) Direct labour hour rate  Dept A $\dfrac{210}{25} = £8.40$

                                    Dept B $\dfrac{175}{50} = £3.50$

                                    Dept C $\dfrac{150}{60} = £2.50$

(ii) Machine hour rate 　　Dept A $\dfrac{210}{100}$ = £2.10

　　　　　　　　　　　　Dept B $\dfrac{175}{40}$ = £4.375

　　　　　　　　　　　　Dept C $\dfrac{150}{10}$ = £15.00

(d) Allotment is the charging of costs to a cost centre when the cost was made specifically for that cost centre.

Allocation – if the amount of a cost is known with certainty, and the department causing the overhead can be specifically identified, the cost is allocated to that department.

Apportionment – some costs cannot be identified as arising from the activities of one specific department. The unallocated costs are apportioned to the various production departments using area, usage, numbers of staff etc.

**2** Togfell Ltd has decided to abandon its present costing system and change to one using absorption costing techniques. The company manufactures three products – Tog A, Tog B and Tog C. Each product has to pass through two production departments before it is completed. These departments are identified as the Cutting Department and the Machining and Finishing Department. Both departments are labour intensive, so it has been decided to use a direct labour hour rate of overhead absorption. Only overheads primarily involved with production will be used. The budgeted overhead costs for the coming year are:

|  | £ |
|---|---|
| Factory power | 59,500 |
| Sales commission | 30,000 |
| Light and heat (factory) | 46,200 |
| Depreciation of equipment | 62,500 |
| Repairs to factory equipment | 17,500 |
| Delivery charges to customers' premises | 21,700 |
| Advertising | 15,000 |
| Supervisory staff costs (factory) | 54,600 |
| Canteen expenses (used by all factory staff) | 39,360 |

The following is data upon which an appropriate basis of apportionment can be determined:

|  | Cutting Dept. | Machining and Finishing Dept. | Administration and Selling Dept. |
|---|---|---|---|
| Labour force (excluding supervisory) | 20 | 50 | 20 |
| Floor space (sq. metres) | 4,000 | 5,000 | 2,000 |
| Book value of equipment (£000) | 80 | 420 | – |
| Equipment (kilo-watt hours (000)) | 25 | 75 | – |
| Supervisory staff | 1 | 5 | – |
| Production time per product (hours) |  |  |  |
| Tog A | 0.6 | 3.5 |  |
| Tog B | 0.5 | 2.9 |  |
| Tog C | 0.4 | 2.4 |  |

The total hours worked by the factory labour force per person is expected to be 1,800.

*Required*

(a) Calculate, to two decimal places, the selected overhead absorption rate for each department (Cutting; and Machining and Finishing) stating the apportionment basis used. (24)

(b) Calculate, to two decimal places, the total unit overhead cost per product. (12)

(c) A report to the managing director briefly describing **three** methods of overhead absorption and in each case stating why each may or may not be adopted. (10)

(AEB)

*Tutorial note*

Note that you need only calculate the overhead absorption rate for the two production departments. The administration and selling departments must be included in the workings for apportioning the overheads. In part (c) remember to use the report format (easy marks).

*Suggested answer*

(a)                    **Togfell Ltd overhead apportionment statement**

| Cost | Basis | Cutting | Machining & Finishing | Administration & Selling |
|------|-------|---------|-----------------------|--------------------------|
| Factory power | Kilowatt/hour | 14,875 | 44,625 | |
| Light and heat | Floor space | 16,800 | 21,000 | 8,400 |
| Depreciation of equipment | Book value | 10,000 | 52,500 | |
| Repairs to equipment | Book value | 2,800 | 14,700 | |
| Supervision | Number of staff | 9,100 | 45,500 | |
| Canteen | Labour force | 8,610 | 22,550 | 8,200 |
| | | 62,185 | 200,875 | 16,600* |

*(not used in this question)

Direct labour hours    1 800 × 20 = 36,000 in cutting dept
                       1,800 × 50 = 90,000 in machining & finishing dept

$$\text{Rate} = \frac{62,185}{36,000} \qquad \frac{200,875}{90,000}$$

= £1.73 in cutting dept    £2.23 in machining & finishing dept

(b) Total unit overhead cost per product:

Tog A £1.73 × 0.6 = £1.038 and £2.23 × 3.5 = £7.805    Total = £8.84
Tog B £1.73 × 0.5 = £0.865 and £2.23 × 2.9 = £6.467    Total = £7.33
Tog C £1.73 × 0.4 = £0.692 and £2.23 × 2.4 = £5.352    Total = £6.04

(c) To
    From
    Date *(i.e. report format)*

*Methods of overhead absorption*

Methods could include:

Output – easy to apply; budget is divided by number of units produced; it is suitable when one homogeneous product is being produced.

Direct labour cost – easy to apply when labour and overhead are closely linked; budgeted overhead is divided by budgeted labour cost; weakness is that some overheads are time based and there are usually different grades of labour involved in production.

Labour hour rate – budgeted overhead is divided by budgeted labour hours; useful when process is labour intensive and machines play a very small part in production.

Machine hour rates – budgeted overhead is divided by budgeted machine hours; useful in capital intensive work because in this type of process the machines incur most of the overheads.

**3** Rimcast Ltd produces castings which depend for their quality on the experience of skilled craftsmen in the moulding department, where assisted by unskilled workers, manual methods of production are used. The castings are then subjected to machine operations in a department where the latest automatic machining methods have been introduced to the extent of almost complete exclusion of direct workers. Castings are then finished using labour intensive methods, and sold at agreed selling prices which are based on absorption costing principles. These prices have been calculated by adding 40% to total factory cost to recover all administration and selling overheads and then allowing for a profit margin of 20% on the final price.

Extracts from next year's budget are as follows:

| | Production departments | | | Service departments | |
| | Moulding | Machining | Finishing | Maintenance | Material handling |
|---|---|---|---|---|---|
| **Hourly rates of pay** | | | | | |
| Craftsmen | £5.00 | – | – | – | – |
| Unskilled workers | £3.00 | – | – | – | – |
| Other direct workers | – | £4.00 | £2.50 | – | – |
| Total direct labour hours | 250,000 | 30,000 | 120,000 | – | – |
| Total machine hours | 40,000 | 200,000 | – | – | – |
| Total departmental overheads | £281,209 | £724,735 | £134,056 | £240,000 | £120,000 |

Service departments provide services to the other departments as follows:

| | **Moulding** | **Machining** | **Finishing** | **Material handling** |
|---|---|---|---|---|
| Maintenance | 15% | 70% | 10% | 5% |
| Material handling | 65% | 15% | 20% | – |

### Required

(a) Calculate suitable overhead absorption rates for each of the production departments. (All calculations should be correct to **one** decimal place.)     (10)

(b) Calculate the selling price to be quoted for a batch of castings which are estimated to require direct materials costing £1,529 and to take the following times in the three departments.

| | **Moulding** | **Machining** | **Finishing** |
|---|---|---|---|
| Machine hours | 30 | 255 | – |
| Craftsmen's hours | 220 | – | – |
| Unskilled workers' hours | 130 | – | – |
| Other direct labour hours | – | 32 | 80 |

(10)
(NEAB)

*Tutorial note*

Part (b) needs quite a lot of workings to arrive at the correct solution – show all your workings in case you make the odd error.

*Suggested answer*

(a)          **Rimcast Ltd calculation of overhead absorption rates for production departments**

| | Moulding | Machining | Finishing | Maintenance | Material handling |
|---|---|---|---|---|---|
| | £ | £ | £ | £ | £ |
| Direct overheads | 281,209 | 724,735 | 134,056 | 240,000 | 120,000 |
| Maintenance | 36,000 | 168,000 | 24,000 | (240,000) | 12,000 |
| Material handling | 85,800 | 19,800 | 26,400 | – | (132,000) |
| | 403,009 | 912,535 | 184,456 | – | – |
| Labour hours | 250,000 | – | 120,000 | – | – |
| Machine hours | – | 200,000 | – | – | – |
| Absorption rates | £1.61 | £4.56 | £1.54 | | |
| (1 decimal place) | £1.60 | £4.60 | £1.50 | | |
| | per labour hour | per machine hour | per labour hour | | |

(b) **Calculation of selling price for a batch of castings**

|  |  | £ | £ |  |
|---|---|---|---|---|
| Direct materials |  |  | 1,529 |  |
| Direct labour: Moulding: Skilled |  | 1,100 |  | (220 hrs × £5.00) |
|  | Unskilled | 390 |  | (130 hrs × £3.00) |
| Machining |  | 128 |  | (32 hrs × £4.00) |
| Finishing |  | 200 |  | (80 hrs × £2.50) |
|  |  |  | 1,818 |  |
| Production overheads: | Moulding | 560 |  | (350 direct labour hrs × £1.60) |
|  | Machining | 1,173 |  | (255 machine hrs × £4.60) |
|  | Finishing | 120 |  | (80 direct labour hrs × £1.50) |
|  |  |  | 1,853 |  |
| Total factory cost |  |  | 5,200 |  |
| Selling and administrative overheads |  |  | 2,080 | (40% of £5,200) |
| Total cost |  |  | 7,280 |  |
| Profit |  |  | 1,820 | (20% of selling price (25% on cost)) |
| Total Selling price |  |  | 9,100 |  |

# BUDGETS AND BUDGETARY CONTROL

## Units in this chapter

10.1 *Budgeting*
10.2 *Budgetary control*

## Chapter objectives

In this chapter we look at budgeting as an aid to management. We see how budgets are a vital part of management accounting. Budgets act as both plans for the future and as a control mechanism.

The key topics and concepts covered in this chapter are:

- planning;
- preparing budgets;
- limiting factors;
- fixed budgets;
- flexible budgets;
- zero-based budgets;
- variances;
- cash budget;
- stock budget;
- debtors' budget;
- creditors' budget
- master budget.

## 10.1 BUDGETING

Planning within an organisation can be either:

- Long-term planning, generally known as, strategic or corporate planning.
- Short-term planning will provide the building blocks or the components of the long-term plan.

Short-term plans are known as budgets. A **budget** is a financial statement. It is prepared and approved in advance of a defined period of time, usually a year, and shows how policies are to be pursued during that time period in order that planned objectives can be attained.

A budget is based on the objectives of the business, and enables a manager to set operational targets for the department and then to control operations by comparing the actual results with those in the budget. Managers involved in the process have to think ahead and to co-ordinate their thinking with other managers. They will prepare operational (functional) budgets.

Budgets provide plans for cash movements. There is a time lag between paying for factors of production (wages, purchases of raw materials, etc) and receiving cash flows from sales of the finished product. Also, cash inflows may be irregular in their timing. Remember that liquidity is often the most critical aspect of business. Lack of cash causes many businesses to go into liquidation.

Budgeting enables management to anticipate future problems and to take appropriate corrective action.

The comparison of actual results with those that were budgeted is a similar process to that undertaken in standard costing (Chapter 11). However, budgets are prepared for the business as a whole while standard costing looks in detail at individual production and manufacturing costs.

Do not confuse budgeting with forecasting; they are not the same.

- A *budget* is a planned outcome of what the organisation hopes to achieve.
- A *budget* will show planned future incomes and expenditures.
- A *forecast* is a prediction of what could happen if a given set of circumstances is obtained in the future.
- A *forecast* does not imply any kind of management intervention.

Operational budgets may be prepared for:

- sales;
- production;
- expenses;
- stock;
- cash;
- debtors;
- creditors;
- research and development; and
- capital expenditure.

The defined time period covered by a budget is generally the next financial year, but some budgets require a much longer time horizon, notably those that involve capital projects and those that involve research and development.

The annual budget is generally supplemented by budgets prepared for a shorter time period. Some businesses prepare monthly budgets or quarterly budgets. These may be necessary if there are expected short-term variations in the operating conditions the business might face.

The information contained in these operational budgets will provide the constituent parts of the master budget (the budgeted trading and profit and loss account and balance sheet).

## PREPARING THE BUDGETS

The board of directors will appoint a budget committee, and charge that committee to prepare a budget for the following financial year. The board of directors will lay down the financial parameters that the committee has to work within.

The committee, which is usually the senior management team of the organisation, prepare a strategy that will achieve the organisation's objectives, bearing in mind the constraints laid down by the board for the next financial year.

The committee will appoint a budget officer who will prepare the master budget from the operational budgets and functional budgets prepared by heads of department. The budget officer may also help departmental managers in the preparation of their budgets.

The committee can either prepare the budgets themselves and rely on departmental heads to implement them, or the committee may let the heads of department prepare their own budgets and submit them for approval. If the operational budgets are prepared by senior managers, it could give them greater control but this method can cause resentment among those who have to operate the budget. If budgets are prepared by lower managers there may be a possibility of targets being set at a more comfortable level, and strategic objectives may not be met.

The budget officer or the committee will ensure that there are no contradictions or inconsistencies between the various subsidiary budgets. If there are problems they must be resolved before the master budget can be prepared.

The budget officer collates the operational budgets into the master budget (the budgeted profit and loss account and budgeted balance sheet). This is then submitted to the budget committee and then to the board of directors for approval.

Constraints may be placed on the key goals of a business by a **limiting factor** (also known as a **principal factor** or **key factor**).

For example, the senior management team of a biscuit manufacturing business could not implement an increase in production of chocolate-covered biscuits by a factor of 250 billion. Why not? What are the constraints? I am sure you can list some: could they sell 250 billion times more biscuits? Will the business be able to obtain sufficient ingredients to make 250 billion more biscuits? Are there sufficient machines to increase production? Etc.

Most businesses have a least one limiting factor. It is important that all the budgets are prepared with a consideration of what the physical constraints might be. The budgeting process will start with the budget of the department which faces the limiting factor. The other budgets will then be prepared around that budget taking into account the limitations imposed. If sales are the limiting factor, the other operational budgets will use the sales budget as a constraining influence. Management must determine the optimum output that can be achieved within the constraint imposed by the limiting factor.

If a factor of production is the limiting factor management must gain maximum benefit from the use of that factor, and the production budget would set the constraints to be borne in mind when the other operational budgets are prepared. (See also Marginal Costing Chapter 13.)

Budgeting involves the managers of a business looking into the future and formulating goals, and then deciding on strategies which will enable them to achieve the desired results.

## 10.2 BUDGETARY CONTROL

**Budgetary control** delegates financial planning to particular managers. It evaluates the performance of managers by comparing the actual results achieved by their department with those set in the budget.

Departments cannot work in isolation. It is essential to coordinate the different activities of a business if optimum performance is to be achieved. If the sales force manage to double the number of orders from one time period to the next, how can they be sure that production can meet the extra goods needed to fulfill the orders? If departmental managers make decisions purely within their own areas of responsibility without reference to other departments, this could lead to the frustration of the overall strategy of the organisation.

A system of budgetary control will ensure that all decision making is related to the corporate plan. It entails the continuous comparison of actual results with budgeted results in control periods (budget periods are broken down into smaller time periods for control purposes), either to allow remedial action to be undertaken in order to achieve the required end result, or to revise the budget.

Budgets may be **fixed** or **flexible**. Flexed budgets are considered further in Chapter 11.

A **fixed budget** remains unchanged whatever output is achieved by the organisation. The use of a **flexible budget** recognises that the application of a fixed budget approach to variable costs can give very misleading results. It recognises that cost patterns may vary with different levels of business activity.

Some organisations use a system of budgeting based on last year's actual results, plus a certain percentage increase, say 5%. The major problem with this approach is that some activities that may be uneconomical or inefficient may be perpetuated merely because they were pursued in the preceding year (some parts of the public sector use this approach).

**Zero-based budgeting** questions each activity as if it were a new one before allocating resources towards it.

If a business prepares short-term budgets (say, on a monthly or quarterly basis) the head of each department will receive a report based on a comparison of actual results and the budget. **Variances** (differences) between actual and budgeted figures will be highlighted. Favourable variances will increase profitability.

**Favourable variances** arise when:

- actual revenue is greater than budgeted revenue, or
- actual expenditure is less than budgeted expenditure.

**Adverse variances** arise when:

- actual revenue is less than budgeted revenue, or
- actual expenditure is greater than budgeted expenditure.

The report received by heads of departments will highlight departures from the budget, and are one measure of managerial effectiveness.

Budgets are based on a prediction of future events and conditions. All predictions are subject to error. This means that variances are inevitable. All variances should be analysed and should provoke action from the managers concerned. The analysis may reveal inefficiencies of some kind in a department – these inefficiencies should be eradicated if possible. The analysis may also reveal efficient operations which can be used throughout the business as examples of good practice.

## BENEFITS OF BUDGETARY CONTROL

- Budgets are a control mechanism for the whole of the business. They regulate the amount of money allocated to departments and draw attention to inefficiencies in departments.
- They allow comparisons between what was planned and what actually happened, thus allowing corrective action to be taken.
- Budgets clearly identify areas of responsibility and help to formalise management plans. The operational budgets make each manager aware of his/her department's role in the attainment of corporate objectives.
- Budgets enable delegation of responsibilities without the loss of control; the budget acting as a constraint, provided the subordinate stays within the budget set by a senior manager.
- Budgets are a vital aid to the co-ordination and communication between departments.
- They help to provide clear targets and can focus the mind on efficient economical methods that will have an effect on costs and productivity.

- Management by exception is facilitated – attention is focused on areas of the business that are not conforming to plan.
- If lower management has responsibility for the preparation of its own functional budgets it may lead to a sense of ownership and commitment to the corporate plan.

## THE DRAWBACKS OF BUDGETARY CONTROL

- Budgets can affect motivation. Staff not involved in the preparation of the budget may resent what they see as restrictions or edicts imposed from above, and this could result in poor performance.
- Budgets may result in the loss of business. If the sales budget has been spent before the end of the budget period, the sales team cannot operate effectively and could lose orders.
- If actual results differ widely from those budgeted, the control function may seem less important to those who operate the budget.

Examination questions tend to concentrate on the preparation of cash budgets, although the preparation of other budgets does appear from time to time in examination papers. Be aware of the format for each type of budget.

The summary layout is similar for all types of budget:

|  |  | **Months** |
|---|---|---|
| Balance brought forward |  |  |
|  | receipts of cash |  |
|  | purchases/production of stock |  |
| Increases | sales to debtors |  |
|  | purchases from creditors |  |
|  |  | **subtotals** |
|  | payments of cash |  |
|  | issues of stock |  |
| Decreases | cash received from debtors |  |
|  | cash paid to creditors |  |
| Balance carried forward |  |  |

You will have to provide a receipts and payments schedule for a cash budget in order to arrive at the figures that go into the summary.

EXAMPLE

Ann Baron plans to open a retail shop on 1 August 1996. She will withdraw £30,000 from her private building society account and pay it into the business bank account.

Ann will sell her goods at a uniform mark-up of 80% on cost price.

She provides you with the following forecasts for the four months ending on 30 November 1996:

(1) On 1 August 1996:
She will pay £3,000 rent for the six months ending 31 January 1997.
She will purchase and pay for shop fixtures and fittings £2,700.
She will purchase a delivery van £8,880, paying an initial deposit of £2,880 on 1 August. She will borrow the balance and repay 24 monthly instalments of £280 (each repayment includes interest of £30 per month) payable on the first of each month thereafter.
She plans to depreciate her fixed assets using the straight line method at the following rates: fixtures and fittings at 10% per annum on cost; delivery van at 25% per annum on cost.

(2) She will employ two assistants. Each will receive a salary of £780 per calendar month.

(3) The purchases for the 4 months are expected to be: August £2,500; September £1,600; October £1,800; November £2,000. Suppliers will be paid one month after the purchases are made.

(4) Sales are expected to be: August £2,700; September £2,970; October £3,240; November £3,600.
Ann anticipates that one third of her sales will be for cash the remainder will be

credit sales. Debtors are expected to pay one month after the sales have been made.

(5) General running expenses for the shop are expected to be: August £230; September £480; October £330; November £600.

(6) Ann with withdraw £560 per calendar month for her own private expenses.

**Required**

(a) A cash budget for the four months ending 30 November 1996.

(b) A stock budget for the four months ending 30 November 1996.

(c) A debtors budget for the four months ending 30 November 1996.

(d) A creditors budget for the four months ending 30 November 1996.

(e) A budgeted trading and profit and loss account for the four months ending 30 November 1996.

(f) A budgeted balance sheet as at 30 November 1996.

**Solution**

(a)      **Ann Baron cash budget for the four months ending 30 November 1996**

| | August £ | September £ | October £ | November £ |
|---|---|---|---|---|
| Schedule of receipts | | | | |
| Capital | 30,000 | | | |
| Cash sales | 900 | 990 | 1,080 | 1,200 |
| Receipts from debtors | | 1,800 | 1,980 | 2,160 |
| | 30,900 | 2,790 | 3,060 | 3,360 |
| Schedule of payments | | | | |
| Rent | 3,000 | | | |
| Fixtures and fittings | 2,700 | | | |
| Van | 2,880 | 280 | 280 | 280 |
| Wages | 1,560 | 1,560 | 1,560 | 1,560 |
| Payments to creditors | | 2,500 | 1,600 | 1,800 |
| General expenses | 230 | 480 | 330 | 600 |
| Drawings | 560 | 560 | 560 | 560 |
| | 10,930 | 5,380 | 4,330 | 4,800 |
| Cash budget | | | | |
| Balance brought forward | – | 19,970 | 17,380 | 16,110 |
| Receipts | 30,900 | 2,790 | 3,060 | 3,360 |
| | 30,900 | 22,760 | 20,440 | 19,470 |
| Payments | 10,930 | 5,380 | 4,330 | 4,800 |
| | 19,970 | 17,380 | 16,110 | 14,670 |

There are other layouts. If your teacher has taught you another acceptable layout and you feel comfortable using it – continue to use it.

(b)      **Stock budget for the four months ending 30 November 1996**

| | £ | £ | £ | £ |
|---|---|---|---|---|
| Balance brought forward | – | 1,000 | 950 | 950 |
| Purchases of stock | 2,500 | 1,600 | 1,800 | 2,000 |
| | 2,500 | 2,600 | 2,750 | 2,950 |
| Sales | 1,500 | 1,650 | 1,800 | 2,000 |
| Balance carried forward | 1,000 | 950 | 950 | 950 |

(c)      **Debtors budget for the four months ending 30 November 1996**

| | £ | £ | £ | £ |
|---|---|---|---|---|
| Balance brought forward | – | 1,800 | 1,980 | 2,160 |
| Sales | 1,800 | 1,980 | 2,160 | 2,400 |
| | 1,800 | 3,780 | 4,140 | 4,560 |
| Cash received from debtors | – | 1,800 | 1,980 | 2,160 |
| Balance carried forward | 1,800 | 1,980 | 2,160 | 2,400 |

(d)              **Creditors budget for the four months ending 30 November 1996**

|                              | £       | £     | £     | £     |
|------------------------------|---------|-------|-------|-------|
| Balance brought forward      | –       | 2,500 | 1,600 | 1,800 |
| Purchases                    | 2,500   | 1,600 | 1,800 | 2,000 |
|                              | 2,500   | 4,100 | 3,400 | 3,800 |
| Cash paid to creditors       | –       | 2,500 | 1,600 | 1,800 |
| Balance carried forward      | 2,500   | 1,600 | 1,800 | 2,000 |

(e)              **Ann Baron budgeted trading and profit and loss account**
                 **for the four months ending 30 November 1996**

|                                    | £      | £      |
|------------------------------------|--------|--------|
| Sales                              |        | 12,510 |
| less Cost of sales:                |        |        |
|     Purchases  | 7,900  |        |
|     less stock 30 November 1996 | 950 | 6,950 |
| Gross profit                       |        | 5,560  |
| less Expenses:                     |        |        |
|     Wages      | 6,240  |        |
|     General expenses | 1,640 |    |
|     Rent       | 2,000  |        |
|     Loan interest | 90  |        |
|     Depreciation:  Fixtures | 90 |  |
|            Delivery van | 740 | 10,800 |
| Net loss                           |        | 5,240  |

(f)              **Ann Baron budgeted balance sheet as at 30 November 1996**

|                                    | £      | £      |
|------------------------------------|--------|--------|
| Fixed assets                       |        |        |
| Fixtures and fittings at cost      | 2,700  |        |
| less depreciation                  | 90     | 2,610  |
| Delivery van at cost               | 8,880  |        |
| less depreciation                  | 740    | 8,140  |
|                                    |        | 10,750 |
| Current assets                     |        |        |
|     Stock      | 950    |        |
|     Debtors    | 2,400  |        |
|     Bank       | 14,670 |        |
| Prepayment - rent                  | 1,000  |        |
|                                    | 19,020 |        |
| less Current liabilities           |        |        |
|     Creditors  | 2,000  | 17,020 |
|                                    |        | 27,770 |
| Capital                            |        | 30,000 |
| less loss                          | 5,240  |        |
|     drawings   | 2,240  | 7,480  |
|                                    |        | 22,520 |
| Loan for delivery van              | 6,000  |        |
| less repayments                    | 750    | 5,250  |
|                                    |        | 27,770 |

*Points to note*
Notice how similar all the summaries are:

Opening balance + increases – decreases = Closing balance.

**Cash budget:**
- Do not get cash budgets confused with cash flow statements
- Always show each month separately; accounting is an information system. The position at each month end is important to the business.
- Examiners usually require the cash transactions due to credit sales and credit purchases to take place one or two months after the appropriate transactions have taken place.

- Depreciation does not figure in the cash budget – there is no movement of cash with depreciation. The entries required are merely book entries.

**Stock budget:**

- Remember that issues of stock are at cost. You may have to reduce the value from selling price to cost price.

**Debtors budget:**

- Include only credit sales.
- If there are any discounts allowed show these separately, but deduct them with the cash.
- Provisions for bad debts should be ignored here and in the cash budget, but must be included on the profit and loss account.

**Creditors budget:**

- Include only credit purchases.
- If there are any discounts received, show them separately but deduct them with the cash.

**Profit and loss account:**

- Make sure you get the heading correct. It should say: *budgeted profit and loss account for xx months ending . . .*
- If the profit and loss account is only for four months then only the expenses for those four months must be included, i.e. rent for four months, depreciation for four months etc.
- Note the split of the loan repayments. The interest is a charge on profits while the capital repayments are deducted from the outstanding capital figure on the balance sheet.

**The balance sheet**

- It is just like every other balance sheet you have drawn up.
- Note the heading. A balance sheet is prepared at one moment in time. It shows the state of affairs of a business at the end of one day. The balance sheet is not prepared over a time period. Balance sheets always have a heading that says Balance sheet as at . . .

---

### Chapter roundup

Chapter 10 has explained the importance of budgeting for management and control purposes.

It has developed the concept of simple budgets into the use of budgets to ensure overall control of a business by passing management responsibilities to lower and middle managers.

You should be able to prepare simple cash, stock and debtors and creditors budgets and use the information from them to prepare a master budget (forecast final accounts).

---

# Illustrative questions

1  Porthcothen Enterprises Ltd plans to open a new factory on 1 August 1994. The finance will be raised by the issue of a 10% debenture of £800,000 in July 1994 (interest payable in July 1995). At the same time the company will purchase plant and machinery costing £520,000 and stock costing £200,000. Both of these items will be paid for in August 1994.

   The company makes the following forecasts for the year ending 31 July 1995.

   (i)  Gross profit will be 25% on cost.

(ii) Credit sales of £150,000 per month and cash sales of £50,000 per month will be achieved.

(iii) Credit customers are expected to pay two months following the month of sale.

(iv) Each month's sales will be replaced by an equivalent monthly purchase (i.e. stocks will remain constant).

(v) Purchases will be paid for in the month following delivery.

(vi) Expenses will be incurred at the rate of £24,000 per month and paid immediately; of these expenses £18,000 will be fixed and the remainder will vary with sales.

(vii) Bad debts will be 2% of credit sales.

(viii) Depreciation, calculated on a straight line basis, will be 10% per annum. The plant and machinery will have no residual value.

*Required*
(a) Prepare a month-by-month cash budget for the year ending 31 July 1995, highlighting the maximum overdraft requirement. (10)
(b) Prepare a forecast profit and loss account for the year ending 31 July 1995. (8)
(c) Prepare a forecast balance sheet as at 31 July 1995. (8)
(d) Reconcile the forecast profit with the forecast bank balance at 31 July 1995; (4)
(e) Calculate the additional sales required to give a return of 15% if the company had chosen to use its own capital instead of borrowing. (You are to assume that all the additional sales would be on credit.) 10)

Calculations should be to the nearest whole number and workings must be shown.

(NEAB)

*Tutorial note*
Always use a month-by-month budget in examinations. Pay particular attention to the time lags involved in the listed transactions. Take care in your treatment of the depreciation charge. Show all your working, especially in (d) and (e).

*Suggested answer*
(a) **Cash budget**

|  | Aug £000 | Sept £000 | Oct .... £000 | June £000 | July £000 |
|---|---|---|---|---|---|
| Receipts |  |  |  |  |  |
| Cash sales | 50 | 50 | 50 ❶ | 50 | 50 |
| Cash from debtors |  |  | 147 | 147 | 147 |
|  | 50 | 50 | 197 | 197 | 197 |
| Payments |  |  |  |  |  |
| Cash to creditors |  | 160 | 160 | 160 | 160 |
| Expenses | 24 | 24 | 24 | 24 | 24 |
| Plant & machinery | 520 |  |  |  |  |
| Stock | 200 |  |  |  |  |
| Debenture interest |  |  |  |  | 80 |
|  | 744 | 184 | 184 | 184 | 264 |
| Balance | 800 | 106 | (28) | 76 | 89 |
| Receipts | 50 | 50 | 197 ❷ | 197 | 197 |
|  | 850 | 156 | 169 | 273 | 286 |
| Payments | 744 | 184 | 184 ❸ | 184 | 264 |
| Balance | 106 | (28) | (15) | 89 | 22 |

This cash budget is fairly straightforward but care must be taken not to become too complacent.

❶ The months November to May inclusive follow the same pattern as October.
❷ Receipts for the next seven months amount to £197,000.
❸ Payments for the next seven months amount to £184,000.

(b)

**Porthcothen Enterprises Ltd forecast trading and profit
and loss account for the year ending 31 July 1995**

|  | £ | £ |
|---|---|---|
| Sales |  | 2,400,000 |
| Less cost of sales |  | 1,920,000 |
| Gross profit |  | 480,000 |
| Less expenses |  |  |
| Expenses | 288,000 |  |
| Bad debts | 36,000 |  |
| Debenture interest | 80,000 |  |
| Depreciation | 52,000 | 456,000 |
| Net profit |  | 24,000 |

(c)

**Balance sheet as at 31 July 1995**

|  | Cost | Depreciation | Net |
|---|---|---|---|
| Fixed assets | £ | £ | £ |
| Plant and machinery | 520,000 | 52,000 | 468,000 |
| Current assets |  |  |  |
| Stock |  | 200,000 |  |
| Debtors |  | 294,000 |  |
| Bank |  | 22,000 |  |
|  |  | 516,000 |  |
| Less Current liabilities: creditors |  | 160,000 | 356,000 |
|  |  |  | 824,000 |
| Less 10% Debentures |  |  | 800,000 |
|  |  |  | 24,000 |
| Reserves: profit and loss account |  |  | 24,000 |

(d) There are often a number of different approaches that can be taken in order to arrive at an answer. This section is a case in point. I show only one approach, if you arrive at the reconciliation from another direction then you would be awarded the appropriate marks.

**Porthcothen Enterprises Ltd reconciliation of net profit and bank
balance as at 31 July 1995**

|  | £ |
|---|---|
| Profit as per forecast profit and loss account | 24,000 |
| Add depreciation | 52,000 |
| amounts owing to creditors | 160,000 |
| bad debts | 36,000 |
| Less amounts owed by debtors | (294,000) |
| Forecast bank balance as per cash budget | 22,000 |

(e) Porthcothen requires a return of 15% on the capital invested.
15% of £800,000 = £120,000.

The company already makes £24,000. This would rise by a further £80,000 if the debenture interest was not required – profits would be £104,000 without the debentures The shortfall in profits that needs to be made up is therefore £16,000. The company is earning 20% gross profit on sales, but this is reduced by 5% to 15% when the bad debts of 2% and variable expenses of 3% (notes (ii) and (vi), £6,000 on sales of £200,000) are taken into account.

We need to increase Porthcothen's profits by £16,000, which requires increased sales of £106,667.

$$\frac{15}{100} \times \text{Sales} = £16,000$$

$$15 \times \text{Sales} = £16,000 \times 100$$

$$\text{Sales} = \frac{£1,600,000}{15}$$

**2** (a) Define the terms *budget centre, functional budget,* and *master budget.* How does the concept of 'budget centre' differ from that of 'cost centre'? (10)

(b) From the following information, you are required to prepare for the six months ending 30 June 1995:
(i) a monthly cash budget; and
(ii) a forecast operating statement to show planned gross profit.

| Sales | Finished Goods | Raw Material Purchases |
|---|---|---|
| **1994:** | £ | £ |
| Oct | 980 | 200 |
| Nov | 960 | 180 |
| Dec | 1,010 | 270 |
| **1995:** | | |
| Jan | 1,120 | 230 |
| Feb | 1,400 | 290 |
| Mar | 1,680 | 350 |
| Apr | 2,520 | 520 |
| May | 2,540 | 530 |
| Jun | 1,960 | 410 |

Additional information:

(1) Production cost per unit for 1995 are expected to be:

| | £ |
|---|---|
| Direct materials | 8 |
| Direct labour | 6 |
| Variable overheads | 4 |
| | 18 |

(2) Raw materials are paid for two months after purchase.
(3) Debtors are expected to have paid for their goods after three months.
(4) Direct labour and variable overheads are paid in the same month as the units are produced.
(5) Production for January-April will be at the rate of 60 units per month; for May and June output will be 70 units per month.
(6) Fixed overheads are £150 per month payable in arrears.
(7) New equipment is to be paid for in March, £220.
(8) Bank balance at 1 January 1995 was £100.
(9) The value of finished units in stock at 1 January 1995 was £900; the value of finished units at 30 June 1995 is expected to be £720. (12)

(c) Why might you have used a different set of sales figures for the cash budget than for the operating statement? (3)

(ULEAC)

*Tutorial note*
Be clear and precise with your definitions. Carefully check the precise meaning of any concept involved before applying to a question.

*Suggested answer*
(a) *Budget centres* are also called responsibility centres and are part of an organisation for which a separate budget is prepared.

A *functional budget* relates to a particular function which is common to a number of different budget centres within an organisation, for example personnel, marketing etc.

The *master budget* is prepared by collating all the budgets from the individual budget centres. It is often called the budgeted trading and profit and loss account and budgeted balance sheet. It is the overall budget for the organisation.

A *cost centre* is a person (or machine), or a group of people (or machines), engaged in a single easily identifiable activity, whose costs can be itemised and to which costs can be allocated for control purposes. A budget centre will use information from cost centres to produce its departmental budget.

(b) (i)

| **Cash budget** | **Jan** | **Feb** | **March** | **April** | **May** | **June** |
|---|---|---|---|---|---|---|
| | £ | £ | £ | £ | £ | £ |
| Receipts from debtors | 980 | 960 | 1,010 | 1,120 | 1,400 | 1,680 |
| Payments | | | | | | |
| Direct materials | 180 | 270 | 230 | 290 | 350 | 520 |
| Direct labour | 360 | 360 | 360 | 360 | 420 | 420 |
| Variable overheads | 240 | 240 | 240 | 240 | 280 | 280 |
| Fixed overheads | 150 | 150 | 150 | 150 | 150 | 150 |
| Equipment | | | 220 | | | |
| | 930 | 1,020 | 1,200 | 1,040 | 1,200 | 1,370 |
| Balance | 100 | 150 | 90 | (100) | (20) | 180 |
| Total receipts | 980 | 960 | 1,010 | 1,120 | 1,400 | 1,680 |
| | 1,080 | 1,110 | 1,100 | 1,020 | 1,380 | 1,860 |
| Total payments | 930 | 1,020 | 1,200 | 1,040 | 1,200 | 1,370 |
| Balance | 150 | 90 | (100) | (20) | 180 | 490 |

(ii) **Forecast operating statement for the six months ending 30 June 1995**

| | £ | £ |
|---|---|---|
| Sales | | 11,220 |
| Opening stock of finished goods | 900 | |
| Purchases of direct materials | 2,330 | |
| Direct labour costs | 2,280 | |
| Variable overheads | 1,520 | |
| Fixed overheads | 900 | |
| Depreciation of equipment | 11 | |
| | 7,941 | |
| Less closing stock of finished goods | 720 | 7,221 |
| Gross profit | | 3,999 |

(c) The realisation concept states that a sale is recognised when the title passes to the purchaser, not when the cash is paid to the seller. Sales are £11,220; the cash received is £7,150; £11,220 is used in the operating statement.

# STANDARD COSTING AND VARIANCE ANALYSIS

## Units in this chapter

11.1 *Standard costing*
11.2 *Variances*
11.3 *The flexed budget*
11.4 *Overhead variances*

## Chapter objectives

In this chapter we see that before a product is made, management will plan how it is to be produced – the amounts of materials to be used, the labour needed to make it, and the overheads that will be used during the manufacturing process. This will allow the management to estimate the likely total production cost for the product.

The key topics and concepts covered in this chapter are:

- management by exception;
- standard hours;
- standard labour cost;
- standard overhead cost;
- variances;
- sub variances;
- price variances;
- quantity variances;
- flexing the budget;
- sales variances;
- fixed and variable overhead variances;
- causes of variances.

## 11.1 STANDARD COSTING

**Standard costing** sets levels of costs and revenues which ought to be achieved when reasonable levels of performance are used, together with efficient working practices, to manufacture a product. It deals with *costs that ought to occur*. It is a carefully prepared prediction of what should happen to individual costs if everything goes according to plan.

The standards set should not be impossible to achieve, otherwise they will have a de-motivating effect on staff.

Standard costing involves some of the processes used in budgeting. The major difference is that budgeting deals with the business as a whole, whereas standard costing relates to the individual cost units.

The managers in businesses set standards for themselves and their employees. Standard costing promotes efficiency, since the standards will be compared with actual performance. If there are variations from the standards, the differences (variances) will be investigated.

If the standard costs agree or are lower than actual costs, then management may decide that investigation will not be necessary. This is an example of **management by exception**. Management can then concentrate their energies on areas where there are adverse variances from the budget.

In standard costing production is often expressed in **standard hours**. This measures the quantity of work that can be achieved at a standard level of performance in one hour. For example, a manager might expect a worker to produce 10 units of output per hour. If the business works on standard minutes this would give 0.167 standard units per minute.

The **standard material cost** is determined by the type of material required, the quality of the material required to complete the job to the customers' satisfaction, and the expected price of the materials. **Standard labour cost** is determined by the grades of labour to be employed to complete the work, and the expected wage rate of each grade of labour employed on the job. **Standard overhead cost** is determined by using the information from the calculations of overhead absorption rates.

## 11.2 VARIANCES

Standard material cost, standard labour cost and standard overhead costs are compared with actual material cost, actual labour cost and actual overhead cost. Any deviations between standard cost and actual cost is called a variance.

Once a variance has been calculated it should be analysed into its constituent parts. This is known as **variance analysis**. Within each **total variance** there are two **sub-variances**, one relating to the price paid, the other relating to the quantity used. The total variance and the sub-variances may be **favourable** (if the price paid or the costs incurred increase profit) or **adverse** (if the price paid or the costs incurred decrease profit). The calculations in order to find total variances should be straightforward.

Standard Cost – Actual cost = Total variance
(if positive then favourable, if negative adverse)

The sub-variances require you to *learn the formulae*. These formulae are presented in two main ways in text books and by teachers; both methods are the same, only the layout is slightly different.

- Price variance = (standard price per unit-actual price per unit) x actual quantity of units
- Quantity variance = (standard quantity – actual quantity) x standard price per unit

If you are comfortable using these formulae in this form then continue to use them. If you have difficulty in remembering the formulae as shown above try this version:

Standard quantity × Standard price  }
Actual quantity × Standard price    }  }  = Quantity variance
Actual quantity × Actual price      }     = Price variance

It can be abbreviated to:

Sq × Sp  }
Aq × Sp  }  }  = Quantity variance
Aq × Ap     }  = Price variance

The same formula may be used this way round:

Aq × Ap  }
Aq × Sp  }  }  = Price variance
Sq × Sp     }  = Quantity variance

You will get the same results.

Both these ways of calculating sub-variances will give the same results. Choose the layout that you find easiest to learn.

## EXAMPLE 1

Standard cost 40 units at £16 per unit. Actual cost 38 units at £19 per unit.

**Point to note**

In this illustration there is no indication whether the units are labour hours or quantities of material.

**Required**

Calculate the total variance; the quantity sub-variance and the price sub-variance.

**Solution**

| Sq × Sp | 40 × 16 | = £640 | } | | |
|---------|---------|--------|---|---|---|
| Aq × Sp | 38 × 16 | = £608 | } } | £32 | Quantity variance favourable |
| Aq × Ap | 38 × 19 | = £722 | } | £114 | Price variance adverse |
| | | | | £82 | Total variance adverse |

Once you have learned this basic formula it can be adapted to all the problems you are likely to encounter with regard to materials, labour and sales in your examination.

- **Quantity** is the correct word to describe amounts of materials.
- **Labour hours** describes the quantity of labour used.
- **Price** is the correct word to describe the cost of materials.
- **Labour rate** or **wage rate** describes the reward to labour.
- The quantity sub-variance will be a **usage variance** for materials and an **efficiency variance** for labour.

Think about these descriptions; they are sensible.

## EXAMPLE 2

A business manufactures a 'hytber', the standard cost of which contains the following:

Direct materials    170 kg at a cost of £4 per kg
Direct labour       58 hours at £7.50 per hour

The actual costs incurred in manufacturing the product were:

Direct materials    165 kg at a cost of £3 per kg
Direct labour       60 hours at £7.00 per hour

**Required**
Calculate:

(a) The total direct material cost variance and its analysis into:
(i) direct material usage variance;
(ii) direct material price variance.

(b) The total direct labour cost variance and its analysis into:
(i) direct labour efficiency variance;
(ii) direct labour rate variance.

**Solution**

(a) Sq × Sp  170kg x £4  = £680 ⎫
    Aq × Sp  165kg x £4  = 660 ⎬   ⎫
    Aq × Ap  165kg x £3  = 495    ⎬

| | |
|---|---|
| Material usage variance | £20 (fav) |
| Material price variance | £165 (fav) |
| Total direct material variance | £185 (fav) |

(a) Sq × Sp  58hrs x £7.50 = £435 ⎫
    Aq × Sp  60hrs x £7.50  = 450 ⎬   ⎫
    Aq × Ap  60hrs x £7.00  = 420    ⎬

| | |
|---|---|
| Labour efficiency variance | £15 (adv) |
| Labour rate variance | £30 (fav) |
| Total direct labour variance | £15 (fav) |

*Point to note*

The same basic formula has been used but the descriptions of the variances have been changed for labour. If direct labour takes more time to complete a job, the workers are being *less* efficient; if they take less time they are being *more* efficient.

Similarly, if I worked in a burger bar at weekends I would tell you of the *rate* I was being paid not the *price* I was paid.

The **usage variance** and the **labour efficiency variance** show how much of the total variance is attributable to the efficient or inefficient use of materials and labour. The **price variance** and the **wage rate variance** show how much of the total variance is due to changes in the price of the materials, or a change in the wage rate paid by the business. Think of reasons for the variances identified above. Why has the business used less material than was planned? Why have more labour hours been used than were planned? We will look at some reasons later.

## 11.3   THE FLEXED BUDGET

### FLEXING THE BUDGET

One of the aims of using a standard costing system is that it should highlight areas of good practice and areas where problems are occurring. The standard costing system makes comparisons between the standard costs (budgeted costs) and the costs which have actually been incurred.

We have already said in an earlier chapter that the only valid comparisons that should be made are like with like.

The same principle applies with standard costing.

### EXAMPLE 1

A manager of a business had budgeted to produce 80,000 pairs of jeans in a year. The budgeted figures for the use of materials was 120,000 m$^2$.

The actual number of jeans produced was 70,000, and the actual material used was 110,000 m$^2$.

Management are extremely pleased with the savings made in the cutting department. They suggest that the cutters all deserve a bonus for being so efficient.

**Required**

Calculate the amount of material saved by the cutting department.

**Solution**

The actual output of jeans is in fact only $^7/_8$ $(^{70,000}/_{80,000})$ of what it ought to have been. One could therefore reasonably expect that only $^7/_8$ of the budgeted amount of material would have been used.

The budgeted use of materials should be flexed to show how much material should have been used for the output achieved. Only if we flex the budget can we say whether material has been saved or not.

To produce 70,000 pairs of jeans the business should have used 105,000 m² of material ($^7/_8$ of 120,000). In fact the cutters used 110,000 m². Rather than using less materials, the cutters have used more and the reasons should be investigated.

## SALES VARIANCES

Sales variances can be determined by using the

$$\text{Sq} \times \text{Sp}$$
$$\text{Aq} \times \text{Sp}$$
$$\text{Aq} \times \text{Ap} \qquad \text{grid.}$$

### EXAMPLE 2

The budgeted sales for Werds was 2,000 units at a selling price of £24. The actual sales were 2 300 at a total revenue of £52,900.

**Required**

(a) the total sales variance

(b) the sales volume variance

(c) the sales margin variance

**Solution**

| | | | | |
|---|---|---|---|---|
| Sq × Sp | 2,000 Werds × £24 = £48,000 | | | |
| Aq × Sp | 2,300 × 24 = 55,200 | | Sales volume variance £7,200 (fav) | |
| Aq × Ap | = 52,900 | | Sales margin variance £2,300 (adv) | |
| | | | £4,900 (fav) | |

The most common questions relating to the calculation and analysis of variances deal with material variances and labour variances. *Learn the formulae.*

## 11.4 OVERHEAD VARIANCES

Overhead variances cause more problems than the other variances already mentioned, because of the way they are absorbed – by means of overhead absorption rates which are applied to particular levels of production.

You can see that differences (variances) could arise because:

- the costs could be different from those planned e.g. the budgeted overhead was thought to be £300,000 in reality it proved to be £375,000

- the budgeted activity during the period could be different to the actual level e.g. labour hours were estimated to be 100,000, and actual labour hours were in fact 98,000.

The formulae used are more complex too. *They also need to be learned.*

The **total variable overhead variance** can be split into:

- **expenditure variances** which occur when actual costs differ from those planned;

- **efficiency variances** which arise because of a change in the actual level of output from the planned level. This variance applies only to variable overheads.

## EXAMPLE 1

The following data refers to the production of 'moyts':

|  | £ |
|---|---|
| Budgeted variable overhead | 60,000 |
| Actual variable overhead | 52,000 |
| Standard labour hours | 12,000 |
| Actual labour hours | 10,000 |

**Required**

Calculate:

(a) the variable overhead expenditure variance for the production of 'moyts'.

(b) the variable overhead efficiency variance for the production of 'moyts'.

**Solution**

(a) This variance shows the difference between the actual overhead incurred and the flexed budgeted overhead.

**The formula is:**

**Variable overhead expenditure variance = actual variable overhead expenditure – (actual hours worked × variable overhead absorption rate)**

Variable overhead expenditure variance = £52,000 – (10,000 × £5)

Variable overhead expenditure variance = £52,000 – £50,000

Variable overhead expenditure variance = £2,000 (adverse)

The actual expenditure was £52,000. The budgeted figure needs to be flexed (only 10/12 of the time budgeted has been used so only 10/12 of the overhead should have been spent). The flexed budgeted figure is therefore 10/12 × £60,000 = £50,000.

(b) This variance shows how the planned number of hours of production time compared to the actual number of hours affects the variable overheads.

**The formula is:**

**Variable overhead efficiency variance = (standard hours of production – actual hours worked) × variable production overhead absorption rate.**

Variable overhead efficiency variance = (12,000 – 10,000) × £5

Variable overhead efficiency variance = 2,000 × £5

Variable overhead efficiency variance = £10,000 (favourable)

2,000 hours have been saved in the production of 'moyts' and each hour has saved the £5 absorbed in those hours.

The total favourable variable overhead is £8,000
(Budgeted variable overhead £60,000 less actual variable overhead £52,000) made up of:
Variable overhead expenditure variance = (£2,000) (adverse)
Variable overhead efficiency variance = £10,000 (favourable)

The **total fixed overhead** can be split into:

- expenditure variance which is the difference between the budgeted fixed overhead and the actual fixed overhead;

- volume variance which is the difference between the actual standard hours and the planned standard hours at the standard hourly rate. This variance applies only to fixed overheads.

## EXAMPLE 2

The following data refers to the production of 'throps':

|  | £ |
|---|---|
| Budgeted fixed overhead | 80,000 |
| Actual fixed overhead | 90,000 |
| Standard labour hours | 20,000 |
| Actual labour hours | 22,000 |

**Required**

Calculate:

(a) the fixed overhead expenditure variance for the production of 'throps';

(b) the fixed overhead volume variance for the production of 'throps'.

**Solution**

(a) This variance arises because of the difference between actual output and the planned output.

**The formula is:**

**Fixed overhead expenditure variance = actual fixed overhead expenditure – budgeted fixed overhead expenditure.**

Fixed overhead expenditure variance = £90,000 – £80,000

Fixed overhead expenditure variance = £10,000 (adverse)

The business has spent £10,000 more on fixed overheads than planned when the budget was drawn up.

(b) This variance reflects the change in levels of activity and the way that the fixed overhead recovery is affected by that activity.

**The formula is:**

**Fixed overhead volume variance = (actual hours of work done – budgeted hours of work to be done) × standard fixed overhead rate.**

Fixed overhead volume variance = (22,000 hours – 20,000 hours) × £4 per hour

Fixed overhead volume variance = 2,000 hours × £4 per hour

Fixed overhead volume variance = £8,000 (favourable)

The actual fixed overhead incurred by the business was £90,000, but £88,000 has been recovered in the labour hour rate (22,000 hours × £4 per hour) giving a total adverse fixed overhead variance of £2,000.

This adverse fixed overhead variance is made up of:

Fixed overhead expenditure variance = (£10,000)

Fixed overhead volume variance = £8,000

Provided you have learned the various formulae, the calculation of variances should be a fairly simple arithmetic process. The most important task is to gain information from the calculations.

The reason why the managers of a business introduce a standard costing system is that it highlights variances between pre-determined costs and the actual costs incurred. It should stimulate investigation as to why the variances have arisen.

Standard costing is a natural extension of budgetary control. Budgetary control seeks to make the whole business, or a department, more efficient. Standard costing goes into much more detail by examining detailed costs of all the constituents parts of the production process for each product. Action can then be taken to correct any adverse variances. It is possible, however, to have a system of budgetary control without having a system of standard costing in operation.

Managers must know what has caused the deviation from the planned figures in order to take remedial action.

In an examination you will be asked to comment upon or make observations about the possible causes of individual variances. Remember, one of the main purposes of variance analysis is to highlight areas of concern. You may also be asked to identify some inter-relationships between different variances.

Many of the comments you will be required to make are speculative since you will not have the complete picture – you will only have the information supplied in the question and this may not be very detailed. Your answer will require quite a lot of thought and common sense.

# CAUSES OF VARIANCES

One of the causes of variances must be the fact that in some cases there are errors in the budgets that have been prepared. The original standard might have been unrealistic. It might have been too tight a budget or too slack. This problem applies to all the variances calculated.

In an examination answer, show the examiner that you are aware of this source of error in all the calculations, but make this a general comment which covers all the variances calculated.

## Direct material usage variance

- Poor materials
- Inefficient workers
- Poor machinery
- Theft of materials
- Deterioration of materials

These comments refer to adverse variances. If you turn them on their head they refer to favourable variances, e.g. favourable variance could be due to use of very good materials, highly skilled workers, new sophisticated machinery, etc.

## Direct material price variance

- Inflation – general or specific to the materials being investigated
- Supplier changing price
- Use of different quality or different type of material
- Change in quantity being purchased
- Movement in currency value for imported materials.

Remember, the above effects can be positive or negative, e.g. the supplier can increase or decrease prices.

## Direct labour efficiency variance:

- Use of higher or lower grade of skilled workers
- Poor or good machinery
- Poor or good working methods
- Poor or good working conditions – low or good morale
- Poor or good quality control

## Direct labour rate variance

- Use of higher or lower grade of skilled workers
- Wage inflation since standard was set
- Overtime or premium rates paid.

## Sales price variance

- Change in price for bulk customers
- Price reductions – end of year sales etc. to attract new market segment or new customer
- Price increases

## Sales volume variance

- Change in marketing strategy
- Seasonal variations
- Competition within sector – lower market share or change in price
- Defective product
- Change in consumer tastes

## Variable overhead expenditure variance

Changes in variable overheads e.g. gas, electricity, water etc.

## Variable overhead efficiency variance

Change in activity levels linked to labour or machine hours worked.

## Fixed overhead expenditure variance

Change in price of fixed overheads, e.g. rent, rates and standing charges.

## Fixed overhead volume variance

Change in activity levels linked with labour efficiency or efficiency of machinery.

---

### Chapter roundup

Chapter 11 shows how managers can determine the reasons why actual results have deviated from the results they expected. Once they know the reasons they can do something about the problem.

    You should be able to calculate total and sub-variances and be able to give some explanation as to why they have occurred. You should also be able to identify the reasons why certain variances will have an influence on other variances.

---

# Illustrative questions

---

1  WBM Electronics plc makes and sells a range of electric heaters. These are marketed as models W, B and M, the current monthly budget being 1000, 1750 and 2000 units respectively. All models require manufacturing operations in two production departments as indicated in the following extract from the standard specifications.

| Department | Standard labour rate per hour | Standard time in minutes Model W | Model B | Model M |
|---|---|---|---|---|
| 1 | £3.50 | 72 | 48 | 36 |
| 2 | £3.80 | 30 | 15 | 18 |

There is no opening or closing work-in-progress. The following actual data has been recorded for the previous month.

| | Model W | Model B | Model M |
|---|---|---|---|
| Finished output (units) | 900 | 1800 | 2100 |

| | Department 1 | Department 2 |
|---|---|---|
| Direct wages incurred | £13,200 | £6,325 |
| Actual hours worked | 3,600 | 1,700 |

*Required*

(a) Define the term 'standard hour' and indicate clearly how, and for what purpose, it is used. (6)

(b) From the data given calculate, for **each** department:
(i) the direct labour rate variance;
(ii) the direct labour efficiency variance. (14)
(NEAB)

*Tutorial note*
Remember to be precise in your use of definitions. Use the formula then fit into it the information given in the question.

*Suggested answer*

(a) A standard hour is a measure of the amount of work that can be done at a standard level of performance in a standard period of time.

The standard hour is used when a variety of products is being produced.

Production may be measured in metres, litres, kilograms etc. depending on the product. The standard hour is used, since it is more convenient to use a measure that can be common to all the products.

(b) **Department 1**

| | | |
|---|---|---|
| 900 units of model W taking 72 minutes each = | 1,080 | hours |
| 1,800 units of model B taking 48 minutes each = | 1,440 | hours |
| 2,100 units of model M taking 36 minutes each = | 1,260 | hours |
| Total standard hours for Department 1 = | 3,780 | hours |

**Department 2**

| | | |
|---|---|---|
| 900 units of model W taking 30 minutes each = | 450 | hours |
| 1,800 units of model B taking 15 minutes each = | 450 | hours |
| 2,100 units of model M taking 18 minutes each = | 630 | hours |
| Total standard hours for Department 2 = | 1,530 | hours |

**Department 1**

Sq × Sp     3,780 × £3.50 = £13,230
labour efficiency variance £630 (favourable)
Aq × Sp     3,600 × £3.50 = £12,600
labour wage rate variance £600 (adverse)
Aq × Ap     3,600 × £3.67 = £13,200

**Department 2**

Sq × Sp     1,530 × £3.80 = £5,814
labour efficiency variance £646 (adverse)
Aq × Sp     1,700 × £3.80 = £6,460
labour wage rate variance £135 (favourable)
Aq × Ap     1,700 × £3.72 = £6,325

**2** HGW Ltd produces a product called a Lexton. The standard selling price and the manufacturing costs of this product are as follows:

| | | £ |
|---|---|---|
| Standard selling price per unit | | 86 |
| Standard production costs: | | |
| Direct material | 1.5 kilos at £12 per kilo | 18 |
| Direct labour | 4.4 hours at £7.50 per hour | 33 |
| Variable overheads | 4.4 hours at £5 per hour | 22 |
| | | 73 |

The projected production and sales for March 1994 were 520 units.
On 1 April 1994 the following actual figures were determined.

| | |
|---|---|
| Sales | 550 units at £85 each |
| Production | 550 units |
| Direct material | 785 kilos at £12.40 per kilo |
| Direct labour | 2,400 hours at £7.80 per hour |
| Overheads | £12,500 (overall variance £400 adverse) |

There was no opening stock of the product Lexton.

*Required*

(a) Prepare an actual profit and loss statement for HGW Ltd for March 1994.     (8)

(b) Calculate the following variances and their respective sub-variances:
   (i)   sales – price and volume;     (6)
   (ii)  direct materials – price and usage;     (6)
   (iii) direct labour – rate and efficiency.     (6)

(c) Prepare a statement reconciling the actual profit calculated in part (a) with the budgeted profit on actual sales. (Use the variances calculated in part (b) and the given overhead variance). (10)

(d) Write a report to the management outlining the factors that need to be considered when standards are being established. (10)

(AEB)

*Tutorial note*

Parts (a) and (b) should be fairly straightforward. The reconciliation statement appears daunting at first – the key is to adjust Budgeted Sales Revenue less Actual Sales Revenue by each of the variances. Remember your report heading!

*Suggested answer*

(a)
### HGW Ltd profit and loss statement for March

| | £ | £ | |
|---|---|---|---|
| Sales | | 46,750 | |
| Less cost of sales | | | |
| Materials | 9,734 | | (785 kilos × £12.40 per kilo) |
| Labour | 18,720 | | (2,400 hours × £7.80 per hour) |
| Variable overhead | 12,500 | | |
| | | 40,954 | |
| Profit | | 5,796 | |

(b) Sales variances

Sq × Sp 520 × £86 = £44,720    sales volume variance = £2,580 (favourable)
Aq × Sp 550 × £86 = £47,300    sales price variance =     £550 (adverse)
Aq × Ap 550 × £85 = £46,750    Total sales variance =   £2,030 (favourable)

Direct materials variances

Sq × Sp    *825 × £12 =    £9,900  *flexed
                            materials usage variance =    £480 (favourable)
Aq × Sp    785 × £12 =    £9,420
                            material price variance =    £314 (adverse)
Aq × Ap    785 × £12.40 = £9,734
                            Total materials variance =    £166 (favourable)

Direct Labour variances

Sq × Sp    *2,420 × £7.50 =  £18,150  *flexed
                            labour efficiency variance =   £150 (favourable)
Aq × Sp    2,400 × £7.50 =   £18,000
                            labour wage rate variance = £720 (adverse)
Aq × Ap    2,400 × £7.80 =   £18,720
                            Total labour variance =      £570 (adverse)

(c)
### Statement reconciling actual and budgeted profit

| | | £ | £ | |
|---|---|---|---|---|
| Budgeted sales | | | 44,720 | |
| Sales variances – | price | (550) (adverse) | | |
| | volume | 2,580 (favourable) | 2,030 (favourable) | |
| Actual sales | | | 46,750 | |
| Less standard cost of actual sales | | | | |
| (550 × £73) | | | 40,150 | |
| | | | 6,600 | |
| Material variances – | usage | 480 (favourable) | | |
| | price | (314) (adverse) | 166 (favourable) | |
| Labour variances – | efficiency | 150 (favourable) | | |
| | wage rate | (720) (adverse) | (570) (adverse) | |
| Overheads | | | (400) (adverse) | |
| Actual profit | | | 5,796 | |

(d) To

From

Date *(i.e. report format)*

*Factors to be considered when establishing standards*

Factors could include:

Systems must be established to provide comprehensive information.

Production system must be fully planned, and there must be a norm for every element in the product.

There must be systems for regular monitoring of standards and suitable amendment procedures must be available.

Work measurement techniques must be used to set standards.

Allowances should be made for natural wastages of materials.

**3** Dour Ltd manufactures moulded furniture including chairs for general purpose use. These chairs are manufactured from a chemical mixture purchased in a prepared state. Details of the contribution made by these chairs to the overall company results for the year ended 31 October 1989 were:

**Contribution statement for chairs for the year ended 31 October 1989**

|                     | £      | £       |
|---------------------|--------|---------|
| Sales               |        | 112,500 |
| less variable costs |        |         |
| Raw materials       | 55,000 |         |
| Direct labour       | 26,000 | 81,000  |
| Contribution        |        | 31,500  |

Additional information:

(1) There were no opening or closing stock of chairs.

(2) The budget and standard cost details prepared prior to 1 November 1988 revealed:
   (i) budgeted sales of chairs 18,000 at £8.00 each;
   (ii) each chair should take 3 kg of chemical mixture at £1.00 per kg;
   (iii) each chair should take 20 minutes of direct labour time;
   (iv) the direct labour rate per hour was £6.00.

(3) In investigating the actual results for the year ended 31 October 1989 the following information came to light:
   (i) 15,000 chairs were sold;
   (ii) 44,000 kg of raw materials was used;
   (iii) 4,000 hours of direct labour time was clocked.

*Required*

(a) Calculate the overall sales variance for the year ended 31 October 1989. (2)

(b) Calculate the overall labour variance for the year ended 31 October 1989 analysing it into:
   (i) rate variance;
   (ii) efficiency variance. (6)

(c) Calculate the overall materials variance for the year ended 31 October 1989 analysing it into:
   (i) price variance;
   (ii) usage variance. (6)

(d) Prepare a statement that shows the budgeted contribution for the year ended 31 October 1989. (4)

(e) Examine the variances calculated in (a), (b) and (c) above and give possible reasons for each. (7)

(AEB)

*Tutorial note*
Some of the figures to be used in your formula have already been calculated for you. Write down your formula and insert into it the information given in the question. In part (e) avoid contradictory reasons.

*Suggested answer*
(a)  Sales variance

| | |
|---|---|
| Budgeted sales revenue = 18,000 × £8.00 = | £144,000 |
| Actual sales revenue = | 112,500 |
| Total adverse sales variance = | £31,500 |

The budgeted figures need to be flexed.

The budgeted figures are based on an output of 18,000 chairs, in fact only 15,000 chairs were produced. That is 15,000/18,000 or 5/6 of the estimated output.

Therefore only 5/6 of the total amount of labour hours and kilograms of materials should have been used in the production of the chairs.

After flexing, the budgeted figure read:
Materials 5/6 × 54,000 kg = 45,000 kilos × £1
Labour 5/6 × 6,000 hrs = 5,000 hrs × £6.00

(b)  Labour variances

Sq × Sp   5,000 hrs × £6.00 =   £30,000
                                  labour efficiency variance =   £6,000 (favourable)
Aq × Sp   4,000 hrs × £6.00 =   £24,000
                                  labour wage rate variance = £2,000 (adverse)
Aq × Ap   4,000 hrs × £6.50 =   £26,000
                                  Total labour variance =   £4,000 (favourable)

(c)  Material variances

Sq × Sp   45,000 kg × £1 =      £45,000
                                  material usage variance =   £1,000 (favourable)
Aq × Sp   44,000 kg × £1 =      £44,000
                                  material price variance =   £11,000 (adverse)
Aq × Ap   44,000 kg × £1.25 = £55,000
                                  Total material variance =   £10,000 (adverse)

(d)  Statement showing budgeted contribution for the year ended 31 October 1989

| | £ | £ |
|---|---|---|
| Sales (18,000 × £8) | | 144,000 |
| Less Variable costs | | |
| Raw materials (18,000 × 3 × £1) | 54,000 | |
| Direct labour (18,000/3 × £6.00) | 36,000 | 90,000 |
| Budgeted contribution | | 54,000 |

(e)  Sales variances could be the result of economic climate – fewer chairs sold despite a reduction in selling price; could be due to competition.

Labour variances could be due to employing more highly skilled workforce – they are more efficient (favourable variance) but have cost more to employ (adverse rate variance).

Material variances could be due to using a better grade of materials – less used but at a higher price. The more highly skilled workforce may have wasted fewer materials.

# CAPITAL INVESTMENT APPRAISAL

## Units in this chapter

12.1 *Capital projects*
12.2 *Payback*
12.3 *Accounting rate of return*
12.4 *Discounted cash flows*
12.5 *Internal rate of return*

## Chapter objectives

We have looked at budgets for most aspects of a business. In this chapter we look at budgeting for capital items.

The key topics and concepts covered in this chapter are:

* reasons for capital investment appraisal;

* payback;

* opportunity cost;

* cash flows;

* time value of money;

* cost of capital.

## 12.1    CAPITAL PROJECTS

Fixed assets are purchased with the intention that they will generate profits for a business for some years into the future. They comprise land, premises, machinery, plant, office equipment, motor vehicles, etc. The managers of a business are always looking for the best value for money when purchasing such assets.

The managers do not have access to infinite financial resources; money is a scarce business resource, so they must plan very carefully in order to ensure that maximum benefits are received from any purchases of capital equipment.

**Capital projects are appraised in terms of potential earning power.**

Managers may need to replace some obsolete machinery or purchase extra machinery to expand production. If there were only one type of machine to choose from there would be no problem. In the real world there are always alternative options to choose from: there are machines of very different prices and different qualities; different machines are capable of producing different quality products and different quantities of the product; different machines have differing life spans. You have probably been confronted by similar factors if you have ever bought a CD player or a camera.

There are four main methods used to appraise a capital project. They are:

- The payback method
- The accounting rate of return method (ARR)
- The net present value method (NPV)
- The internal rate of return method (IRR)

Check with your teacher or syllabus which methods you need to know.

All of these method require predictions about the future. How accurate can predictions be? If forecasts are wildly inaccurate there could be serious problems for the business because:

- large sums of cash are generally involved;

- decisions often require a commitment to a particular course of action or policy for a number of years into the future. Sometimes the commitment is of an almost irreversible nature;

- the investment will have an effect on profits into the future and this will have an effect on the business dividend policy as well as having an effect on the retained profits.

Managers of a business will usually use more than one of the methods in order to arrive at a decision which could affect the welfare of the business for many years to come.

Only the additional expenditure that may be incurred and the additional revenue that the project may generate is considered, whichever method is used. The additional expenditure may include opportunity cost.

**Opportunity cost** is the cost of making a decision about how to use limited resources expressed in terms of the benefit lost by not making the next best decision.

For example, if a machine is currently generating a net revenue of £150,000 and the managers of a business wish to use that machine in a new project, the lost (foregone) revenue of £150,000 must be included as part of the costs of the new project.

The net present value and internal rate of return both take into account the time value of money. (Payback can also be calculated by using discounted returns.)

There are always competing demands for the resources within a business. A resource used in one area of the business is not available for use elsewhere. Money used on one project is not available to be used on anything else. This inevitably means competition between alternative strategies. The alternatives need to be evaluated, appraised, and compared. They need to be ranked in order to determine the order of priority. The criteria used may not be purely financial. In some cases the financial criteria may come low down in the list of factors to be considered. Top priority may be a legal obligation, as in the case of ensuring that health and safety legislation is complied with. Even so, different alternative implementation plans may be available.

## 12.2  PAYBACK

The payback period is the length of time required for the total cash flows generated by the project to equal the initial capital outlay, i.e. how long will it take for the project to pay for itself?

This is the method which is widely used in practice since most businesses are concerned with short time horizons. Also, the longer the time horizon the less predictable are any outcomes, and earlier receipts could allow reinvestment of funds received. Note that *cash flows* are used in this method, *not profits*.

**Advantages** of using the payback method of capital appraisal include:

- It is simple and fairly easy for non-accountants to understand.

- It also recognises that cash received early in the asset life cycle is preferable to cash received later.

- All future predictions carry an element of risk. This method identifies the project with the quickest payback – the project with the shortest risk period.

- Cash flows can be an objective measure of performance, whereas profits are dependent on the accounting policies pursued by the managers of the business.

   **Disadvantages** include:

- It does not take into account the time value of money.
- It does not consider any cash flows that take place after the payback period.

### EXAMPLE

Clive Dixon is considering the purchase of a new wire extrusion machine for his business. There are two models that will suit his purpose.

| | Machine fg/8<br>Cost £45,000<br>Estimated net cash flows<br>£ | Machine lgz/56<br>Cost £52,000<br>Estimated net cash flows<br>£ |
|---|---|---|
| Year 1 | 19,000 | 22,000 |
| Year 2 | 22,000 | 24,000 |
| Year 3 | 24,000 | 26,000 |
| Year 4 | 26,000 | 28,000 |

**Required**

Calculate the payback period for each of the two machines.

**Solution**

**Machine fg/8**

Payback = 2 years 2 months

   At the end of year 2 £41,000 had been 'paid back' by the machine. Another £4,000 is needed to complete the payback. £4,000 represents 1/6 of the following year's cash flow, it is assumed that 1/6 of the cash flow will be generated in 1/6 of the year.

**Machine lgz/56**

Payback = 2 years × 2.77 months.

## 12.3 THE ACCOUNTING RATE OF RETURN

This method is in some respects similar in approach to the calculation of return on capital employed. It shows the return on the investment expressed as a percentage of the average investment over the period being considered.

   **Advantages** of using the accounting rate of return include:

- It is simple to use.
- It takes into account the aggregate earnings of the project.

   **Disadvantages** include:

- It does not take into account the time value of money.
- It does not recognise the timing of the cash flows, e.g. project A has forecast profits for one year only of £20,000 – average profit £20,000. Project B has the following forecast profit pattern: year 1, £1,000; year 2, £1,000; year 3, £2,000; year 4, £3,000; year 5, £98,000 – average, profit £21,000.
- It does not recognise the length of the earning life of the asset (see above).

### EXAMPLE

Use the same information as in the example used for payback.

**Required**

Computations using the accounting rate of return for each of the two wire extrusion machines.

**Solution**

### Average profits for each machine

| | fg/8 | | | | lgz/56 | | |
|---|---|---|---|---|---|---|---|
| Year | Net cash flow | Depreciation | Profit | Year | Net cash flow | Depreciation | Profit |
| | £ | £ | £ | | £ | £ | £ |
| 1 | 19,000 | 11,250 | 7,750 | 1 | 22,000 | 13,000 | 9,000 |
| 2 | 22,000 | 11,250 | 10,750 | 2 | 24,000 | 13,000 | 11,000 |
| 3 | 24,000 | 11,250 | 12,750 | 3 | 26,000 | 13,000 | 13,000 |
| 4 | 26,000 | 11,250 | 14,750 | 4 | 28,000 | 13,000 | 15,000 |
| | | | 46,000 | | | | 48,000 |

Average profits £46,000/4 = £11,500     Average profits £48,000/4 = £12,000

### Average investment in each machine

| fg/8 | Year | Cost | Aggregate depreciation | Net book value |
|---|---|---|---|---|
| | | £ | £ | £ |
| | 1 | 45,000 | 11,250 | 33,750 |
| | 2 | | 22,500 | 22,500 |
| | 3 | | 33,750 | 11,250 |
| | 4 | | 45,000 | – |
| | | | | 67,500 |

Average investment = £67,500/4 = £16,875

| lgz/56 | Year | Cost | Aggregate depreciation | Net book value |
|---|---|---|---|---|
| | | £ | £ | £ |
| | 1 | 52,000 | 13,000 | 39,000 |
| | 2 | | 26,000 | 26,000 |
| | 3 | | 39,000 | 13,000 |
| | 4 | | 52,000 | – |
| | | | | 78,000 |

Average investment = £78,000/4 = £19,500

The accounting rate of return for each machine is:

fg/8     $\dfrac{\text{Average annual profit}}{\text{Average investment}} = \dfrac{£11,500}{£16,875} = 68.15\%$

lgz/56     $\dfrac{\text{Average annual profit}}{\text{Average investment}} = \dfrac{£12,000}{£19,500} = 61.54\%$

## 12.4   DISCOUNTED CASH FLOWS

Most people would agree that £100 to spend today is better than having the prospect of £100 to spend in a year's time. Why? There is uncertainty about the future. There is an element of risk involved. If you could guarantee that today's £100 could be invested and that it would be worth £200 in a year's time, then you might be prepared to wait a year to receive your money.

Managers of a businesses invest to provide security through profits and cash flows for the future. We all invest to provide more money in the future; we hope that the money in the future will be worth waiting for.

In giving up the money today we expect a reward. The reward is the interest that we will earn on our investment. Just as you invest in, say, a building society, knowing that you will get your investment back plus, say, 3.5%, managers of a business invest in projects that will pay the investment back plus a return.

Managers evaluate a project by comparing the investment with the return the investment will bring in the future.

| | You | | Business Manager |
|---|---|---|---|
| | £ | | £ |
| Investment | 100 | Investment | 100,000 |
| Year 1 return at 3.5% | 3.50 | Year 1 Net cash inflow | 40,000 |
| Year 2 return | 7.12 | Year 2 Net cash inflow | 40,000 |
| Year 3 return | 10.87 | Year 3 Net cash inflow | 40,000 |

If you had left your investment in the building society to grow then your investment could be withdrawn and you would have £110.87. The business manager has recouped £120,000 from the business investment. Have these investments been worthwhile?

One consideration that you both should have considered is whether there were alternative investments that might have given you both greater returns. The opportunity cost of capital should be considered. In this case we do not know what the alternatives were, but your £10.87 and the business manager's £120,000 should be discounted to see how they compare with the original investment.

It may be preferable for you to have £100 now rather than a possible £110.87 in three years time. The business managers may prefer to have £100,000 now to use in an alternative project than the prospect of £120,000 spread over a three year period.

The problem that we identified as being a disadvantage of both the payback and the accounting rate of return methods of appraisal, was that neither recognised the time value of money.

In order to make a meaningful comparison between the original investment and the future returns of cash there is a need to discount the cash flows so that they are equivalent to a cash flow now. We can then compare like with like.

The discounting factor used in net present value (NPV) calculations is generally based on a weighted average cost of capital available to the business.

## EXAMPLE 1

Chang and Co Ltd has the following capital structure:

| | £ |
|---|---|
| Ordinary shares | |
| (currently paying a dividend of 12% per annum) | 500,000 |
| 7% Preference shares | 250,000 |
| 8% Debenture stock | 200,000 |
| Bank loan (current rate of interest payable 11%) | 50,000 |

**Required**
Calculate the weighted average cost of capital for Chang and Co Ltd.

**Solution**

| | Nominal value | Rate of return paid | Cost of capital per annum |
|---|---|---|---|
| Ordinary shares | 500,000 | 12% | 60,000 |
| Preference shares | 250,000 | 7% | 17,500 |
| Debenture stock | 200,000 | 8% | 16,000 |
| Bank loan | 50,000 | 11% | 5,500 |
| | 1,000,000 | | 99,000 |

$$\text{Average cost of capital} = \frac{\text{Cost of capital per annum}}{\text{Nominal value of capital}} = \frac{£99,000}{£1,000,000} = 9.9\%$$

It shows that it would cost Chang and Co Ltd 9.9% per annum to raise the required capital if it were to undertake a new project

*Points to note*

- The example is correct in principle. However, the interest on debenture stock is a profit and loss account expense; it reduces profits; it reduces the amount of tax payable by the company. Therefore the figure used in the calculation should be net of taxation.

- In an examination the cost of capital will be given to you as part of the question.

- You may be given a number of discounting factors to choose from. Choose the one which is identified in the question as the cost of capital.

There is a misconception that the discounted cash flow is used to take into account the effects of inflation on the results. This is not so; the effects of inflation are self-correcting, profits do not change in real terms.

Think about this simple example: if revenues were £50, costs £20, profit would be £30.

If inflationary pressures increased prices by 100%: revenues would rise to £100, costs would rise to £40, what happens to profits?

What we have considered is what the return would be if we invested money in a building society or the managers invested in a business project. We are working from the present into the future. Discounting uses the same principles but in reverse, working back from the future to the present time. We look at future sums of money and calculate the amount which needs to be invested now in order to realise the future sum.

If we look at the table for the present value of £1 for, say 6%, 7%, and 8% they will show:

|  | 6% | 7% | 8% |
|---|---|---|---|
| Period 1 | 0.943 | 0.935 | 0.926 |
| 2 | 0.890 | 0.873 | 0.857 |
| 3 | 0.840 | 0.816 | 0.794 |
| 4 | 0.792 | 0.763 | 0.735 |
| 5 | 0.747 | 0.713 | 0.681 |

If you required £1 in 5 years, and the interest rate was 6%, you would have to invest 74.7 pence today.

If you required £10 in 3 years time and the interest rate was 8% you would have to invest £7.94 today (0.794 for £1 so 0.794 × 10 for £10).

If you required to have £100 in 4 years time and the interest rate was 7% you would have to invest £76.30 (0.763 for £1 so 0.763 × 100 for £100).

Working these figures in reverse, £1 in 5 years has a (present) value of 74.7 pence today. £10 in 3 years time has a (present) value of £7.94 today. £100 in 4 years time has a (present) value of £79.40 today.

Present value gives the value of a future sum of money at today's values. The future sum is discounted to take into account interest rates. If the discount rate was 10%, then £100 received in one year's time has a value now of £90.90. The sum of £100 received in two years' time would have a present value of £82.60. Similarly, an expense of £100 in a year's time is like spending £90.90 today. Spending £100 in two years' time is like spending £82.60 today.

The net present value technique compares the investment (at today's price) with future net cash inflows (at today's prices ).

## EXAMPLE 2

Edna Chevalier is considering whether to invest in a new moulding machine costing £10,000. She estimates that the future cash flows to be:

|  | Revenue receipts £ | Operating payments £ |
|---|---|---|
| Year 1 | 4,000 | 3,000 |
| 2 | 5,000 | 3,200 |
| 3 | 6,000 | 3,500 |
| 4 | 7,000 | 3,800 |
| 5 | 7,500 | 4,000 |

Her cost of capital is 10%. All costs are paid and revenues received on the last day of each year. The following is an extract from the present value tables of £1 at 10%:

|  | 10% |
|---|---|
| Year 1 | 0.909 |
| 2 | 0.826 |
| 3 | 0.751 |
| 4 | 0.683 |
| 5 | 0.621 |

**Required**

Advise Edna whether to invest in the new moulding machine.

**Solution**

| Year | Cash flows £ | Present value factor | Net present value £ |
|------|------|------|------|
| 0 (now) | (10,000) | 1 | (10,000) |
| 1 | 1,000 | 0.909 | 909 |
| 2 | 1,800 | 0.826 | 1,487 |
| 3 | 2,500 | 0.751 | 1,878 |
| 4 | 3,200 | 0.683 | 2,186 |
| 5 | 3,500 | 0.621 | 2,174 |
| | | | (1,366) |

Edna should not invest in the new moulding machine. It would yield a negative net present value.

*Point to note*

Calculations are not done for the receipts and payments – they are netted out since the discounting factor applies to both sets of figures.

## EXAMPLE 3

DEF Ltd are considering a project which has an initial outlay of £50,000. The annual net receipts for the next five years are estimated to be £15,000 per year. The cost of capital for DEF Ltd is 11%.

The following is an extract from the present value table of £1 at 11%:

| | 11% |
|------|------|
| Year 1 | 0.901 |
| 2 | 0.812 |
| 3 | 0.731 |
| 4 | 0.659 |
| 5 | 0.594 |

**Required**

Calculations to show whether DEF Ltd should undertake the project.

**Solution**

| Year | Cash flows £ | Present value factor | Net present value £ |
|------|------|------|------|
| 0 | (50,000) | 1 | (50,000) |
| 1 | 15,000 | 0.901 | 13,515 |
| 2 | 15,000 | 0.812 | 12,180 |
| 3 | 15,000 | 0.731 | 10,965 |
| 4 | 15,000 | 0.659 | 9,885 |
| 5 | 15,000 | 0.594 | 8,910 |
| | | | 5,455 |

On financial grounds DEF Ltd should go ahead with the project.

Examination questions often ask candidates to make choices between a number of alternative projects or machines. The same procedure is repeated for each of the alternatives. The results are then ranked in order of their net present value results taking the best ones first. A construction company with limited resources might only be able to complete 8 contracts in a five year period. It would base its tenders on the top 8 projects in its NPV ranking.

## EXAMPLE 4

The managers of the Gina Hill Company wish to purchase two new machines. They have drawn up a shortlist of 4 machines which are capable of producing the quality of goods they desire. The company's cost of capital is 12%.

The following extract is from the present value tables for £1:

| | 12% |
|---|---|
| Year 1 | 0.893 |
| 2 | 0.797 |
| 3 | 0.712 |
| 4 | 0.636 |

The following information is available:

| Machine | | AR/86 | SB/88 | CT/102 | UD/79 |
|---|---|---|---|---|---|
| | | £ | £ | £ | £ |
| Purchase price | | 40,000 | 45,000 | 52,000 | 60,000 |
| Forecast net cash flows | Year 1 | 20,000 | 21,500 | 22,000 | 27,000 |
| | 2 | 20,000 | 21,500 | 22,000 | 27,000 |
| | 3 | 20,000 | 21,500 | 22,000 | 27,000 |
| | 4 | 20,000 | 21,500 | 22,000 | 27,000 |

**Required**

Using discounted cash flow techniques advise the managers of the Gina Hill Company which two machines they should purchase.

**Solution**

(The workings have been omitted. Do the calculations yourself and see if you get the same results.)

| | AR/86 | SB/88 | CT/102 | UD/79 |
|---|---|---|---|---|
| | £ | £ | £ | £ |
| Year 0 | (40,000) | (45,000) | (52,000) | (60,000) |
| 1 | 17,860 | 19,200 | 19,646 | 24,111 |
| 2 | 15,940 | 17,136 | 17,534 | 21,519 |
| 3 | 14,240 | 15,308 | 15,664 | 19,224 |
| 4 | 12,720 | 13,674 | 13,992 | 17,172 |
| | 20,760 | 20,318 | 14,836 | 22,026 |

The machines would be ranked:

| 1 | UD/79 | £22,026 |
|---|---|---|
| 2 | AR/86 | 20,760 |
| 3 | SB/88 | 20,318 |
| 4 | CT/102 | 14,836 |

The managers should purchase the UD/79 and the AR/86.

All the machines are acceptable in financial terms, because they all produce a positive NPV, and under different circumstances they would all have been worth purchasing.

## 12.5 THE INTERNAL RATE OF RETURN

A business must make profits to survive. The business must ensure that the projects it undertakes will be profitable.

If the cost of capital is 10%, the return on each project must cover its cost of capital, that is the return must be greater than 10%. Management must know what rate of return any project will yield. (Some text books deal with this method of capital investment appraisal under the heading of **yield**.)

The expected yield can then be compared with the cost of capital. The process is to calculate the present value of future cash flows which, when discounted back to the present, will equal zero. The rate that equals zero is the rate of return on that project.

This process is relatively simple using a computer spreadsheet. Performed 'manually', it is a process of trial and error by guessing the rate of return and doing the NPV calculations. If the calculation does not equate to zero another attempt is made, and so on, until a rate is found which does equate to zero (or so close as to be irrelevant).

EXAMPLE

The cost of capital for Ardnas Ltd. is 14%. The managers are considering a 3 year project which will cost £56,000. The net cash flows are expected to be:

|  | £ |
|---|---|
| Year 1 | 20,000 |
| 2 | 25,000 |
| 3 | 30,000 |

The following are extracts from the present value tables for £1.

|  | 12% | 13% | 14% | 15% | 16% |
|---|---|---|---|---|---|
| Year 1 | 0.893 | 0.885 | 0.877 | 0.870 | 0.862 |
| 2 | 0.797 | 0.783 | 0.769 | 0.756 | 0.743 |
| 3 | 0.712 | 0.693 | 0.675 | 0.658 | 0.641 |

**Required**

Calculate the internal rate of return on the new project being considered by Ardnas Ltd.

**Solution**

If we try 12%:

|  | Cash flows £ | Present value factor | Net present value £ |
|---|---|---|---|
| Year 0 | (56,000) | 1 | (56,000) |
| 1 | 20,000 | 0.893 | 17,860 |
| 2 | 25,000 | 0.797 | 19,925 |
| 3 | 30,000 | 0.712 | 21,360 |
|  |  |  | 3,145 |

The internal rate of return is greater than 12%.

If we try 16%:

|  |  |  |  |
|---|---|---|---|
| Year 0 | (56,000) | 1 | (56,000) |
| 1 | 20,000 | 0.862 | 17,240 |
| 2 | 25,000 | 0.743 | 18,575 |
| 3 | 30,000 | 0.641 | 19,230 |
|  |  |  | (955) |

Close, but the internal rate of return is below 16%.

Try 15%:

|  |  |  |  |
|---|---|---|---|
| Year 0 | (56,000) | 1 | (56,000) |
| 1 | 20,000 | 0.870 | 17,400 |
| 2 | 25,000 | 0.756 | 18,900 |
| 3 | 30,000 | 0.658 | 19,740 |
|  |  |  | 40 |

Close enough – the internal rate of return is just above 15%.

The project should be accepted since the actual rate of return on the project exceeds Ardnas Ltd's cost of capital.

This method is also popular in practice, although managers would use a spreadsheet to do their calculations.

---

## Chapter roundup

Chapter 12 has looked at the various methods that managers will use to make decisions on whether to undertake a capital investment. It also considered how managers decide between competing projects.

You should be able to use the payback and discounted cash flow methods to make decisions, and be aware of the limitations of each.

# Illustrative questions

1  Newcastle Engineering Company is considering two capital expenditure proposals. Both proposals are expected to last for five years.
   The following information is available.

|  | X | Y |
|---|---|---|
|  | £ | £ |
| Initial investment | 100,000 | 110,000 |
| Profit year 1 | 20,000 | 30,000 |
| Profit year 2 | 25,000 | 25,000 |
| Profit year 3 | 30,000 | 20,000 |
| Profit year 4 | 15,000 | 20,000 |
| Profit/(loss) year 5 | 5,000 | (2,000) |
| Estimated scrap value at end of year 5 | 10,000 | 10,000 |

Depreciation is charged on the straight line basis.
The company estimates the cost of capital at 14% per annum; discount factors at 14% are as follows.

| year 1 | 0.8772 |
|---|---|
| year 2 | 0.7695 |
| year 3 | 0.6750 |
| year 4 | 0.5921 |
| year 5 | 0.5194 |

*Required*
(a) Calculate for both proposals:
   (i)   the payback period;
   (ii)  the accounting rate of return; and
   (iii) the net present value. (10)

(b) Compare and contrast the above three methods of investment appraisal and state with reasons which proposal you would recommend. (5)
(NICCEA)

*Tutorial note*
You will have to calculate the annual depreciation in order to adjust the profit figures. This is necessary in order to arrive at the cash flows derived from each project.
   You are expected to arrive at a conclusion in part (b).

*Suggested answer*
(a)  Newcastle Engineering Company.

|  | Proposal X | | Proposal Y | |
|---|---|---|---|---|
| Year | Profit after depreciation | Cash flow | Profit after depreciation | Cash flow |
| 1 | 20,000 | 38,000 | 30,000 | 50,000 |
| 2 | 25,000 | 43,000 | 25,000 | 45,000 |
| 3 | 30,000 | 48,000 | 20,000 | 40,000 |
| 4 | 15,000 | 33,000 | 20,000 | 40,000 |
| 5 | 5,000 | 23,000 | (2,000) | 18,000 |

Depreciation is a non-cash expense and needs to be added back to find the cash flow.

(i)  **Project X payback period**
     Initial investment of £100,000 is paid back during year 3. Payback is 2 years and 19,000/48,000 of year 3. Payback period 2.395 years.
     **Project Y payback period**
     Initial investment of £110,000 is paid back during year 3 also. Payback is 2 years and 15,000/40,000 of year 3. Payback period 2.375 years.

(ii) Accounting rate of return

**Project X**

Average annual profit £19,000

Average capital invested £46,000

Depreciation £18,000 per annum

Capital invested  yr1 £100,000 – £18,000 = £82,000

yr2 £82,000 – £18,000 = £64,000

yr3 £64,000 – £18,000 = £46,000

yr4 £46,000 – £18,000 = £28,000

yr5 £28,000 – £18,000 = £10,000

Average annual investment £230,000/5

Accounting rate of return = £19,000/£46,000 = 41.3%

**Project Y**

Average annual profit £18,600

Average capital invested £50,000

Depreciation £20,000 per annum

Capital invested  yr1 £110,000 – £20,000 =£90,000

yr2 £90,000 – £20,000 = £70,000

yr3 £70,000 – £20,000 = £50,000

yr4 £50,000 – £20,000 = £30,000

yr5 £30,000 – £20,000 = £10,000

Average annual investment £250,000/5

Accounting rate of return = £18,600/£50,000 = 37.2%

(iii) Net present value

| Year | Cash | Project X Discount factor | NPV | Cash | Project Y Discount factor | NPV |
|---|---|---|---|---|---|---|
| 0 | (100,000) | 1 | (100,000) | (110,000) | 1 | (110,000) |
| 1 | 38,000 | 0.8772 | 33,334 | 50,000 | 0.8772 | 43,860 |
| 2 | 43,000 | 0.7695 | 33,089 | 45,000 | 0.7695 | 34,628 |
| 3 | 48,000 | 0.6750 | 32,400 | 40,000 | 0.6750 | 27,000 |
| 4 | 33,000 | 0.5921 | 19,539 | 40,000 | 0.5921 | 23,684 |
| 5 | 33,000 | 0.5194 | 17,140 | 28,000 | 0.5194 | 14,543 |
| | | | 35,502 | | | 33,715 |

(b) Points should include:

*Payback* is simple to use and calculate. It measures the time taken for the initial capital investment to be repaid by the cash flows generated by the investment. Its drawbacks include the fact that it ignores the time value of money, it does not measure the overall return on the project and it does not recognise any cash flows that occur after the payback period.

*Accounting rate of return* is also easily calculated but there are a number of variations in popular use. Unlike the other two methods it uses profits which are a more subjective measure than cash flows. It does not take into account the timing of cash flows.

The *net present value method* of appraisal takes the time value of money into consideration by discounting the cash flows. This attaches greater importance to immediate cash flows than later cash flows. The cash flows are discounted by using the businesses cost of capital, and this gives rise to the problem that the rate may change in the future.

It should be remembered that projections into the future are of a speculative nature. Future cash flows are difficult to predict, the life of the project is sometimes uncertain etc.

Proposal X gives the best return using both ARR and DCF methods.

**2** Andre Lefevre runs a car valeting business and now wishes to expand his operations into car hire. He is considering purchasing a small fleet of five identical cars. His accountant has provided him with the following information on each of three models under consideration.

| Model | Country of manufacture | Cost per car £ |
|---|---|---|
| Armada | UK | 7,000 |
| Biarritz | Spain | 12,000 |
| Carioka | Japan | 16,000 |

Additional information:

(1) Dealers are prepared to allow the following discounts on the purchase of a fleet of five cars.

| | % |
|---|---|
| Armada | 5 |
| Biarritz | 10 |
| Carioka | 15 |

(2) Market research has indicated that likely demand for the hire of each fleet will yield the following total incomes per year:

| | £ |
|---|---|
| Armada | 30,000 |
| Biarritz | 35,000 |
| Carioka | 44,000 |

(3) It is intended to sell the cars immediately at the end of three years. Estimated selling prices for each car then being:

| | £ |
|---|---|
| Armada | 2,500 |
| Biarritz | 5,000 |
| Carioka | 7,000 |

(4) Insurance premiums are to be paid at the start of each year and are expected to rise over the next three years. Insurance for each fleet is expected to cost:

| | Year 1 £ | Year 2 £ | Year 3 £ |
|---|---|---|---|
| Armada | 7,000 | 8,050 | 9,257 |
| Biarritz | 9,000 | 10,350 | 11,902 |
| Carioka | 10,500 | 12,075 | 13,886 |

(5) Servicing and fuel charges are also expected to rise over the next three years. Servicing and fuel charges for each fleet are expected to cost:

| | Year 1 £ | Year 2 £ | Year 3 £ |
|---|---|---|---|
| Armada | 4,050 | 4,155 | 4,270 |
| Biarritz | 5,400 | 5,520 | 5,652 |
| Carioka | 6,700 | 6,870 | 7,057 |

(6) All cash flows except insurance arise at the end of the relevant year.

(7) The rate of interest applicable is 12% per annum.

(8) The following extract is from the present value table for £1.

| Year | 12% |
|---|---|
| 1 | 0.893 |
| 2 | 0.797 |
| 3 | 0.712 |

*Required*

(a) A financial statement using the net present value method for **each** fleet of cars being considered. (35)

(b) A report for Andre Lefevre advising him which fleet of cars should be purchased. Indicate any reservations you may have regarding the net present value method of evaluating a project. (7)

(c) A discussion of any other factors which may influence Andre in his decision. (8)

(AEB)

*Tutorial note*

Do your workings using the figures given then convert each annual total to the present value. Note that insurance is paid at the start of each year. Remember to use the report format. The reservations are to do with the uncertainty of future events. Use simple 'other factors' – the ones you might consider yourself when buying a car!

*Suggested answer*

(a) Net present value calculations for car fleets

| Car | Year 0 | Year 1 | Year 2 | Year 3 | Total |
|---|---|---|---|---|---|
| **Armada** | £ | £ | £ | £ | £ |
| Cost | (33,250) | | | | |
| Insurance | (7,000) | (8,050) | (9,257) | | |
| Fuel & servicing | | (4,050) | (4,155) | (4,270) | |
| Hire fees | | 30,000 | 30,000 | 30,000 | |
| Trade in | | | | 12,500 | |
| | (40,250) | 17,900 | 16,588 | 38,230 | |
| | × 1 | × 0.893 | × 0.797 | × 0.712 | |
| | (40,250) | 15,985 | 13,221 | 27,220 | 16,176 |
| **Biarritz** | | | | | |
| Cost | (54,000) | | | | |
| Insurance | (9,000) | (10,350) | (11,902) | | |
| Fuel & servicing | | (5,400) | (5,520) | (5,652) | |
| Hire fees | | 35,000 | 35,000 | 35,000 | |
| Trade in | | | | 25,000 | |
| | (63,000) | 19,250 | 17,578 | 54,348 | |
| | × 1 | × 0.893 | × 0.797 | × 0.712 | |
| | (63,000) | 17,190 | 14,010 | 38,696 | 6,896 |
| **Carioka** | | | | | |
| Cost | (68,000) | | | | |
| Insurance | (10,500) | (12,075) | (13,886) | | |
| Fuel & servicing | | (6,700) | (6,870) | (7,057) | |
| Hire fees | | 44,000 | 44,000 | 44,000 | |
| Trade in | | | | 35,000 | |
| | (78,500) | 25,225 | 23,244 | 71,943 | |
| | × 1 | x 0.893 | x 0.797 | x 0.712 | |
| | (78,500) | 22,526 | 18,526 | 51,223 | 13,775 |

(b) To

From

Date *(i.e. report format)*

Advice on purchase of car fleet

On financial grounds Andre should purchase the fleet of Armada cars. This fleet gives the highest NPV value. It also has the shortest payback period.

NPV reservations could include accuracy of future predictions; both incomes and expenses. Accuracy of discount factor. Is it likely to change over the three years?

(c) Other factors to be considered might include:

Andre may wish to buy British; he may perceive problems with foreign vehicles, e.g. cost of servicing, speed of servicing, availability of spares etc.

Popularity of models with the public; safety features; size of each car; ease of drive etc.

Environmental factors; use of unleaded petrol etc.

# ABSORPTION AND MARGINAL COSTING

## Units in this chapter

13.1 *Variable and fixed costs*
13.2 *Marginal costing*
13.3 *Uses of marginal costing*

## Chapter objectives

We saw in Chapter 9 that estimated overheads were allocated/apportioned to various cost centres and then absorbed into jobs/units produced etc. They are attached to products.

When using absorption costing techniques the distinct behavioural characteristics of fixed costs and variable costs are not recognised. Indeed some costs are charged to the unit produced even when there may be no direct relationship between the costs and the unit. The factory overheads are absorbed into total production cost. Absorption costing is also known as **full costing**.

These costs, together with the under or over recovery of overheads, are included in the final financial accounts. They are historic figures; they occurred in the year just gone. A different approach is needed when making decisions for the future. In this chapter we look at marginal costing as a management accounting tool.

The key topics and concepts covered in this chapter are:

- variable costs;
- fixed costs;
- contribution;
- special contracts;
- make or buy;
- choices between alternatives;
- use of scarce resources;
- penetration pricing;
- break-even by calculation;
- break-even by graph.

## 13.1 VARIABLE AND FIXED COSTS

**Variable costs** are those costs which vary directly with levels of activity, e.g. direct materials.

If production is 1,000 units and each unit costs £10 then total variable costs would be £10,000. If production rises to 1500 units then total variable costs would be £15,000. If production fell to 800 units then total variable costs would be £8,000.

Other examples of direct costs would include direct labour if workers are paid on piece work rates (in examination questions direct labour costs are generally treated as variable costs) and royalties. you may recognise this as forming the prime costs in a manufacturing account.

**Fixed costs** do not vary directly with levels of activity (within certain limits). They are period costs and are written off in the accounting period to which they relate. Do not fall into the trap of saying that fixed costs never change. Rent can change if extra capacity is needed or a business shrinks and moves to smaller premises.

An example of a fixed cost would be rent. Say production was 100 units and the rent was £25,000. If production rose to 1,500 units the rent would still be £25,000. If production fell to 800 units, the rent would still be £25,000.

Fixed costs are also known as sunk costs; the business is committed to paying fixed costs whatever level of activity is achieved. In many cases they can be disregarded when solving problems involving changes in output.

In order for a business to be profitable all costs must be recovered in the final selling price paid by the customer. Absorbing costs into products is an attempt to ensure that each product does recover a proportion of the overall costs incurred in running the whole business.

Absorption costing does have some weaknesses:

- The calculations are based on a predicted level of output. The result does not apply to variations in that output, also, the predictions or any apportionment methods used may be inaccurate

- Absorption costing does not take into account the different characteristics shown by fixed costs, variable costs, and semi-variable costs at differing levels of output.

## 13.2 MARGINAL COSTING

Marginal costing does make a clear distinction between variable costs and fixed costs. No attempt is made to allocate fixed costs to cost centres or cost units.

The **marginal cost** of an item is the extra cost incurred by a business in producing one extra unit of production above the planned production level.

Marginal costs usually comprise *extra* materials, *extra* labour costs, *extra* direct expenditure, *extra* variable costs in selling and distributing the product, and the *extra* variable overhead for general administration, when there is an increase in production.

Fixed costs generally remain unchanged so there is no extra cost incurred with an increase in the level of production. For example:

| Output units | Fixed cost £ | Variable cost £ | Total cost £ | Marginal cost per unit £ |
|---|---|---|---|---|
| 100 | 1,000 | 100 | 1,100 | |
| | | | | 1 |
| 101 | 1,000 | 101 | 1,101 | |
| | | | | 1 |
| 102 | 1,000 | 102 | 1,102 | |
| | | | | etc. |

You will notice that the variable costs change – there are extra variable costs – but the fixed costs remain unchanged. The variable costs *are* the marginal costs (in this example).

> **Contribution** is the difference between selling price and variable costs. Contribution should correctly be named 'contribution towards fixed costs and profit'. The contribution is available to pay the fixed costs; once they are all covered then contribution becomes profit.

## EXAMPLE 1

|  | | £ |
|---|---|---|
| The selling price of one unit of production of an HI/10 is | | 36 |
| The variable costs per unit of the product are – | Direct materials | 8 |
| | Direct labour | 12 |
| | Royalties | 2 |
| | Fixed costs | 10 |

**Required**

Calculate the contribution earned by one unit of the product.

**Solution**

Contribution per unit = Selling price per unit – Variable costs per unit
Contribution per unit = 36 – 22 (8 + 12 + 2)
Contribution per unit = 14

## EXAMPLE 2

The Arual Company produces a single product. The following information relates to the product in May.

|  |  | £ |
|---|---|---|
| Sales: 1,000 units at | | 60 per unit |
| Costs per unit: | Direct materials | 12 |
| | Direct labour | 18 |
| | Royalties | 5 |
| | Fixed costs | 15 |

All production is sold.

**Required**

An income statement showing clearly the total contribution and profit for May at 1,000 units production.

**Solution**

### Income statement for May

|  | £ | £ |
|---|---|---|
| Sales | | 60,000 |
| Less:  Direct materials | 12,000 | |
| Direct labour | 18,000 | |
| Royalties | 5,000 | 35,000 |
| Contribution | | 25,000 |
| Less fixed costs | | 15,000 |
| Profit | | 10,000 |

## EXAMPLE 3

As above – but 1,400 units sold at £60.

**Required**

An income statement showing clearly the total contribution and profit for May at 1,400 units production.

**Solution**

| | £ | £ |
|---|---|---|
| Sales | | 84,000 |
| Less Direct materials | 16,800 | |
| Direct labour | 25,200 | |
| Royalties | 7,000 | 49,000 |
| Contribution | | 35,000 |
| Less Fixed Costs | | 15,000 |
| Profit | | 20,000 |

The contribution has risen but *not* the fixed costs. The identification of contribution is vital in these circumstances. Marginal costing splits total costs into the two elements of fixed costs and variable costs to assist the decision-making process.

## 13.3   USES OF MARGINAL COSTING

Marginal costing techniques are used in the following circumstances:
- In costing special one-off contracts or jobs.
- In make or buy decisions making.
- In choosing between competing alternatives.
- When a business has a factor limiting production levels.
- When employing penetration or destroyer pricing strategies.
- To calculate the break-even level of output.

These all tend to be short-term decisions.

### SPECIAL 'ONE-OFF' CONTRACTS OR PROJECTS

EXAMPLE 1
Neleh Engineering manufacture one product: an MIT. The following information relates to a production level of 10,000 MITs.

| | £ |
|---|---|
| Selling price per MIT | 75 |
| Costs per unit: Direct materials | 25 |
| Direct labour | 17 |
| Royalties | 4 |
| Fixed costs | 14 |

There is spare capacity in the factory. A French retailer has indicated that he will purchase 2,000 MITs if the selling price to him was £50.

**Required**
Advise the managers of Neleh Engineering whether they should accept the order.

**Solution**
The order should be accepted since the special order will make a positive contribution of £4 per unit.

Workings:
Contribution = Selling price per unit – variable costs per unit
Contribution = £50 – £46
Contribution = £4

This special order has no need to cover the fixed costs since *they are already absorbed in the 'normal' selling price*. The special contract is providing Neleh Engineering with an extra £4, per unit, net income it would forego if the contract was not taken. You can see from the following revenue statements that it would be a worthwhile project to accept.

|  | **Without the order** | | | **With the order** | |
|---|---:|---:|---|---:|---:|
|  | £ | £ |  | £ | £ |
| Sales |  | 750,000 | Sales |  | 850,000 |
| less  Direct materials | 250,000 |  | less  Direct materials | 300,000 |  |
| Direct labour | 170,000 |  | Direct labour | 204,000 |  |
| Royalties | 40,000 | 460,000 | Royalties | 48,000 | 552,000 |
| Contribution |  | 290,000 | Contribution |  | 298,000 |
| less  Fixed costs |  | 140,000 | less  Fixed costs |  | 140,000 |
| Profit |  | 150,000 | Profit |  | 158,000 |

### Points to note

- The fixed costs will not change with the increased level of output
- The profit will increase by the amount of the total contribution from the French order. (£4 per unit × 2,000 units).

Care must be taken when accepting an order based on Marginal Costing for the following reasons:

- The order should not displace other business, if it does the lost revenue also becomes a marginal cost.
- The business should have spare production capacity.
- There needs to be a clear separation of customers so that other customers do not get to know of the lower price.
- The customer needs to know that this is only a one-off and that it will not constitute a 'normal' price in the future – it should not set a precedent so that the customer expects or demands the same price later.
- That competitors do not match the price and start a price war where all producers suffer.
- The customer should not be in a position to sell to other customers at a price below the regular price.

> All costs must be covered, so overheads must be covered. A business cannot work by costing *all* production at marginal cost.

A special contract may be accepted with a negative contribution to keep:
- a skilled workforce or
- machines working or
- in the hope of stimulating further orders at the full cost price later.

## MAKE OR BUY DECISIONS

A business may have an opportunity to buy the product that it manufactures itself at the moment.

The business should consider the extra costs and revenues that apply to this problem.

EXAMPLE 2

Siok Chin manufactures silk shirts for retail clothing outlets. Her costs and revenues for the next financial year are estimated to be as follows:

|  | £ |
|---|---|
| Sales 30,000 shirts at | 25 each |
| Direct material costs | 4 per shirt |
| Direct labour costs | 11 per shirt |
| Other direct costs | 3 per shirt |
| Fixed costs | 5 per shirt |
| Total production cost per shirt | 23 |
| Profit per shirt | 2 |
| Total profits | 60,000 |

Her brother, Tee, who still lives in Malaysia, has said that he can supply Siok Chin with the shirts at a total cost to her of only £20 each.

Siok Chin believes that if she purchases the shirts from her brother her profits will increase to £150,000 per year (selling price £25 less purchase price £20 = £5 × Sales of 30,000 shirts).

**Required**

Advise Siok Chin whether on financial grounds she should accept her brother's offer.

**Solution**

Siok Chin would be financially worse off if she accepted her brother's offer.

Manufacturing the shirts herself each shirt makes a contribution of £7
(Selling price £25 per unit – Marginal (variable) costs per shirt £18)

Buying the shirts from her brother each shirt would make a contribution of £5
(Selling price £25 per unit – Marginal (variable) costs per shirt £20)

Once again you can prove this by preparing a forecast income statement:

| Make | £ | £ | Buy in | £ |
|---|---|---|---|---|
| Sales | | 750,000 | Sales | 750,000 |
| Less Direct material costs | 120,000 | | | |
| Direct labour costs | 330,000 | | Less Purchase price | 600,000 |
| Other direct costs | 90,000 | 540,000 | | |
| Contribution | | 210,000 | Contribution | 150,000 |
| Less Fixed costs | | 150,000 | Less Fixed costs | 150,000 |
| Profit | | 60,000 | | 0 |

*Points to note*

- The example assumes that any resources released by buying the shirts from Tee cannot be used elsewhere by Siok Chin.

- The fixed costs (sunk costs) will have to be met whether the shirts are made or bought in.

- If the manufacturing space could be sub let this would be a marginal (extra) revenue too and should be included with our sales figure in the 'buy in' calculation.

- If extra costs were incurred in keeping the manufacturing area safe whilst unused this would also represent a marginal (extra) cost.

## EXAMPLE 3

As above, but Siok Chin can sublet her manufacturing space. The rent she will receive is £12,000.

**Required**

Calculate the contribution and profit that will be made if Siok Chin purchases the shirts from her brother and sub lets her manufacturing space.

**Solution**

Contribution would be £162,000 (original contribution £150,000 + £12,000 rent).
Profit would be £12,000 (contribution £162,000 – £150,000 fixed costs)

## EXAMPLE 4

As in original scenario, but Siok Chin employs a security firm to keep her manufacturing unit safe from vandals; this will cost £16,000 per annum. She also estimates that extra maintenance costs will amount to £6,500.

**Required**

Calculate the contribution and profit if Siok Chin purchases the shirts from her brother.

**Solution**

|  | £ | £ |
|---|---|---|
| Sales |  | 750,000 |
| Less   purchase price |  | 600,000 |
| Cost of sales |  | 150,000 |
| Less   other marginal costs: |  |  |
| security | 16,000 |  |
| maintenance | 6,500 | 22,500 |
| Contribution |  | 127,500 |
| Less fixed costs |  | 150,000 |
| Loss |  | 22,500 |

Purchasing the shirts from Tee does give a positive contribution but it is insufficient to cover the total fixed costs. Siok Chin's business would make a loss if she purchased the shirts from her brother.

**Point to note**

All extra costs and revenues which occur because of any proposed change in business circumstances must be included in the calculations.

## MAKING A CHOICE BETWEEN COMPETING COURSES OF ACTION

The managers of a business may be faced with making a choice between competing strategies. In order to arrive at a decision only marginal costs need to be considered.

Any common costs may be disregarded in the calculation. However once the decision has been arrived at the total costs will have to be included since we said earlier '. . . all costs must be covered . . .'

EXAMPLE 5

Michael Jones has decided to start a small furniture manufacturing business. He will specialise in only one product. He will choose to produce either tables, chairs, or stools. He supplies you with the following information:

|  | Tables | Chairs | Stools |
|---|---|---|---|
|  | £ | £ | £ |
| Selling price per unit | 280 | 120 | 60 |
| Direct material costs per unit | 70 | 8 | 6 |
| Direct labour costs per unit | 40 | 25 | 8 |
| Total fixed costs | 40,000 | 40,000 | 40,000 |

**Required**

(a) Advise Michael which product he should manufacture.

(b) A forecast revenue statement showing the contribution and the profit based on the advise given in part (a).

**Solution**

Since the fixed costs of £40,000 is a cost that is common to all the alternatives it can be disregarded in the calculation to decide which product should be produced.

| (a) Contribution statements | Tables | Chairs | Stools |
|---|---|---|---|
|  | £ | £ | £ |
| Selling price per unit | 280 | 120 | 60 |
| Marginal costs per unit | (110) | (33) | (14) |
| Contribution per unit | 170 | 87 | 46 |

Michael should produce the furniture that gives him the largest contribution, i.e. tables.

(b)

**Forecast revenue statement for the production of tables**

|  |  | £ | £ |
|---|---|---|---|
| Sales |  |  | 140,000 |
| Less | Direct material costs | 35,000 |  |
|  | Direct labour costs | 20,000 | 55,000 |
| Contribution |  |  | 85,000 |
| Less Fixed costs |  |  | 40,000 |
| Profit |  |  | 45,000 |

# WHEN A BUSINESS HAS A LIMITED AMOUNT OF A FACTOR OF PRODUCTION

A business may be faced by a short-term shortage of one of the factors of production. There could be a shortage in the supply of raw materials; there could be a shortage of labour with a particular necessary skill; or there could be a lack of storage space. The shortage will limit the business's ability to maximise its profits.

It is essential that the managers of a business use the limited resource to obtain maximum advantage for the business.

## EXAMPLE 6

The Petaling Company manufactures four products. The products use the same type of skilled labour. At the present time there is a shortage of the skills necessary to produce the four products.

The following information relates to the Petaling Company:

| Product | A | B | C | D |
|---|---|---|---|---|
| Selling price per unit (£) | 175 | 210 | 245 | 280 |
| Demand for product (units) | 4,000 | 6,000 | 5,000 | 3,000 |
| Material usage per unit (kg) | 8 | 10 | 12 | 12 |
| Labour hours per unit | 4 | 3 | 6 | 5 |
| Variable overheads per unit (£) | 9 | 11 | 6 | 8 |

Material costs per kg = £8.00
Labour costs per hour = £7. 00
The available skilled labour hours is restricted to 35,000 hours.

### Required
A statement showing the level of production for each product which will maximise profits for the Petaling Company.

### Solution
Contribution earned per product:

|  |  | A £ |  | B £ |  | C £ |  | D £ |
|---|---|---|---|---|---|---|---|---|
| Selling price per unit |  | 175 |  | 210 |  | 245 |  | 280 |
| Marginal (variable) costs |  |  |  |  |  |  |  |  |
| Material costs per unit | 64 |  | 80 |  | 96 |  | 96 |  |
| Labour costs per unit | 28 |  | 21 |  | 42 |  | 35 |  |
| Variable overheads per unit | 9 | 101 | 11 | 112 | 6 | 144 | 8 | 139 |
| Contribution per unit |  | 74 |  | 98 |  | 101 |  | 141 |
| Contribution per hour of skilled labour used |  | £18.50 £74/4 |  | £32.67 £98/3 |  | £16.83 £101/6 |  | £28.20 £141/5 |
| Ranking |  | 3rd |  | 1st |  | 4th |  | 2nd |

The Petaling Company should produce: 6,000 units of product B, total hours used 18,000; 3,000 units of product D, total hours used 33,000. There are only 2,000 hours of skilled labour hours remaining.

The Petaling Company should produce 500 units of A, total hours used 35,000.

In some examination questions the amounts of materials and labour may not be given, in this case the contribution for every pound (£) spent would be calculated.

233

In this example:

Product A will earn £2.64 contribution for every £1 spent on skilled labour.
Product B will earn £4.67 contribution for every £1 spent on skilled labour.
Product C will earn £2.40 contribution for every £1 spent on skilled labour
Product D will earn £4.03 contribution for every £1 spent on skilled labour.

The products will still be ranked B, then D, then A, and finally C.

## PENETRATION OR DESTROYER PRICING

When business managers wish to gain a foothold in a new market, they may adopt a marginal approach to the costing of the product.

### EXAMPLE 7

A British company has had a great deal of success with a product in the home market. The product sells for £48.00. Other information relating to the product:

Variable costs per unit   £22.00
Fixed costs per unit     £12.00

The managers decide to launch the product in Spain.

**Required**
Calculate the lowest price that the company could charge in the Spanish market without reduction in total business profits.

**Solution**
Provided the company can cover the marginal costs incurred in penetrating the Spanish market the company will be no worse off. It could charge £22.00 – this would cover the company's variable costs.

This could penetrate the market. It could mean that other products with the same brand name manufactured by the British company might have an advantage. It also might mean that once consumer loyalty has been established in Spain for the product the price can be increased.

The managers of a business can also use the same tactics to destroy a competitor.

## BREAK EVEN

The break-even point is the level of sales or units sold at which the business neither makes a profit nor a loss. It can be ascertained in the following ways (all are popular with examiners).

### The unit contribution method

$$\text{Break even} = \frac{\text{Total fixed costs}}{\text{Contribution per unit}} = \text{Number of units required to be sold}$$

### The contribution/sales method (also called the profit/volume method)

$$\text{Break even} = \frac{\text{Total fixed costs}}{\text{Total contribution/sales}} = \text{Value of sales}$$

### Graphical means

*Do not use this method unless instructed to do so* – it is very time consuming and can be less accurate than the other two methods.

### EXAMPLE 8

The following information relates to the production of 100,000 ginglets, the single product of Kerweeds plc.

| | £ |
|---|---|
| Selling price per unit | 25 |
| Raw material costs per unit | 4 |
| Direct labour costs per unit | 7 |
| Variable manufacturing overhead per unit | 3 |
| Fixed manufacturing overhead per unit | 4 |
| Variable sales overhead per unit | 1 |
| Fixed sales overhead per unit | 2 |

**Required**

(a) Calculate the break-even point for ginglets.

(b) Prepare a graph showing the break-even point for ginglets. Indicate on your graph the margin of safety.

**Solution**

(a) The easiest method is to calculate and use the unit contribution. If you can find the unit costs easily use this method.

Contribution per ginglet = Selling price per unit − Variable costs per unit
Contribution per ginglet = £25 − £15 (4 + 7 + 3 + 1)
Contribution per ginglet = £10

Total fixed costs = (Fixed manufacturing overhead + fixed sales overhead) × 100,000
Total fixed costs = (£4 + £2) × 100,000
Total fixed costs = £6 per ginglet × 100,000 ginglets
Total fixed costs = £600,000

$$\text{Break-even point} = \frac{\text{Total fixed costs}}{\text{Contribution per unit}} = \frac{£600,000}{£10} = 60,000 \text{ ginglets.}$$

*Points to note*

- This method gives you the answer in units. If you need the sales revenue required to break even the units must be multiplied by the selling price per unit

- Sales revenue required to break even = 600,000 × £25 = £1,500,000.
    Take care to use the **TOTAL fixed costs**. Many examination candidates use the fixed costs per unit and lose easy marks through carelessness.

- Some questions give a revenue statement to base the calculations on:

**Kerweeds plc revenue statement for ginglets**

| | £ | £ |
|---|---|---|
| Sales | | 341,800 |
| Less Raw material costs | 54,688 | |
| Direct labour costs | 95,704 | |
| Variable manufacturing overhead | 41,016 | |
| Variable sales overhead | 13,672 | 205,080 |
| Contribution | | 136,720 |
| Less Fixed manufacturing overhead | 400,000 | |
| Fixed sales overhead | 200,000 | 600,000 |
| Loss | | 413,280 |

Using the contribution/sales method:

$$\frac{\text{Contribution}}{\text{Sales}} = \frac{\text{Sales} - \text{Variable costs}}{\text{Sales}} = \frac{£341,800 - 205,080}{£341,800}$$

$$\frac{\text{Contribution}}{\text{Sales}} = \frac{£136,720}{£341,800}$$

$$\frac{\text{Contribution}}{\text{Sales}} = 0.4$$

$$\text{Break-even point} = \frac{\text{Total fixed costs}}{\text{Contribution/sales ratio}}$$

$$\text{Break-even point} = \frac{\pounds 600,000}{0.4}$$

Break-even point = £1,500,000 sales revenue.

This method gives you the level of sales revenue required to break even. If the number of units to break even is required, divide the revenue by the unit selling price.

$$\text{Break-even point} = \frac{\pounds 1,500,000}{\pounds 25} = 60,000 \text{ ginglets}$$

(b) Only use the graphical method of finding the break-even point when it is asked for in the question. You need to build up the information in stages. Generally there will be marks scored at each stage, so work carefully. The accuracy of your results depends on the care you take.

The vertical axis of your graph (the $y$ axis when you draw algebraic graphs) is always used for the costs and revenue values.

The horizontal axis of your graph (the $x$ axis in algebra) is used to show the sales output.

Where the vertical and horizontal axes meet is called the origin and has a value of zero on both axes. It is marked 0.

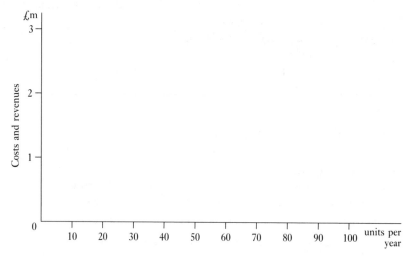

It is important to remember that the data must be scaled evenly otherwise the graph that you draw will be distorted and will give incorrect results.

Graphs are a visual aid. They must be accurate and easy to read. Make your graph as large as the graph paper will allow.

The next stage is put in your heading. This can be copied almost word for word from the question, i.e. graph showing the break-even point for ginglets.

Now plot the points showing fixed costs, then variable costs, and finally the sales.

Since, in examinations, fixed costs remain the same whatever level of sales is achieved when we plot this part of the graph it will appear as a straight line running parallel to the horizontal axis.

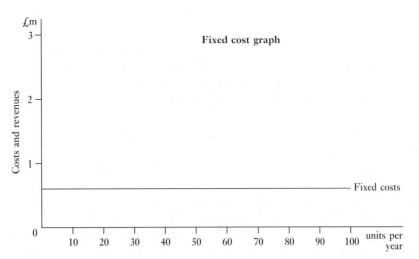

Now the variable costs need to be plotted. In order to plot the variable cost graph a few calculations need to be done. You have probably used the same techniques when drawing graphs in mathematics.

| Sales output | 0 | 10,000 | 40,000 |
|---|---|---|---|
| Variable costs (£15 per unit) | 0 | 150,000 | 600,000 |
| Fixed costs | 600,000 | 600,000 | 600,000 |
| Total costs | 600,000 | 750,000 | 1,200,000 |

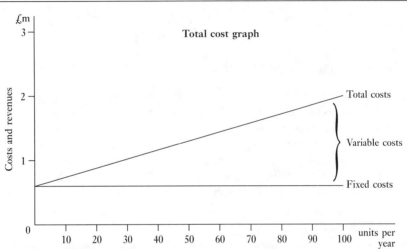

We now have the total cost graph plotted. Mark each graph as you complete it. The final graph to be drawn is the sales revenue graph.

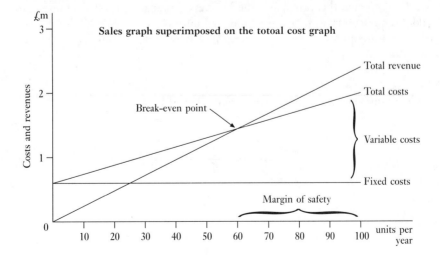

Combining the three straight-line graphs produces the break-even graph. Indicate clearly on your graph the break-even point and the margin of safety.

**The margin of safety** is the difference between the break-even point and the sales actually achieved or forecast to be achieved. In the example, sales could drop to 90,000 ginglets and the company would still be profitable; to 70,000 ginglets, the company is still in profit; to 60,001 ginglets, the company is still profitable. When the output of ginglets falls to 59,999 the company is now in the danger zone; it is making losses.

Questions sometimes ask for the level of output which will achieve a particular profit level. Remember the correct name for contribution? *Contribution towards fixed costs and profits.* We use this in the calculation.

### EXAMPLE 9

Using the data given for production of 100,000 ginglets previously.

**Required**
Calculate the number of ginglets to be sold in order that Kerweeds plc will earn a profit of £70,000

**Solution**

$$\text{Break-even point} + £70,000 = \frac{\text{Total fixed costs} + £70,000}{\text{Contribution per unit}}$$

$$\text{Output to achieve required level of profit} = \frac{£600,000 + £70,000}{£10}$$

$$= \frac{£670,000}{£10}$$

$$= 67,000 \text{ ginglets}$$

## Limitations of break-even charts

- There is an assumption that all data behaves in a linear manner. Unit costs may fall as output increases. Some costs may be stepped in nature: one supervisor may be needed until sales reach 40,000 units, after which another supervisor should be employed. When output reaches 80,000 units perhaps another supervisor should be employed etc. In the practice there are many influences on costs and revenues – changes in technology, changes in levels of productivity. The break-even chart assumes that the only factor affecting costs and revenues is sales volume.

- There is an assumption that all production is sold. The break-even chart does not take into account changing stock levels.

- Break-even charts generally only relate to a single product. (It is possible to produce a multi-product graph, but this is outside the scope of your syllabus).

A break-even chart does not show clearly the amount of profit or loss made by the business. To overcome this problem some businesses prepare a profit/volume graph. This graph plots the relationship between profits and output.

The profits are plotted along the vertical axis and the output is plotted along the horizontal axis.

### EXAMPLE 10

The following information relates to the production of Krams.

| Production in units | 1,000 | 2,000 | 3,000 | 4,000 | 5,000 |
|---|---|---|---|---|---|
| | £ | £ | £ | £ | £ |
| Sales | 8,000 | 16,000 | 24,000 | 32,000 | 40,000 |
| Variable costs | 4,000 | 8,000 | 12,000 | 16,000 | 20,000 |
| Fixed costs | 9,000 | 9,000 | 9,000 | 9,000 | 9,000 |

**Required**
A profit/volume chart for Krams.

Solution

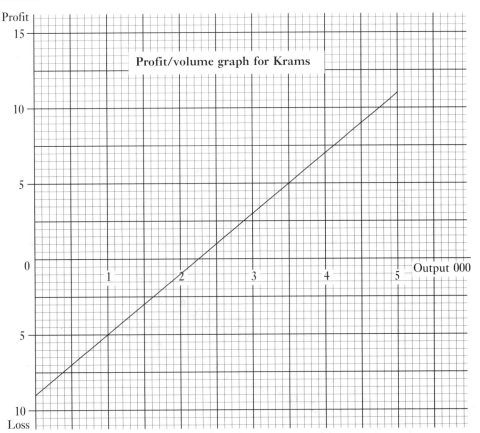

At zero level of output the loss is £9,000. At zero level of production the fixed costs still have to be paid.

Plot any other two points, say, 1,000 units and 5,000 units:

at 1,000 unit output the loss is (£5,000) Sales £8,000 – (£4,000 and £9,000);

at 5,000 unit output the profit is £11,000 Sales £40,000 – (£20,000 and £9,000).

---

## Chapter round up

Chapter 13 has dealt with marginal costing and its uses. This is another popular area with examiners.

It is important that you recognise the types of questions asked. They tend to be on the acceptance of an order at less than 'normal' price.

Remember that 'marginal' means extra.

You should be able to calculate and use contribution in arriving at a decision.

---

# Illustrative questions

**1**  Meir Market Gardeners Ltd commenced business on 1 June 1993 and entered into a contract with a supermarket chain to supply potatoes, cabbages and cauliflowers. The contract called for a minimum of 18,000 boxes and a maximum of 45,000 boxes of each product per annum. Meir has only 3,600 square metres of land available. At the end of the year to 31 May 1994 the following information was available.

Areas devoted to product

| | |
|---|---|
| Potatoes | 1,800 square metres |
| Cabbages | 900 square metres |
| Cauliflowers | 900 square metres |
| | 3,600 square metres |

Number of boxes produced

| | |
|---|---|
| Potatoes | 36,000 |
| Cabbages | 27,000 |
| Cauliflowers | 32,400 |
| | 95,400 |

Sales of each product

| | |
|---|---|
| Potatoes | £86,400 |
| Cabbages | £32,400 |
| Cauliflowers | £48,600 |
| | £167,400 |

The company's financial accountant has prepared the following total profit and loss account for the year ended 31 May 1994.

| | £ | £ |
|---|---|---|
| Sales | | 167,400 |
| Less: Direct materials | 48,960 | |
| Direct wages – cultivating | 34,200 | |
| Direct wages – packing | 18,900 | |
| Boxes | 9,540 | |
| Salaries | 6,480 | |
| Heating | 10,800 | |
| Maintenance | 1,800 | |
| Depreciation | 6,300 | |
| Rates | 3,600 | |
| Distribution costs | 11,450 | |
| Administration costs | 8,370 | 160,400 |
| Profit | | 7,000 |

The directors are planning for the next year and are making the following assumptions.

(i) The yield for each product per square metre will remain the same as the previous year.
(ii) No cost or selling price increases are expected.
(iii) The three direct costs and the cost of boxes will continue to vary with output.
(iv) All other costs are expected to remain the same.

The directors have asked you, as management accountant, to calculate the profit for each product using the following data.

| Item | Potatoes £ | Cabbages £ | Cauliflowers £ |
|---|---|---|---|
| Direct materials | 27,000 | 6,300 | 15,660 |
| Direct wages – cultivating | 16,200 | 9,000 | 9,000 |
| Direct wages – packing | 10,800 | 3,600 | 4,500 |

| | Basis of apportionment |
|---|---|
| Boxes | Number of boxes |
| Salaries | 1/3 to each |
| Heating | Area |
| Maintenance | Area |
| Depreciation | Area |
| Rates | Area |
| Distribution costs | Number of boxes |
| Administration costs | Sales income |

Whilst you think that this information will be useful you believe that for decision making purposes a marginal costing approach, identifying contributions, will give more relevant information.

*Required*

(a) Provide the directors with the profit per product line as requested. (12)

(b) Provide the directors with a statement showing the optimum product mix which will give the maximum annual profit under the conditions of the present contract. (15)

(c) Present a profit and loss account which shows the results of the data in your answer to part (b). (10)

(d) Explain the concept of contribution per limiting factor. (3)

(NEAB)

*Tutorial note*
You must understand how to calculate contribution. This is the key to all marginal costing questions.

Optimum product mix will use the limiting factor to gain the greatest contribution. Remember a statement does not mean a written statement.

*Suggested answer*

(a) **Meir Market Gardeners Ltd profit per product line**

| | Potatoes £ | | Cabbages £ | | Cauliflowers £ | |
|---|---|---|---|---|---|---|
| Sales | | 86,400 | | 32,400 | | 48,600 |
| Less Variable costs | | | | | | |
| Direct materials | 27,000 | | 6,300 | | 15,660 | |
| Cultivating wages | 16,200 | | 9,000 | | 9,000 | |
| Packing wages | 10,800 | | 3,600 | | 4,500 | |
| Boxes | 3,600 | 57,600 | 2,700 | 21,600 | 3,240 | 32,400 |
| Contribution | | 28,800 | | 10,800 | | 16,200 |
| Fixed costs | | | | | | |
| Salaries | 2,160 | | 2,160 | | 2,160 | |
| Heating | 5,400 | | 2,700 | | 2,700 | |
| Maintenance | 900 | | 450 | | 450 | |
| Depreciation | 3,150 | | 1,575 | | 1,575 | |
| Rates | 1,800 | | 900 | | 900 | |
| Distribution costs | 4,320 | | 3,240 | | 3,890 | |
| Administration costs | 4,320 | 22,050 | 1,620 | 12,645 | 2,430 | 14,105 |
| Net profit/(loss) | | 6,750 | | (1,845) | | 2,095 |

(b) **Statement showing optimum product mix**

Limiting factor is the available land:
20 boxes of potatoes can be grown per square metre;
30 boxes of cabbage can be grown per square metre;
36 boxes of cauliflowers can be grown per square metre.

| | Potatoes | Cabbages | Cauliflowers |
|---|---|---|---|
| Contribution | £28,800 | £10,800 | £16,200 |
| Area under cultivation per crop | 1,800m² | 900m² | 900m² |
| Contribution per m² | £16 | £12 | £18 |
| Ranking | 2 | 3 | 1 |

So grow as many cauliflowers as possible, but Meir must produce 18,000 boxes of cabbage.

45,000 boxes
18,000 boxes

Cauliflowers will take up  1,250 square metres (45,000/36)
Cabbages will take up     600 square metres (18,000/30)
so there will be       1,750 square metres left to grow potatoes.

Meir should produce 35,000 boxes of potatoes (1,750 × 20)

Optimum product mix is 45,000 boxes of cauliflowers, 35,000 boxes of potatoes and 18,000 boxes of cabbage.

(c) Profit and loss account

|  |  | £ | £ |
|---|---|---|---|
| Sales – | Cauliflowers | 67,500 | |
| | Potatoes | 84,000 | |
| | Cabbage | 21,600 | 173,100 |
| Less variable costs | | | |
| | Cauliflowers | 45,000 | |
| | Potatoes | 56,000 | |
| | Cabbage | 14,400 | 115,400 |
| Contribution | | | 57,700 |
| Less fixed costs | | | 48,800 |
| Net profit | | | 8,900 |

(d) Maximum use must be made of a limiting factor by employing it in the area where it will yield maximum contribution for every unit used.

**2** Barmik Ltd produces three products, and for the coming year its budget shows the following:

| | Total £ | Product A £ | Product B £ | Product C £ |
|---|---|---|---|---|
| Sales | 100,000 | 60,000 | 25,000 | 15,000 |
| Direct material | 42,000 | 23,000 | 10,000 | 9,000 |
| Direct labour | 20,000 | 10,000 | 8,000 | 2,000 |
| Variable overheads | 10,500 | 4,000 | 5,000 | 1,500 |
| Fixed overheads | 15,000 | 7,500 | 6,000 | 1,500 |
| Total costs | 87,500 | 44,500 | 29,000 | 14,000 |
| Profit/(Loss) | 12,500 | 15,500 | (4,000) | 1,000 |

Fixed overheads are absorbed on the basis of a percentage on direct labour. A suggestion has been made that Product B should be eliminated.

*Required*

(a) Using graph paper, produce a break-even chart for the company for the coming year, showing the break-even point based on the original **total** budget. (5)

(b) Calculate the revised profit for each of the Products A and C, assuming that Product B is eliminated. (4)

(c) Using graph paper, produce a new **total** break-even chart assuming that Product B is eliminated. (5)

(d) Show, **by calculation**, the break-even point at the original budget level and the break-even point if Product B is eliminated. (6)

(NEAB)

*Tutorial note*
Score the easy marks first by making sure that the heading and axes are marked. Plot the fixed costs then the total costs and finally the total revenue. Indicate clearly the break even point.

*Suggested answer*

(a)

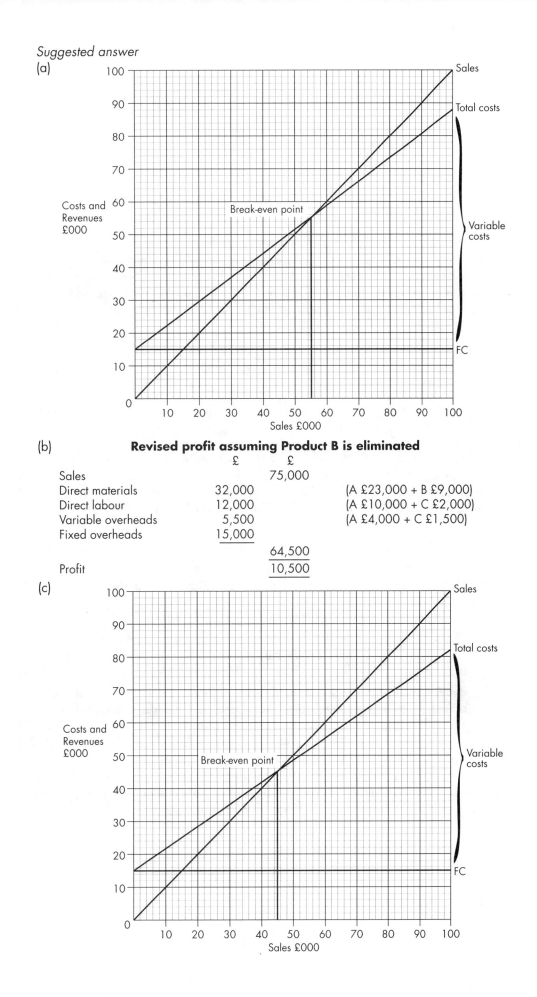

(b)

**Revised profit assuming Product B is eliminated**

| | £ | £ | |
|---|---|---|---|
| Sales | | 75,000 | |
| Direct materials | 32,000 | | (A £23,000 + B £9,000) |
| Direct labour | 12,000 | | (A £10,000 + C £2,000) |
| Variable overheads | 5,500 | | (A £4,000 + C £1,500) |
| Fixed overheads | 15,000 | | |
| | | 64,500 | |
| Profit | | 10,500 | |

(c)

(d) $\dfrac{\text{Contribution}}{\text{Sales}} = \dfrac{£100,000 - £72,500}{£100,000} = 0.275$

Break-even point $= \dfrac{\text{Fixed costs}}{\text{Contribution/sales ratio}} = \dfrac{£15,000}{0.275}$

$= £54,545.45$ sales revenue

**Excluding B**

$\dfrac{\text{Contribution}}{\text{Sales}} = \dfrac{£75,000 - £49,500}{£75,000} = 0.34$

Break-even point $= \dfrac{\text{Fixed costs}}{\text{Contribution/sales ratio}} = \dfrac{£15,000}{0.34}$

$= £44,117.65$ sales revenue

**3** Joanne Hornby has written the best selling book *The Langdale Chronicles*, an historical novel set in seventeenth-century Cumbria. It is published by Greystone publishers.

The following unit costs and revenues apply to the publication based on a production run of 650,000 books.

|  | £ |
| --- | --- |
| Materials | 1.70 |
| Labour | 3.50 |
| Royalties | 1.30 |
|  | 6.50 |
| Factory overheads | 2.40 |
|  | 8.90 |

The selling price of the book is £13.00. All factory overheads are fixed costs.

420,000 books were sold. The remainder of the books remain in the publisher's warehouse. The Fireside Book Club wish to buy the remaining stock of books to sell to their members and make an offer to Greystone publishers of £7.50 per copy.

*Required*

(a) Based on the publisher's costings, how many books must be sold to break even? Show the basis of your calculation. (6)

(b) (i) Based on the relevant data, advise the publisher whether the book club offer should be accepted. (6)

 (ii) What other benefits might the publisher obtain from accepting the book club offer? (6)

(c) Prepare an income statement for the publisher assuming that the book club offer is accepted. (12)

(d) Explain clearly the main characteristics of absorption costing and marginal costing. Answers should indicate the circumstances in which each should be used. (20)

(AEB)

*Tutorial note*

The bulk of the marks are for part (d) and you should allocate 18 minutes of your total time to it. Plan you answer to avoid repetition of the same point. Make your point, explain what you mean and use examples to illustrate your point.

*Suggested answer*

(a) Break even level of sales $= \dfrac{\text{Fixed costs}}{\text{Contribution per unit}} = \dfrac{£1,560,000}{£6.50}$

$= 240,000$ books

(b) 
| Selling price to book club | £7.50 |
| --- | --- |
| Marginal costs | £6.50 |
| Contribution per book | £1.00 |

The marginal extra costs are for materials, labour and royalties only.

(i) So, based on the above calculation the book club offer ought to be accepted. The offer makes a positive contribution towards fixed costs and profit. In fact, this contribution is all profit since 420,000 books were sold and the break even point was 240,000 books. Once 240,000 books had been sold all fixed costs had been covered

(ii) The other benefits that might accrue to the publisher could include
A larger market for all books published by this publisher.
Lower unit costs if sales do increase in the future.
Will help publisher's cash flow.
Could save costs by freeing up storage space.

(c) **Income statement for *The Langdale Chronicles* publication**

| | | |
|---|---:|---:|
| Sales | | 7,185,000* |
| Less variable costs | | |
| Materials | 1,105,000 | |
| Labour | 2,275,000 | |
| Royalties | 845,000 | 4,225,000 |
| Contribution | | 2,960,000 |
| Less fixed costs | | 1,560,000 |
| Profit | | 1,400,000 |

*(Original sales £5,460,000, book club sales £1,725,000.)

(d) **Absorption costing**
Points could include:
Absorption costing attempts to apportion estimated costs to cost centres or products, and this can present difficulties.
There are no definitive rules on how to apportion overheads; it is arbitrary but is guided by common sense.
All costs are absorbed in arriving at the estimated total cost of production.
Is used to help determine selling price.
May help in making a 'buy or make' decision.
It is necessary for stock valuation purposes in a manufacturing business.

**Marginal costing**
The costs incurred in producing one extra unit of the product.
Marginal costs must be covered by marginal revenues to be acceptable.
Marginal cost pricing is used for 'one off' jobs or contracts, penetration pricing, determining optimum sales mix, and determining break even position.
But there must be spare capacity and the marginal cost work should not displace full-cost priced work; it should only be undertaken when no other work is available at the normal selling price.
In order to be profitable a business must cover all its costs during a financial time period; all work taken cannot be costed using marginal costing techniques.

## CHAPTER 14

# SOCIAL ACCOUNTING

## Units in this chapter

14.1 *Non-financial aspects of accounting*
14.2 *Social awareness*
14.3 *Social costs*
14.4 *Social costs and profitability*

## Chapter objectives

In this chapter we consider how, over the last few decades, businesses have become increasingly aware of the world outside the business world.

We will outline the impact that business decisions will have on people inside and outside the workplace and on the local environment. We will also look at the importance of realising the wider implications of business activity.

Key topics and concepts covered in this chapter are:

*   people;
*   environmental issues;
*   global concerns.

## 14.1 NON-FINANCIAL ASPECTS OF ACCOUNTING

Businesses increasingly need to consider not only the financial aspects of the organisation but also the non-financial factors. Traditionally, they prepare financial statements that concentrate on the monetary aspects of business in order to make decisions. This is a one-dimensional approach. The non-financial aspects are an increasingly important element of the decision-making process for businesses.

Businesses affect all our lives, in one way or another, whether we are directly involved or not. Consumers and society in general are becoming more aware of the environmental damage that is often the by-product of business activity. We are also conscious, more than ever before, of the danger of depleting our non-renewable resources at an unsustainable rate.

## 14.2 SOCIAL AWARENESS

As consumers become more aware of environmental implications, producers are under pressure to show that they are accepting their social responsibility and are manufacturing their products with an appreciation of more than just financial factors.

Profitability is not the only concern of businesses now. There has been a move in recent years to consider the impact that businesses have on our lives. We are consumers, perhaps employees, and we all live in an environment which is influenced in a multitude of ways by the business world.

Businesses may be profitable but what of the 'hidden costs'? In securing the profits what are the costs inflicted on people outside the organisation as well as those working within it? What are the costs to the immediate environment and the wider world?

## 14.3    SOCIAL COSTS

What are the **social costs** involved in carrying out business?

*Stress* in the workforce?

*Pollution* in the workplace, e.g. dust, fumes etc?

Does the business have an effect on the immediate environs of the business e.g. *noise, dirt etc*?

Does the business have an environmental impact of global significance, e.g. *acid rain*?

## 14.4    SOCIAL COSTS AND PROFITABILITY

You may be cynical and say that businesses do not care about these things so long as they make sufficient profit, but **these factors do affect profitability**.

If the workforce are unhappy about the environment they work in they are less likely to work at full capacity and so *productivity will suffer*. If working conditions are poor there may be a *high staff turnover and/or absenteeism*. New staff may need to be trained in the ways of the business, thus incurring *recruitment and training costs*.

If the environment near the business is poor, perhaps *recruitment* of new staff will suffer. There might be *bad local publicity* affecting product sales in the locality.

If the problems are not resolved satisfactorily the publicity may become more widespread, affecting sales even more.

With larger firms there may well be a more global reaction, as we saw in 1995 with Shell, when a significant number of consumers refused to purchase Shell's products, thus bringing economic pressure to bear on Shell's decision to dispose of the Brent Spar oil platform. Businesses cannot afford to ignore the views of their customers. If consumers decide to unite in opposition against a producer/supplier and cease to purchase from the business this will inevitably reduce its sales and ultimately its profits. No business can afford to ignore this type of action from pressure groups in the long term.

The major problem that a business faces, in evaluating the consequences of following a particular line of action, is that **it is very difficult to put a price on many of the factors** that we have mentioned. We saw earlier, as accountants, that we do not include in our accounts things that cannot be measured in monetary terms (the money measurement concept).

If a factory closes we can calculate the savings in variable costs and in the longer term the savings in fixed costs. We can calculate with some degree of accuracy the redundancy payments. How do we measure the *distress* that a typist or shop floor worker experiences?

If a business buys a new computer system the cost can be calculated. The savings on staff time can be costed, but once again how can we put a value on the redundant workers' *feelings* or the *frustration* felt by employees who find the operation of computer software a nightmare?

If a business opens an out of town superstore, how do we value the *convenience* that many will experience by being able to do all their shopping in one outing? Balance this against the cost to your grandparents who can now no longer shop at the local corner shop, because it had to close down – its prices were much higher than those charged at the superstore.

## EXAMPLE

The Sainsway supermarket chain has acquired a greenfield site on the edge of Artown. It is planning to open a superstore on this site in September 1996. If planning permission is granted it will create 135 new permanent jobs.

**Required**

(a) Discuss the non-financial factors that Sainsways might consider in opening their superstore.

(b) Outline the non-financial factors that might be experienced by small businesses in the surrounding area after Sainsways open their new store.

**Solution**

(a) Points that ought to be mentioned could include:

Social benefits: extra employment during construction and on completion leading to extra income; the multiplier effect would lead to economic well-being for locality; reduced unemployment figures.

Social costs: loss of the amenity of the greenfield site; increase in the infrastructure surrounding the site; loss of view for those adjacent to the site; increase in traffic and exhaust pollution.

(b) Closure of 'corner shop' facilities as they are unable to compete, leading to unemployment of shop assistants. Extra travel costs to the out-of-town site.

*Point to note*

Some questions are based on the closure of an unprofitable business, often in an already deprived area. You would then include factors such as the loss of a local amenity, inconvenience to local residents, the effect on house prices.

There are others area of social responsibility which are covered by legislation. If unheeded they could result in legal action being taken against the business. These include such areas as health and safety, Government restrictions on trade (e.g. arms trade with Iraq), consumer and employment law.

---

### Chapter roundup

This chapter has dealt with an aspect of accounting that is likely to appear as part of a question that tests other elements of your syllabus. For example, you may be asked to undertake an investment appraisal for a power station and then to comment on the non-financial factors that also should be considered.

---

# Illustrative question

You work as a Product Accountant at Stafford plc. The company is investigating ways of improving the profitability of one of its products. The following budgeted data is available for production and sales of 15,000 units for the next financial year.

|                   | £'000 |
|-------------------|------:|
| Direct materials  | 450   |
| Direct labour     | 375   |
| Variable overheads| 225   |
|                   | 1,050 |
| Fixed overheads   | 300   |
|                   | 1,350 |
| Sales             | 1,800 |

The following options are being considered with a view to increasing profitability. The company has the capacity to increase production by 20% on budgeted levels.

(i) Increase advertising by £80,000 per annum, together with introducing a sales commission of £5 per unit. The selling price would be increased by £8 per unit, and sales quantity would be expected to increase by 10%.

(ii) Invest in new equipment which would reduce direct labour costs by 20% and variable overheads by 20%. Fixed overheads would increase by 25%. The sales quantity and price would be unchanged.

(iii) The Purchasing Manager has indicated that if a long-term contract was agreed with a single supplier then material costs would be reduced by 10%. If two-thirds of this saving was passed on to customers, then sales would be expected in increase by 1,000 units per annum. Fixed costs would be unchanged.

(iv) A major retailer has offered to place a special order for 3,000 units at £100 per unit. Under the terms of the offer the units would subsequently be sold by the retailer as 'own brand'. The existing sales quantity and price would not be affected, and due to increased production volume direct material costs would decrease by £1 per unit for all units manufactured. Fixed costs would increase by £50,000.

(v) Subcontract the making of all units to an outside supplier at a cost of £75 per unit and maintain budgeted sales price and quantity. The workshop and machinery currently in use cannot be used to produce anything else and the product workforce would be made redundant.

(vi) The profit attributable to the product for the previous year was £440,000. The volume of sales is to be increased such that under budgeted data, the profit would be increased by 10% for the next financial year.

*Required*
(a) Based on the original budget, calculate:
    (i) profit;
    (ii) contribution per unit;
    (iii) break-even in both units and sales value.     (5)

(b) Taking each suggestion independently, complete a profit statement for options (i) to (v), showing the contribution in each case. For suggestion (vi) calculate the sales quantity necessary to increase profit as indicated.     (18)

(c) Comment on the implications for the company of undertaking options (iv) and (v), and for the local community of undertaking option (v).     (8)
    (Oxford)

*Tutorial note*
The question is testing your ability to recognise and calculate contribution. Work through part (b) methodically and carefully, considering each option separately. The second part of (c) is looking at the social implications of option (v).

*Suggested answer*
(a) (i) Profit = £450,000 (£1,800,000 – £1,350,000)

    (ii) Contribution per unit = £50 ((£1,800,000 – £1,050,000) ÷ 15,000)

    (iii) Break-even = 6,000 units (£300,000 ÷ 50)
              = £720,000 (6,000 units × £120)

(b) (i)

| | £ | £ |
|---|---|---|
| Sales | | 2,112,000 |
| Direct materials | 450,000 | |
| Direct labour | 450,000 | |
| Variable overheads | 225,000 | 1,125,000 |
| Contribution | | 987,000 |
| Fixed overheads | | 380,000 |
| Profit | | 607,000 |

(ii)

| | £ | £ |
|---|---|---|
| Sales | | 1,800,000 |
| Direct materials | 450,000 | |
| Direct labour | 300,000 | |
| Variable overheads | 180,000 | 930,000 |
| Contribution | | 870,000 |
| Fixed overheads | | 375,000 |
| Profit | | 495,000 |

(iii)

| | £ | £ |
|---|---|---|
| Sales | | 1,890,000 |
| Direct materials | 405,000 | |
| Direct labour | 300,000 | |
| Variable overheads | 180,000 | 885,000 |
| Contribution | | 1,005,000 |
| Fixed overheads | | 300,000 |
| Profit | | 705,000 |

(iv)

| | £ | £ |
|---|---|---|
| Sales | | 2,100,000 |
| Direct materials | 522,000 | |
| Direct labour | 450,000 | |
| Variable overheads | 270,000 | 1,242,000 |
| Contribution | | 858,000 |
| Fixed overheads | | 350,000 |
| Profit | | 508,000 |

(v)

| | £ |
|---|---|
| Sales | 1,800,000 |
| Variable costs | 1,125,000 |
| Contribution | 675,000 |
| Fixed overheads | 350,000 |
| Profit | 325,000 |

(vi) Extra profit needed £44,000.
Extra contribution needed £44,000.
Contribution per unit £50.
So sales volume needs to increase by 880 units.

(c) *Implications for company*

For option (iv) points would include:
- Will existing sales volume be affected in the future?
- Reaction of existing customers if they gain knowledge of the 'special price'.
- Length of contract – once contract ceases, material prices will rise.
- Increased contribution and profit – more security for employees and the business in general.

For option (v):
- Decreased contribution and profit – less security for employees and the business in general.
- Redundancy – increased costs for one year.
- Under-utilisation of resources
- Loss of skills etc.

*Implications for local community*
- Unemployment in workforce – if workers are skill-specific then perhaps no work in area.
- Labour migration.
- Effect on other local businesses due to loss of spending power – downward multiplier effect.
- Loss of morale in local community etc.

# TEST RUN

*In this section:*

Test Your Knowledge Quiz

Test Your Knowledge Quiz Answers

Progress Analysis

Mock Exam

Mock Exam Suggested Answers

■ This section should be tackled towards the end of your revision programme, when you have covered all your syllabus topics, and attempted the practice questions at the end of the relevant chapters.

■ The Test Your Knowledge Quiz contains short-answer questions on a wide range of syllabus topics. You should attempt it without reference to the text.

■ Check your answers against the Test Your Knowledge Quiz Answers. If you are not sure why you got an answer wrong, go back to the relevant unit in the text: you will find the reference next to our answer.

■ Enter your marks in the Progress Analysis chart. The notes below will suggest a further revision strategy, based on your performance in the quiz. Only when you have done the extra work suggested should you go on to the final test.

■ The Mock Exam is set out like two real exam papers. It contains a wide spread of topics and question styles, as used by the examination boards. You should attempt these papers under examination conditions. Read the instructions carefully. Attempt the papers in the time allowed, and without reference to the text.

■ Compare your answers to our Mock Exam Suggested Answers. We have provided tutorial notes to each, showing why we answered the questions as we did and indicating where your answer may have differed from ours.

# TEST YOUR KNOWLEDGE QUIZ

1 Show the journal entries that are necessary to correct the following error. Discounts received of £23 have been posted to the debit of the discount allowed account.

2 At the 1 January 1995 a business had a provision for doubtful debts of £470. At the 31 December 1995 the business requires the provision to be £320. Show the provision for bad debts account as it would appear at 31 December 1995.

3 Define depreciation.

4 A, B, and C are in partnership sharing profits and losses equally. On 1 February D is admitted as a partner. The partners agree that goodwill at the 31 January be valued at £36,000. The new partnership agreement provides that profits be shared in the ratio of 4:3:3:2 respectively. It was further agreed that no goodwill account should remain in the books of the partnership. Calculate change to the partners' capital account balances at 1 February immediately after the admittance of D as a partner.

5 Why would a partnership keep separate capital and current accounts?

6 Outline four ways in which a limited company might raise additional capital.

7 Outline two measures that the managers of a limited company might take to improve business liquidity.

8 Give two ways in which a business might improve its mark-up.

9 Explain what is meant by the 'going concern' concept.

10 Explain what is meant by the concept of 'materiality'.

11 Why is a profit on sale of an asset deducted from the year's profit on a cash flow statement?

12 In FRS 1, what are 'cash' and 'cash equivalents'?

13 What is meant by a perpetual and a periodic method of stock valuation?

14 'The LIFO system of stock valuation means that the last stocks purchased are always sold first.' Discuss.

15 What is the purpose of overhead absorption?

16 Distinguish between allocation, apportionment and absorption.

17 Why might the managers of a business prepare budgets?

18 Why might the managers of a business introduce a system of budgetary control?

19 Why is it deemed necessary to undertake a capital investment appraisal?

20 Give one disadvantage of using:

(i) payback and

(ii) NPV methods of capital investment appraisal.

21 Define contribution.

22 Outline three uses of marginal costing.

23 What are the two sub-variances of the direct material total variance?

24 Why do managers use a standard costing system?

25 Why is it important to provide for depreciation?

26 Why is it important for a partnership to have a written agreement?

27 Which basic accounting concepts and conventions should be applied when valuing stock?

28 Explain the term 'share premium'.

29 Define the term 'provision'.

30 Give the formula used to calculate the rate of stock turnover.

31 Outline one advantage and one disadvantage of using a standard costing system.

32 Explain the term 'net realisable value'.

33 What type of business is likely to use a machine hour rate for overhead absorption of its overheads?

34 A business has the following unit cost and revenue pattern: fixed costs = £10, variable costs = £7, selling price = £22. Calculate the unit contribution.

35 Outline the factors which might have caused an adverse labour efficiency variance.

## TEST YOUR KNOWLEDGE QUIZ ANSWERS

1

|  | Dr | Cr |  |
|---|---|---|---|
| Suspense | 46 | | |
| Discount received | | 23 | |
| Discount allowed | | 23 | (1.6) |

2 **Provision for doubtful debts**

| | | | |
|---|---|---|---|
| 31 December 1995 P & L a/c | 150 | 1 January 1995 Balance b/d | 470 |
| 31 December 1995 Balance c/d | 320 | | |
| | 470 | | 470 |
| | | 1 January 1996 Balance b/d | 320 |
| | | | (1.4) |

3 Depreciation is the apportioning of the cost of an asset over its useful lifetime. (1.2)

4 A's capital account would remain unchanged (+£12,000 – £12,000).
B's capital account would increase by £3,000 (+£12,000 – £9,000).
C's capital account would increase by £3,000 (+£12,000 – £9,000).
D's capital account would decrease by £6,000 (0 – £6,000). (4.5)

5 To facilitate the calculation of partners' interest on capital. To show clearly if any partner's drawings are exceeding his profits earned in the partnership. (4.3)

6 Borrow long-term from a bank or other financial institution.
Borrow from the general public by issuing debentures.
Issue shares.
Sell surplus fixed assets. (5.7, 5.10)

7 As in 6 above, plus reduce debtors' credit period and negotiate increase in time taken to pay creditors.

8 Raise selling price. Find cheaper suppliers. (6.3)

9 Business is assumed to continue in existence into the foreseeable future, so value assets at cost. (3.2)

10 Capital expenditure items are material if their inclusion or exclusion in the appropriate accounts would mislead any of the users of the accounts. (3.2)

11 Profit arising from the sale of a fixed asset is not in itself a flow of cash, it is merely a book entry. The money received from the purchaser is a cash flow. The profit is a debit entry. The money received from the purchaser is a cash flow. The profit on disposal increases overall profit, but does not increase the cash received by the business. To calculate the cash generated by the business the profit must be deducted from the net profit for the year. (7.2)

12 'Cash' refers to cash in hand and any deposits repayable to the business on demand. 'Cash equivalents' are short term, very liquid investments which can be converted into cash without notice. (7.2)

13 A perpetual method of stock valuation recalculates the value of stocks held by the business after each purchase is received or each issue of stock is made. When stock is taken only once a year the periodic method is used. (8.2)

14 LIFO is a method of valuation. It does not necessarily mean that stock will be issued to customers or jobs in that order. (8.2)

15 To ensure that overheads are charged to cost units so that the overheads can be recovered in the final selling price. (9.3)

16 When overheads can be charged directly to a department or cost centre they are allocated; when overheads cannot be directly allocated to a department or cost centre they are apportioned by using area, cost, horsepower etc. When all overheads have been allocated or apportioned they are then absorbed into the product in order that the total cost can be arrived at. (9.1, 9.3)

17 For planning and control purposes. (10.1, 10.2)

18 Budgetary control delegates financial planning to managers. It may be introduced to evaluate performance, and act as an aid to co-ordinate the work of all departments, thus ensuring that all work undertaken relates to the corporate plan. (10.2)

19 It is a method used to try to ensure that the business gets value for money when purchasing fixed assets. (12.1)

20 Payback does not take into account the time value of money. Much of the data used to calculate the NPV of a project is speculative. (12.2, 12.4)

21 Contribution is the amount by which the selling price exceeds the variable costs of a product, or amount by which total revenue exceeds total variable costs. (13.2)

22 Whether to accept a special contract or not.

Deciding on a product mix when confronted by a shortage of a scarce resource.

Calculating the break-even point of a single product. (13.3)

23 Material price variance and material usage variance. (11.2)

24 Standard costing promotes efficiency and identifies deviations between the standards set and the actual performance. Variances can then be investigated. (11.1)

25 Answer could include: to ensure a true and fair view of a business's profit; to spread the cost of the asset over its useful life; to accord with the accruals concept. (1.2)

26 Answer could include: it identifies the rights, roles and duties of each partner; it outlines the responsibilities of each partner; it should prevent disputes amongst partners. (4.1)

27 Consistency and prudence. (3.2)

28 A share premium arises when a limited company issues shares at a price greater than their nominal value. (5.6)

29 A provision is an amount set aside out of profits for a known expense, the amount of which is uncertain. (1.1)

30 Cost of sales ÷ average stock. (6.5)

31 Advantages could include: managers participate in setting and agreeing standards; may be used for tendering for new contracts; identifies adverse variances – allows remedial action to be taken; identifies favourable variances – highlighting good practice.

Disadvantages could include: expensive to implement, time-consuming. (11.1)

32 Selling price less any expenses incurred in getting the goods ready for sale. (8.6)

33 A capital-intensive business. (9.3)

34 £15 (£22 – £7) (13.2)

35 Use of lower-skilled workers than budgeted for. Use of poorer materials than budgeted for. Use of badly maintained or worn out machinery. (11.5)

## PROGRESS ANALYSIS

| Question | My answer ✓ or ✗ ? | Question | My answer ✓ or ✗ ? | Question | My answer ✓ or ✗ ? |
|---|---|---|---|---|---|
| 1 | | 13 | | 25 | |
| 2 | | 14 | | 26 | |
| 3 | | 15 | | 27 | |
| 4 | | 16 | | 28 | |
| 5 | | 17 | | 29 | |
| 6 | | 18 | | 30 | |
| 7 | | 19 | | 31 | |
| 8 | | 20 | | 32 | |
| 9 | | 21 | | 33 | |
| 10 | | 22 | | 34 | |
| 11 | | 23 | | 35 | |
| 12 | | 24 | | | |

My total marks is . . . . . . . out of 35.

### If you scored 0–9

You need to do some more work. The Mock Exam is intended as a test of exam technique: it will be wasted if your basic syllabus coverage is insufficient. Starting at Chapter 1, look at the list of Units at the beginning of each chapter, and if any of them look unfamiliar, make a note to go back over that chapter.

### If you scored 10–18

You need to do a little more work. The Mock Exam is intended as a test of exam technique: it will not be really useful until you have filled in the current gaps in your syllabus coverage. If you have time, go through the list of Units at the beginning of each chapter, and plan to revise all those that look unfamiliar. If you don't think you'll have time to do this, look through the Illustrative Questions at the end of each chapter, and the notes on points to include: this will be a 'whistle-stop tour' through key areas of the syllabus. You should then attempt the Test Your Knowledge Quiz again.

### If you scored 19–27

You are just about ready to attempt the Mock Exam, but to get the best out of it, you might like to be a little more confident about your recall of some topics. If you have time, look through the Illustrative Questions at the end of each chapter, and the notes on points to include: this will be a good guide to which syllabus areas are still unfamiliar. If you don't think you'll have time to do this, you should go back to the chapter whose reference is given in the Test Your Knowledge Quiz Answers for the ones you got wrong, and look over those chapters again. You should then be ready to go on to the Mock Exam.

### If you scored 28–35

Congratulations. You have sufficient grasp of the syllabus topics to get real value out of attempting the Mock Exam in exam conditions. For your own satisfaction, though, you should go back to the specific Unit referred to in the Test Your Knowledge Quiz Answers for any question you got wrong: reassure yourself that there is no real gap in your knowledge.

## LETTS EXAMINATIONS BOARD
General Certificate of Education Examination

## ADVANCED LEVEL
## ACCOUNTING

### Paper 1
Time allowed: 3 hours

This paper contains two sections.

In section A answer **all** questions. In section B answer **two** questions.

You are advised to allocate your time as follows:

Section A: one and a half hours
Section B: one and a half hours

Mark allocations for each question are shown in brackets.

Show **all** your workings.

Make and state any necessary assumptions.

### Paper 2
Time allowed: 3 hours

In section A answer **all** questions.
In section B answer **one** question.
In section C answer **one** question.

You are advised to spend 45 minutes of your time on each question.

Mark allocations are shown in brackets.

Show all your workings.

Make and state any necessary assumptions.

## PAPER 1

### Section A

Attempt ALL the questions in this Section.
You are advised to spend half of your time on this Section.

1 Denise Exton sells furniture. Over the past two years she has seen a large increase in bad debts. The following figures refer to the past two financial years:

|  | Year ended 31 December 1994 | Year ended 31 December 1995 |
|---|---|---|
|  | £ | £ |
| Cash sales | 210,000 | 235,000 |
| Credit sales | 16,000 | 38,000 |
| Debtors | 14,000 | 16,000 |
| Bad debts written off during the year | 1,285 | 3,830 |

A provision for doubtful debts has been maintained throughout the period and on 1 January 1994 the balance was £275.

Because of the increase in bad debts written off Denise has increased her provision for doubtful debts to 10% of debtors in 1994 and 20% in 1995; she is also is considering selling on a cash basis only.

*Required*

(a) The bad debts account and the provision for doubtful debts account for the years ended 31 December 1994 and 31 December 1995. (12)

(b) Advise Denise whether she should continue to sell on credit. (10)

(c) State and explain two accounting concepts that necessitate the creation of a provision for doubtful debts at the end of an accounting period. (8)

2 During the year ended 31 January 1996 the following unrelated accounting problems have been encountered by a company:

(1) the closing stock figure of £210,000 has been valued using the first in first out (FIFO) method of stock valuation. It is now proposed to revalue the stock at £170,000 by changing the basis of valuation to last in first out (LIFO).

(2) On 30 November 1995 the company negotiated and received a loan for £50,000. The terms are that repayments of £8,940 (capital repayment £7,500, £1,440 interest charge) be paid quarterly in arrears. The first payment is due on 29 February 1996. Since no repayments have been made during the financial year, the only entry regarding the loan appears on the balance sheet as at 31 January 1996 under the heading: Creditors: amounts falling due after more than one year £50,000.

(3) The company owns a highly specialised piece of machinery. It has a book value of £4,000. One of the directors has heard that a similar machine has recently been sold for £18,000. It is proposed that the machine be revalued in the company's accounts.

*Required*

Discuss the extent to which each of the proposals outlined above fails to comply with generally accepted accounting principles. (30)

**3** Wastell and Wallace commenced trading on 1 January 1995 as dealers in antique brass beds.

During the year ended 31 December 1995 the following transactions took place:

| 1 January | Bought | 100 beds at £200 each |
| 1 February | Sold | 40 beds at £600 each |
| 1 April | Sold | 50 beds at £650 each |
| 1 June | Bought | 80 beds at £250 each |
| 1 July | Sold | 70 beds at £650 each |
| 1 September | Bought | 100 beds at £300 each |
| 1 November | Sold | 95 beds at £650 each |

The partnership expenses during the year ended 31 December 1995 totalled £62,500. The replacement cost of an antique brass bed on 31 December 1995 was £350. All the business transactions during 1995 have been on a cash basis.

*Required*

(a) Statements showing the net profit for the year ended 31 December 1995 for each of the following methods of stock valuation:
   (i)  FIFO (first in first out) and
   (ii) LIFO (last in first out).                                    (20)

(b) Outline the major advantages and disadvantages of historical cost accounting.                                    (20)

## Section B

Attempt **two** questions. All questions carry 50 marks each.

**4** The draft balance sheet as at 31 January 1996 of Ellesmere plc is as follows:

| Fixed assets | Cost | Depreciation | Net |
|---|---|---|---|
| £ | £ | £ | |
| Freehold buildings | 460,000 | 92,000 | 368,000 |
| Machinery | 667,000 | 312,800 | 354,200 |
| | 1,127,000 | 404,800 | 722,200 |
| Current assets | | | |
| Stock | | 340,400 | |
| Debtors | | 481,390 | |
| Bank | | 43,010 | |
| | | 864,800 | |
| Creditors | | 151,800 | 713,000 |
| | | | 1,435,200 |
| Creditors falling due after more than one year | | | 230,000 |
| | | | 1,205,200 |
| Capital and reserves | | | |
| Ordinary shares of £1 each fully paid | | | 920,000 |
| Profit and loss account | | | 285,200 |
| | | | 1,205,200 |

After the above draft balance sheet had been prepared the following discoveries were made:

(1) Depreciation has been provided on machinery for the year ended 31 January 1996 at 12 1/2% per annum using the reducing balance method, instead of 10% per annum using the straight line method in accordance with the company's policy.

(2) The revaluation of the freehold buildings at £575,000 had not been taken into account.

(3) The stock includes a machine costing £57,500 (selling price £80,500) which was transferred on 1 February 1995 to machinery and used in the Ellesmere workshop. There were no other fixed asset acquisitions or disposals during the

year ended 31 January 1996. No accounting entries have been made yet for this transfer.

(4) Goods costing £9,200 were sent on a sale or return basis to Greystone Ltd in December 1995 and remain unsold. In Ellesmere plc's books the goods have been regarded as sold to Greystone Ltd at £12,190.

(5) A bonus (scrip) issue in August 1995 of one ordinary share of 1 for every 10 previously held has not been recorded in Ellesmere's books.

(6) Provision has not yet been made in Ellesmere's books for a proposed final dividend of 10p per share for the year ended 31 January 1996.

*Required*

(a) A corrected balance sheet as at 31 January 1996 of Ellesmere plc.　(38)

(b) Explain the difference between a bonus issue and a rights issue of shares.　(12)

**5** Winifred Rigg is a sole trader. She has not kept full accounting records during her first year of trading. She commenced business on 1 February 1995 with a van which she valued at £9,400 and £8,000 cash taken from her private building society account.

A summary of the business bank account for the year ended 31 January 1996 is as follows:

| 1995 | £ | | £ |
|---|---|---|---|
| 1 February | | | |
| Deposit | 8,000 | Expense | 62,900 |
| Receipts from cash sales | 32,460 | Loan repayments | 4,500 |
| Receipts from debtors | 27,906 | 31 January 1996 Balance c/d | 966 |
| | 68,366 | | 68,366 |
| 1996 | | | |
| 1 February Balance b/d | 966 | | |

Before banking the receipts from cash sales Winifred withdrew £800 cash per calendar month for her personal use, and spent a total of £9,320 on general expenses. In addition Winifred took stock valued at £1,500 for her own use during the year.

On 1 May 1995 Winifred negotiated a loan over two years. The repayment terms being £500 per month including £50 per month interest. The whole of this amount was used to purchase fixtures.

The expense items in the summarised bank account comprises rent at £240 per calendar month, payments to creditors for purchases of stock and the purchase of fixtures in addition to those financed by the loan.

Winifred provides you with further information:

(1) a uniform gross profit of 25% on sales is earned;

(2) at 31 January 1996 the following figures were available:

| | |
|---|---|
| trade debtors were | £1,714 |
| trade creditors were | £7,180 |
| stock was | £4,750 |

(3) the van is to be depreciated at 25% of its book value. The fixtures are to be depreciated at 10% of their cost.

*Required*

(a) A trading and profit and loss account for the year ended 31 January 1996 for Winifred Rigg.　(20)

(b) A balance sheet as at 31 January 1996.　(15)

(c) Advise Winifred Rigg on the advisability of keeping proper accounting records.　(15)

**6** Mary Taylor is considering purchasing a small trading business in Melmerby. She has received the following information relating to the business, together with comparative figures of similar businesses in the county.

All the statistics relate to the year ended 31 January 1996.

| | Melmerby business | Similar businesses |
|---|---|---|
| $\dfrac{\text{Net profit}}{\text{Capital employed}}$ | 25% | 32% |
| $\dfrac{\text{Net profit}}{\text{Sales}}$ | 15% | 16% |
| $\dfrac{\text{Gross profit}}{\text{Cost of Sales}}$ | 30% | 28% |
| $\dfrac{\text{Expenses}}{\text{Sales}}$ | 8% | 7% |
| $\dfrac{\text{Debtors at year end}}{\text{Sales}}$ | 5% | 4% |
| $\dfrac{\text{Creditors at year end}}{\text{Purchases}}$ | 5% | 10% |
| $\dfrac{\text{Fixed assets}}{\text{Net current assets}}$ | 400% | 1,000% |
| Stockturn | 10 times | 10 times |

Mary Taylor is unable to obtain a copy of the final accounts for the Melmerby business. She is aware, however, that the stock was valued at £29,000 at 31 January 1996 and this was an increase of £16,000 over the year

Note: The bank balance is a balancing figure in current assets.

*Required*

(a) The trading and profit and loss account for the year ended 31 January 1996 and a balance sheet as at that date for the Melmerby business. (36)

(b) A comparison of the results of the Melmerby business for the year ended 31 January 1996 with those given for similar businesses within the county (14)

## PAPER 2

### Section A

Attempt ALL questions in this Section.
You are advised to spend half your time on this Section.

**1** Crofthouse Ltd. launched a new product two years ago. The details are as follows:

| Based on an output of | Year ended 28 Feb 1995<br>2,000 units | Year ended 28 Feb 1995<br>2,500 units |
|---|---|---|
| | £ | £ |
| Unit selling price | 48 | 54 |
| Direct material costs per unit | 8 | 10 |
| Direct Labour costs per unit | 12 | 12 |
| Variable overheads per unit | 15 | 18 |
| Fixed costs per unit | 10 | 9 |

The management team believe that the cost pattern for 1996 will remain unchanged for the foreseeable future.

The sales manager suggests that if the selling price were dropped to £50 in the year ending 28 February 1997 sales could increase to 2,750 units.

*Required*

(a) Calculate the break-even point in units and in total sales revenue for the years ended 28 February 1995 and 29 February 1996. (10)

(b) Calculate the profit or loss for each of the years ended 28 February 1995 and 29 February 1996. (25)

(c) Advise the management of Crofthouse Ltd whether to pursue the sales manager's plans for the year ending 28 February 1997. Your answer should be supported by reasons and workings. (15)

**2** The following is the balance sheet as at 31 December 1995 for Russell plc.

| 1994<br>£000 | | £000 | £000 | £000 |
|---|---|---|---|---|
| | Fixed Assets | | | |
| 320 | Land | | | 320 |
| 1,152 | Buildings | | | 1,552 |
| 592 | Plant and machinery | | | 560 |
| 2,064 | | | | 2,432 |
| | Current assets | | | |
| 480 | Stock | 672 | | |
| 192 | Debtors | 352 | | |
| 32 | Bank | – | | |
| | | | 1,024 | |
| 704 | | | | |
| | Creditors: amounts falling due within one year | | | |
| 150 | Taxation | 130 | | |
| – | Bank overdraft | 192 | | |
| 170 | Creditors | 174 | | |
| 72 | Proposed dividend | 96 | | |
| 392 | | | 592 | |
| 312 | | | | 432 |
| 2,376 | | | | 2,864 |
| | Creditors: amounts falling due after more than one year | | | |
| 570 | 10% Debentures | | | 570 |
| 1,806 | | | | 2,294 |
| | Capital and reserves | | | |
| 800 | Ordinary shares of £1 each fully paid | | | 1,200 |
| 560 | Share premium | | | 160 |
| – | Revaluation reserve | | | 480 |
| 446 | Profit and loss account | | | 454 |
| 1,806 | | | | 2,294 |

Additional information:

(1) Movements of fixed assets during the year ended 31 December 1995 were as follows:

| Buildings | £ |
|---|---:|
| Cost 1 January 1995 | 1,312 |
| Revaluation | 480 |
| | 1,792 |
| | |
| Provision for depreciation 1 January 1995 | 160 |
| Depreciation for the year | 80 |
| | 240 |

| Plant and machinery | |
|---|---:|
| Cost 1 January 1995 | 960 |
| Additions | 160 |
| Disposal | (80) |
| | 1,040 |
| | |
| Provision for depreciation 1 January 1995 | 368 |
| Depreciation on disposal | (64) |
| Depreciation for the year | 176 |
| | 480 |

The plant and machinery disposed of during the year was sold for £9,000.

(2) An interim dividend of £40,000 was paid on 3 August 1995

(3) There was a bonus issue of shares during October 1995 of one new share for every two held.

*Required*

(a) A cash flow statement for the year ended 31 December 1995. (35)

(b) Draft a report addressed to the production manager explaining the uses of a cash flow statement. (15)

## Section B

Answer ONE question in this Section.

**3** Sandie Ltd makes a single product. The unit budget details are as follows:

| | £ | £ |
|---|---:|---:|
| Selling price | | 60 |
| Direct material costs | 18 | |
| Direct labour costs | 8 | |
| Direct production expenses | 12 | |
| Variable selling expenses | 8 | 46 |
| Contribution | | 14 |

Additional information:

(1) Unit sales are expected to be:

| January | February | March | April | May |
|---|---|---|---|---|
| 1,500 | 2,000 | 1,500 | 1,200 | 2,400 |

(2) Credit sales will account for 75% of total sales.
Debtors are expected to pay in the month following sale.

(3) Stock levels will be arranged so that the production in one month will meet next month's sales demand.

(4) Purchase of Direct materials in one month will just meet the next month's production requirements.

(5) Suppliers of direct materials will be paid in the month following purchase.

(6) Labour costs will be paid in the month in which they are incurred.

(7) All other expenses will be paid in the month following that in which they are incurred.

(8) Fixed costs are £3,500 per month including £400 depreciation. Fixed costs are paid in the month in which they are incurred.

(9) There was a bank overdraft of £780 at 31 January 1995.

*Required*

(a) Cash budget for the three months ending 30 April 1996 for Sandie Ltd.     (35)

(b) Explain three ways in which a cash budget could be of use to the management of Sandie Ltd.     (15)

**4**  Wildriggs plc processes chemicals. Management are considering investing in a new machine which will increase production capacity from 20,000kg to 50,000kg in equal stages over the next three years.

The new machinery would cost £1,500,000. A deposit of 50% of the total cost would be paid on delivery and the balance paid at the end of the first year.

The cost per kg of the product would be:

|  | £ |
|---|---|
| Direct materials | 40 |
| Direct labour | 10 |
| Overheads | 20 |

These prices are expected to remain constant over the next three years.

Market research shows that the increased production could be sold at the following prices per kg:

|  | £ per kg |
|---|---|
| Year 1 | 120 |
| Year 2 | 115 |
| Year 3 | 110 |

If the new machine is purchased fixed costs are expected to increase by the following amounts:

|  | £000 |
|---|---|
| Year 1 | 150 |
| Year 2 | 130 |
| Year 3 | 140 |

It should be assumed that all costs are paid and revenues received at the end of each year.

The company's cost of capital is 12%.

The following is an extract from the present value table for £1:

|  | 12% |
|---|---|
| Year 1 | 0.893 |
| Year 2 | 0.797 |
| Year 3 | 0.712 |

*Required*

(a) Using the NPV (net present value) method advise Wildriggs plc. whether they should purchase the new machine.     (35)

(b) Draft a memorandum addressed to the directors of Wildriggs plc outlining any reservations you may have regarding the net present value method of evaluating a project.     (15)

## Section C

Answer ONE question in this Section.

**5**  Irthington plc is a manufacturing company that uses 23 machines in its production process. It uses machine hour rates to absorb the production overheads in job costs.

The following details are available for machine AB/10:

(1) The cost of the machine is £36,000, it has an estimated life of 10 years. The straight line method of depreciation is applied.

(2) The total machine department overheads are:

|  | £ |
| --- | --- |
| Heat and light | 18,480 |
| Supervisory salaries | 22,126 |

The area of the department is 9,680m² of which the AB/10 occupies 110m². The number of machines used in the department is 23.

(3) The annual cost of repairs for the AB/10 is £620.

(4) The machine running time is 2,100 hours per annum.

(5) The power cost is 9p per hour.

(6) The labour rate for machinists is £5.20 per hour, and machinists can control 4 machines.

(7) The annual premium for all the machines in the department is £17,400. (The total cost of all the machines in the department is £1,044,000)

(8) A typical job carried out on an AB/10 machine is coded 135/Gr. This job involves using 8kg of materials costing £37.50 per kg; 12 machine hours; and 4 hours assembly work using labour paid at £3.80 per hour.

*Required*

(a) Prepare a statement showing the machine hour rate for AB/10 (correct to 2 decimal places). (25)

(b) Calculate the job cost of 135/Gr. (15)

(c) Identify the possible reasons why Irthington plc has used machine hour rates in its costing. (10)

**6** Helen and Tim are in partnership sharing profits and losses in the ratio of 2:1 after allowing Tim a salary of £8,000 per annum.

The following is the summarised partnership balance sheet as at 29 February 1996:

|  | £ | £ |  | £ | £ |
| --- | --- | --- | --- | --- | --- |
| Fixed assets |  |  | Capital |  |  |
| Premises | 41,000 |  | Helen | 32,000 |  |
| Machinery | 32,800 | 73,800 | Tim | 16,000 | 48,000 |
|  |  |  | Current accounts |  |  |
|  |  |  | Helen | 4,000 |  |
|  |  |  | Tim | 1,000 | 5,000 |
| Current assets |  |  | Current liabilities |  |  |
| Stock | 20,500 |  | Creditors | 30,100 |  |
| Debtors | 8,200 | 28,700 | Bank overdraft | 19,400 | 49,500 |
|  |  | 102,500 |  |  | 102,500 |

The profits of the business have been low during recent years but a new business opportunity is available from 1 September 1996 requiring an additional investment of £40,000. The anticipated net profits from the new investment are £24,000 per annum and it is expected that the other profits earned by the partnership will be £16,000 per annum for the foreseeable future. All profits will accrue evenly throughout the year.

Helen and Tim are considering two alternative methods of financing the investment.

### Alternative 1

To accept Laura into the partnership with effect from 1 September 1996 on the following basis:

(1) Laura will pay into the partnership £50,000 cash as capital.

(2) Interest will be paid on partner's fixed capital at the rate of 8% per annum.

(3) The balance of profits and losses are to be shared equally between partners.

(4) The premises are to be revalued at £80,000 immediately prior to Laura's admission.

### Alternative 2

To borrow £40,000 from a bank at a fixed nominal rate of interest of 10% over 5 years, repayable in equal monthly instalments. In addition Helen and Tim will have to employ a part time supervisor at an annual salary of £8,000 per annum.

*Required*

(a) The forecast profit and loss appropriation account for the year ended 28 February 1997 assuming that Laura is admitted to the partnership on the terms outlined above. (25)

(b) A financial statement comparing the income to be received by Helen and Tim under the two alternatives for each of the year's ending 28 February 1997 and 28 February 1998. (25)

## MOCK EXAM SUGGESTED ANSWERS

### PAPER 1

#### Tutorial notes

In Section A you must attempt all three questions. Note the marks available for each question and multiply by 0.9 minutes (for example question 1 should take no longer than 27 minutes).

Remember to take careful note of any key instruction words in questions and to respond accordingly, e.g. outline, discuss, advise etc.

In question 2 there are three proposals for a total of 30 marks, so spend one-third of your 27 minutes on each.

When you have completed question 3 you should be half way through the time allocated to Paper 1.

Your remaining time should be divided equally between your choice of questions from Sections B and C.

Plan very carefully your responses in the written sections. It is worth spending a few minutes planning exactly what you intend to say. This will ensure that you do not repeat the same point several times. The plan will also enable you to marshall the facts into a logical sequence.

When giving a definition, be brief and to the point. It is often useful to give an example as this can add clarity to your expression and confirm your understanding to the examiner.

### Section A

**1** (a)

**Denise Exton – bad debts**

| | | | | |
|---|---|---|---|---|
| 31 Dec '94 Sundry debtors | 1,285 | 31 Dec '94 P&L a/c | | 1,285 |
| 31 Dec '95 Sundry debtors | 3,830 | 31 Dec '95 P&L a/c | | 3,830 |

**Provision for doubtful debts**

| | | | | |
|---|---|---|---|---|
| | | 1 Jan '94 Bal b/d | | 275 |
| 31 Dec '94 Bal c/d | 1,400 | 31 Dec '94 P&L a/c | | 1,125 |
| | 1,400 | | | 1,400 |
| | | 1 Jan '95 Bal b/d | | 1,400 |
| 31 Dec '95 Bal c/d | 3,200 | 31 Dec '95 P&L a/c | | 1,800 |
| | 3,200 | | | 3,200 |
| | | 1 Jan '96 Bal b/d | | 3,200 |

(b) Advice should include:
Increase in bad debts.
Reduction in profit through bad debts and provision for doubtful debts. If she wished to sell it would not look good.
Credit sales have more than doubled. As a proportion of overall sales they have increased from 7% to 14%.
Can she afford not to sell on credit?

(c) Prudence – take figure that understates rather than overstates profits; anticipate possible losses.
Accruals – matching expenses and revenues in the same accounting period.

**2** (1) Consistency – use the same method over time – facilitates comparisons. LIFO not accepted by Inland Revenue, nor by SSAP 9, so would have to redraft accounts for submission. Continue with FIFO.

(2) Accruals – matching revenues and expenses within the same accounting period. The interest is an expense but not yet an expenditure. Entry on the Balance Sheet

should have two repayments (£5,000) deducted from capital sum. The P & L a/c should have two months interest (£960) shown as an expense.

(3) Going concern – assumes the business is going to operate for an indefinitely long period of time. Since the business is not going to cease trading- continue to value the machine at cost and depreciate in the normal manner.

**3** FIFO – use the periodic method.

280 beds purchased – 255 sold = 25 in stock at latest price £300 = £7,500

| LIFO | Purchases | Issues | Stock | |
|------|-----------|--------|-------|--|
| 1 Jan | 100 @ £200 | | £20,000 | (100 @ £200) |
| 1 Feb | | 40 @ £200 | £12,000 | (60 @ £200) |
| 1 Apl | | 50 @ £200 | £2,000 | (10 @ £200) |
| 1 Jun | 80 @ £250 | | £22,000 | (10 @ £200 + 80 @ £250) |
| 1 Jul | | 70 @ £250 | £4,500 | (10 @ £200 + 10 @ £250) |
| 1 Sep | 100 @ £300 | | £34,500 | (10 @ £200 + 10 @ £250 + 100 @ £300 |
| 1 Nov | | 95 @ £300 | £6,000 | (10 @ £200 + 10 @ £250 + 5 @ £300) |

**Trading and profit and loss account**
**for the year ended 31 December 1995**

| | FIFO £ | LIFO £ | | FIFO £ | LIFO £ |
|--|------|------|--|------|------|
| Purchases | 70,000 | 70,000 | Sales | 163,750 | 163,750 |
| Less stock | 7,500 | 6,000 | | | |
| Cost of sales | 62,500 | 64,000 | | | |
| Gross profit | 101,250 | 99,750 | | | |
| | 163,750 | 163,750 | | 163,750 | 163,750 |
| Expenses | 62,500 | 62,500 | Gross profit | 101,250 | 99,750 |
| Net profit | 38,750 | 37,250 | | | |
| | 101,250 | 99,750 | | 101,250 | 99,750 |

(b) Advantages of historical cost accounting include:
Has been used for long time – everyone is used to it and, generally, understands it.
The methods used are free of subjectivity.
Fairly straightforward for computational purposes.

Disadvantages include:
Ignores the time factor.
Ignores changes in the value of assets and liabilities.
May not be sound for decision making purposes.
It does not make a distinction between operating profit and holding gains made.
Maintaining 'monetary capital' may conceal declining real capital.

## Section B

**4** (a) **Ellesmere plc balance sheet as at 31 January 1996**

| Fixed assets | Cost £ | Depreciation £ | Net £ |
|--------------|--------|----------------|-------|
| Freehold buildings | 575,000 | | 575,000 |
| Machinery | 724,500 | 334,650 | 389,850 |
| | 1,299,500 | 334,650 | 964,850 |
| Current assets | | | |
| Stock | | 292,100 | |
| Debtors | | 469,200 | |
| Bank | | 43,010 | |
| | | 804,310 | |

|  |  |  |  |
|---|---|---|---|
| Creditors falling due within one year |  |  |  |
| Creditors | 151,800 |  |  |
| Proposed dividend | 101,200 | 253,000 | 551,310 |
|  |  |  | 1,516,160 |
| Creditors falling due after more than one year |  |  | 230,000 |
|  |  |  | 1,286,160 |
| Capital and reserves |  |  |  |
| Ordinary shares of £1 each fully paid |  |  | 1,012,000 |
| Revaluation reserve |  |  | 207,000 |
| Profit and loss account |  |  | 67,160 |
|  |  |  | 1,286,160 |

(b) Bonus issue – no additional finance raised; the issue capitalises reserves; the balance sheet gives a more realistic picture re shareholders' interests; the existing shareholders' interests are preserved.

Rights issue – provides additional finance; existing shareholders can increase their investment in the company at an attractive price; shareholders can sell the rights; gives existing shareholders the opportunity to sell some shares yet keep an interest in the company.

**5** (a)

## Winifred Rigg Trading and profit and loss account
### for the year ended 31 January 1996

|  | £ | £ |
|---|---|---|
| Sales |  | 81,000 |
| Less cost of sales |  |  |
| Purchases | 67,000 |  |
| Less goods for own use | 1,500 |  |
|  | 65,500 |  |
| Less stock | 4,750 | 60,750 |
| Gross profit |  | 20,250 |
| Less expenses |  |  |
| Rent | 2,880 |  |
| General expenses | 9,320 |  |
| Interest | 450 |  |
| Depreciation  Van | 2,350 |  |
| Fixtures | 1,100 | 16,100 |
| Net profit |  | 4,150 |

(b)

### Balance sheet as at 31 January 1996

|  | £ | £ |
|---|---|---|
| Fixed assets |  |  |
| Fixtures at cost | 11,000 |  |
| Less depreciation | 1,100 | 9,900 |
| Motor van at cost | 9,400 |  |
| Less depreciation | 2,350 | 7,050 |
|  |  | 16,950 |
| Current assets |  |  |
| Stock | 4,750 |  |
| Debtors | 1,714 |  |
| Bank | 966 |  |
|  | 7,430 |  |
| Less creditors | 7,180 | 250 |
|  |  | 17,200 |
| Less loan |  | 6,750 |
|  |  | 10,450 |
| Capital |  | 17,400 |
| Add profit |  | 4,150 |
|  |  | 21,550 |
| Less drawings |  | 11,100 |
|  |  | 10,450 |

(c) Management purposes.
Greater awareness of all that goes on in the business.
Control can be exercised more efficiently if a complete picture is available.
May be necessary for inland revenue and VAT purposes.

**6** (a)

**Melmerby business trading and profit and loss account
for the year ended 31 January 1996**

| | £ | £ |
|---|---|---|
| Sales | | 273,000 |
| Less cost of sales | | |
| Stock 1 February 1995 | 13,000 | |
| Purchases | 226,000 | |
| | 239,000 | |
| Stock 31 January 1996 | 29,000 | 210,000 |
| Gross profit | | 63,000 |
| Less expenses | | 21,840 |
| Net profit | | 41,160 |

**Balance sheet as at 31 January 1996**

| | £ | £ |
|---|---|---|
| Fixed Assets | | 131,712 |
| Current assets | | |
| Stock | 29,000 | |
| Debtors | 13,650 | |
| Bank balance | 1,578 | |
| | 44,228 | |
| Less creditors | 11,300 | 32,928 |
| | | 164,640 |
| Capital | | 164,640 |

(b) Comments should focus on the following points amongst others.
Positive points re the Melmerby shop:
It has a better gross profit rate.
Better utilisation of fixed assets.
It has a better working capital ratio and a better acid test ratio.

Negative points:
Melmerby has a lower ROCE.
Its expenses are higher.
Both the debtors settlement period and the creditors payment periods are worse than the other businesses.

# PAPER 2

## Tutorial notes

All questions of Paper 2 carry the same number of marks. You should therefore spend an equal amount of time on each question. The same points apply as in Paper 1, as the same concepts are being tested in both papers.

Within each question allocate your time according to the marks available (mark available × 0.9 minutes). In the written section always state the obvious – there are always marks for this. When answering any question assume that the examiner has little or no knowledge of accounting. This will ensure that you explain yourself in sufficient detail.

Although the suggested answers are given in note form, please ensure that your answers are developed fully.

## Section A

**1** (a) Break even:

Year ended 28 Feb 1995: $\dfrac{\text{Total fixed costs}}{\text{Contribution per unit}}$ $\dfrac{£20,000}{£13}$ = 1,539 units

Year ended 28 Feb 1996: $\dfrac{\text{Total fixed costs}}{\text{Contribution per unit}}$ $\dfrac{£22,500}{£14}$ = 1,607 units

Year ended 28 Feb 1997: $\dfrac{\text{Total fixed costs}}{\text{Contribution per unit}}$ $\dfrac{£22,500}{£10}$ = 2,250 units

Total revenue to break even:

| | |
|---|---|
| Year ended 28 Feb 1995 | 1,539 × £48 = £73,846 |
| Year ended 28 Feb 1996 | 1,607 × £54 = £86,778 |
| Year ended 28 Feb 1997 | 2,250 × £50 = £112,500 |

(b) Profit = Production beyond break even × Contribution

| | |
|---|---|
| Year ended 28 Feb 1995 | 461 × £13 = £5,993 |
| Year ended 28 Feb 1996 | 893 × £14 = £12,502 |
| Year ended 28 Feb 1997 | 500 × £10 = £5,000 |

### Point to note

The figures for 1997 were not asked for in parts (a) or (b) but the figures will be used in (c).

(c) The business should not pursue the sales manager's plans since the break-even point will be higher than in previous years. Also, the profit would be lower than that previously earned.

**2** (a) **Russell plc cash flow statement for year ended 31 December 1995**

| | £000 | £000 |
|---|---|---|
| Net cash inflow from operating activities ❶ | | 246 |
| Returns on investments and servicing of finance | | |
|     Dividends paid | (112) | |
|     Debenture interest | (57) | |
| Net cash outflow from returns on investments and servicing of finance | | (169) |
| Taxation | | |
|     Corporation tax paid | | (150) |
| Investing activities | | |
|     Payments to acquire tangible fixed assets | (160) | |
|     Receipts from the sales of tangible fixed assets | 9 | |
| Net cash outflow from investing activities | | (151) |
| Net cash outflow before financing | | (224) |
| Financing | | – |
| Decrease in cash and cash equivalents ❷ | | (224) |

❶  Reconciliation of operating profit to net cash inflow from operating activities

| | £000 |
|---|---|
| Operating profit | 8 ✓ |
| Depreciation charges Buildings | 80 ✓ |
| Machinery | 176 ✓ |
| Loss on sale of asset | 7 ✓ |
| Increase in creditors | 4 ✓ |
| Increase in stock | (192) ✓ |
| Increase in debtors | (160) ✓ |
| Tax liability | 130 ✓ |
| Interim dividend paid | 40 ✓ |
| Proposed final dividend | 96 ✓ |
| Debenture interest paid | 57 |
| Net cash inflow from operating activities | 246 |

❷ Analysis of changes in cash and cash equivalents during the year

|  | £ |
|---|---|
| Balance 1 January 1995 | 32,000 |
| Net cash outflow | (224,000) |
| Balance 31 December 1995 | (192,000) |

(b) Cash flow statements concentrate on liquidity, which is very important because lack of liquid funds often causes businesses to fail.

It provides a link between the two balance sheets. The profit and loss account provides one link, the cash flow statement provides another.

It explains why profits and losses are different from flows of cash

It shows how assets have changed during the year. It identifies acquisitions and disposals of assets.

It shows how the company has raised finance, i.e. selling shares or debentures. It also shows any repayment of loans and share capital .

It shows the extent to which a company is financing itself by internal sources and the extent to which finance is being obtained from external sources during the year.

## Section B

**3** (a)     **Sandie Ltd cash budget for three months ending 30 April 1996**

| Receipts: | Feb £ | Mar £ | April £ |
|---|---|---|---|
| Cash sales | 30,000 | 22,500 | 18,000 |
| Payments from debtors | 67,500 | 90,000 | 67,500 |
|  | 97,500 | 112,500 | 85,500 |
| Payments: |  |  |  |
| Creditors | 36,000 | 27,000 | 21,600 |
| Direct labour costs | 12,000 | 9,600 | 19,200 |
| Direct production costs | 24,000 | 18,000 | 14,400 |
| Variable – selling costs | 12,000 | 16,000 | 12,000 |
| Fixed costs | 3,100 | 3,100 | 3,100 |
|  | 87,100 | 73,700 | 70,300 |
| Cash budget: |  |  |  |
| Balance | (780) | 9,620 | 48,420 |
| Receipts | 97,500 | 112,500 | 85,500 |
|  | 96,720 | 112,500 | 133,920 |
| Payments | 87,100 | 73,700 | 70,300 |
| Balance | 9,620 | 48,420 | 63,620 |

(b) As part of budgetary control – helps set targets – very important part of total budget.

For planning purposes:

Shows cash flows and highlights times when there will be a shortage – loan or overdraft can be arranged well in advance.

If surplus cash is shown arrangements can be made to use this to the best advantage of the business.

**4** (a)

| | | Net cash flow | Discount factor | NPV |
|---|---|---|---|---|
| Year 0 | Capital cost | (750,000) | × 1 | (750,000) |
| Year 1 | Capital cost | (750,000) | | |
| | Materials | (400,000) | | |
| | Labour | (100,000) | | |
| | Overheads | (200,000) | | |
| | Fixed costs | (150,000) | | |
| | Sales | 1,200,000 | | |
| | | (400,000) | × 0.893 | (357,200) |
| Year 2 | Materials | (800,000) | | |
| | Labour | (200,000) | | |
| | Overheads | (400,000) | | |
| | Fixed costs | (130,000) | | |
| | Sales | 2,300,000 | | |
| | | 770,000 | × 0.797 | 613,690 |
| Year 3 | Materials | (1,200,000) | | |
| | Labour | (300,000) | | |
| | Overheads | (600,000) | | |
| | Fixed costs | (140,000) | | |
| | Sales | 3,300,000 | | |
| | | 1,060,000 | × 0.712 | 754,720 |
| | | | | 261,210 |

(b) Memorandum format rewarded:

To:                          Date:

From:

Regarding:

Points should include:

How accurate are the forecasts?

Assumes a level of demand that may not materialise – is only an estimate.

Will there be changes in cost behaviour with different levels of production?

Consideration of the opportunity cost of alternative strategies.

Will the cost of capital change over the period of the investment?

Will technology change making chosen machines obsolete? etc.

## Section C

**5** (a)          **Statement showing the machine hour rate for an AB/10**

| | £ | Basis |
|---|---|---|
| Depreciation | 3,600 | Cost |
| Heat and light | 210 | Area |
| Supervisors salaries | 962 | Number of machines |
| Repairs | 620 | Actual |
| Power | 189 | Running time |
| Insurance | 600 | Value |
| | 6,181 | Total cost per annum |

Machine hour rate = $\dfrac{£6,181}{2,100}$ = £2.94 per hour

(b)          **Job cost of 136/Gr**

| | £ |
|---|---|
| 8kg of materials at £37.50 per kg | 300 |
| 12 machine hours – labour | 15.60 |
| Assembly work | 15.20 |
| 12 machine hours – absorption | 35.28 |
| | 366.08 |

(c) Discussion on fact that machine hour rates are more appropriate to an organisation which is capital intensive, since this is where the majority of the overheads will be incurred. The overheads will be related to the functioning of the machinery.

**6** (a) **Alternative 1:**

### Helen and Tim forecast appropriation account for the half year ended 31 August

|  |  | £ | £ |
|---|---|---:|---:|
| Net profit |  |  | 8,000 |
| Salary – Tim |  | 4,000 |  |
| Share of profits – | Helen | 2,667 |  |
|  | Tim | 1,333 | 8,000 |

### Helen, Tim and Laura forecast appropriation account for the half year ended 28 February 1997

|  |  | £ | £ |
|---|---|---:|---:|
| Net profit |  |  | 20,000 |
| Interest on capital – | Helen | 2,320 |  |
|  | Tim | 1,160 |  |
|  | Laura | 2,000 |  |
| Share of profits – | Helen | 4,840 |  |
|  | Tim | 4,840 |  |
|  | Laura | 4,840 | 20,000 |

### Alternative 2:

|  | £ | £ |
|---|---:|---:|
| Net profit |  |  |
| (16,000 + 12,000 – 4,000 – 2,000) |  | 22,000 |
| Salary – Tim | 8,000 |  |
| Share of profits – Helen | 9,333 |  |
| Tim | 4,667 | 22,000 |

(b) **Alternative 1:**

|  |  | Helen | Tim |
|---|---|---:|---:|
|  |  | £ | £ |
| Year 1 | Share of profits | 2,667 | 1,333 |
|  | Salary | – | 4,000 |
|  | Interest on capital | 2,320 | 1,160 |
|  | Share of profits | 4,840 | 4,840 |
|  |  | 9,827 | 11,333 |
| Year 2 | Interest on capital | 4,640 | 2,320 |
|  | Share of profits | 9,680 | 9,680 |
|  |  | 14,320 | 12,000 |

### Alternative 2:

|  |  | £ | £ |
|---|---|---:|---:|
| Year 1 | Salary | – | 8,000 |
|  | Share of profits | 9,333 | 4,667 |
|  |  | 9,333 | 12,667 |
| Year 2 | Salary | – | 8,000 |
|  | Share of profits | 18,667 | 9,333 |
|  |  | 18,667 | 17,333 |

# INDEX

absorption
  fixed and variable costs 226–7
  overheads 178–81
accounting
  bases/policies 58
  concepts 57–68
  functions of 112–13
  social issues 246–50
accounting rate of return (ARR)
  215–16
Accounting Standards Board
  (ASB) 58, 131, 132
accruals concept 38, 59
accumulated fund 37, 43
acid test ratio 118
adjusting events 62
adjustment accounts 38, 40, 44
algebraic method, overheads
  176–8
allocation, overhead costs 173–5
allotment 100
amalgamation, partnerships 80–3
analysis, cash changes 134–7
apportionment, overheads 173–8
appropriation account see profit
  and loss appropriation account
ARR see accounting rate of return
ASB see Accounting Standards
  Board
assets 23, 59, 99
see also fixed assets
AVCO see weighted average cost

bad debts 23–5, 142
balance sheet
  budgeted 193–5, 197
  cash-based business 38, 42
  clubs and societies 46
  limited company 95–6
  partnerships 71
bonus shares 103–4, 139–40
break-even 234–9
budgets 188–95, 203–4, 213
business entity concept 60

call account, share issue 100–1
capital, cost 213–21
  accounts 71–2
capital invesment appraisal
  213–221
capital investment 19, 61
capital redemption reserve 98
capital reserves 97
capitalisation 62, 103
cash accounts 38, 40
cash budget 193–4
cash deficiencies 46–7
cash flow statements 131–43
cash-based businesses 36–43
clubs 43–6

Companies Acts 58, 93, 104,
  156–7
concepts 57–64
conservatism see prudence
  concept
consistency concept 58, 59
contingencies 63
continuous apportionment 176–7
contra items, control accounts 27
contribution 228–9, 238
contribution/sales method 234
control accounts 26–9, 38, 40, 44
cost centre 173–4
cost of sales adjustment 124
costing
  absorption 178–81, 226–7
  marginal 227–39
  standard 201
costs
  see also labour; materials;
  overheads
  fixed/variable 227–9
  hidden 247
  stepped 238
credit transactions 27
creditors 45, 119, 135–6, 193, 195
current accounts 71–2
current cost accounting 124
current purchasing power
  accounting 124
current ratio 118

debentures 99, 143
debtors 23, 45, 118, 193, 195
debts, bad 23–5, 142
depreciation 58, 61–2
  cash flow statements 134–5
  current cost accounting 124
  provision 19–23
direct costs 227
direct labour 158, 161, 207
direct material variances 207
directors, limited companies 92
discounted cash flows 216–20
disposals 20–2, 138–9, 140–2
dissolution, partnerships 78–80
dividends 95, 114, 120–1
  cash flow statements 136, 143
dual aspect concept 61

earnings per share (EPS) 120, 130
efficiency variance 202–3, 205,
  208
elimination method 176–7
environmental issues 246–7
EPS see earnings per share
equal instalments, depreciation 20
equity see ordinary shares
errors, correction 27–32
expenditure variances 204, 208

FIFO see first in first out
final accounts 38–42, 43–6, 70
financial ratios 114, 117–19
financial statements, users 112
finished goods 163–4
first in first out (FIFO) 154–6
fixed assets 98–9, 213–14
  depreciation 19–23, 61–2
  disposal 21–2, 138–9, 140–2
fixed budget 190
fixed costs 227–9
flexed budgets 203–4
flexible budget 190
FRS 1 Cash Flow Statements
  131–43
functional budget 198

gearing 110, 114, 119–20
gearing adjustment 124
general reserve 97
going concern concept 58–9
goodwill 63, 75–8
government grants 61
graphical method, break-even
  point 234, 236–9
guaranteed minimum weekly
  wage 160

HCA see historic cost accounting
hidden costs 247
high day rate 159–60
historic cost accounting (HCA)
  123–4

idle time 159
incentive schemes 159–61
income and expenditure account
  43, 46
incomplete records 36–48
indirect labour 158
inflation 123–4, 217–18
instalments, share issue 100–1
interest cover 121
internal rate of return (IRR) 214,
  220–1
investment ratios 114, 119–21
IRR see internal rate of return

labour 159, 178–9, 202
  standard cost 201
  variances 202–3, 207
land, revaluation 139–40
last in first out (LIFO) 154–6
liability 92, 93
LIFO see last in first out
limited companies 91–106
limiting factors 190, 233–4
liquidity 117–19, 132
long-term contracts 61
long-term planning 189

machine hour rate 179
make/buy decisions 230–2
management 112–13, 188–91, 201
manufacturing accounts 161–5
margin ratio 117
margin of safety 238
marginal costing 227–39
mark-up ratio 117
master budget 189–90
matching concept *see* accruals
    concept
materiality concept 60
materials 153–4
    standard cost 201
    variances 207
money measurement concept 60,
    247

net margin ratio 117
net present value method (NPV)
    214, 216–20, 223, 224
net realisable value 61, 156, 157,
    164
non-adjusting events 62–3
non-trading organisations 43–6
NPV *see* net present value
    method

one-off projects 229–30
operating profit 137–8
operational budgets 189
opportunity cost 214
ordinary shares 95
overhead adjustment account 181
overheads 161, 173–81
    marginal costing 230
    standard cost 201
    variances 204–6, 208
overtime 159
ownership, limited company 92

P/E *see* price/earnings ratio
partnerships 69–84
payback method 214–15
penetration pricing 234
performance evaluation 113–23
period costs 158, 182
periodic stock valuation 154–5
perpetual stock valuation 154–5
piece work remuneration 160
planning 188–9
post-balance sheet events 62–3
preference shares 95, 104
premium, share price 95–6
premium bonus schemes 160–1
price variance 201–3
price/earnings ratio (P/E) 120
primary ratio 114, 116
prime cost 161
product costs 158
productivity 158
profit 137–8, 142
    unrealised 162–5
profit and loss account 42, 194–5
profit and loss appropriation
    account 70, 72, 93–4
profit sharing ratio 70, 73
profit/volume method 234, 238–9

profitability ratios 114, 116–17,
    128
provision
    bad debts 24–5, 142
    depreciation 19–23
    discounts 25–6
    unrealised profit 162–4
prudence concept 23, 58, 59–60,
    164
published accounts 99–100

quantity variance 201–3
quick asset ratio 118

ratio analysis 113–23
realisation account, partnerships
    79, 80, 82
realisation concept 60, 164
receipts and payments account 43
reconciliation statement 133,
    137–8
redemption, shares 104–5
reducing balance method 20
repeated distribution 176–7
research and development 62
reserves 19, 96–8
resource utilisation 114, 233–4
retained profits 96–7, 136, 143
return on capital employed
    (ROCE) 116
return on owner's equity (ROOE)
    116–17
revaluation account 74
revaluation reserve 98, 139–40
revenue expenditure 61, 62
revenue reserve 93, 97
rights issue 100–1
ROCE *see* return on capital
    employed
ROOE *see* return on owner's
    equity
royalties 162, 227

sales variances 204, 207
scrip issue 103
service department costs 175–8
set-offs, control accounts 27
share capital 92, 95, 100–4
    cash flow statements 136, 143
share premium account 97–8
shareholders 92, 95, 104, 113
shares 95, 100–5
simplified method, overheads
    176–7
simultaneous equation method,
    overheads 176–8
social accounting 246–8
societies 43–6
special contracts 229–30
SSAP 2 Disclosure of Accounting
    Policies 58–60
SSAP 4 Accounting for
    Government Grants 61
SSAP 9 Stocks and Long-term
    Contracts 61, 156–7
SSAP 12 Accounting for
    Depreciation 19, 61–2

SSAP 13 Accounting for
    Research and Development 62
SSAP 17 Accounting for Post-
    balance Sheet Events 62–3
SSAP 18 Accounting for
    Contingencies 63
SSAP 22 Accounting for
    Goodwill 63
standard costing 201
standard hour 201
Statements of Accounting
    Practice (SSAPs) *see* SSAP...
stepped costs 238
stewardship 113
stock 47–8, 135, 193
    turnover rate 119
    valuation methods 58, 61,
    154–8, 164
stores ledger 153–5
straight line, depreciation 20
strategic planning 189, 232–3
subscriptions account 45
sunk costs *see* fixed costs
surplus, club accounts 43
suspense accounts 29–32

takeover, partnership 83–4
taxation, cash flow statements
    136, 138, 143
time value, money 214, 216–17
time-based remuneration 159–60
trading accounts 42
transfer pricing 162
trial balance 29–32

unit contribution method 234
unit costs 152
unit produced rate 179
unrealised profit 162–5
usage variance 202–3
users, financial statements 112

valuation
    assets 59, 98, 99
    finished goods 163–4
    land 139–40
    stock 58, 61, 154–8, 164
    work in progress 157–8
variable costs 227–9
variances 200–8
voting rights 95, 104

wages 158–61, 202–3
weighted average cost (AVCO)
    154–7
WIP *see* work in progress
work in progress (WIP) 157–8
working capital 118, 124, 136–7
working conditions 247

yield, dividends 114, 120–1, 130
yield method *see* internal rate of
    return

zero-based budgeting 191